CAMBRIDGE

Brighter Thinking

A Level Further Mathematics for OCR A

Mechanics Student Book (AS/A Level)

Jess Barker, Nathan Barker, Michele Conway, Janet Such Course consultant: Vesna Kadelburg

CAMBRIDGE
UNIVERSITY PRESS

University Printing House, Cambridge CB2 8BS, United Kingdom

One Liberty Plaza, 20th Floor, New York, NY 10006, USA

477 Williamstown Road, Port Melbourne, VIC 3207, Australia

314–321, 3rd Floor, Plot 3, Splendor Forum, Jasola District Centre, New Delhi – 110025, India

79 Anson Road, #06–04/06, Singapore 079906

Cambridge University Press is part of the University of Cambridge.

It furthers the University's mission by disseminating knowledge in the pursuit of education, learning and research at the highest international levels of excellence.

www.cambridge.org
Information on this title: www.cambridge.org/9781316644416 (Paperback)
www.cambridge.org/9781316644270 (Paperback with Cambridge Elevate edition)

First published 2017

20 19 18 17 16 15 14 13 12 11 10 9 8 7

Printed in Great Britain by CPI Group (UK) Ltd, Croydon CR0 4YY

A catalogue record for this publication is available from the British Library

ISBN 978-1-316-64441-6 Paperback
ISBN 978-1-316-64427-0 Paperback with Cambridge Elevate edition

Additional resources for this publication at www.cambridge.org/education

This resource is endorsed by OCR for use with specification AS Level Further Mathematics A (H235) and specification A Level Further Mathematics A (H245). In order to gain OCR endorsement, this resource has undergone an independent quality check. Any references to assessment and/or assessment preparation are the publisher's interpretation of the specification requirements and are not endorsed by OCR. OCR recommends that a range of teaching and learning resources are used in preparing learners for assessment. OCR has not paid for the production of this resource, nor does OCR receive any royalties from its sale. For more information about the endorsement process, please visit the OCR website, **www.ocr.org.uk.**

Contents

Introduction

You have probably been told that mathematics is very useful, yet it can often seem like a lot of techniques that just have to be learned to answer examination questions. You are now getting to the point where you will start to see where some of these techniques can be applied in solving real problems. However, as well as seeing how maths can be useful, we hope that anyone working through this book will realise that it can also be incredibly frustrating, surprising and ultimately beautiful.

The book is woven around three key themes from the new curriculum:

Proof

Maths is valued because it trains you to think logically and communicate precisely. At a high level, maths is far less concerned about answers and more about the clear communication of ideas. It is not about being neat – although that might help! It is about creating a coherent argument that other people can easily follow but find difficult to refute. Have you ever tried looking at your own work? If you cannot follow it yourself it is unlikely anybody else will be able to understand it. In maths we communicate using a variety of means – feel free to use combinations of diagrams, words and algebra to aid your argument. And once you have attempted a proof, try presenting it to your peers. Look critically (but positively) at some other people's attempts. It is only through having your own attempts evaluated and trying to find flaws in other proofs that you will develop sophisticated mathematical thinking. This is why we have included lots of common errors in our 'work it out' boxes – just in case your friends don't make any mistakes!

Problem solving

Maths is valued because it trains you to look at situations in unusual, creative ways, to persevere and to evaluate solutions along the way. We have been heavily influenced by a great mathematician and maths educator, George Polya, who believed that students were not just born with problem solving skills – these skills were developed by seeing problems being solved and reflecting on the solutions before trying similar problems. You may not realise it but good mathematicians spend most of their time being stuck. You need to spend some time on problems you can't do, trying out different possibilities. If after a while you have not cracked it then look at the solution and try a similar problem. Don't be disheartened if you cannot get it immediately – in fact, the longer you spend puzzling over a problem the more you will learn from the solution. You may, for example, never need to integrate a rational function in future, but we firmly believe that the problem solving skills you will develop by trying it can be applied to many other situations.

Modelling

Maths is valued because it helps us solve real-world problems. However, maths describes ideal situations and the real world is messy! Modelling is about deciding on the important features needed to describe the essence of a situation and turning that into a mathematical form, then using it to make predictions, compare to reality and possibly improve the model. In many situations the technical maths is actually the easy part – especially with modern technology. Deciding which features of reality to include or ignore and anticipating the consequences of these decisions is the hard part. Yet some fairly drastic assumptions – such as pretending a car is a single point or that people's votes are independent – can result in models that are surprisingly accurate.

More than anything else, this book is about making links. Links between the different chapters, the topics covered and the themes just discussed, links to other subjects and links to the real world. We hope that you will grow to see maths as one great complex but beautiful web of interlinking ideas.

Maths is about so much more than examinations, but we hope that if you take on board these ideas (and do plenty of practice!) you will find maths examinations a much more approachable and possibly even enjoyable experience. However, always remember that the results of what you write down in a few hours by yourself in silence under exam conditions is not the only measure you should consider when judging your mathematical ability – it is only one variable in a much more complicated mathematical model!

How to use this book

Throughout this book you will notice particular features that are designed to aid your learning. This section provides a brief overview of these features.

In this chapter you will learn how to:

- calculate the work done by a force
- calculate kinetic energy
- use the work-energy principle

Learning objectives
A short summary of the content that you will learn in each chapter.

Before you start...

GCSE	You should know how to convert units of distance, speed and time.	1 Convert 15 000 metres to kilometres.
A Level Mathematics Student Book 1	You should know how to calculate the weight of an object from its mass, and know the unit of weight.	2 Calculate the weight of a car of mass 1150 kg, stating the unit with your answer.

Before you start
Points you should know from your previous learning and questions to check that you're ready to start the chapter.

WORKED EXAMPLE

The left-hand side shows you how to set out your working. The right-hand side explains the more difficult steps and helps you understand why a particular method was chosen.

Key point

A summary of the most important methods, facts and formulae.

PROOF

Step-by-step walkthroughs of standard proofs and methods of proof.

Explore

Ideas for activities and investigations to extend your understanding of the topic.

WORK IT OUT

Can you identify the correct solution and find the mistakes in the two incorrect solutions?

Tip

Useful guidance, including on ways of calculating or checking and use of technology.

Each chapter ends with a **Checklist of learning and understanding** and a **Mixed practice exercise**, which includes **past paper questions** marked with the icon.

In between chapters, you will find extra sections that bring together topics in a more synoptic way.

Focus on ...

Unique sections relating to the preceding chapters that develop your skills in proof, problem solving and modelling.

CROSS-TOPIC REVIEW EXERCISE

Questions covering topics from across the preceding chapters, testing your ability to apply what you have learned.

You will find AS Level and A Level **practice questions** towards the end of the book, as well as a **glossary** of key terms (picked out in colour within the chapters), and **answers** to all questions. Full **worked solutions** can be found on the Cambridge Elevate digital platform, along with a **digital version** of this Student Book.

Maths is all about making links, which is why throughout this book you will find signposts emphasising connections between different topics, applications and suggestions for further research.

Rewind

Reminders of where to find useful information from earlier in your study.

Focus on...

Links to problem solving, modelling or proof exercises that relate to the topic currently being studied.

Fast forward

Links to topics that you may cover in greater detail later in your study.

Did you know?

Interesting or historical information and links with other subjects to improve your awareness about how mathematics contributes to society.

Colour-coding of exercises

The questions in the exercises are designed to provide careful progression, ranging from basic fluency to practice questions. They are uniquely colour-coded, as shown here.

1 A uniform rectangular lamina has vertices at (7, 2), (8, 4), (4, 6) and (3, 4). Find the coordinates of the centre of mass of the lamina.

10 Find the increase of elastic potential energy when a light elastic string of natural length 1.8 m and modulus of elasticity 125 N is extended from 2.05 m to 2.8 m.

13 An object P of mass 1.2 kg is attached to one end of a light elastic string of natural length 1.25 m with its other end attached to a fixed point, O. The modulus of elasticity of the string is 65 N. P is dropped from O. Find the extension of the string when the object reaches its maximum velocity.

18 A light elastic spring with natural length 18 cm rests on a smooth horizontal table. One end is attached to a fixed point A and a 280 g mass is attached at the other end B, held 12 cm from A. The modulus of elasticity of the spring is 550 N.

10 Road surface conditions are being assessed for a horizontal bend in a road that is formed by an arc of a circle of radius 25 m. The road surface could be made of asphalt or concrete. The coefficient of friction between car tyres and asphalt is 0.72, and between car tyres and concrete 0.85.

14 A vertical hollow cylinder of radius 0.4 m is rotating about its axis. A particle rough inner surface of the cylinder. The cylinder and P rotate with the same The coefficient of friction between P and the cylinder is μ.

Black – drill questions. Some of these come in several parts, each with subparts i and ii. You only need attempt subpart i at first; subpart ii is essentially the same question, which you can use for further practice if you got part i wrong, for homework, or when you revisit the exercise during revision.

Green – practice questions at a basic level.

Blue – practice questions at an intermediate level.

Red – practice questions at an advanced level.

Purple – challenging questions that apply the concept of the current chapter across other areas of maths.

Yellow – designed to encourage reflection and discussion.

A – indicates content that is for A Level students only

AS – indicates content that is for AS Level students only

1 Work, energy and power 1

In this chapter you will learn how to:

- calculate the work done by a force
- calculate kinetic energy
- use the work–energy principle
- equate gravitational potential energy to work done against gravity
- perform calculations using power.

Before you start...

GCSE	You should know how to convert units of distance, speed and time.	1 Convert 15 000 metres to kilometres.
A Level Mathematics Student Book 1	You should know how to calculate the weight of an object from its mass, and know the unit of weight.	2 Calculate the weight of a car of mass 1150 kg, stating the unit with your answer.
A Level Mathematics Student Book 1	You should be able to use Newton's second law of motion: $F = ma$	3 A resultant force of 50 N acts on an object of mass 2.5 kg. Calculate the acceleration of the object.
A Level Mathematics Student Book 2	You should be able to resolve a force into components at right angles to each other.	4 A force of 8 N acts on a particle at an angle of 20° to the positive horizontal direction. What are the horizontal and vertical components of the force?

The relationship between work and energy

You have already studied the effect of a force or system of forces in A Level Mathematics.

In this chapter, you will learn the definition of the work done by a force, which is a quantity that is measured in joules, the same units that are used for energy. You will learn about propulsive and resistive forces. You will learn about the relationship between work done and two different types of energy: kinetic energy and gravitational potential energy. You will also learn about power, which is the rate of doing work.

Ideas of work, energy and power are crucial in engineering, enabling engineers to design machines to do useful work. Hydroelectric power stations work by converting the work done by falling water, first into kinetic energy as the hydroelectric turbines rotate and then into electricity.

Fast forward

A In Chapter 6, you will learn about elastic potential energy and its conversion to kinetic energy.

Section 1: The work done by a force

Work is done by a force when the object it is applied to moves. The amount of **work done** is the product of the force and the distance moved in the direction of the force.

Some forces promote movement, while others resist it. For example, when you cycle into a breeze, your pedalling promotes movement but the breeze acts against your movement. Forces that promote movement are called **propulsive forces** and those that resist movement are known as **resistive forces.**

Other propulsive forces include the **tension** in a rope being used to drag an object across the ground and the driving force of a vehicle engine. The driving force of an engine is often described as its **tractive force.** Other resistive forces include friction, vehicle braking and resistance by moving through still air or a liquid.

Key point 1.1

For a force acting in the direction of motion:

work done = force × distance

Work done is measured in joules (J).

1 joule = 1 newton × 1 metre, i.e. 1 J = 1 N m

For example a force of 5 N acting on an object that moves 15 m in the direction of the force does $5 \times 15 = 75$ J of work. Doubling the force to 10 N over the same distance would double the amount of work done to 150 J. Likewise, doubling the distance moved to 30 m with an unchanged force of 5 N would double the amount of work done to 150 J.

WORKED EXAMPLE 1.1

A box is pushed 5 m across a horizontal floor by a horizontal force of 25 N. Calculate the work done by the force.

Work done = force × distance

$= 25 \times 5$ — Use the definition of work done.

$= 125$ J — State units of work done (J) with your answer.

WORKED EXAMPLE 1.2

A truck driver driving along a horizontal road applies a braking force of 75 kN for 25 m. Calculate the work done by the brakes, giving your answer in kJ.

75 kN = 75 000 N — Convert 75 kN to 75 000 N as you need to work in standard units.

Work done by brakes — Use the definition of work done.

= braking force × distance

= 75 000 × 25

= 1 875 000 J — Change J to kJ.

= 1880 kJ (3 s.f.)

WORKED EXAMPLE 1.3

A 50 kg crate is lifted 12 m by a rope and pulley system. Calculate the work done against gravity.

Work done = force × distance

∴ work done against gravity

= weight × height gained — Apply the definition of work done to the gravitational force. The force needed to lift the crate is equal to the crate's weight and the distance moved is height gained.

Weight of crate = 50 × 9.8

= 490 N — Calculate the weight of the crate, based on the usual approximation for the acceleration due to gravity of 9.8 m s^{-2}.

Work done against gravity

= weight × height gained

= 490 × 12 — Use the definition of work done.

≈ 5880 J

Key point 1.2

When a mass, m, is raised or lowered through a height h:

work done against or by gravity = weight × height = $mg \times h$

Fast forward

In Section 3 you will learn the equivalence of work done against gravity and gravitational potential energy.

WORKED EXAMPLE 1.4

A competitor of mass 75 kg dives from a 10-metre-high diving board into a pool. Air resistance averages 12 N as he descends 10 m through the air. Resistance from the water then averages 3000 N as he descends 2 m further. Calculate:

a the total work done by gravity as the diver descends 12 metres

b the total work done against air and water resistance during this descent.

a Work done by gravity $= 75g \times 12$

$= 8820$ J

Use mgh to calculate the work done by gravity.

b Work done against air resistance $= 12 \times 10$

$= 120$ J

Use force × distance to calculate the work done against each of the resistances.

Work done against water resistance $= 3000 \times 2$

$= 6000$ J

Total work done against resistances $= 6120$ J

WORKED EXAMPLE 1.5

A van of mass 1250 kg travels along a straight road. The driving force of the vehicle engine is 500 N and resistance to motion is 220 N, on average. The van travels 1.5 km from one delivery to the next, descending 8 m in height. Find:

a the work done by the vehicle engine

b the work done by gravity

c the work done against resistance.

a 1.5 km = 1500 m

Convert distance to metres.

Work done by vehicle engine $= 500 \times 1500 = 750\,000$ J

Use force × distance to calculate the work done by the vehicle engine.

b Work done by gravity $= 1250g \times 8$

$= 98\,000$ J

Use mgh to calculate the work done by gravity.

c Work done against resistance $= 220 \times 1500$

$= 330\,000$ J

Use force × distance to calculate the work done against resistance.

EXERCISE 1A

1. A parcel is dragged 5 metres across a horizontal floor by a horizontal rope. The tension in the rope is 12 N. Calculate the work done by the tension in the rope.
2. Susan climbs a vertical rock 32 m high. Susan's mass is 65 kg. Calculate the work done by Susan against gravity.
3. Sunil descends a vertical ladder. His mass is 82 kg and the work done by gravity is 2150 J. Find the height Sunil descends.
4. A ball of mass 100 g is dropped from a window. Calculate the work done by gravity as the ball falls vertically to the ground 6 m below.
5. A puck slides 50 metres across an ice rink, against a resistive force of 2.5 N. Calculate the work done against resistance.
6. A cyclist travelling on horizontal ground applies a driving force of 25 N against a headwind of 10 N and a resistance from friction of 5 N. The cyclist travels 1.2 km. Find:

   a the work done by the cyclist **b** the total work done against wind and friction.
7. A fish basket is raised from the sea floor to a fishing boat at sea level, 18 metres above. The mass of the basket is 15 kg. The resistance to motion from the seawater is 50 N. Calculate the total work done, against gravity and water resistance, in raising the fish basket.
8. A driving force of 400 N does 50 kJ of work moving a van along a horizontal road from A to B. Resistance to motion averages 185 N. Calculate the work done against resistance as the van moves from A to B.

Section 2: Kinetic energy and the work–energy principle

Kinetic energy is the energy an object has because it is moving.

Key point 1.3

An object of mass m moving with speed v has kinetic energy $\frac{1}{2}mv^2$.

If mass is measured in kg and speed is measured in m s^{-1}, kinetic energy is measured in joules.

Tip

If speed is not given in m s^{-1}, you should convert to m s^{-1} before you start the rest of your calculations.

WORKED EXAMPLE 1.6

A particle of mass 1.5 kg is moving with kinetic energy 48 joules. Calculate the speed of the particle.

$$\text{Kinetic energy} = \frac{1}{2}mv^2$$

Use the formula for kinetic energy.

$$48 = \frac{1}{2} \times 1.5 \times v^2$$

$$\therefore v^2 = 64 \quad \text{so} \quad v = 8 \text{ m s}^{-1}$$

Substitute and rearrange to find speed.
As mass was given in kg and kinetic energy in joules, speed is in m s^{-1}. Speed is a positive scalar, so the negative option of the root can be disregarded.

WORKED EXAMPLE 1.7

A cyclist slows down from 25 km h^{-1} to 10 km h^{-1}. The combined mass of the cyclist and her bicycle is 95 kg. Calculate the loss of kinetic energy.

Let u be the starting speed and v be the final speed:

$u = \frac{25}{3.6} = 6.944$ m s^{-1} and

$v = \frac{10}{3.6} = 2.777$ m s^{-1}

To convert km h^{-1} to m s^{-1} you must multiply by the conversion factor $\frac{1000}{3600}$, which simplifies to division by 3.6.

Loss of kinetic energy $= \frac{1}{2}mu^2 - \frac{1}{2}mv^2$

Loss of kinetic energy = initial kinetic energy – final kinetic energy

Loss of kinetic energy $= \frac{1}{2} \times 95 \times 6.944^{-2}$

$- \frac{1}{2} \times 95 \times 2.78^2 = 1920$ J (3 s.f.)

A

WORKED EXAMPLE 1.8

Calculate the increase in kinetic energy when a boat of mass 2 tonnes changes velocity from $3\mathbf{i} + 4\mathbf{j}$ m s^{-1} to $4.5\mathbf{i} + 4.5\mathbf{j}$ m s^{-1}. Give your answer in kJ.

$(\text{Starting speed})^2 = 3^2 + 4^2 = 25$

$(\text{Final speed})^2 = 4.5^2 + 4.5^2 = 40.5$

Use Pythagoras' theorem to convert the velocity vectors to speeds. You need the square of the *speed,* not the velocity vector, for the kinetic energy formula.

Gain in kinetic energy $= \frac{1}{2}m(v^2 - u^2)$

You can write $\frac{1}{2}mv^2 - \frac{1}{2}mu^2$ in factorised form.

2 tonnes = 2000 kg

Convert 2 tonnes to 2000 kg.

Gain in kinetic energy $= \frac{1}{2} \times 2000 \times (40.5 - 25)$

$= 15.5$ kJ

Divide by 1000 to convert joules to kJ.

The **work-energy principle** is an essential idea in Mechanics that enables us to calculate the work necessary to cause a change in kinetic energy.

Key point 1.4

The net work done by all the forces acting on a particle, including its own weight, is equal to the change in kinetic energy of the particle.

work done $= \frac{1}{2}mv^2 - \frac{1}{2}mu^2$

WORKED EXAMPLE 1.9

A particle of mass 1.6 kg at rest on a smooth horizontal plane is acted on by a constant horizontal force of 8 N. Find the speed of the particle after it has travelled 5 metres.

Work done $= 8 \times 5 = 40$ J — Work done = force × distance

$40 = \frac{1}{2} \times 1.6 \times v^2$

$v^2 = 50$ — Work-energy principle: since the particle is starting from rest, work done $= \frac{1}{2}mv^2$

$\Rightarrow v = 7.07$ m s^{-1} (3 s.f.)

WORKED EXAMPLE 1.10

Stephen is driving his car along a horizontal road at 55 km h^{-1} when he notices a broken-down vehicle, just off the road, 150 m ahead. Stephen and his car have a mass of 1025 kg and the total resistance to motion is assumed constant at 500 N. Stephen believes he should slow down and that he can slow down sufficiently without applying the brakes. Calculate Stephen's speed, in km h^{-1}, as he reaches the broken-down vehicle, taking account of the resistance to motion.

Assume that Stephen allows the resistance to motion to slow his car down over 150 m. There is no driving or braking force.

Work done against resistance
= resistive force × distance
$= 500 \times 150$
$= 75\,000$ J — Calculate the work done against resistance.

$u = 55$ km h^{-1} $= \frac{55}{3.6} = 15.28$ m s^{-1} — Convert the initial speed u of 55 km h^{-1} to m s^{-1}.

Loss of kinetic energy $= \frac{1}{2} \times m \times (u^2 - v^2)$ — Write down the expression for loss of kinetic energy.

$75\,000 = \frac{1}{2} \times 1025 \times (u^2 - v^2)$ — Work-energy principle: work done against resistance = loss of KE

$u^2 - v^2 = \frac{2 \times 75\,000}{1025} \approx 146.34$

$v^2 = 15.28^2 - 146.3$ — Substitute for u. Rearrange and solve for v.

$v = 9.33$ m s^{-1}

$v = 9.33 \times 3.6$ km h^{-1} — Convert back to km h^{-1}.

$v = 33.6$ km h^{-1} (3 s.f.)

EXERCISE 1B

1. Calculate the kinetic energy of a cyclist and her bicycle having a combined mass of 70 kg, travelling at 12 m s^{-1}. Give your answer in kJ.

2. Calculate the mass of an athlete who is running at 8.5 m s^{-1}, with kinetic energy 3500 J.

3. Calculate the speed of a bus of mass 20 tonnes with kinetic energy 1100 kJ. Give your answer in km h^{-1}.

4. A box of mass 5 kg is pulled from A to B across a smooth horizontal floor by a horizontal force of magnitude 10 N. At point A, the box has speed 1.5 m s^{-1} and at point B the box has speed 2.8 m s^{-1}. Ignoring all other resistive forces, find:
   - **a** the increase in kinetic energy of the box
   - **b** the work done by the force
   - **c** the distance AB.

A 5. Calculate the loss of kinetic energy when a boat of mass 3.5 tonnes reduces in velocity from $(3\mathbf{i} + 4\mathbf{j})$ m s^{-1} to $(2.5\mathbf{i} + 3\mathbf{j})$ m s^{-1}.

6. A car driver brakes on a horizontal road and slows down from 20 m s^{-1} to 12 m s^{-1}. The mass of the car and its occupants is 1150 kg.
   - **a** Find the loss in kinetic energy.
   - **b** Given that the work done against resistance to motion is 50 kJ, find the work done by the brakes.

7. A child of mass 35 kg descends a smooth slide, after propelling herself from the top at 1.6 m s^{-1}. Ignoring air resistance, calculate her speed at the bottom of the slide, which is 2.1 metres lower down than the top.

8. A bullet of mass 10 grams passes horizontally through a target of thickness 5 cm. The speed of the bullet is reduced from 240 m s^{-1} to 90 m s^{-1}. Calculate the magnitude of the average resistive force exerted on the bullet.

9. A train with mass 100 tonnes is travelling at 108 km h^{-1} on horizontal tracks, when the driver sees a speed reduction sign. The train's speed must be reduced to 75 km h^{-1} over 500 m. Resistance to motion is approximately 8 kN. Calculate the braking force required, in kN.

10. A package of mass 500 grams slides down a parcel chute of length 3.5 metres, starting from rest. The bottom of the chute is 2.2 metres below the top. The speed of the package at the bottom of the chute is 4.5 m s^{-1}. Find the resistance to motion on the chute.

11. Use the equation of motion, $F = ma$, together with the formula, $v^2 = u^2 + 2as$, to derive the relation: $Fs = \frac{1}{2}m(v^2 - u^2)$.

12. Eddy cycles up a hill. His mass, together with his bicycle, is 92 kg. His driving force is 125 N and resistance from friction is 45 N. Eddy travels 350 metres along the road, which rises through a vertical height of 32 metres. His starting speed is 8.2 m s^{-1}. Find his final speed.

Section 3: Potential energy, mechanical energy and conservation of mechanical energy

Consider an object of mass m falling freely under gravity from height h_1 to height h_2, with starting speed u and final speed v.
Since the only external force acting on the object is gravity, the work-energy principle becomes:

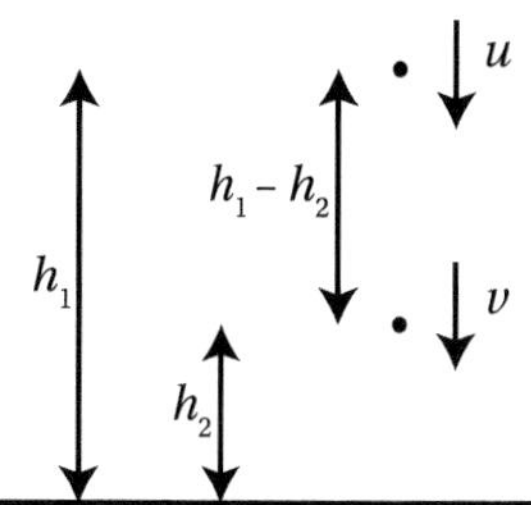

work done by gravity = increase in kinetic energy

$$\Rightarrow mg(h_1 - h_2) = \frac{mv^2}{2} - \frac{mu^2}{2}$$

Rearranging this gives:

$$mgh_1 - mgh_2 = \frac{mv^2}{2} - \frac{mu^2}{2}$$

$$\Rightarrow \quad mgh_1 + \frac{mu^2}{2} = mgh_2 + \frac{mv^2}{2}$$

Each side of this equation is the sum of two terms, one of which is kinetic energy. The other term is gravitational potential energy. **Gravitational potential energy** (GPE) is the energy an object has by virtue of its position. For an object of mass m raised a distance h, the increase in GPE is equal to the product of its weight, mg, and the distance h.

Tip

You can choose any height as your ground (zero) level but it is usually best to choose the lowest height reached by the moving object.

Key point 1.5

Gravitational potential energy (GPE) = mgh

where h is the height above ground (zero) level.

The principle of the conservation of **mechanical energy** states that, if there are no external forces other than gravity doing work on an object during its motion, then the sum of kinetic energy and gravitational potential energy remains constant.

Key point 1.6

If the only force acting on an object is its weight then mechanical energy is conserved:

GPE + KE = $mgh + \frac{1}{2}mv^2$ = constant

where h is the vertical height above the zero level.

This diagram may help you to understand the formula for conservation of mechanical energy more easily. As an object descends in height it speeds up, so gravitational potential energy is converted into kinetic energy. As an object ascends in height it slows down, so kinetic energy is converted into gravitational potential energy.

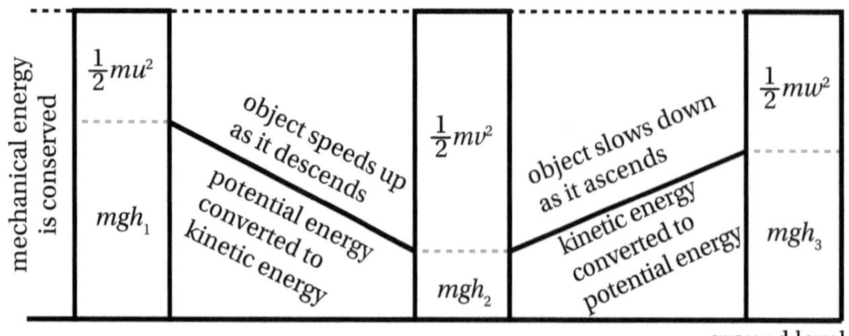

WORKED EXAMPLE 1.11

Faisal throws a ball of mass 125 grams vertically upwards from ground level with a speed of 12.5 m s⁻¹. Assuming no external forces apply:

a calculate the speed of the ball after it has risen 5 metres

b calculate the maximum height gained by the ball.

a Starting KE $= \frac{1}{2} \times 0.125 \times 12.5^2$

$= 9.766$ J

Starting KE $= mgh +$ KE at 5 m — Use conservation of mechanical energy over the first 5 m of the ascent.

$9.766 = 0.125g \times 5 +$ KE at 5 m — Take the gravitational potential energy at ground level to be zero.

KE at 5 m $= 3.641$ J — Calculate the kinetic energy of the ball at 5 m.

$\frac{1}{2}mv^2 = 3.641$ — Use the formula for KE with the speed at 5 m equal to v.

$v = \sqrt{\frac{2 \times 3.641}{0.125}}$

$= 7.63$ m s⁻¹ (3 s.f.) — Calculate the speed of the ball.

b Starting KE $= mgh_{max}$ — Use conservation of mechanical energy over the whole ascent (final kinetic energy is zero). At the maximum height, all the initial kinetic energy will have been converted into gravitational potential energy.

$9.766 = 0.125g \times h_{max}$

$\Rightarrow h_{max} = 7.97$ metres (3 s.f.) — Calculate the maximum height gained.

Using energy to solve problems

The principle of conservation of mechanical energy applies to the situation where the only force acting on an object is its weight.

You have already used the work-energy principle to solve problems involving external forces, such as friction and driving forces. You are now ready to combine the work-energy principle and the principle of conservation of energy. Any change in the mechanical energy of a system is the result of work done by external forces:

$(GPE_1 + KE_1)$ + work done by driving forces - work done against resistive forces $= (GPE_2 + KE_2)$

The formula can also be written as:

The change in the total energy of an object = the work done on the object by external forces.

Tip

External forces are any forces acting on an object other than its own weight.

WORKED EXAMPLE 1.12

A 1.5 kg package is attached to one end of an inextensible string. The string and package are being raised by the action of a pulley. The tension in the string is 18 N. Find the height gained by the package as it increases in speed from 1.2 m s^{-1} to 3.2 m s^{-1}.

Increase in KE $= \frac{1}{2} \times 1.5 \times (3.2^2 - 1.2^2)$
$= 6.6$ J

Calculate the increase in kinetic energy.

Change in GPE $= mgh = 1.5gh$ joules

Calculate the change in gravitational potential energy.

Work done $= T \times h = 18h$

Calculate the work done in raising the package.

$18h = 1.5gh + 6.6$

Work done on object = change in total energy

$18 \times h - 1.5g \times h = 6.6$

$h = \frac{6.6}{18 - 1.5g} \approx 2$ m

WORKED EXAMPLE 1.13

Helen cycles from rest at the top of a sloping track, 35 m above the valley floor. She pedals downhill, then continues along a horizontal track, before ascending 10 m on an uphill track and stopping. The total distance she travels is 500 m, and the average resistance to motion is 55 N. The combined mass of Helen and her bicycle is 62 kg. Calculate the total work done by Helen, and the average driving force she applies.

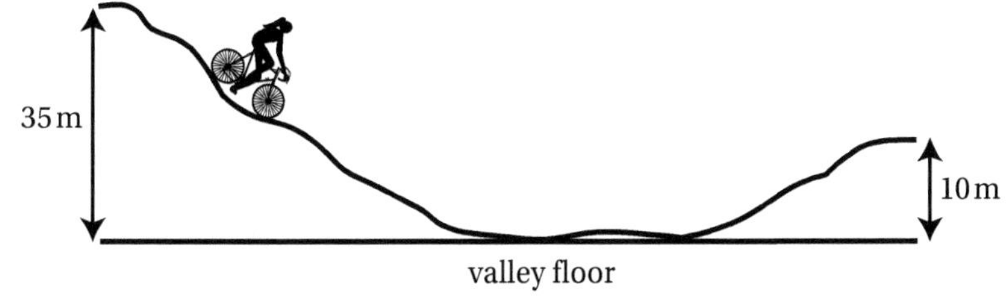

Continues on next page ...

$mgh_1 + \text{KE}_1 + \text{work done by Helen} - \text{work done against resistance} = mgh_2 + \text{KE}_2$

Use the work-energy principle and the principle of conservation of energy.

$\text{KE}_1 = \text{KE}_2 = 0$

Helen has no kinetic energy at the start of her ride and none at the end.
You do not need to consider her motion throughout her ride: just at the start and at the end.

Work done against resistance
$= \text{resistive force} \times \text{distance}$
$= 55 \times 500$
$= 27\,500 \text{ J}$

Calculate the work done against resistance. The distance used is the total distance along the road.

$62 \times (35 - 10) + \text{work done by Helen}$
$= 27\,500$

Let both initial and final kinetic energy be zero and rearrange:
$mgh_1 - mgh_2 + \text{work done by Helen}$
$= \text{work done against resistance}$
$mgh_1 - mgh_2$ is the loss of potential energy of Helen and her bicycle.

$\text{Work done by Helen} = 27\,500 - 15\,190$
$= 12\,310 \text{ J}$

Helen's average driving force
$= \dfrac{\text{work done by Helen}}{\text{distance}}$
$= \dfrac{12\,310}{500}$
$= 24.6 \text{ N (3 s.f.)}$

Use Helen's work done, together with her distance travelled (500 m) to calculate her average driving force.

Conservation of energy is an important principle throughout Physics. Work done by a moving object against resistance, which is lost mechanical energy, is converted to other forms of energy such as thermal energy and sound. This means that total energy is still conserved.

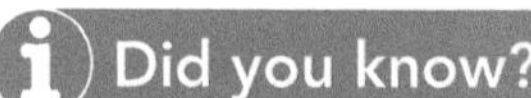

Did you know?

The mechanical equivalent of heat was first proposed by James Joule and explains the relationship between mechanical energy and thermal energy.

EXERCISE 1C

1. Calculate the increase in potential energy when a mass of 5 kg is raised 25 m.
2. Calculate the loss of potential energy when a mass of 2 tonnes is lowered 10 m.
3. A boy of mass 68 kg gains 3600 J of potential energy when climbing a vertical rope. Calculate the height he gains.

4 A toy train loses 1.5 J of potential energy when it descends a spiral track losing 50 cm in height. Find the mass of the toy train.

5 Richard strikes a golf ball off an elevated tee. The golf ball has mass 45 grams and Richard imparts an initial speed of 35 m s^{-1} to the ball.

a Find the initial kinetic energy of the golf ball.

The ball lands on the green 25 metres below the tee. Assume there is no significant air resistance.

b Calculate the loss of potential energy of the ball when it lands on the green.

c Calculate the kinetic energy of the ball when it lands on the green.

d Calculate the speed of the golf ball when it lands on the green.

6 Anita dives off a highboard into a diving pool. When Anita leaves the board she has a speed of 7.5 m s^{-1} and she is 8 metres above the water surface. Anita's mass is 60 kg.

a Find Anita's kinetic energy as she leaves the board.

b Calculate Anita's kinetic energy as she enters the water.

c Calculate Anita's speed as she enters the water.

d What modelling assumptions have you made to simplify your calculations?

7 Wing serves a 58 gram tennis ball with a speed of 9.5 m s^{-1} from a height 3 metres above the level of the tennis court. Assuming there are no resistive forces acting on the ball, calculate:

a the kinetic energy of the ball as Wing serves it

b the potential energy lost by the ball as it descends to the level of the court

c the kinetic energy of the ball as it strikes the court

d the speed of the tennis ball as it strikes the court.

8 Preeti descends a slide starting from rest. Her mass is 58 kg. Overall, her change in vertical height is 5.8 m and her speed at the bottom of the slide is 6.5 m s^{-1}. Calculate the work done against resistance during her descent.

9 A package of mass 0.8 kg is projected down a smooth sloping parcel chute with a speed of 2.2 m s^{-1}. The bottom of the chute is 7.5 m vertically below the top. Assuming there are no external resistive forces, calculate:

a the loss of potential energy of the package

b the speed of the package at the bottom of the chute.

10 Karol slides on his sledge down a straight track of length 210 m, descending 32 m. The combined mass of Karol and his sledge is 72 kg. Karol's starting speed is 2.8 m s^{-1} and his speed at the end of his descent is 10.5 m s^{-1}. Calculate the average resistance to motion, R N, during Karol's descent.

11 Loretta and her bicycle have a combined mass of 75 kg. Loretta cycles up a straight hill AB, accelerating from rest at A to 4 m s^{-1} at B. The level of point A is 5.5 m below the level of B. Find:

a the increase in kinetic energy of Loretta and her bicycle as she cycles from A to B

b the increase in potential energy of Loretta and her bicycle.

During her ride, the resistance to motion is constant at 60 N parallel to the road surface and Loretta does 8500 J of work.

c Calculate the distance from A to B.

Section 4: Work done by a force at an angle to the direction of motion

The problems you have worked with so far have had all forces in the direction of movement, either promoting motion or resisting it directly. But in many cases the forces causing motion are not in the direction of motion. Examples are:

- a man dragging a sledge along horizontal ground by pulling on a rope that is angled upwards
- a child descending a slide under gravity; the child's weight acts vertically downwards but she travels down the slide at an angle to the vertical.

If a force is applied at an angle θ to the direction of motion as shown, the resolved component of the force that does work is $F\cos\theta$. The resolved component that is perpendicular to the direction of motion, $F\sin\theta$, does no work.

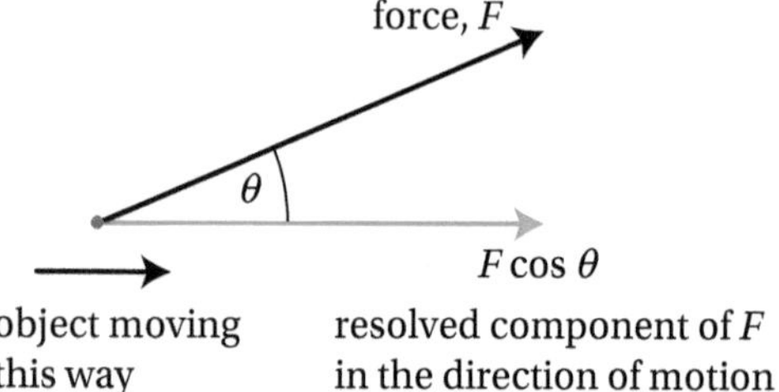

Key point 1.7

If a force is acting at an angle θ to the direction of movement:

work done = force × cos θ × distance

Rewind

Resolving forces is covered in A Level Mathematics Student Book 2, Chapter 21.

Fast forward

A In Chapter 6 you will learn that the formula for work done by a force at an angle to movement is the scalar product of the force vector and the displacement vector.

WORKED EXAMPLE 1.14

Jamal is dragging his son on a sledge on horizontal ground. He is pulling a rope, attached to the sledge, at an angle of 30° to the horizontal. The tension in the rope is 50 N. Find the work Jamal does dragging the sledge 85 m.

Work done = force × cos θ × distance

Use the definition of work done by a force acting at an angle to the direction of motion.

$\Rightarrow$ Work done = $50 \times \cos 30 \times 85$

= 3680 J (3 s.f)

WORKED EXAMPLE 1.15

A girl of mass 20 kg descends a straight smooth slide, starting from rest. The slide is 5 m in length and inclined at 10° to the horizontal. Use work and energy to calculate the speed of the girl at the bottom of the slide.

Working	Explanation
Let θ be the angle between the vertical and the slope. $\theta = 80°$	The slope makes an angle of 10° with the horizontal but 80° with the vertical.
Work done by girl's weight $= \text{weight} \times \cos\theta \times \text{distance}$ $= 20g \times \cos 80 \times 5$ $= 170.2 \text{ J}$	Calculate the work done by gravity. Use the component of the weight acting down the slope.
$170.2 = \frac{1}{2} \times 20 \times v^2$	Use the work-energy principle: work done by gravity = increase of kinetic energy
$v = 4.13 \text{ m s}^{-1}$ (3 s.f.) The girl is travelling at 4.13 m s^{-1} at the bottom of the slide.	

WORKED EXAMPLE 1.16

A box of mass 500 g is projected with speed 2.5 m s^{-1} up a smooth inclined plane. The plane slopes at 20° to the horizontal. Calculate how far the box travels up the plane by considering conservation of energy.

Working	Explanation
The slope makes an angle of 20° with the horizontal but 70° with the vertical.	The component of the weight that does work acts down the plane, at an angle of 70° to the weight.
$GPE_1 = 0$	Let gravitational potential energy at start of movement be zero ($GPE_1 = 0$).
At the end of the movement: $GPE_2 = 0.5g \times \cos 70 \times x$ $= 1.676x$	Let x m be the distance the box travels up the plane. As the box travels x metres up the plane, its gravitational potential energy increases. This is equivalent to the work done against the weight of the box: weight $\times \cos\theta \times$ distance
$KE_1 = GPE_2$ $\frac{1}{2} \times 0.5 \times 2.5^2 = 1.676x$ $x = 0.932$ m (3 s.f.) The box travels 0.932 m up the plane.	Compare mechanical energy when the box is projected with mechanical energy when it comes to rest: $GPE_1 + KE_1 = GPE_2 + KE_2$ $KE_2 = 0$ (when the box comes to rest).

EXERCISE 1D

1 A force of 25 newtons is acting at a constant 20° to the line of movement of a particle that moves 5 metres. Calculate the work done by the force.

2 A force of 1.8 kN is acting at a constant 25° to the line of movement of a particle that moves 1.2 metres. Calculate the work done by the force. Give your answer in kJ.

3 A particle is acted on by a force of 12 newtons acting at a constant angle of 15° to its direction of movement. The force does 850 joules of work. Find the distance moved by the particle.

4 A particle is acted on by a force of F newtons acting at a constant angle of 8° to its direction of movement. The force does 1250 joules of work moving the particle 55 metres. Find the value of F.

5 A particle is acted on by a force of 10.5 newtons acting at a constant angle to its direction of movement. The force does 750 joules of work moving the particle through 125 metres. Find the constant angle.

6 Calculate the increase in potential energy when a mass of 500 grams is moved 10 m up a plane inclined at 25° to the horizontal.

7 Calculate the loss of potential energy when a mass of 1.5 kg descends 20 m along a plane inclined at 35° to the horizontal.

8 A car is towed at constant speed along a horizontal straight road. The tow rope is at 30° to the horizontal and the tension in the tow rope is 180 N. The work done by the force is 4800 N. Calculate the distance moved by the car.

9 A block of mass 3 kg is released from rest on a smooth plane inclined at 18° to the horizontal, and descends 50 m down the plane. Calculate:

a the loss of potential energy of the block

b the gain in kinetic energy of the block.

10 A block of mass 20 kg is dragged up a smooth slope from rest at X to Y. The distance XY is 28 m and the slope is inclined at 6° to the horizontal. The rope used to drag the block is parallel to the slope and has a tension of 30 N. Find:

a the work done by the tension in the rope

b the change in potential energy of the block

c the speed of the block at Y.

Section 5: Power

Power is the rate of doing work. Average power is defined as the total work done by a force divided by the time taken.

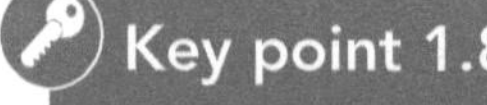

Key point 1.8

When the force applied is constant:

$$\text{average power} = \frac{\text{work done}}{\text{time taken}}$$

Power is measured in watts (W). 1 joule per second is equal to 1 watt.

Did you know?

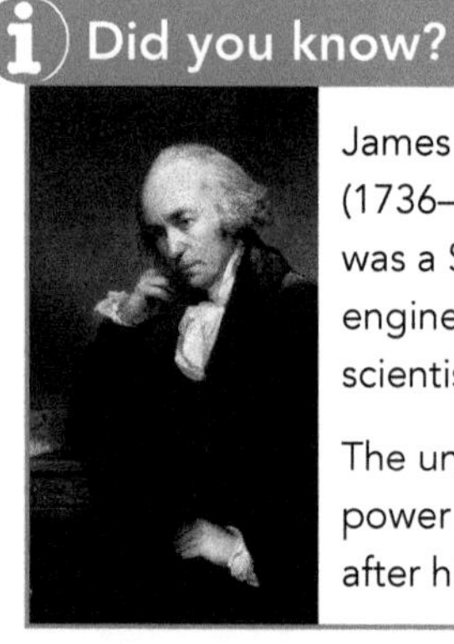

James Watt (1736–1819) was a Scottish engineer and scientist.

The unit of power is named after him.

Often you consider power in relation to a driving force but it applies equally to any force acting on an object.

WORKED EXAMPLE 1.17

A crane lifts a 2.5 tonne concrete block 35 m in 250 seconds. Calculate the average power rating of the crane during the lift, giving your answer in kW.

Work done against gravity $= \text{weight} \times \text{height gained}$
$= 2500g \times 35$
$= 87\,500g$ J

Calculate the work done by the crane lifting the block against gravity.

$\text{Power} = \dfrac{87\,500\,g}{250}$
$= 3430$ W or 3.43 kW

Use the definition of power $= \dfrac{\text{work done}}{\text{time taken}}$.

WORKED EXAMPLE 1.18

The engine brakes on a truck have a power rating of 25 kW. Calculate the total work done in 5 seconds by the braking force at this average power rating, giving your answer in kJ.

$\text{Power} = \dfrac{\text{work done}}{\text{time}}$
Work done $= \text{power} \times \text{time}$

Rearrange the definition of power to make work done the subject.

Work done by brakes $= 25\,000 \times 5$
$= 125\,000$ J or 125 kJ

Convert your answer to kJ.

WORKED EXAMPLE 1.19

A pump is used to raise water from a well. In one minute, 1500 litres of water is raised 8 metres before being ejected into a tank at a speed of 7.5 m s^{-1}. The density of water is 1000 kg m^{-3}.

a Calculate the gain of potential energy of the water per second.
b Calculate the gain of kinetic energy of the water ejected per second.
c Calculate the power of the pump, in watts.

There are 1000 litres in 1 m^3, with a mass of 1000 kg.
1500 litres of water has a mass of 1500 kg.

Work out the mass of 1500 litres of water.

a Gain of PE of water per second $= \dfrac{1500g \times 8}{60}$
$= 1960$ J

Use mgh to calculate the gain in potential energy of the water per second.

b Gain of KE of water per second $= \dfrac{\frac{1}{2} \times 1500 \times 7.5^2}{60}$
$= 703.125$ J

Use $\frac{1}{2}mv^2$ to calculate the gain of kinetic energy of the water per second.

c Work done by pump per second
$= 1960 + 703.125$
$= 2660$ J
Therefore power $= 2660$ W (3 s.f.)

Use conservation of mechanical energy:
work done by the pump = gain in GPE + gain in KE
The gain of total mechanical energy per second is the power of the pump.

You can make use of an alternative formula for power when solving problems.

From the definitions of power and work done:

$$\text{power} = \frac{\text{work done}}{\text{time taken}} = \frac{\text{force} \times \text{distance}}{\text{time taken}} = \text{force} \times \frac{\text{distance}}{\text{time}} = \text{force} \times \text{speed}$$

This definition allows you to work out power at a specific point in time if you know the force and the speed. This is often referred to as 'instantaneous power' and can be used to work out power when either the force or the velocity varies over time.

Key point 1.9

power = tractive force × speed

WORKED EXAMPLE 1.20

Chris is cycling at a constant speed of 8 m s^{-1} on a horizontal road with a power output of 200 W. Calculate the total resistance to Chris and his bicycle in newtons.

$200 = \text{tractive force} \times 8$

$\Rightarrow \text{tractive force} = 25\text{ N}$

power = tractive force × speed

Tractive force − total resistive force = 0

∴ tractive force = total resistive force

∴ total resistive force = 25 N

From $F = ma$, as Chris is travelling at constant speed the resultant force is zero.

WORKED EXAMPLE 1.21

Julia is riding her motorbike along a horizontal road with constant speed 90 km h^{-1}, at an engine power of 15 kW. Julia decides to overtake and increases to full power, 20 kW. Assuming the resistance to motion is unchanged, calculate Julia's acceleration. Julia and her motorbike have a combined mass of 465 kg.

$90\text{ km h}^{-1} = 25\text{ m s}^{-1}$

Convert Julia's speed to m s^{-1}.

Power = tractive force × speed

$\Rightarrow \text{tractive force} = \frac{\text{power}}{\text{speed}}$

Use the definition of power, but rearrange to make tractive force the subject.

For the motorbike:

$\text{tractive force} = \frac{15\,000}{25}$

$= 600\text{ N}$

Calculate the tractive force of Julia and her motorbike when she is travelling at constant speed.

Tractive force − resistance to motion = 0

∴ tractive force = resistance to motion

∴ resistance to motion = 600 N

As Julia is cruising at constant speed the resultant force is zero. Hence calculate the resistive force.

Continues on next page ...

When Julia increases to full power:

$\text{tractive force} = \frac{\text{power}}{\text{speed}} = \frac{20\,000}{25} = 800\text{ N}$

resultant force

$= \text{tractive force} - \text{resistance to motion}$

$= 800 - 600$

$= 200\text{ N}$

Using $F = ma$

$200 = 465 \times \text{acceleration}$

$\text{Acceleration} = 0.430\text{ m s}^{-2}$

When Julia increases the power, the tractive force increases so that it is greater than the resistive force, and she accelerates. Calculate the resultant force.

Use $F = ma$ to calculate Julia's acceleration.

WORKED EXAMPLE 1.22

A car of mass 1250 kg is travelling along a straight horizontal road against a resistance to motion of $kv^{\frac{1}{2}}$ N, where v is the speed of the car and k is a constant. When the engine is producing a power of 13.5 kW, the car has speed 12.5 m s^{-1} and is accelerating at 0.45 m s^{-2}.

a Find the value of k.

The maximum constant speed of the car on this road is 28 m s^{-1}.

b Find the engine's maximum power, giving your answer in kW.

The car now descends a hill, which is inclined at a constant angle $\alpha°$ below the horizontal. The car engine is working at maximum power and the vehicle moves with constant speed 36.5 m s^{-1}.

c Find the value of α, to 1 decimal place.

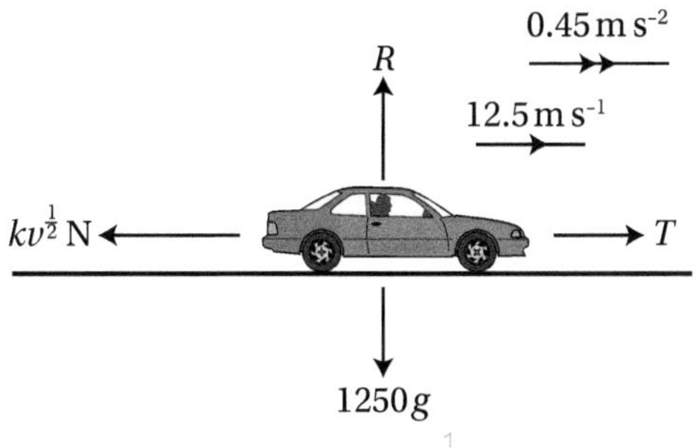

Let T be the tractive force of the car engine. Resistance varies with $v^{\frac{1}{2}}$.

a $\text{Resultant force} = T - kv^{\frac{1}{2}}$

Resultant force = T – resistance

$T = \frac{\text{power}}{\text{speed}}$

Rearrange the formula: power = force × speed

$\Rightarrow T = \frac{13\,500}{12.5}$

$= 1080\text{ N}$

Calculate T.

$\text{Resultant force} = \text{mass} \times \text{acceleration}$

$1080 - k \times 12.5^{\frac{1}{2}} = 1250 \times 0.45$

Use $F = ma$.

$k = \frac{1080 - 1250 \times 0.45}{12.5^{\frac{1}{2}}}$

$= 146.4$ or 146 units

Rearrange to find the value of k.

Continues on next page ...

Mixed practice 1

1. A woman drags a suitcase at constant speed in a straight line along horizontal ground by means of a plastic tether attached to the suitcase. The tether makes an angle of 25° with the horizontal and the tension in the tether is 50 N. Calculate the work done in moving the suitcase 150 m.

2. A car is pulled at constant speed along a horizontal straight road by a force of 200 N inclined at 35° to the horizontal. Given that the work done by the force is 5000 J, calculate the distance moved by the car.

© OCR, GCE Mathematics, Paper 4729, June 2008

3. Find the average power exerted by a rock climber of mass 80 kg when climbing a vertical distance of 60 m in 4 minutes.

4. A block is being pushed in a straight line along horizontal ground by a force of 18 N inclined at 15° below the horizontal. The block moves a distance of 6 m in 5 s with constant speed. Find:

   i the work done by the force,

   ii the power with which the force is working.

© OCR, GCE Mathematics, Paper 4729/01, January 2013

5. A and B are two points on a line of greatest slope of a smooth inclined plane, with B a vertical distance of 8 m below the level of A. A particle of mass 0.75 kg is projected down the plane from A with a speed of 2 m s^{-1}. Find:

   i the loss in potential energy of the particle as it moves from A to B,

   ii the speed of the particle when it reaches B.

© OCR, GCE Mathematics, Paper 4729/01, June 2013

6. The power developed by the engine of a car as it travels at a constant speed of 32 m s^{-1} on a horizontal road is 20 kW.

   i Calculate the resistance to the motion of the car.

   The car, of mass 1500 kg, now travels down a straight road inclined at 2° to the horizontal. The resistance to the motion of the car is unchanged.

   ii Find the power produced by the engine of the car when the car has speed 32 m s^{-1} and is accelerating at 0.1 m s^{-2}.

© OCR, GCE Mathematics, Paper 4729/01, June 2013

7. A car of mass 1600 kg moves along a straight horizontal road. The resistance to the motion of the car has constant magnitude 800 N and the car's engine is working at a constant rate of 20 kW.

   i Find the acceleration of the car at an instant when the car's speed is 20 m s^{-1}.

   The car now moves up a hill inclined at 4° to the horizontal. The car's engine continues to work at 20 kW and the magnitude of the resistance to motion remains at 800 N.

   ii Find the greatest steady speed at which the car can move up the hill.

© OCR, GCE Mathematics, Paper 4729, June 2012

8 A stone of mass 50 kg starts from rest and is dragged 35 m up a slope inclined at 7° to the horizontal by a rope inclined at 25° to the slope. The tension in the rope is 120 N and the resistance to the motion of the stone is 20 N. Calculate:

a the work done by the tension in the rope

b the change in the potential energy of the stone

c the speed of the stone after it has moved 35 m up the slope.

9 A car of mass 1250 kg travels along a straight road inclined at 2° to the horizontal. The resistance to the motion of the car is kv N, where v m s^{-1} is the speed of the car and k is a constant. The car travels at a constant speed of 25 m s^{-1} up the slope and the engine of the car works at a constant rate of 21 kW.

i Calculate the value of k.

ii Calculate the constant speed of the car on a horizontal road.

10 A car of mass 1500 kg travels along a straight horizontal road. The resistance to the motion of the car is $kv^{\frac{1}{2}}$ N, where v m s^{-1} is the speed of the car and k is a constant. At the instant when the engine produces a power of 15 000 W, the car has speed 15 m s^{-1} and is accelerating at 0.4 m s^{-2}.

i Find the value of k.

It is given that the greatest steady speed of the car on this road is 30 m s^{-1}.

ii Find the greatest power that the engine can produce.

11 The resistance to the motion of a car is $kv^{\frac{3}{2}}$ N, where v m s^{-1} is the car's speed and k is a constant. The power exerted by the car's engine is 15 000 W, and the car has constant speed 25 m s^{-1} along a horizontal road.

i Show that $k = 4.8$.

With the engine operating at a much lower power, the car descends a hill of inclination α, where $\sin\alpha = \frac{1}{15}$. At an instant when the speed of the car is 16 m s^{-1}, its acceleration is 0.3 m s^{-2}.

ii Given that the mass of the car is 700 kg, calculate the power of the engine.

12 The maximum power produced by the engine of a small aeroplane of mass 2 tonnes is 128 kW. Air resistance opposes the motion directly and the lift force is perpendicular to the direction of motion. The magnitude of the air resistance is proportional to the square of the speed and the maximum steady speed in level flight is 80 m s^{-1}.

i Calculate the magnitude of the air resistance when the speed is 60 m s^{-1}.

The aeroplane is climbing at a constant angle of 2° to the horizontal.

ii Find the maximum acceleration at an instant when the speed of the aeroplane is 60 m s^{-1}.

13 The resistance to the motion of a car of mass 600 kg is kv N, where v m s^{-1} is the car's speed and k is a constant. The car ascends a hill of inclination α, where $\sin\alpha = \frac{1}{10}$. The power exerted by the car's engine is 12 000 W and the car has a constant speed 20 m s^{-1}.

i Show that $k = 0.6$.

The power exerted by the car's engine is increased to 16 000 W.

ii Calculate the maximum speed of the car while ascending the hill.

The car now travels on horizontal ground and the power remains 16 000 W.

iii Calculate the acceleration of the car at an instant when its speed is 32 m s^{-1}.

14 A car of mass 1200 kg has a maximum speed of 30 m s^{-1} when travelling on a horizontal road. The car experiences a resistance of kv N, where v m s^{-1} is the speed of the car and k is a constant. The maximum power of the car's engine is 45 000 W.

i Show that $k = 50$.

ii Find the maximum possible acceleration of the car when it is travelling at 20 m s^{-1} on a horizontal road.

iii The car climbs a hill, which is inclined at an angle of 10° to the horizontal, at a constant speed of 15 m s^{-1}. Calculate the power of the car's engine.

15 A space shuttle of mass 400 kg is moving in a straight line in space. There is no resistance to motion, and the mass of the shuttle is assumed to be constant. With its motor working at a constant rate of 650 kW the shuttle's speed increases from 120 m s^{-1} to 160 m s^{-1} in a time t seconds.

a Calculate the value of t.

b Calculate the acceleration of the shuttle at the instant when its speed is 150 m s^{-1}.

16 A car of mass 1100 kg has maximum power of 44 000 W. The resistive forces have constant magnitude of 1400 N.

i Calculate the maximum steady speed of the car on the level.

The car is moving on a hill of constant inclination α to the horizontal, where $\sin\alpha = 0.05$.

ii Calculate the maximum steady speed of the car when ascending the hill.

iii Calculate the acceleration of the car when it is descending the hill at a speed of 10 m s^{-1} working at half the maximum power.

17 A car of mass 800 kg experiences a resistance of magnitude kv^2 N, where k is a constant and v m s^{-1} is the car's speed. The car's engine is working at a constant rate of P W. At an instant when the car is travelling on a horizontal road with speed 20 m s^{-1} its acceleration is 0.75 m s^{-2}. At an instant when the car is ascending a hill of constant slope 12° to the horizontal with speed 10 m s^{-1} its acceleration is 0.25 m s^{-2}.

i Show that $k = 0.900$, correct to 3 decimal places, and find P.

The power is increased to $1.5P$ W.

ii Calculate the maximum steady speed of the car on a horizontal road.

18 A cyclist and her bicycle have a combined mass of 70 kg. The cyclist ascends a straight hill AB of constant slope, starting from rest at A and reaching a speed of 4 m s^{-1} at B. The level of B is 6 m above the level of A. For the cyclist's motion from A to B, find

i the increase in kinetic energy,

ii the increase in gravitational potential energy.

During the ascent the resistance to motion is constant and has magnitude 60 N. The work done by the cyclist in moving from A to B is 8000 J.

iii Calculate the distance AB.

© OCR, GCE Mathematics, Paper 4729/01, June 2007

19 **i** A car of mass 800 kg is moving at a constant speed of 20 m s^{-1} on a straight road down a hill inclined at an angle α to the horizontal. The engine of the car works at a constant rate of 10 kW and there is a resistance to motion of 1300 N. Show that $\sin \alpha = \frac{5}{49}$.

ii The car now travels up the same hill and its engine now works at a constant rate of 20 kW. The resistance to motion remains 1300 N. The car starts from rest and its speed is 8 m s^{-1} after it has travelled a distance of 22.1 m. Calculate the time taken by the car to travel this distance.

© OCR, GCE Mathematics, Paper 4729/01, June 2014

20 A car of mass 1500 kg travels up a line of greatest slope of a straight road inclined at 5° to the horizontal. The power of the car's engine is constant and equal to 25 kW and the resistance to the motion of the car is constant and equal to 750 N. The car passes through point A with speed 10 m s^{-1}.

i Find the acceleration of the car at A.

The car later passes through a point B with speed 20 m s^{-1}. The car takes 28 s to travel from A to B.

ii Find the distance AB.

© OCR, GCE Mathematics, Paper 4729, January 2012

21 A car of mass 700 kg is moving along a horizontal road against a constant resistance to motion of 400 N. At an instant when the car is travelling at 12 m s^{-1} its acceleration is 0.5 m s^{-2}.

i Find the driving force of the car at this instant.

ii Find the power at this instant.

The maximum steady speed of the car on a horizontal road is 35 m s^{-1}.

iii Find the maximum power of the car.

The car now moves at maximum power against the same resistance up a slope of constant angle $\theta°$ to the horizontal. The maximum steady speed up the slope is 12 m s^{-1}.

iv Find θ.

© OCR, GCE Mathematics, Paper 4729, January 2010

22 A particle of mass 500 grams moves along the x-axis under the action of a propulsive force F. The particle's displacement, x metres, depends on time, t seconds, as follows:

$x = 3t^2 + 2t$

Find the power of force F when $t = 5$ seconds.

 A van of mass 1500 kg travels along a horizontal road against a constant resistive force of 225 N. The van travels with constant acceleration from rest, at time $t = 0$ seconds, to 15 m s^{-1} at time $t = 30$ seconds. It then travels at constant speed for 120 seconds before decelerating to rest over 25 seconds.

The speed–time graph illustrates the motion.

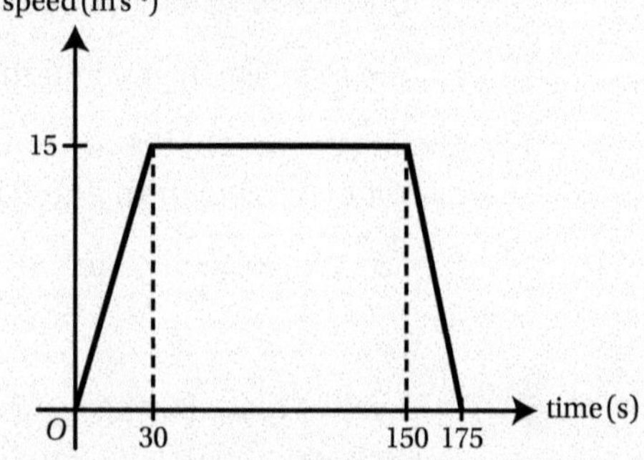

Calculate the power of the vehicle engine when:

a $t = 20$ seconds

b $t = 120$ seconds.

Calculate the power of the van's brakes when:

c $t = 160$ seconds.

2 Dimensional analysis

In this chapter you will learn how to:

- understand the concept of dimensions
- use the language and symbols of dimensional analysis
- understand the connections between units and dimensions
- check the validity of a formula by using dimensional considerations
- predict formulae by using dimensional analysis.

Before you start…

A Level Mathematics Student Book 1	You should be able to work with indices and surds.	1 Simplify: a $\frac{r^5 r^8}{r^9}$ b $(r^4)^3$ c $8^{-\frac{4}{3}}$ d $\frac{3\sqrt{6}}{\sqrt{27}}$
GCSE	You should be able to rearrange formulae.	2 Make x the subject of the formula: $y=\frac{x^2 z t^3}{t+1}$
GCSE	You should be able to solve simultaneous equations.	3 Solve the equations: $2x+3y=2$ $3x-2y=16$
GCSE	You should be able to express direct and indirect proportion in mathematical terms.	4 P is inversely proportional to r^2. If $P=2$ when $r=2$, what is the value of P when $r=6$?
GCSE	You should know common area and volume formulae.	5 For a sphere of radius 3 cm, give in terms of π expressions for: a the volume b the surface area.
A Level Mathematics Student Book 1	You should be familiar with the standard SI units of mass (kg), length (m) and time (s).	6 What are the SI units of velocity?
A Level Mathematics Student Book 2	You should know the definition of a radian.	7 What is the angle, in radians, of a sector of a circle of radius 4 cm and arc length 5 cm?

Continues on next page ...

A Level Mathematics Student Book 1	You should know the definitions and units of velocity and acceleration.	8 A particle moving in a straight line with constant velocity travels 10 m in 2 seconds. What is its velocity? State the units. 9 A particle moving in a straight line with constant acceleration increases its velocity from 8 m s^{-1} to 15 m s^{-1} in 10 seconds. What is the acceleration? State the units.
A Level Mathematics Student Book 1	You should know the definition and units of force.	10 A mass of 3 kg is acted on by a constant force of 12 N. What is its acceleration? State the units.
Chapter 1	You should know the definitions of kinetic energy $\left(\frac{1}{2}mv^2\right)$ and potential energy (mgh).	11 A mass of 3 kg is held at a height of 2 metres vertically above the ground. The particle is released from rest. By equating its loss in potential energy to its gain in kinetic energy, find its speed at the instant when it hits the ground.

What is 'dimensional analysis'?

In dimensional analysis you look at the type of unit used to measure a quantity rather than the specific units. You use it as a mathematical way of checking that equations and formulae are correct, and are combining 'like' quantities, and also to predict and establish formulae.

Section 1: Defining and calculating dimensions

The **dimensions** of a given quantity describe what sort of quantity you are measuring, so any distance or length, whatever its units, has the dimension of length and has the symbol **L**.

You can use square brackets to mean 'the dimension of' so [distance] = **L**.

The dimension of distance is **L**. The diameter of a pin, the radius of a circle, the length of a running track, the distance from London to Hong Kong are all distances that would be measured in different units, but which are all measurements of length or distance and have the dimension **L**.

The other common dimensions that you use in Mechanics are **M** for mass and **T** for time.

The mass of a spider, the mass of an elephant, the mass of a planet might all be measured in different units - there is even a unit of mass in America called a slug - but are all measurements of mass with the dimension **M**.

Similarly time, whether measured in seconds, days or centuries, has the dimension **T**.

In some branches of science, other dimensions are used, for example, the dimensions of temperature, electric current, intensity of light and amount of matter.

Did you know?

There is a connection between dimensional analysis and the greenhouse effect.

The concept of dimensional analysis is often attributed to Joseph Fourier, a famous French Mathematician and Physicist. He is probably best known for Fourier series and Fourier analysis, which is widely used in Mathematics and Physics, and for his work on heat flow.

Fourier is widely recognised as being the first scientist to suggest that the Earth's atmosphere would act as an insulation layer – the idea now known as the greenhouse effect.

Key point 2.1

The dimensions of quantities in Mechanics can be expressed in terms of **M** for mass, **L** for length and **T** for time.

You use square brackets to abbreviate the phrase 'the dimension of', so [time] = **T**.

Finding dimensions

A **scalar quantity** is a quantity that only has magnitude but not direction, whereas a **vector quantity** is a quantity that has both magnitude and direction.

Vector quantities such as velocity and **displacement** have the same dimension as their scalar equivalents (speed and distance).

To find the dimensions of quantities that are multiplied or divided, you combine their dimensions in the same way as the quantities are combined.

WORKED EXAMPLE 2.1

State the dimensions of:

a velocity **b** acceleration **c** force.

a If an object is moving with constant velocity v in a straight line and it moves a distance s in time t, then you have the relationship:

$$v = \frac{s}{t}$$

State an equation for velocity.

$$[v] = \left[\frac{s}{t}\right] = \frac{\mathrm{L}}{\mathrm{T}} = \mathrm{LT}^{-1}$$

Write down the dimensions of the right-hand side of the equation and simplify. The dimension of distance is **L** and of time is **T**. You can use negative indices with dimensions.

In more general terms:

$$v = \frac{ds}{dt}$$

$\frac{\mathrm{d}s}{\mathrm{d}t}$ has the same dimension as $\frac{s}{t}$.

$$[v] = \left[\frac{ds}{dt}\right] = \left[\frac{s}{t}\right] = \frac{\mathrm{L}}{\mathrm{T}} = \mathrm{LT}^{-1}$$

b $a = \frac{dv}{dt}$

$\frac{\mathrm{d}v}{\mathrm{d}t}$ has the same dimensions as $\frac{v}{t}$.

$$[a] = \left[\frac{dv}{dt}\right] = \left[\frac{v}{t}\right] = \frac{\mathrm{LT}^{-1}}{\mathrm{T}} = \mathrm{LT}^{-2}$$

c $F = ma$

State an equation for force ...

$$[\text{Force}] = [m][a] = \mathrm{MLT}^{-2}$$

and take dimensions of both sides of the equation.

WORKED EXAMPLE 2.2

Find the dimensions of:

a area

b kinetic energy.

a $[\text{Area}] = [\text{length}][\text{length}] = \text{L}^2$ — Area formulae always involve multiplying two lengths together or squaring a length.

b Kinetic energy $= \frac{1}{2}mv^2$ — State the formula for kinetic energy.

$[\text{Kinetic energy}] = \left[\frac{1}{2}\right][m][v^2] = [m][v]^2$ — To find the dimensions you need to multiply the dimension of m by the square of the dimensions of v. $\frac{1}{2}$ is a constant so it has no dimensions and does not affect the calculation of dimensions.

$[m][v]^2 = \text{M}(\text{LT}^{-1})^2 = \text{ML}^2\text{T}^{-2}$ — Remove the brackets and simplify the result.

Dimensionless quantities

If all the dimensions cancel out, then the quantity is said to be dimensionless. This is true of many quantities in Mechanics that are described as coefficients. Examples are the coefficient of restitution (which you will meet in Chapter 3, Section 3) and the coefficient of friction.

Rewind

The coefficient of friction is covered in A Level Mathematics Student Book 2, Chapter 21. In this chapter, you will be given the definition when required.

The limiting value of the frictional force F_{Lim} between two surfaces is proportional to the normal reaction force R between them. This can be written $F_{\text{Lim}} = \mu R$, where μ is the coefficient of friction.

$$\mu = \frac{F_{\text{Lim}}}{R}$$

Since F and R are both forces:

$$[\mu] = \frac{[F_{\text{Lim}}]}{[R]} = \frac{\mathbf{MLT}^{-2}}{\mathbf{MLT}^{-2}} = \mathbf{M}^0\mathbf{L}^0\mathbf{T}^0\ (=1)$$

So μ is dimensionless.

You can leave out dimensionless quantities when you are working out the dimensions of a formula or expression, or you can put in the number 1 to represent the dimensionless quantity.

Key point 2.2

'Pure' numbers, such as 2 and π in the formula $C = 2\pi r$, are dimensionless.

EXERCISE 2A

1 Find the dimensions of the following quantities or state if they are dimensionless:

a linear acceleration (a)

b acceleration due to gravity (g)

c force (ma)

d weight

e momentum (mv)

f π in the formula $C = 2\pi r$

g volume

h density (mass per unit volume)

i moment of a force F (force $\times$ distance)

j pressure (force per unit area)

2 What are the dimensions of $\sin\theta$?

3 What are the dimensions of $\tan^2\theta$?

4 a What are the dimensions of potential energy (mgh)?

b Are these the same as the dimensions of kinetic energy?

5 a What are the dimensions of work done? (work done = force $\times$ distance)

b How does this compare to the dimensions of kinetic or potential energy?

6 The refractive index n of a material is defined as $n = \frac{c}{v}$ where c is the speed of light in a vacuum and v is the speed of light through the material. Find $[n]$.

7 What are the dimensions of $\frac{dF}{dt}$ where F is a force and t is time?

8 a Given that all forms of mechanical energy have the same dimensions, find the dimensions of mechanical energy.

b The mechanical energy stored in an elastic string of initial length l extended by a distance x is $\frac{\lambda x^2}{2l}$ where λ is the modulus of elasticity of the string. Find the dimensions of λ.

9 Newton's law of gravitational attraction states that the force of attraction between two masses m_1 and m_2 which are a distance r apart is $\frac{Gm_1m_2}{r^2}$ where G is a constant. Find the dimensions of G.

10 The energy-frequency relationship for slow-moving particles is given by the formula $\lambda = \frac{h}{mv}$ where λ is the wavelength, m is the mass of the particle, v is velocity of the particle and h is Planck's constant. What are the dimensions of h?

Tip

Once you have established the dimensions of a quantity then the dimensions will be the same however you calculate it.

Forces all have the same dimensions however they are described, for example friction, tension, thrust, reaction force.

Section 2: Units and dimensions of sums, differences and angles

Sums and differences

Key point 2.3

You can only add and subtract terms that have the same dimensions.

If two or more quantities with the same dimensions are added or subtracted, then the resulting sum or difference will have the same dimensions.

If you add two or more lengths, then the answer is also a length with dimension **L**. If you add and subtract several forces the answer is also a force.

You can add 10 minutes to 3 hours or you can add 6 kilometres to 5 miles but you cannot add 10 seconds to 6 metres to give any meaningful result. You can only add or subtract quantities if they have the same dimensions.

Only terms having the same dimensions can be added or subtracted to give a consistent formula. You can use this principle to check whether or not a formula is dimensionally consistent. This is called an error check.

The sum $u + v$ where u and v are speeds is also a speed and has the dimension of speed.

In dimensional terms:

$$[u+v]=[u]+[v]=\mathbf{LT}^{-1}+\mathbf{LT}^{-1}=\mathbf{LT}^{-1}$$

The sum $\sum_{i=1}^{n} m_i v_i$ has the same dimensions as mv:

$$[m][v]=(\mathbf{M})(\mathbf{LT}^{-1})=\mathbf{MLT}^{-1}$$

The integral $\int_0^t v\,\mathrm{d}t$ is a sum and has the same dimension as $v\,\mathrm{d}t$, which is

$$[v][\mathrm{d}t]=(\mathbf{LT}^{-1})\mathbf{T}=\mathbf{L}$$

For sums and differences, you should check that the dimensions of the terms that you are adding or subtracting are the same. Then the dimensions of the answers will also be the same.

Tip

Many dimensional analysis questions look very complicated as they involve formulae, often with indices. Do not let the look of the question put you off, it's about applying rules!

Key point 2.4

For products and quotients you multiply or divide the dimensions.

WORKED EXAMPLE 2.3

If a, r, r_1, r_2 and h are lengths and m_1 and m_2 are masses, check that the terms being added have the same dimensions and find the dimensions of the expression.

a $ar^2 + arh$ **b** $\dfrac{m_1r_1 + m_2r_2}{m_1 + m_2}$ **c** $\sqrt{\dfrac{r_1^3 + r_2^3}{r_1 + r_2}}$

a $[ar^2 + arh] = [ar^2] + [arh] = \mathrm{L}^3 + \mathrm{L}^3 = \mathrm{L}^3$

The dimensions of both terms are $\mathbf{L}^3$ so the dimension of their sum is also $\mathbf{L}^3$.

b $\left[\dfrac{m_1r_1 + m_2r_2}{m_1 + m_2}\right] = \dfrac{[m_1r_1] + [m_2r_2]}{[m_1] + [m_2]}$

$= \dfrac{\mathrm{ML}}{\mathrm{M}} = \mathrm{L}$

The dimensions of both terms in the numerator are **ML**, so the dimension of their sum is also **ML**. The dimensions of both terms in the denominator is **M** so the dimension of their sum is also **M**. The dimension of the quotient is **L**.

c $\left[\sqrt{\dfrac{r_1^3 + r_2^3}{r_1 + r_2}}\right] = \sqrt{\dfrac{[r_1^3 + r_2^3]}{[r_1 + r_2]}}$

$= \sqrt{\dfrac{[r_1^3] + [r_2^3]}{[r_1] + [r_2]}} = \sqrt{\dfrac{\mathrm{L}^3}{\mathrm{L}}} = \mathrm{L}$

The dimension of both terms of the numerator is $\mathbf{L}^3$, so the dimension of their sum is also $\mathbf{L}^3$. The dimension of both terms of the denominator is **L** so the dimension of their sum is also **L**. You divide $\mathbf{L}^3$ by **L** giving $\mathbf{L}^2$ and take the square root.

WORKED EXAMPLE 2.4

Is the equation $v^2 = u^2 + 2gt$, where u and v are velocities, g is the acceleration due to gravity and t is time, dimensionally consistent?

Checking the dimensions of each term:

To check an equation for consistency you need to find the dimensions of each term and show that they are all of the same dimensions.

Velocity involves dividing distance by time so has dimensions LT^{-1}

$[v^2] = [v]^2 = (\mathrm{LT}^{-1})^2 = \mathrm{L}^2\mathrm{T}^{-2}$

Find the dimensions of v^2 by squaring the dimensions of v.

Similarly $[u^2] = \mathrm{L}^2\mathrm{T}^{-2}$

The dimensions of u^2 will be the same as those of v^2 as they are both velocities.

$[2gt] = [2][g][t] = [g][t]$

$[g][t] = (\mathrm{LT}^{-2})\mathrm{T} = \mathrm{LT}^{-1}$

The dimension of $2gt$ is found by multiplying the dimensions of 2, g (acceleration) and t.

As the dimensions of the three terms are not the same the equation is not dimensionally consistent so cannot be correct.

Dimensions of angles and trigonometric functions

The definition of an angle in radians is the ratio:

$$\text{angle in radians} = \frac{\text{arc length}}{\text{radius}}$$

As both arc length and radius are lengths then the dimensions of angle are $\frac{\mathbf{L}}{\mathbf{L}} = \mathbf{L}^0$ (= 1). An angle is therefore dimensionless.

All trigonometric functions are dimensionless for the same reason – they are the ratio of two quantities with the same dimensions.

Rewind

Radians were introduced in A Level Mathematics Student Book 2.

Key point 2.5

An angle has units but is dimensionless.

WORKED EXAMPLE 2.5

What are the dimensions of angular velocity, $\omega = \frac{d\theta}{dt}$, where θ is an angle in radians?

Angular velocity $\omega = \frac{d\theta}{dt}$ radians per second where θ is the angle in radians.

Define the quantity involved – angular velocity is rate of change of angle and has the symbol ω.

$[\omega] = \frac{[d\theta]}{[dt]} = \frac{1}{\mathbf{T}} = \mathbf{T}^{-1}$

Equate the dimensions of all terms in the equation.

Did you know?

The metric system originated during the French Revolution of the 1790s in order to provide a unified system of measures that used the metre and kilogram as standard units of length and mass, respectively. SI stands for 'Système Internationale' d'unités, which are the units commonly used by the scientific communities of most developed nations. The main base units are metres for length, kilograms for mass and seconds for time. The system, sometimes known as MKS after the units, was the result of an initiative to standardise units started in the late 1940s, at which time the UK was using feet, pounds and seconds as standard and most of Europe were using cgs – centimetres, grams and seconds, or mixtures of centimetres and metres, grams and kilograms, and seconds.

Definitions of some SI units

Some common **SI** units have particular names.

- A **newton** is the unit of force. 1 newton (N) is the force required to give a mass of 1 kilogram an acceleration of 1 metre per second. Force is mass × acceleration.

- The **joule** is the unit of work and energy. 1 joule (J) is the work done (or energy transferred) to an object when a force of 1 newton acts on that object in the direction of motion for a distance of 1 metre. Work done is force × distance.
- The **newton metre** is the unit of a moment (or torque). It is the effect of a force of 1 newton applied perpendicularly to a moment arm of 1 metre. The moment of a force about a point is force × perpendicular distance to the line of action of that force.
- The **watt** is the unit of power. 1 watt (W) is a rate of energy transfer or a rate of working of 1 joule per second.
- The **pascal** is the unit of pressure. 1 pascal is the pressure exerted by a force of 1 newton acting on an area of 1 square metre. Pressure is force per unit area.

EXERCISE 2B

In this exercise, the letters represent the following quantities:

- u and v for velocities
- a for acceleration
- r, s, h, x and y for distance or displacement
- θ for angles
- F for force
- t for time
- m for mass

1 If r, l and h are measurements of length, state the dimensions of:

a $r + l + h$ **b** $h^2 + rl$ **c** $r^2 l - h^3$

2 If m and m_i are masses, x_i are distances, and v and v_i are speeds, state the dimensions of:

a $m_1 v_1 + m_2 v_2$ **b** $\frac{1}{2}mv_2^2 - \frac{1}{2}mv_1^2$

c $\sum_1^n m_i x_i^2$ **d** $\int v \, dt$

3 If m_i are masses and x_i are distances, determine the dimensions of:

$$\frac{\sum_1^n m_i x_i}{\sum_1^n m_i}$$

4 Find the dimensions of each term in the following equations and hence determine which of the equations are dimensionally consistent.

a $v^2 = u^2 + 2as$

b $s = ut + \frac{1}{2}at$

c $\frac{1}{2}mv^2 - \frac{1}{2}mu^2 = mgh$

Explore

In this chapter, you are using M, L and T as dimensions. These are three of the seven basic dimensions: the other four are electrical current, thermodynamic temperature, amount of substance and luminous intensity.

You could use other quantities as your basic dimensions if they are independent, that is, if you cannot equate the dimensions of any one to a product of powers of the dimensions of the other two.

For example force, momentum and time are not independent as [force] = [momentum][time]$^{-1}$.

Can you express quantities, such as acceleration, in terms of products of powers of density (ρ), length (L) and force (F)?

d Impulse (force × time) = change in momentum

e $T = 2\pi\sqrt{\frac{l^2}{g}}$ (T is a time, l is a length and g is the acceleration due to gravity)

5 a What is the dimension of angular acceleration, commonly written as $\ddot{\theta}$?

b Is the formula $\ddot{\theta} = -\frac{g}{l}\theta$ dimensionally consistent? Give a dimensional argument for your answer.

6 In simple harmonic motion (SHM) the restoring force measured towards the centre of the motion is proportional to the displacement, x, measured away from the centre of the motion.

a Write this as an equation, in terms of m, x and t, using k as the constant of proportionality.

b What are the dimensions of k?

7 Angular momentum is defined as $I\omega$ where I is the moment of inertia $\left(\sum mr^2\right)$ and ω is angular velocity.

a What are the dimensions of angular momentum?

b Are these the same as the dimensions of linear momentum?

c Explain why angular momentum is sometimes call 'moment of momentum'.

8 The rotational kinetic energy of a rigid body about an axis is defined as $\frac{1}{2}I\omega^2$ where I is the moment of inertia $\left(\sum mr^2\right)$ of the body about that axis and ω is the angular velocity.

a What are the dimensions of rotational kinetic energy?

b Are these the same as the dimensions of translational kinetic energy?

9 Young's modulus, E, for a solid is defined as $E = \frac{\text{stress}}{\text{strain}}$.
Stress is the pressure in the solid and strain is defined as the ratio of extension to the original length.

a Write a formula for E in terms of F, A, l, and x, if F is the force exerted on the solid, A is its cross-sectional area, l is the original length and x is the extension.

b What are the dimensions of E?

10 A student writes the equation for the path of a projectile as:

$$y = x\tan\theta - \frac{gx}{2v^2}\sec^2\theta$$

a Which term in this equation is dimensionally inconsistent?

b Suggest an alteration to one variable in this term that would make it dimensionally consistent.

Tip

You can derive dimensions of a quantity either from its formula or from its units. Any formula for that quantity will have the same dimensions. The volume of an icosahedron will have the same dimensions as the dimensions of a cube: L^3. You only need to know that it is a volume to state its dimensions; you do not need the specific formula.

WORK IT OUT 2.1

A particle of mass m is fixed at the midpoint of an elastic string of natural length $2l$. The string is then fixed to two points A and B on a smooth horizontal surface, such that $AB = 2a$ and $a > l$. When the particle is displaced through a small distance x along the perpendicular bisector of AB it begins to perform small oscillations. λ is the modulus of elasticity of the string and has the dimensions of force. Use dimensional analysis to determine which option could give the correct formula for the periodic time of these oscillations.

Which solution is correct? Can you identify the errors in the incorrect solutions?

Solution 1	Solution 2	Solution 3
$T = 2\pi\sqrt{\dfrac{ma^2l}{2\lambda(a-l)}}$	$T = 2\pi\sqrt{\dfrac{mal}{2\lambda(a-l)}}$	$T = 2\pi\sqrt{\dfrac{mal}{2\lambda(a-l)^2}}$

Section 3: Finding dimensions from units and derivatives and predicting formulae

Finding dimensions from units

This is similar to finding the dimensions of a quantity from its formula.

WORKED EXAMPLE 2.6

The pascal is a unit of pressure. Pressure is force per unit area $\left(\dfrac{\text{force}}{\text{area}}\right)$. The poiseuille (PI) is the (very rarely used) SI unit of dynamic viscosity. It is equivalent to pascal seconds (Pa s). What are the dimensions of the poiseuille?

To find the dimensions of dynamic viscosity you do not need to know its formula, or even what it is, as long as you know its units. You are told that it is measured in pascal seconds.

$$\text{pressure} = \frac{\text{force}}{\text{area}}$$

A pascal is a unit of pressure so you can find its dimensions from the definition of pressure = force per unit area.

$$[\text{Pa}] = \frac{[\text{force}]}{[\text{area}]} = \frac{[\text{mass}][\text{acceleration}]}{[\text{area}]}$$

$$[\text{Pa}] = \frac{\text{MLT}^{-2}}{\text{L}^2} = \text{ML}^{-1}\text{T}^{-2}$$

Simplify the dimensions of a pascal.

$$[\text{poiseuille}] = [\text{Pa}][\text{s}] = \text{ML}^{-1}\text{T}^{-2}\text{T} = \text{ML}^{-1}\text{T}^{-1}$$

Then multiply by the dimension of seconds to give the required dimensions.

You have seen that angles have units but not dimensions. This makes it difficult to predict units from dimensions. For example, angular velocity, ω, has dimension $\mathbf{T}^{-1}$ but units of radians per second. Frequency also has dimension $\mathbf{T}^{-1}$ but has units of hertz (sometimes called cycles per second).

Key point 2.6

You can predict dimensions from units or formulae but it is not always possible to predict units from dimensions.

Tip

Do not assume that a quantity represented by a letter is dimensionless unless you are told specifically that it is.

The tension T in an elastic string of initial length l that has been stretched to $(l + x)$ is given by the formula:

$$T = \lambda \frac{x}{l}$$

where λ is the modulus of elasticity for the string. λ is a physical constant, and if the string were made of a different material, then it would have a different value. λ has the same units and dimensions as the tension. Other examples of physical constants are surface tension and the gravitational constant.

Fast forward

A You will study the tension in an elastic string in Chapter 6.

WORKED EXAMPLE 2.7

a What are the dimensions of λ, the modulus of elasticity?
b State the units of λ.

a The tension (force) T in an elastic string or spring of initial length l that has been stretched to $(l+x)$ is given by the formula: — First state a formula involving λ.

$$T = \lambda \frac{x}{l}$$

$$\lambda = \frac{Tl}{x}$$ — Then rearrange it to give a formula for λ.

$$[\lambda] = \frac{[T][l]}{[x]} = \frac{\mathsf{MLT}^{-2} \times \mathsf{L}}{\mathsf{L}} = \mathsf{MLT}^{-2}$$ — Find the dimensions of each term and combine.

b The units are newtons as $\frac{l}{x}$ is dimensionless. — As l and x have the same dimensions their quotient will be dimensionless so T and λ will have the same units, i.e. newtons, which is in keeping with the dimensions.

Finding dimensions of second derivatives

Rewind

You learned about non-uniform acceleration in A Level Mathematics Student Book 1.

You saw in an earlier example that the dimensions of acceleration are $\mathbf{LT}^{-2}$. You know that acceleration can be written as $a = \frac{d^2x}{dt^2}$. How do you find the dimensions of acceleration from $a = \frac{d^2x}{dt^2}$?

$$\frac{d^2x}{dt^2} = \frac{d}{dt}\left(\frac{dx}{dt}\right) \text{ so } \left[\frac{d^2x}{dt^2}\right] = \left[\frac{d}{dt}\left(\frac{dx}{dt}\right)\right] = \left[\frac{x}{t^2}\right] = \frac{\mathbf{L}}{\mathbf{T}^2} = \mathbf{LT}^{-2}$$

Using dimensions to predict formulae

Key point 2.7

You can use dimensional analysis to predict formulae by equating the dimensions of the terms of the proposed formula.

Tip

Remember that numerical constants, and other dimensionless quantities such as trigonometric functions, ratios and angles, can be left out of the calculation or given the dimension 1.

When you use dimensional analysis to construct a formula, you need to look at all possible factors that could affect the system, even if you then decide that the effects of some of them are negligible and so can be omitted. For example, if you are proposing a formula for the time of oscillation of a simple pendulum the obvious factors to include are the mass of the pendulum, the acceleration due to gravity and the length of the string. Other considerations would be air resistance, the mass of the string and the smoothness and shape of the mass at the end of the string, but you could reasonably assume that the effect of air resistance on a small, smooth object is negligible and that the mass of the string is small enough to have no real effect on the motion of the pendulum.

WORKED EXAMPLE 2.8

Pressure, P, is measured in newtons per metre squared. Surface tension, S, is defined as force per unit length: $\left(\frac{\text{force}}{\text{length}}\right)$.

a What are the dimensions of pressure?

b What are the dimensions of surface tension?

c The pressure P inside an ideal soap bubble is given by the formula $P = 2R^{\alpha}S^{\beta}$ where R is the radius of the sphere and S is the surface tension. Find the values of α and β and hence find the formula for P.

a $[\text{pressure}(P)] = \frac{[\text{newtons}]}{[\text{metres}^2]} = \frac{[\text{force}]}{[\text{length}]^2}$

$[P] = \frac{[\text{mass} \times \text{acceleration}]}{[\text{length}]^2} = \frac{\text{M} \times \text{LT}^{-2}}{\text{L}^2} = \text{ML}^{-1}\text{T}^{-2}$

Use the units of pressure given to write an expression for the dimensions. Newtons are units of force or mass × acceleration. Metres are units of length. Simplify the indices to give a single expression for the dimensions.

b $[\text{surface tension}(S)] = \frac{[\text{force}]}{[\text{length}]}$

$= \frac{[\text{mass} \times \text{acceleration}]}{[\text{length}]}$

$[S] = \frac{\text{MLT}^{-2}}{\text{L}} = \text{MT}^{-2}$

Use the definitions of force and length to find the dimensions of surface tension in the same way.

c $P = 2R^{\alpha}S^{\beta}$

Write down the formula given in the question.

$[P] = [R]^{\alpha}[S]^{\beta}$

Write the dimensional equation. Remember that 2 is dimensionless so can be left out.

Continues on next page ...

$ML^{-1}T^{-2} = L^{\alpha}(MT^{-2})^{\beta}$

for M: $1 = \beta$

for L: $-1 = \alpha$

for T: $-2 = -2\beta$

$\therefore \alpha = -1$ and $\beta = 1$

$\therefore P = 2R^{-1} \times S^{1} = \frac{2S}{R}$

Equate the indices of M, L and T.

Put these values of α and β back into the given formula and simplify.

WORKED EXAMPLE 2.9

A simple pendulum consists of a particle of mass m suspended at the end of an inextensible string of length l. The pendulum is initially hanging at rest and then it is displaced through a small angle θ and released to make small oscillations.

Given that the formula for the periodic time, T, of these oscillations is independent of θ for small values of θ, derive a formula for T using a dimensional argument.

$T \propto m^{\alpha} l^{\beta} g^{\gamma}$

$\therefore T = A\, m^{\alpha} l^{\beta} g^{\gamma}$ where A is a constant.

You need to consider what T is likely to depend on. The factors involved are mass, m, length of pendulum, l, and g so it is sensible to propose that T is proportional to a product of powers of these. Other factors, such as air resistance, are likely to be negligible. If the pendulum was in a viscous medium, such as oil, then the resistance of the medium would also have to be considered.

$T = A\, m^{\alpha} l^{\beta} g^{\gamma}$

$[T] = \mathrm{T}$

The periodic time T has dimension **T**.

$\mathrm{T} = [Am^{\alpha} l^{\beta} g^{\gamma}] = [A][m^{\alpha}][l^{\beta}][g^{\gamma}]$

The dimensions of both sides of the equation must be the same and are equal to **T**.

A is dimensionless

$[m] = \mathrm{M}$

$[l] = \mathrm{L}$

$[g] = \mathrm{LT^{-2}}$

State the dimension of each of the terms ...

$\mathrm{T} = \mathrm{M^{\alpha} L^{\beta} (LT^{-2})^{\gamma}} = \mathrm{M^{\alpha} L^{\beta+\gamma} T^{-2\gamma}}$

then combine them as the formula states and simplify.

$\mathrm{T^{1}} = \mathrm{T^{-2\gamma}} \Rightarrow 1 = -2\gamma \Rightarrow \gamma = -\frac{1}{2}$

Equating indices of **T** gives the value of γ.

$\mathrm{M^{0}} = \mathrm{M^{\alpha}} \Rightarrow \alpha = 0$

Equating indices of **M** gives the value of α.

$\mathrm{L^{0}} = \mathrm{L^{\beta+\gamma}} \Rightarrow 0 = \beta + \gamma \Rightarrow \beta = \frac{1}{2}$

Equating indices of **L** gives the value of β.

The values are:

$\alpha = 0 \quad \beta = \frac{1}{2} \quad \gamma = -\frac{1}{2}$

so $T = Am^{0}\, l^{\frac{1}{2}} g^{-\frac{1}{2}} = A\sqrt{\frac{l}{g}}$

Substitute these values into the equation and state a formula for T.

WORKED EXAMPLE 2.10

A particle moves in a straight line with constant acceleration a m s^{-2}. The initial velocity of the particle is u m s^{-1}. Derive a formula for the velocity, v m s^{-1}, of the particle after t seconds.

$v - u \propto a^x t^y$

$\therefore v - u = Aa^x t^y$ where A is a constant.

You need to consider the change in velocity after t seconds. The only variables involved are a and t. u is a constant. Again, air resistance can be regarded as negligible.

The dimensions of $v = u$ are LT^{-1} so the dimension of $Aa^x t^y$ is also LT^{-1}

The dimensions of all terms must be the same for consistency.

$[Aa^x t^y] = L^1T^{-1} = [A][a]^x [t]^y = [A][LT^{-2}]^x T^y$

Equate the dimensions…

L: $1 = x$

… and equate indices.

T: $-1 = -2x + y \therefore y = 1$

$\therefore v - u = Aat$ or $v = u + Aat$ where A is a constant.

State the equation and rearrange.

EXERCISE 2C

1. The watt is a unit of 1 joule per second. What are the dimensions of watts?
2. The sievert is a unit of 1 joule per kilogram. What are the dimensions of sieverts?
3. What are the dimensions of $\frac{d^2\omega}{dt^2}$, where ω is an expression for angular velocity?
4. A yank is defined to be the rate of change of force with time. What are the dimensions of yanks?
5. The area of a triangle can be written as Area $= \frac{1}{2}ab\sin C$, where a and b are side lengths and C is an angle. By stating the dimensions of each of the components, i.e. area, $\frac{1}{2}$, a, b and $\sin C$, and combining them, show that this formula is dimensionally consistent.
6. In a simple harmonic motion the displacement x can be written as $x = a\sin\omega t$, where x is the displacement and a is the amplitude (greatest distance from the centre of oscillation).
   - **a** Using a dimensional argument, explain why this formula is dimensionally consistent.
   - **b** Is it possible to determine the dimensions of ω from this equation?
7. The sine formula states that $\frac{a}{\sin A} = \frac{b}{\sin B} = \frac{c}{\sin C} = 2R^\alpha$ where R is the radius of the circumcircle of a triangle with angles A, B and C, and side lengths a, b and c, and α is a constant. Find, using dimensional analysis, the value of α, showing the steps in your argument clearly.
8. Decibels (dB) are used to describe how loud a noise is. A formula for sound level in decibels is:

   sound intensity in dB $= 10\log_{10}\left(\frac{I}{I_0}\right)$

   where I is the sound output in watts and I_0 is the threshold-level sound output in watts.
   - **a** What are the dimensions of decibels?
   - **b** A speaker has a sound output of 100 000 times the threshold level. Express this in decibels.

9 **a** What are the dimensions of acceleration?

An equation for oscillations of a damped simple harmonic motion when a system is displaced through a small distance x is $\frac{d^2x}{dt^2}+A\frac{dx}{dt}=-Bx$ where A and B are constants. Given that this equation is dimensionally consistent find:

b the dimensions of A

c the dimensions of B.

10 A light inextensible string of length l is fixed at one end and has a particle of mass m fixed at the other end. The mass m is moving at constant speed v in a horizontal circle of radius r and the string is fully extended. The string makes an angle θ with the downward vertical. Given that $\tan\theta = v^{\alpha}r^{\beta}g^{-1}$, use a dimensional argument to find a formula for $\tan\theta$ in terms of v, r and g, where g is the acceleration due to gravity.

Section 4: Summary of dimensions and units

The following exercise forms a summary of common units and dimensions.

EXERCISE 2D

1 Copy and complete the following table.

Quantity	Dimension	SI unit
Time		
Mass		
Weight (mg)		newton (N)
Length (displacement)		
Area		
Volume		
Velocity		
Acceleration	LT^{-2}	
Acceleration due to gravity		m/s^2 or m s^{-2}
Force (ma)		newton (N)
Kinetic energy $\left(\frac{1}{2}mv^2\right)$		joule (J)
Gravitational potential energy (mgh)		
Work done (force × distance moved)		joule (J)
Moment of a force (force × distance)		newton metre (N m)
Power $\left(\text{rate of doing work: } \frac{dW}{dt}\right)$		watt (W)
Momentum (mv)		kg m s^{-1}
Impulse (force × time)		newton second (N s)
Moment of inertia $\left(\sum mr^2\right)$		
Angular velocity $\left(\omega=\frac{d\theta}{dt}\right)$		
Density $\left(\frac{\text{mass}}{\text{volume}}\right)$		

Quantity	Dimension	SI unit
Pressure $\left(\frac{\text{force}}{\text{area}}\right)$		pascal (Pa)
Time period (time for one complete cycle)		
Frequency $\left(\frac{1}{\text{time period}}\right)$		hertz (Hz)
Surface tension $\left(\frac{\text{force}}{\text{length}}\right)$		

Checklist of learning and understanding

- In Mechanics, dimensions describe a quantity in terms of three basic dimensions **M**ass, **L**ength and **T**ime. Other dimensions are used in other branches of Mathematics and Science.
- You use square brackets to denote 'the dimensions of', so [time] = **T**.
- You can only add and subtract terms that have the same dimensions and the resulting sum or difference will also have the same dimensions.
- For products and quotients you multiply or divide the dimensions.
- A formula must be dimensionally consistent to be valid.
- Angles and numerical constants are dimensionless.
- If two quantities are equal, then they have the same dimensions.
- You can find the dimensions of a quantity from its definition, from an equation describing it or from its units.
- Quantities can have units but be dimensionless. For example, angles in radians are dimensionless.
- You cannot predict units from dimensions, as some dimensionless quantities have units.
- In dimensional calculations, you can give dimensionless quantities the dimensional value 1.
- You can use dimensional analysis to predict formulae by equating dimensions on both sides of a proposed formula.

Mixed practice 2

1. State the dimensions of:

   a $2\pi\sqrt{\frac{l}{g}}$, where l is a length and g is the acceleration due to gravity

   b $\frac{\mathrm{d}^2v}{\mathrm{d}t^2}$, where v is an expression for speed.

2. Heron's (or Hero's) formula for the area of a triangle with sides of length a, b, and c is

   Area $=\sqrt{s(s-a)(s-b)(s-c)}$ where s is half the perimeter. Show, with full explanation, why this formula is dimensionally consistent.

3. a Tension in a string is a force. What are the dimensions of tension?

   b In the following formulae, T is the tension in a string, m is a mass, v is a velocity, r is a length and θ is an angle. Which of the formulae is dimensionally consistent? If the formula is inconsistent, state which term is inconsistent.

   i $T-mg\cos\theta=\frac{mv}{r}$ ii $T-mg\cos\theta=\frac{mv^2}{r}$ iii $T-g\cos\theta=\frac{mv^2}{r}$

4. a What are the dimensions of potential energy?

   b In the cgs (centimetres, grams and seconds) system a particle has potential energy of 5.2×10^8 ergs. What is this in joules?

5. In a simple harmonic motion of a mass m the restoring force is proportional to the displacement. At time t, the displacement x and the acceleration a are given by:

   $$x=A\cos\left(\sqrt{\frac{k}{m}}t\right)$$

   $$a=-\frac{k}{m}A\cos\left(\sqrt{\frac{k}{m}}t\right)$$

   Find the dimensions of:

   a A b k.

6. The radial force on a particle moving in a circle is thought to be of the form $F=m^{\alpha}v^{\beta}r^{\gamma}$. By writing each of the components in term of its dimensions, and equating indices, form three equations to find the values of α, β and γ and hence find the formula for F.

7. a What are the dimensions of force?

   b Newton's law of gravitational attraction states that the force of attraction, F, between two bodies of masses m_1 and m_2 is dependent on the masses, the distance r between them and the constant G so that it can be written as:

   $F=G^{\alpha}m_1^{\beta}m_2^{\gamma}r^{\delta}$

   Write down, with reasons, the relationship between β and γ.

   c Given that the dimensions of G are $\mathbf{M}^{-1}\mathbf{L}^{3}\mathbf{T}^{-2}$, use a dimensional proof to find a formula for F.

8 **a** What are the dimensions of angular acceleration?

b An equation for oscillations of a damped pendulum of length l displaced by a small angle θ is given by $\frac{\mathrm{d}^2\theta}{\mathrm{d}t^2} + A\frac{\mathrm{d}\theta}{\mathrm{d}t} = -B\theta$, where A and B are constants. Given that this equation is dimensionally consistent, find the dimensions of A.

c By expressing B as a product of powers of l and g, where g is the acceleration due to gravity, find an expression for B in terms of l and g.

9 Surface tension is defined as force per unit length.

a What are the dimensions of surface tension?

b When liquid forms a puddle on a clean horizontal surface, the depth d of the puddle has a maximum value that can be written as:

$d = AS^{\alpha}\rho^{\beta}g^{\gamma}$

where A is a dimensionless constant, S is surface tension, g is the acceleration due to gravity and ρ is the density of water. Use dimensional analysis to find a formula for d.

c If $d = 5.4$ mm when $S = 0.073$ N m^{-1} and 1 m^3 of water has a mass of approximately 1000 kg, find the value of A.

10 Tension is a force.

a What are the dimensions of tension?

b Frequency, f, has dimension T^{-1}. Mersenne's law states that the fundamental frequency of a string is of the form $f = \frac{1}{2}l^{\alpha}F^{\beta}\mu^{\gamma}$, where $\frac{1}{2}$ is a dimensionless constant, l is the length of the string, F is the tension in the string and μ is the mass per unit length of the string. Use dimensional analysis to find the values of α, β and γ and hence find the formula for f.

11 **a** Pressure is force per unit area, measured in the unit pascal. What are the dimensions of pressure?

b Dynamic viscosity μ is measured in pascal seconds. What are the dimensions of μ?

c The terminal velocity v_T of a small spherical particle, of radius r and density ρ, falling vertically down though a medium of density ρ_1 and dynamic viscosity μ, is given by:

$$v_T = A\frac{r^{\alpha}g^{\beta}(\rho - \rho_1)}{\mu}$$

where A is a dimensionless constant and g is the acceleration due to gravity. Use dimensional analysis to find the values of α and β.

12 The formula for the lifting force F generated on a wing of an aeroplane is of the form $F = k\rho^{\alpha}v^{\beta}A^{\gamma}$, where k is a dimensionless constant, ρ is the air density, v is the air speed and A is the surface area of the wing. Use dimensional analysis to find the values of α, β and γ and hence find the formula for F.

13 Surface tension, S, is defined as force per unit length.

a State the dimensions of S.

b State the dimensions of density.

c The average height, h, of a liquid in a capillary tube can be written as $h = AS\rho^{\alpha}r^{\beta}g^{\gamma}$, where A is a dimensionless constant for the liquid, S is the surface tension, ρ is the density of the liquid, r is the internal radius of the tube and g is the acceleration due to gravity. Use a dimensional argument to find the values of α, β and γ and hence find the formula for h.

d In this question part use $g = 9.8\ \text{m s}^{-2}$, and give your final answer to an appropriate degree of accuracy. $1\ \text{m}^3$ of water has a mass of approximately 1000 kg. Water rises up a vertical capillary tube that has a diameter of 0.3 mm. Given that $A = 2$ and $S = 0.072\ \text{N m}^{-1}$, what is the height of water in the tube, in millimetres?

3 Momentum and collisions 1

In this chapter you will learn how to:

- understand momentum and impulse in mathematical terms with units
- understand that linear momentum is conserved in a collision between objects that are free to move
- understand that impulse on a body is equal to the change in momentum
- understand Newton's experimental law for collisions
- analyse and solve problems involving simple collisions in a straight line
- analyse and solve problems involving simple cases of connected particles.

Before you start...

GCSE	You should be able to solve simultaneous equations both for two linear equations and for one linear and one quadratic equation.	1 Solve the equations: $4x+5y=8$ $6x+4y=5$ 2 Solve the equations: $x^2+3y=2$ $y=2x-3$
GCSE	You should know the equations of linear motion with constant acceleration.	3 A particle of mass 2 kg is dropped from a height of 6 metres above a pond. What is the speed of the particle at the instant when it hits the water?
A Level Mathematics Student Book 1	You should understand the definitions and units of velocity, acceleration and force.	4 State the units of: a velocity b acceleration c force.
A Level Mathematics Student Book 1	You should know Newton's second law: force = mass × acceleration	5 A constant force of 15 N acts on a particle of mass 2 kg. What is the acceleration of the particle?
Chapter 1	You should know the definition of kinetic and potential energy.	6 The speed of a particle of mass 0.1 kg is $4\ \text{m s}^{-1}$. What is its kinetic energy?

What are momentum and impulse?

You use and understand the concepts of impulse and momentum instinctively in everyday life. If you hit a ball with a tennis racquet, you know that the ball will move in the direction in which you hit it, and the harder you hit it, the faster and further it will go because it receives a greater impulse.

A ball rolling down a slope gathers momentum. A hammer hitting a nail sends the nail forward in the direction of the blow and the hammer bounces back slightly in our hands. Events such as playing snooker or air hockey, applying the brakes in a vehicle, pile-driving the foundations of a building, hitting or kicking a ball, the wind blowing the sails of a boat and carrying it forward, can all be modelled using these two concepts.

Section 1: Momentum and impulse

If you apply a force to a stationary object, the object will try to move in the direction of the force. If the force continues to act in the same direction and there is no resistance, the object will move more and more quickly.

WORKED EXAMPLE 3.1

An object of mass m is moving at u m s^{-1} on a smooth surface in a straight line and a constant force F N is applied to it in the direction of the motion for t seconds. If the final velocity of the object is v m s^{-1} show that $Ft = mv - mu$.

$F = ma$	State Newton's second law $F = ma$. The acceleration is constant, since F and m are both constant.
$v = u + at$	Use the equations of motion in a straight line with constant acceleration to find the final velocity v from the initial velocity u.
$mv = mu + mat$	Multiply this equation through by m.
$mv = mu + Ft$	Substitute F for the term ma.
$Ft = mv - mu$	Rearrange the equation as shown.

Momentum is the product of mass and velocity and is measured in kg m s^{-1}.

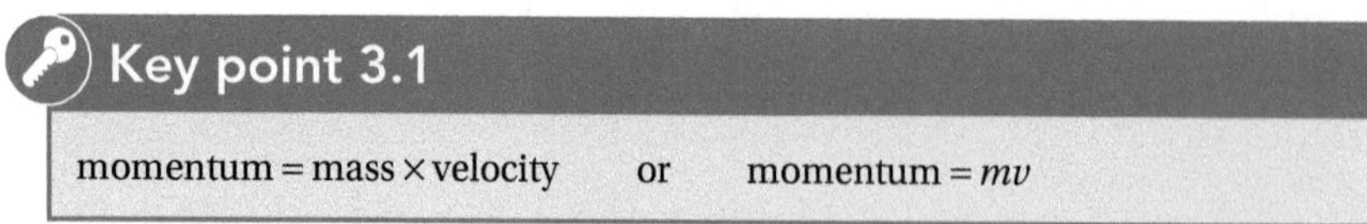
Key point 3.1

momentum = mass × velocity or momentum = mv

Impulse is the product of force and time, has the symbol I, and is measured in N s (newton seconds).

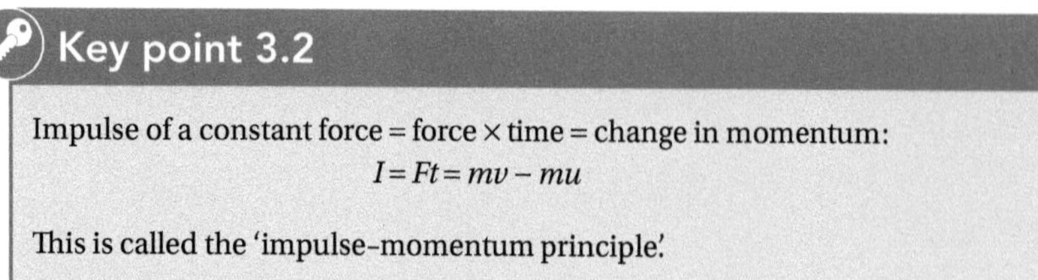
Key point 3.2

Impulse of a constant force = force × time = change in momentum:

$$I = Ft = mv - mu$$

This is called the 'impulse-momentum principle'.

Although the units for momentum and impulse appear to be different, they are in fact equivalent.

Momentum, force, impulse and velocity are all vectors and can be expressed in vector format.

Tip

1. As force, impulse and momentum are all vector quantities their direction matters, so it is often helpful to draw a diagram. Remember to label a direction on the diagram as positive.
2. Always check the units and convert to kilograms, metres and seconds, if necessary.

WORKED EXAMPLE 3.2

A football of mass 450 g is travelling along the ground at 20 m s^{-1}. What is its momentum?

positive direction →

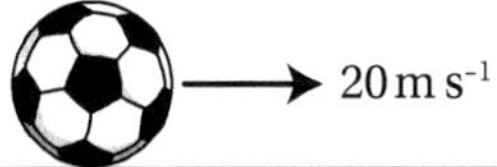

20 m s^{-1}

Working	Explanation
$450\text{ g} = 0.45\text{ kg}$	Convert the mass from g to kg.
Momentum = mass × velocity or just mv	State the formula.
Momentum $= 0.45 \times 20 = 9\text{ kg m s}^{-1}$	Substitute values into the stated formula.

WORKED EXAMPLE 3.3

A particle of mass m kg is at rest on a smooth, horizontal surface. It is hit with an impulse of I N s. What is its velocity immediately after the impulse?

Working	Explanation
Impulse = change in momentum $I = mv - mu$	State the impulse-momentum principle.
Initial momentum $= m \times 0 = 0$ Final momentum $= m \times v = mv$ Change in momentum $= mv - 0 = mv$	Work out the change in momentum by subtracting the initial momentum from the final momentum.
So $I = mv$ giving $v = \frac{I}{m}$ m s^{-1}	Equate the impulse to the change in momentum.

Modelling

When you make a mathematical model you look at a simplified situation. Initially, you model all objects as point masses and do not take into account their size or what they are made of. As you learn more about the situation you can make better models and can put in more accurate data.

Focus on ...

You will learn more about mathematical modelling in Focus on ... Modelling 1.

Tip

You don't have to draw a complicated diagram, as long as it is clear. For example, in Worked example 3.4 the boats could be replaced by dots.

WORKED EXAMPLE 3.4

A toy sailing boat of mass 800 g is blown along by a constant wind acting horizontally with a force of 0.2 N. If the boat is initially at rest, find its velocity after 10 seconds.

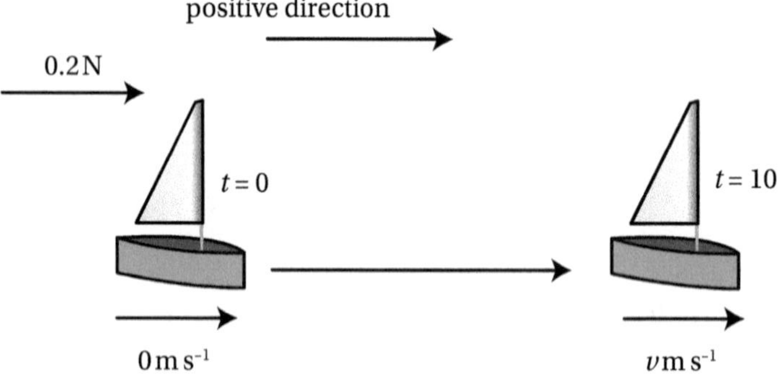

$u = 0$

$m = 800\text{ g} = 0.8\text{ kg}$

$F = 0.2$

$t = 10$ — State the values you are given and convert g to kg.

Let final velocity $= v$ — Define any unknowns.

Impulse = change in momentum — State the formula.

$Ft = mv - mu$

$2 = 0.8v - 0.8 \times 0 = 0.8v$

so $v = 2.5\text{ m s}^{-1}$ in the direction of the wind. — Substitute the values and calculate. As you are asked for velocity, you must also state the direction.

WORKED EXAMPLE 3.5

A football of mass 450 g is travelling in a straight line along the ground at 20 m s^{-1} when it is kicked along the line of motion and starts to move with a speed of 25 m s^{-1}. Calculate the impulse given to the football by the footballer's kick if:

a the ball is now moving in the opposite direction

b the ball continues to move in the same direction.

a

Draw a diagram to illustrate the situation.

+ve →

Choose a positive direction.

$m = 450\text{ g} = 0.45\text{ kg}$

Check the units and change g to kg.

$u = 20\text{ m s}^{-1}$

$v = -25\text{ m s}^{-1}$

State the values you know. v has a negative sign as the football is moving in the negative direction after it is kicked.

Change in momentum $= mv - mu$

To find the impulse you need to find the change in momentum.

$mv - mu = (0.45 \times -25) - (0.45 \times 20)$

Substitute the values and calculate.

$= -11.25 - 9$

$= -20.25$

Impulse $= -20.25$ N s or 20.25 N s in the opposite direction to the approaching ball.

The impulse is negative, which tells you that it is in the opposite direction to the original direction of the ball. This means the ball was moving towards the footballer, who then kicked it back along the line of motion. You need to give the direction as well as the magnitude of the impulse.

b

before

after

Draw a new diagram to illustrate the second situation.

+ve →

$m = 450\text{ g} = 0.45\text{ kg}$

Check the units and change g to kg.

$u = 20\text{ m s}^{-1}$

$v = 25\text{ m s}^{-1}$

State the values you know. v now has a positive sign as it is moving in the positive direction.

Continues on next page ...

Change in momentum $= mv - mu$	To find the impulse you need to find the change in momentum.
$mv - mu = (0.45 \times 25) - (0.45 \times 20)$ $= 11.25 - 9 = 2.25$	Substitute the values and calculate.
Impulse $= 2.25$ N s or 2.25 N s in the same direction as the initial movement of the ball.	The impulse is positive, which tells you that it is in the same direction as the original direction of the ball. This means the ball was moving away from the footballer, who then kicked it in the same direction.

Tip

Remember that velocity and impulse are vector quantities so you must show the direction by using plus and minus signs and use these in your calculations.

EXERCISE 3A

1 Calculate the momentum of the following in kg m s^{-1}. Make sure you change to standard units (kg, m, s) before you start, if necessary.

a A rocket of mass 15 kg and velocity 150 m s^{-1}

b A cat of mass 4.5 kg and velocity 5 m s^{-1}

c A marble of mass 10 g and velocity 20 m s^{-1}

d A car of mass 1200 kg and velocity 60 km h^{-1}

e A rhino of mass 1.4 tonnes running at 20 m s^{-1}.

2 A bullet of mass 5 g is fired from a rifle. Its momentum is 4.5 N s as it leaves the rifle. What is its velocity?

3 A car is moving at a velocity of 15 m s^{-1}. Its momentum is 12 000 N s. What is its mass in metric tonnes?

4 What impulse is generated by an engine that exerts a force of 6 N for 20 seconds?

5 What impulse is generated by an engine that exerts a force of 6 N for 2 minutes?

6 The table shows the velocity in m s^{-1} of a particle of mass m kg before and after an impulse is applied to it. Calculate the impulse in N s each case. The arrow indicates direction and the first one is done for you.

Positive direction →		
Initial velocity (m s^{-1})	**Final velocity (m s^{-1})**	**Impulse (N s)**
4 →	6 →	$(+6m) - (+4m) = +2m$
4 →	2 →	
4 →	← 6	
← 8	← 3	
← 3	8 →	

7 A sailing boat of mass 600 kg is stationary on the sea when it is blown by a wind that exerts a constant force of 10 N. What is the speed of the boat, in m s^{-1}, after 5 minutes?

8 A motor boat, of mass 600 kg, is moving in a straight line at a speed of 8 m s^{-1}. The drag of the water produces a constant force of 10 N in the direction opposite to the direction of motion of the boat. How long does it take for the speed of the boat to halve?

9 A gyrfalcon of mass 1.2 kg is flying at 15 m s^{-1} with a following wind that exerts a constant force of 0.6 N in the direction in which the gyrfalcon is flying. What is the gyrfalcon's speed, in m s^{-1}, 10 seconds later?

10 A gyrfalcon of mass 1.2 kg is flying at 15 m s^{-1} into a wind that exerts a constant force of 0.6 N in the direction opposite to the flight of the gyrfalcon. What is the gyrfalcon's speed, in m s^{-1}, 10 seconds later?

11 A football of mass 500 g is kicked along the ground and hits a vertical wall at right angles. As it hits the wall, its speed is 20 m s^{-1} and it bounces straight back with a speed of 15 m s^{-1}. What is the impulse of the wall on the ball?

12 A bowling ball of mass 2 kg is rolled along the ground and hits a vertical wall at right angles. As it hits the wall, its speed is 15 m s^{-1} and it bounces straight back with a speed of 10 m s^{-1}. What is the impulse of the wall on the ball?

13 A motorbike of mass 250 kg slows down from 25 m s^{-1} to 15 m s^{-1} in 20 seconds. What is the magnitude, in newtons, of the constant braking force?

14 A motorbike of mass 200 kg accelerates from 18 km h^{-1} to 72 km h^{-1} in 20 seconds. What is the magnitude, in newtons, of the constant accelerating force produced by the engine?

Section 2: Collisions and the principle of conservation of momentum

In a game of snooker, if the cue ball hits a stationary red ball it exerts a force on the red ball that causes it to move along the line of the collision. From Newton's third law, there is an equal and opposite reaction force on the cue ball. As the time for which the collision force acts is the same for both balls - i.e. the time the two balls are in contact - then the impulse I (force $\times$ time) on the two balls is also the same but in opposite directions.

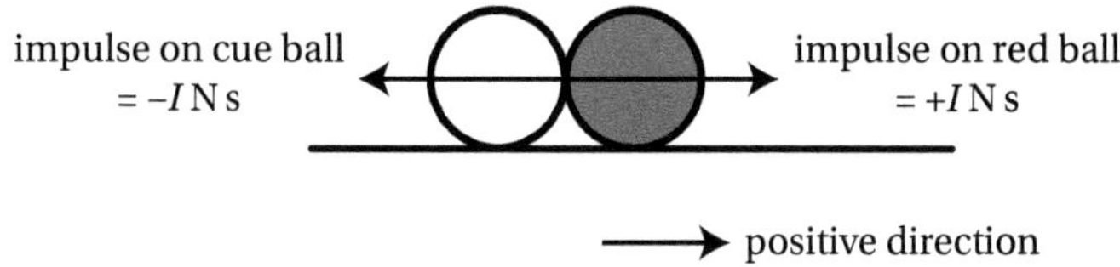

Total impulse on the two balls along the line of the collision is $-I + I = 0$

As the total impulse is zero, there is no change in total momentum, which means that linear momentum is conserved in a collision between two objects when they are both free to move.

This is called 'the principle of conservation of linear momentum.' We can see this by considering the following argument.

Did you know?

Cannon on Spanish galleons were originally mounted on the highest part of the ship to give the best possible advantage over the enemy. It was soon realised that the impulse of the cannon's recoil on the ship at such a height was making the ship unstable and likely to capsize, so the cannon were moved down to the lower decks.

Consider a collision between two objects, A and B, of mass m_1 and m_2, moving with velocities u_1 and u_2 in the same straight line. If their respective velocities after the collision are v_1 and v_2 then:

The impulse on A = the change in momentum of $A = m_1v_1 - m_1u_1$

The impulse on B = the change in momentum of $B = m_2v_2 - m_2u_2$

The impulse on A = –(the impulse on B)

$$m_1v_1 - m_1u_1 = -(m_2v_2 - m_2u_2)$$

$$m_1v_1 - m_1u_1 = -m_2v_2 + m_2u_2$$

Rearranging gives:

$$m_1u_1 + m_2u_2 = m_2u_2 + m_2v_2$$

$m_1u_1 + m_2u_2$ is the total momentum before the collision and $m_1v_1 + m_2v_2$ is the total momentum after the collision.

Key point 3.3

If there are no external impulses then total momentum before collision = total momentum after collision

$$m_1u_1 + m_2u_2 = m_1v_1 + m_2v_2$$

WORKED EXAMPLE 3.6

A ball of mass $3m$ kg is moving at 10 m s^{-1} when it collides with a second ball of mass $2m$ kg moving towards it on the same straight line with a velocity of 6 m s^{-1}. If the second ball now moves in the opposite direction at 6 m s^{-1}, find:

a the final speed of the ball of mass $3m$ kg

b in terms of m, the magnitude of the impulse on the ball of mass $3m$.

positive direction ⟶

Draw a clear diagram with the positive direction marked and values in standard units.

3m → 10 m s^{-1} 6 m s^{-1} ← 2m

initial

final

a Let the final velocity of the mass $3m$ be v.

Define the unknown.

Total momentum before collision = total momentum after collision

Use the principle of conservation of linear momentum.

$m_1u_1 + m_2u_2 = m_1v_1 + m_2v_2$

State the formula.

Continues on next page ...

$3m \times 10 + 2m \times (-6) = 3m \times v + 2m \times 6$

$30m - 6(2m) = 3mv + 2m(6)$

$18m = 3mv + 12m$

$v = 2 \text{ m s}^{-1}$

Substitute the values, remembering that direction is indicated by sign.

Solve for v.

The ball of mass $3m$ moves at 2 m s^{-1} in the direction of its initial motion.

So the final speed is 2 m s^{-1}.

Note that you were asked for speed, so you do not include the minus sign with your answer.

b Find the impulse on the $2m$ mass.

Impulse = change in momentum

= final momentum − initial momentum

$= 2m(6) - 2m(-6)$

$= 24m$ N s

The impulse on the two balls is equal and opposite so it is sensible to find the impulse on the $2m$ mass as you are given its velocities. This will give the correct answer even if you have made a mistake calculating the velocity of the mass $3m$. However, you can use the impulse on the ball of mass $3m$ to check your answer.

The impulse on the ball of mass $3m$ is equal and opposite so is $-24m$ N s or $24m$ N s in the negative direction. Its magnitude is $24m$ N s.

If you are asked for the magnitude, you do not give the minus sign with your answer.

WORKED EXAMPLE 3.7

A snooker cue ball of mass 160 g travelling at 10 m s^{-1} hits a red ball of mass 170 g travelling in the same direction at 6 m s^{-1}. If the red ball continues to move in the same direction but at 9 m s^{-1} find:

a the magnitude of the impulse on the red ball

b the magnitude of the impulse on the cue ball

c in terms of m, the speed of the cue ball after the collision.

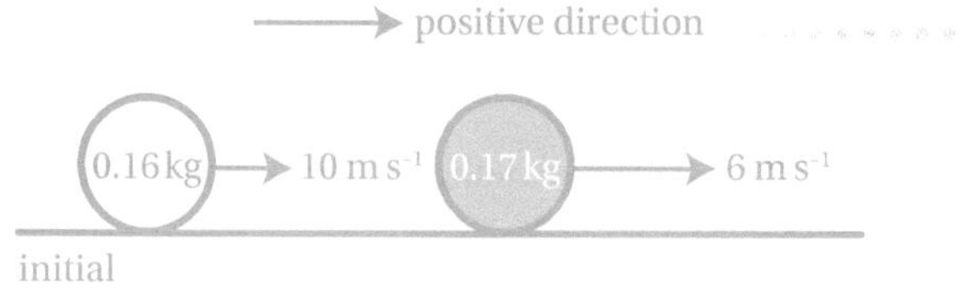

Draw diagrams to show the situation clearly. Make sure that you label a direction as positive.

The masses 160 g and 170 g are written as 0.16 kg and 0.17 kg.

Continues on next page ...

a Impulse = change in momentum

$I = mv - mu$

$= 0.17 \times 9 - 0.17 \times 6$

$= 1.53 - 1.02$

$= 0.51$ N s

The impulse on the red ball is 0.51 N s, in the direction of the motion.

For the red ball only, work out the impulse by finding the change in momentum.

b The impulse on the cue ball is equal and opposite and so it is −0.51 N s. The magnitude of this is 0.51 N s.

The impulse on the cue ball is equal and opposite to the impulse on the red ball. The magnitude is the modulus of this so you omit the minus sign in the answer. Only omit the minus sign if you are asked for the magnitude, otherwise leave it in as it indicates direction.

c The impulse on the cue ball = −0.51 N s

Let the final speed of the cue ball be v.

State the values you know and define the unknown quantity.

Impulse = final momentum − initial momentum

Initial momentum = 0.16×10

Final momentum = $0.16v$

State the formula and the values.

$I = mv - mu$

$-0.51 = 0.16v - 0.16 \times 10$

Put impulse equal to the change in momentum. Here you do need to write the minus sign.

$0.16v = -0.51 + 0.16 \times 10$

$0.16v = -0.51 + 1.6$

$v = 6.8$ m s^{-1} (to 1 d.p.)

Rearrange to find v. The final speed is positive showing that the cue ball continues to move in the same direction but is slower than before.

WORK IT OUT 3.1

Two particles of masses m_1 and m_2 collide. Their speeds before the collision are 4 m s^{-1} and 3 m s^{-1}, respectively, and they are moving in the same direction, which is taken as the positive direction. After the collision, their speeds are v_1 and v_2, respectively.

Solutions 1, 2 and 3 give three possible sets of values for v_1 and v_2. Which solution is possible? Explain why the other two solutions are not possible.

	Solution 1	Solution 2	Solution 3
v_1 m s^{-1}	+5	+4.5	−2
v_2 m s^{-1}	+2	+5	+4

Masses that combine

In some situations, two objects 'move off together' or 'coalesce' after a collision. This means that they combine into one object, rather like two raindrops running down a window that combine to form a single drop. When objects coalesce in a collision, their masses are added together after the collision.

WORKED EXAMPLE 3.8

A toy truck of mass 2 kg is travelling at 10 m s^{-1} when it hits a stationary toy truck of mass 3 kg. If the two trucks move off together, what is their speed immediately after the collision?

positive direction →

2 kg → 10 m s^{-1} 3 kg → 0 m s^{-1}

initial

5 kg → v m s^{-1}

final

Draw a diagram with masses, speeds and the positive direction labelled.

Total momentum before collision = total momentum after collision

Use the principle of conservation of linear momentum.

$m_1u_1 + m_2u_2 = m_1v_1 + m_2v_2$

State the formula.

Let v be the speed of the combined trucks.

Define the unknown quantity.

$(2\times10)+(3\times0)=5\times v$

$5v=20$

$v=4\,\text{m s}^{-1}$

Substitute the values and calculate.

WORKED EXAMPLE 3.9

A cat, of mass 700 g, is sitting on a toy train of mass 2.5 kg that is free to move on a straight horizontal track. The train is at rest when the cat jumps off the train. The direction of the cat is horizontal and in the direction of the track. The velocity of the cat is 2 m s^{-1}. What is the velocity of the train immediately after the cat jumps off?

Draw a diagram.

$(0.7\times0)+(2.5\times0)=(0.7\times2)+2.5v$

$0=1.4+2.5v$

Apply the principle of conservation of linear momentum.

$\Rightarrow v=-0.56$

Solve for v.

The velocity of the train is 0.56 m s^{-1} in the opposite direction to the cat's jump.

Further examples: multiple collisions and using change in kinetic energy

Harder examples often involve multiple collisions. Here you need to split the problem into parts and treat each collision as a separate event. As usual, you need to draw clear diagrams and set out your working clearly.

Change in kinetic energy is considered in Chapter 1.

WORKED EXAMPLE 3.10

Three particles, P, Q and R, of masses m, $2m$ and $3m$ kg, are moving with velocities 2.5 m s^{-1}, 2 m s^{-1} and 1 m s^{-1}, respectively, as shown in the diagram.

positive direction ⟶

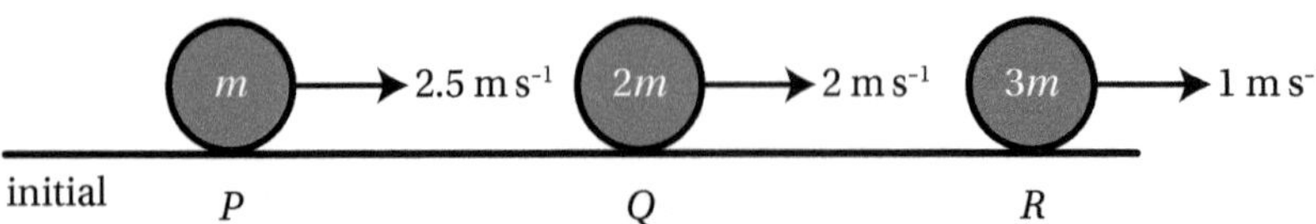

P collides with the mass Q, which then goes on to collide and coalesce with particle R. The combined particle moves with speed 1.5 m s^{-1}.

a What is the speed of Q after the first collision?

b What is the kinetic energy lost by P in the collision with Q?

a Collision 1:

positive direction ⟶

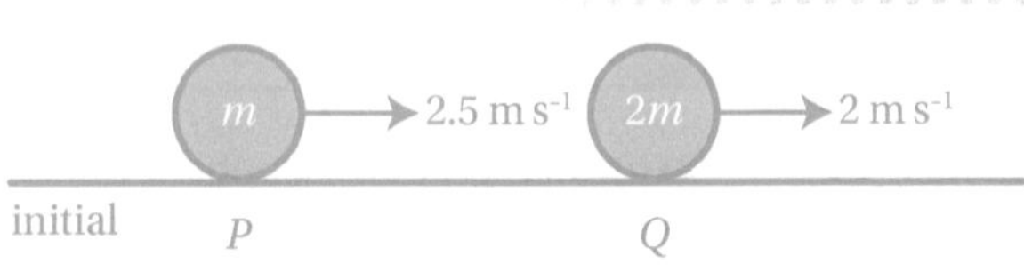

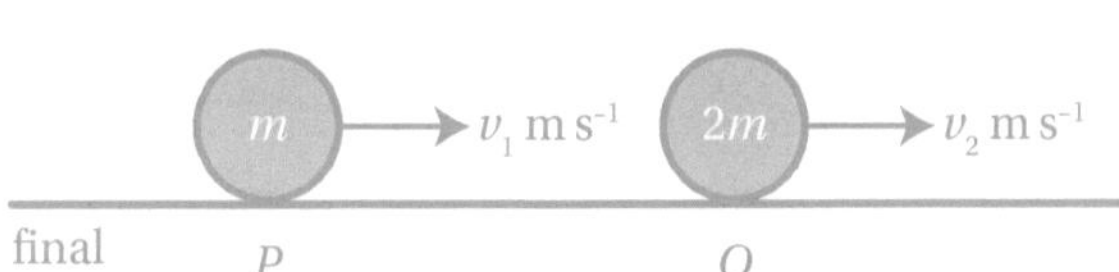

Always draw a diagram to show the situation. Both collisions need two sets of diagrams. Label the speeds clearly, with their directions, and mark the positive direction. The signs of the final answers will give the direction of the motion.

Draw the diagram for the first collision.

Let v_1 m s^{-1} be the speed of P and v_2 m s^{-1} be the speed of Q after the collision.

Collision between P and Q:

Total momentum before collision = total momentum after collision

Use the principle of conservation of momentum. State the formula.

$$m_1u_1 + m_2u_2 = m_1v_1 + m_2v_2$$

$$2.5m + 2(2m) = mv_1 + 2mv_2$$

$$2.5 + 4 = v_1 + 2v_2 \quad (1)$$

Simplify by dividing through by m. You now have one equation in two unknowns so you need more information to solve for the two velocities.

Continues on next page ...

Collision between Q and R: — Draw the diagram for the second collision.

positive direction ⟶

$2m$ ⟶ v_2 m s^{-1} $3m$ ⟶ 1 m s^{-1}

initial Q R

$5m$ ⟶ 1.5 m s^{-1}

final

Total momentum before collision = total momentum after collision — Use the principle of conservation of momentum.

$2mv_2 + 3m \times 1 = 5m \times 1.5$

$2v_2 = 7.5 - 3$ — Solve for v_2.

$2v_2 = 4.5$

so $v_2 = 2.25$ m s^{-1}

b Substituting into equation (1): — To find the loss in kinetic energy of P you need to find the velocity of P after the collision with Q.

$6.5 = v_1 + 2 \times 2.25$

$6.5 = v_1 + 4.5$

$v_1 = 2$

Kinetic energy (KE) $= \frac{1}{2}mv^2$ — State the formula for kinetic energy.

Initial KE of P is $\frac{1}{2}m(2.5)^2 = 3.125m$ — Find the initial KE ...

Final KE of P is $\frac{1}{2}m(2)^2 = 2m$ — ... and the final KE ...

Loss in KE $= 3.125m - 2m$ — ... and subtract.

$= 1.125m$ J

Modelling in collision questions

If you are dealing with collisions between spheres, unless you are told otherwise, you assume that:

- the spheres are smooth
- the impulse during the collision acts along the line of centres
- none of the spheres is spinning.

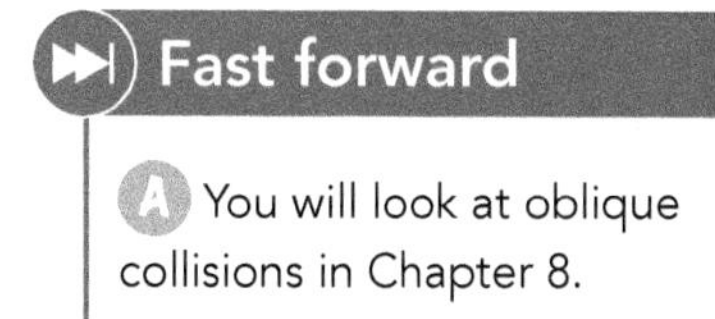

EXERCISE 3B

1. Use the conservation of linear momentum to fill in the following table. m_1 and m_2 are the masses in kg of two particles moving in the same straight line with initial speeds u_1 and u_2, respectively. The particles collide and their speeds after their collision are v_1 and v_2, respectively. The speeds are given in m s^{-1} and the signs indicate direction.

m_1	m_2	u_1	u_2	v_1	v_2
3	4	+10	+2		+6
2	4	+6	−2	−2	
2	5		+2	+0.5	+5
2		+8	−2	−1	+1.6

2. A ball, A, of mass 1.5 kg travelling at 3 m s^{-1} collides with a stationary ball, B, of mass 2 kg. Ball A is brought to rest in the collision. What is the speed of ball B immediately after the collision?

3. A ball, A, of mass 2 kg moving at 8 m s^{-1} collides with a ball, B of mass 2.5 kg moving towards it at a velocity of 10 m s^{-1} in the same straight line. If ball A then moves in a direction opposite to its original at a velocity of 6 m s^{-1}, what is the final speed of ball B?

4. A cat of mass 3.5 kg jumps onto a stationary toy train of mass 1.5 kg that is free to move on a straight horizontal track. The speed of the cat in the direction of the track immediately before it lands on the truck is 20 m s^{-1}. What is the speed of the cat and the train, in the direction of the track, immediately after it lands?

5. A croquet ball of mass 450 g is at rest when a croquet mallet hits it with a force, instantly producing an impulse of 3 N s.
   - **a** What is the exact speed of the ball at the instant it leaves the croquet mallet?
   - **b** The ball immediately hits another croquet ball of mass 400 g that is at rest. If the second ball moves off at 3 m s^{-1}, what is the speed of the first ball immediately after the collision?

6. A particle, A, of mass 0.7 kg is moving with speed 8 m s^{-1} towards particle B, of mass 0.9 kg, which is moving towards A in the same straight line, at a speed of 6 m s^{-1}. The particles coalesce. What is the magnitude and direction of the speed of the combined particles?

7. Particle A, of mass 0.8 kg is moving with speed 8 m s^{-1} towards particle B. Particle B is moving towards particle A, in the same straight line, with speed 6 m s^{-1}. The two collide and after the collision the two particles move in opposite directions, each with speed 4 m s^{-1}. What is the mass of particle B?

8. A truck of mass 600 kg is travelling along a straight track at a speed of 60 km h^{-1} when it collides with a second, stationary, truck of mass 800 kg, which then starts to move with speed 30 km h^{-1}. What is the speed of the first truck immediately after the impact?

9. A skateboard of mass 2 kg is moving at 14 m s^{-1} when it hits a ball of mass 200 g, which is at rest. Immediately after the collision the skateboard moves at 12 m s^{-1} in the same straight line and in the same direction. What is the speed of the ball immediately after the collision?

10. A football of mass 380 g moving at v m s^{-1} hits a second football of mass 420 g moving directly towards it, in the same straight line, at 8 m s^{-1}. After the collision the two footballs both have a speed of $0.75v$ but in opposite directions. Find the value of v. What assumption have you made about the two footballs?

11. A particle A of mass m kg is moving along a straight line with speed 5 m s^{-1}. It collides with another particle, B, of mass 3 kg moving towards A on the same straight line at a speed of 3 m s^{-1}. After the collision the particles coalesce and move at a speed of v m s^{-1}.
    - **a** Find expressions for the two possible values of v, in terms of m.
    - **b** If in each case the magnitude of v is 2 m s^{-1}, find the two possible values of m.

Section 3: Restitution, kinetic energy and impulsive tension

In this section you will consider examples of three different types of collisions: a perfectly elastic collision, a perfectly inelastic collision and one that is neither perfectly elastic nor perfectly inelastic. In a **perfectly elastic collision**, no kinetic energy is lost from the system. The kinetic energy of the individual spheres may change but the total of their kinetic energies will remain the same. Consider the example shown in the diagram.

→ positive direction

2 kg → 10 m s⁻¹ 3 kg → 6 m s⁻¹

initial

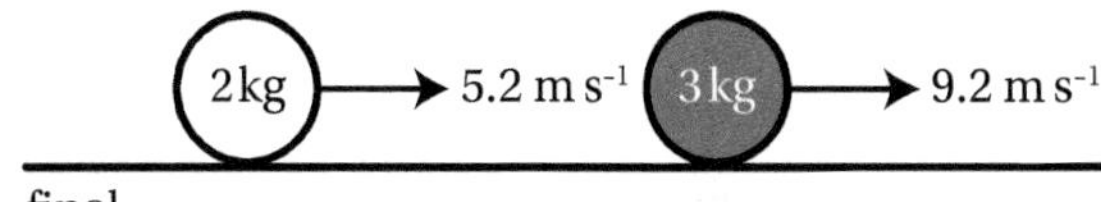

final

Initial momentum $= 2\times 10 + 3\times 6 = 38$ N s

Final momentum $= 2\times 5.2 + 3\times 9.2 = 38$ N s, so momentum is conserved.

Initial kinetic energy $=\frac{1}{2}\times2\times10^2+\frac{1}{2}\times3\times6^2=154$ J

Final kinetic energy $=\frac{1}{2}\times2\times(5.2)^2+\frac{1}{2}\times3\times(9.2)^2=154$ J so there is no loss in kinetic energy.

In a **perfectly inelastic** collision, the spheres coalesce.

→ positive direction

2 kg → 10 m s⁻¹ 3 kg → 6 m s⁻¹

initial

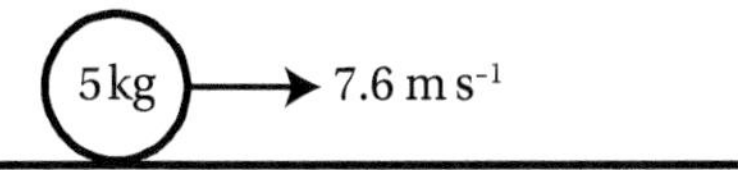

final

Initial momentum $= 2\times 10 + 3\times 6 = 38$ N s

Final momentum $= 5\times 7.6 = 38$ N s, so momentum is conserved.

Initial kinetic energy $=\frac{1}{2}\times2\times10^2+\frac{1}{2}\times3\times6^2=154$ J

Final kinetic energy $=\frac{1}{2}\times 5\times(7.6)^2=144.4$ J, so kinetic energy is lost.

Newton discovered that the outcome of a collision depends on the material that the objects are made of. The next example is of a collision that is neither perfectly elastic nor perfectly inelastic.

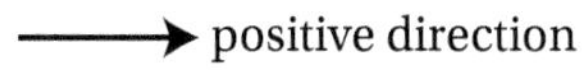

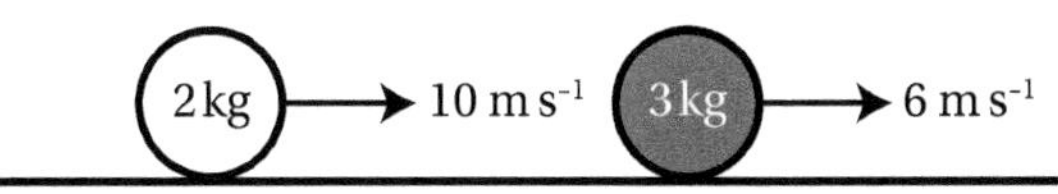

initial

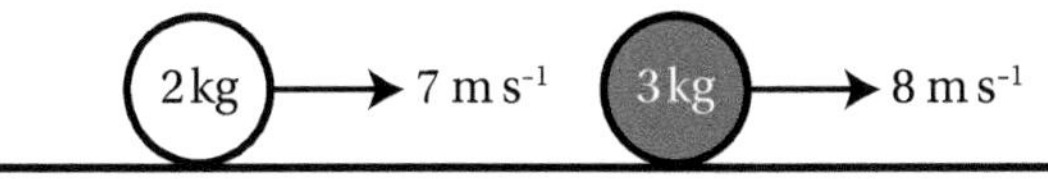

final

Initial momentum $= 2 \times 10 + 3 \times 6 = 38$ N s

Final momentum $= 2 \times 7 + 3 \times 8 = 38$ N s, so momentum is conserved.

Initial kinetic energy $= \frac{1}{2} \times 2 \times 10^2 + \frac{1}{2} \times 3 \times 6^2 = 154$ J

Final kinetic energy $= \frac{1}{2} \times 2 \times 7^2 + \frac{1}{2} \times 3 \times 8^2 = 145$ J, so kinetic energy is lost.

Again momentum is conserved but kinetic energy is lost. The loss in kinetic energy is slightly lower than if the particles had coalesced.

Newton discovered, by carrying out a series of experiments, that there is a constant ratio between the speed of approach and speed of separation of the spheres before and after the collision that is independent of the masses of the two spheres but depends on the materials from which the spheres are made. The constant is called the coefficient of restitution.

Key point 3.4

Newton's experimental law of collisions states that:

$$\frac{\text{speed of separation}}{\text{speed of approach}} = -e \quad \text{or} \quad \frac{v_1 - v_2}{u_1 - u_2} = -e \quad 0 \leqslant e \leqslant 1$$

where e is a constant called the coefficient of restitution.

The value of e varies depending on the material properties of the objects involved in the collision.

For a perfectly elastic collision $e = 1$ and there is no loss of total kinetic energy.

If the spheres coalesce then $e = 0$, the collision is inelastic, and there is maximum loss of kinetic energy. This is sometimes called a perfectly inelastic collision, but for this course the phrase inelastic collision will be used.

In other collisions, for which $0 < e < 1$, the total kinetic energy of the system decreases.

Did you know?

Some collisions are called 'super elastic' because they cause a gain in kinetic energy in the system, usually due to another mechanism that causes potential energy to be released as kinetic energy.

The study of these super elastic collisions is outside the scope of this course but information can be found on the internet.

Checking that kinetic energy is not gained during collisions can be a useful error check.

Applying Newton's experimental law

Consider a collision between two particles of masses m_1 and m_2 with initial velocities u_1 and u_2 and final velocities v_1 and v_2.

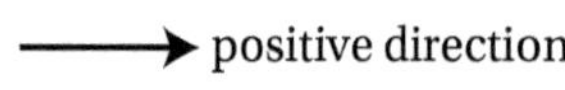

initial

final

Applying Newton's experimental law (NEL) gives:

$$\frac{v_1 - v_2}{u_1 - u_2} = -e$$

Unless $v_2 > v_1$ the spheres will not separate. Similarly, unless $u_1 > u_2$ the spheres will not collide.

Tip

When using Newton's experimental law be careful to get the velocities in the correct order with the correct signs. Use a clearly labelled diagram showing directions clearly.

WORKED EXAMPLE 3.11

Two spheres of masses $3m$ and $2m$ are moving towards each other with speeds 4 m s^{-1}and 5 m s^{-1}, respectively. After the collision, they move away from each other with speeds 2.5 m s^{-1} and 3.5 m s^{-1}, respectively.

a What is the value of the coefficient of restitution between the two spheres?

b In terms of m, what is the kinetic energy loss for the particle of mass $3m$?

positive direction

initial

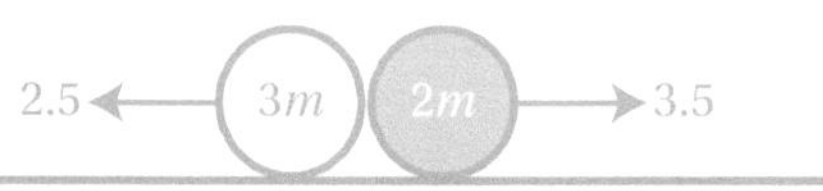

final

Draw a clear diagram. There is no need to put units on the diagram as long as you have checked that the units are consistent. For example, use either grams and kilograms but not a mixture.

a Newton's experimental law:

$$\frac{v_1 - v_2}{u_1 - u_2} = -e$$

State Newton's experimental law.

$u_1 = +4,\ u_2 = -5,\ v_2 = +3.5\text{ m s}^{-1},$
$v_1 = -2.5\text{ m s}^{-1}$

State the values. Remember that signs indicate direction. Do not leave this step out as it helps to prevent errors with signs.

$$-e = \frac{-2.5 - 3.5}{4 - (-5)} = -\frac{6}{9} = -\frac{2}{3}$$

$$e = \frac{2}{3}$$

Remember that the final velocities go on the top line.

b Initial KE of the $3m$ mass $= \frac{1}{2}3m \times 4^2 = 24m$ J

Find the initial KE ...

Final KE of the $3m$ mass $= \frac{1}{2}3m \times 2.5^2 = 9.375m$ J

... and the final KE ...

Loss in KE $= 24m - 9.375m$

$= 14.625m$ J

... and subtract.

Tip

Always check that e is positive and between 0 and 1. If it isn't, check that you have substituted correctly and have the fraction the correct way up.

WORKED EXAMPLE 3.12

Two spheres, A and B, of masses 0.4 kg and 0.5 kg respectively, are moving towards each other with velocities 6 m s^{-1} and 3 m s^{-1} respectively. They collide and the kinetic energy lost in the collision is 9 J.

a What are the speeds and directions of A and B immediately after the collision?
b What does this tell you about the coefficient of restitution between A and B?

positive direction →

Draw a clear diagram and choose a direction to be positive.

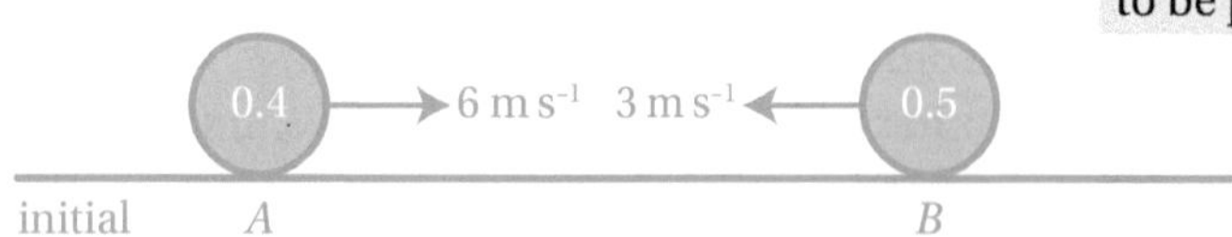

final

a Total momentum before collision = total momentum after collision

Use the principle of conservation of momentum. State the formula.

$$m_1u_1 + m_2u_2 = m_1v_1 + m_2v_2$$

$$(0.4\times 6) - (0.5\times 3) = 0.4v_1 + 0.5v_2$$

$$24 - 15 = 9 = 4v_1 + 5v_2 \quad (1)$$

Multiply through by 10 to simplify the numbers.

$$\text{Initial KE} = \frac{1}{2}\times 0.4\times 6^2 + \frac{1}{2}\times 0.5\times 3^2$$

$$= 9.45 \text{ J}$$

Find the KE before the collision.

Initial KE – final KE = 9 J, so final KE = 0.45 J

Find the KE after the collision by subtracting the amount of KE lost from the initial KE.

$$\text{Final KE} = \frac{1}{2}\times 0.4\times v_1{}^2 + \frac{1}{2}\times 0.5\times v_2{}^2$$

$$0.45 = 0.2v_1^2 + 0.25v_2^2 \quad (2)$$

Write an expression for the KE after the collision and equate this to 0.45.

By solving the system of two equations, we find that $v_1 = 1$ and $v_2 = 1$. The speeds of A and B are both 1 m s^{-1} in the direction of A's initial motion.

You now have two equations, one linear (1) and one quadratic (2), for the two unknown velocities. You need to solve these simultaneously.

b As the velocities have the same value and are in the same direction this means that the particles coalesce (become one) so $e = 0$.

You now need to state the value of e, the coefficient of restitution, and comment on your answer.

WORKED EXAMPLE 3.13

Two spheres of mass 300 g and 500 g are moving in the same direction in the same straight line with velocities 5 m s^{-1} and 4 m s^{-1}, respectively. The coefficient of restitution between the spheres is 0.6. What are the velocities of the spheres immediately after the impact?

initial

final

Draw a clear diagram. Show the positive direction. Convert units as necessary.

$u_1 = 5, u_2 = 4$

State the values you are given.

Total momentum before collision = total momentum after collision

$$m_1u_1 + m_2u_2 = m_1v_1 + m_2v_2$$

$$0.3 \times 5 + 0.5 \times 4 = 0.3v_1 + 0.5v_2 \quad (1)$$

$$0.3v_1 + 0.5v_2 = 3.5 \quad (2)$$

Use the principle of conservation of momentum.
Substitute into the equation and simplify.

Newton's experimental law:

State Newton's experimental law.

$$\frac{v_1 - v_2}{u_1 - u_2} = -e$$

$u_1 = +5, u_2 = +4$

$$\frac{v_1 - v_2}{5 - 4} = -0.6$$

$$v_1 - v_2 = -0.6$$

State the known values with their signs.

$$v_2 = v_1 + 0.6 \quad (3)$$

Substitute in the values and simplify.

Substitute (3) into (2):

$$0.3v_1 + 0.5(v_1 + 0.6) = 3.5$$

$$3v_1 + 5(v_1 + 0.6) = 35$$

$$8v_1 = 32$$

Multiply through by 10 to make the numbers easier and solve.

$v_1 = 4$ m s^{-1} and $v_2 = 4.6$ m s^{-1}, both in the same direction as the initial motion.

Check back in (1):

LHS $0.3 \times 5 + 0.5 \times 4 = 3.5$

RHS $0.3 \times 4 + 0.5 \times 4.6 = 3.5$

You should check your answers by substituting back into the unsimplified conservation of momentum equation (1).

Collisions between a moving object and a fixed object

If a body hits a fixed wall, momentum is not conserved because the wall cannot usually move. However, Newton's experimental law still holds, so you can calculate velocities for impacts involving a fixed object using the coefficient of restitution.

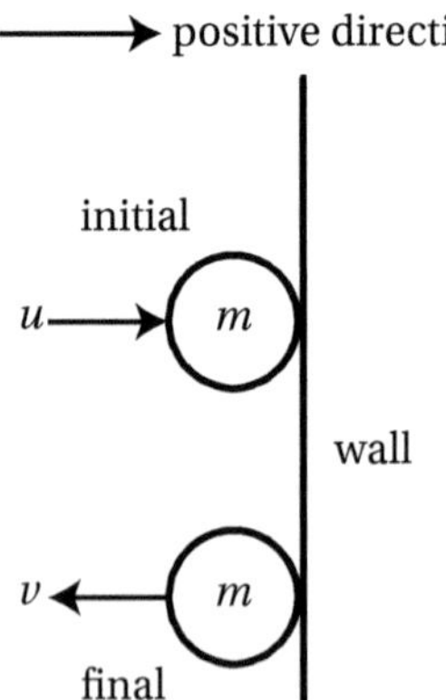

Consider a particle of mass m kg moving with velocity u m s^{-1} on a smooth horizontal plane as it collides with a fixed wall at right angles and bounces back off the wall with a velocity of $-v$ m s^{-1}. The coefficient of restitution between the wall and the particle is e.

Newton's experimental law states that:

$$\frac{v_1 - v_2}{u_1 - u_2} = -e$$

$u_2 = v_2 = 0$ (as the wall does not move), $u_1 = u$ and $v_1 = -v$, so the equation reduces to:

$$\frac{-v_1}{u_1} = e \quad \text{or} \quad v = -eu$$

where u and v are the velocities of the particle before and after the collision with the wall.

The impulse of the wall on the particle is equal to change in momentum of the particle:

$$\begin{aligned} I &= \text{final momentum} - \text{initial momentum} \\ &= -mv - mu \\ &= -meu - mu \\ &= -mu(e+1) \end{aligned}$$

Key point 3.5

If an object, P, moving with velocity u, collides at right angles with a fixed object, then P rebounds with velocity $-eu$ where e is the coefficient of restitution between P and the fixed object.

$$v = -eu$$

Explore

Newton's cradle is a set of spheres suspended from a frame. You can find videos on the internet showing it in action.

Can you explain the behaviour of Newton's cradle when one sphere is set in motion?

What happens if two (or more) of the spheres are displaced at the same time?

WORKED EXAMPLE 3.14

A football of mass 450 g moving with velocity 25 m s^{-1} hits a fixed wall at right angles. If the coefficient of restitution between the football and the wall is 0.8, find:

- **a** the speed at which the ball rebounds from the wall
- **b** the magnitude and direction of the impulse of the ball on the wall
- **c** the loss in kinetic energy of the football.

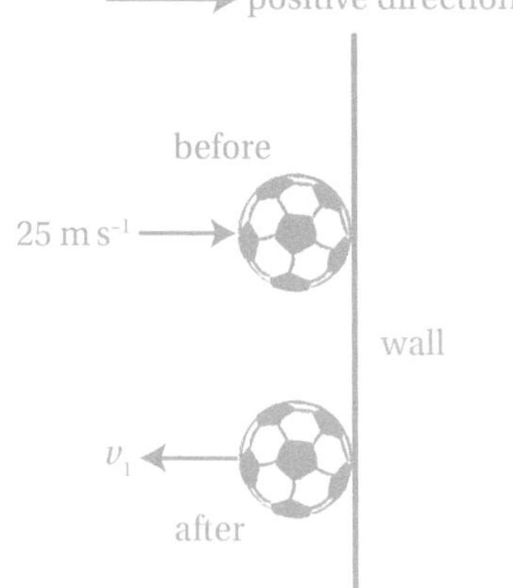

Always draw a diagram so you don't get confused with signs. Always show the positive direction with an arrow.

a Newton's experimental law:

$v = -eu$

You cannot use conservation of momentum as the wall is not free to move but you can use Newton's experimental law.

$v_1 = -e(25)$

Substitute in the numbers.

$v_1 = -0.8(25) = -20$

So the ball rebounds with speed 20 m s^{-1}.

b Impulse = change in momentum

The impulse of the ball on the wall is equal and opposite to the impulse of the wall on the ball.

The impulse of the wall on the ball is:

$0.45(-20) - 0.45(25) = -9 - 11.25$

To find impulse you need force × time or change in momentum. As the wall does not move, you can only find the change in momentum of the football.

Find the impulse of the wall on the ball.

$= -20.25$ N s

The impulse of the ball on the wall is equal and opposite to this.

Therefore the impulse of the ball on the wall is 20.25 N s towards the wall.

c Initial KE $= \frac{1}{2}mu^2 = \frac{1}{2} \times 0.45 \times 25^2 = 140.625$

To find the loss in kinetic energy you subtract the final KE from the initial KE the ball.

Final KE $= \frac{1}{2}mu^2 = \frac{1}{2} \times 0.45 \times 20^2 = 90$

Loss in KE $= 140.625 - 90 = 50.625$ J

WORKED EXAMPLE 3.15

Small spheres P, of mass $3m$, and Q, of mass $2m$ are lying in a smooth horizontal groove, which is a straight line ending in a vertical wall that is at right angles to the groove. P is projected with velocity u m s^{-1} towards Q, which is initially at rest. The coefficient of restitution between P and Q is 0.4. Q then hits the wall and rebounds. The coefficient of restitution between Q and the wall is 0.5.

a What is the velocity of Q as it rebounds off the wall?

b State, with reasons, whether or not there will be any further collisions between P and Q.

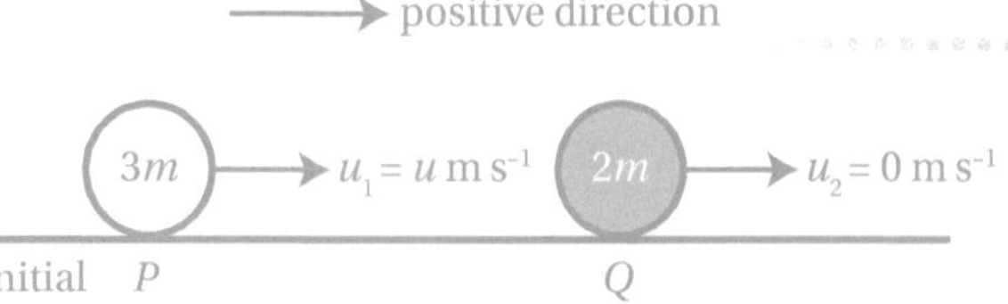

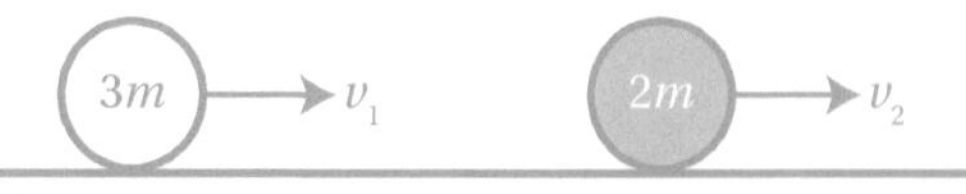

Draw a clear diagram of the first collision only. Do not try to cram both collisions into one diagram. It can help to label u_1, u_2, v_1 and v_2 on the diagram to get Newton's law the correct way round.

a Total momentum before 1st collision = total momentum after 1st collision

Use the principle of conservation of momentum.

$$m_1u_1 + m_2u_2 = m_1v_1 + m_2v_2$$

State the equation.

$$3mu + 2m(0) = 3mv_1 + 2mv_2$$

$$3u = 3v_1 + 2v_2 \quad (1)$$

Substitute in the values given and divide through by m as every term contains m. There is no need to define the unknowns if they are clearly shown on the diagram.

Newton's experimental law:

State the principle and the equation.

$$\frac{v_1 - v_2}{u_1 - u_2} = -e$$

$$\frac{v_1 - v_2}{u - 0} = -0.4$$

Substitute in the values and simplify.

$$v_1 - v_2 = -0.4u$$

$$v_1 = v_2 - 0.4u \quad (2)$$

Substitute (2) into (1):

Substitute the expression for v_1 into (1).

$$3u = 3(v_2 - 0.4u) + 2v_2$$

$$5v_2 = 4.2u \Rightarrow v_2 = 0.84u$$

Find v_2.

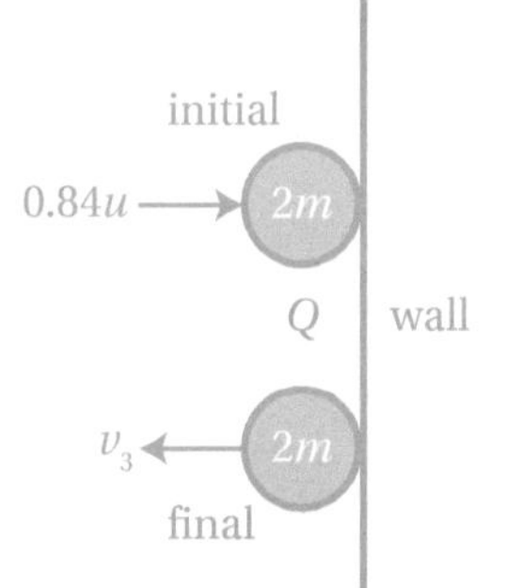

Now deal with the collision with the wall. Draw a new diagram.

Continues on next page ...

Newton's experimental law: — Momentum is not conserved as the wall is fixed so you use Newton's experimental law.

$v = -eu$ — State the equation.

$v_3 = -0.5(0.84u)$

$= -0.42u$ — Put in the values and solve for v_3. Don't forget to include u with your answer.

The final velocity of Q is $0.42u$ m s^{-1} away from the wall. — Explain that the minus sign indicates direction and state that direction.

b From (2),

$v_1 = v_2 - 0.4u$

$= 0.84u - 0.4u$

$= +0.44u$ — To find out if there are any further collisions you need to know the velocity of P after the first collision and then compare the final velocities of P and Q.

The final velocity of P is $0.44u$ m s^{-1} towards the wall.

As P is moving towards the wall and Q is moving away from the wall they will be moving towards each other so there will be at least one further collision. — The direction of P and Q is important as well as the speed. Here the two particles are moving towards each other so they will collide again whatever their speeds.

WORKED EXAMPLE 3.16

A ball of mass 400 g is dropped from rest at a height of 2 m onto a smooth horizontal surface. It instantly bounces back vertically and reaches a height of 1.5 m.

a What is the impulse of the ball on the ground at the instant of the collision? Take g as 10 m s^{-2} and leave your answer in surd form.

b Taking g as 10 m s^{-2}, calculate the coefficient of restitution between the ball and the ground from the information given, leaving your answer in surd form.

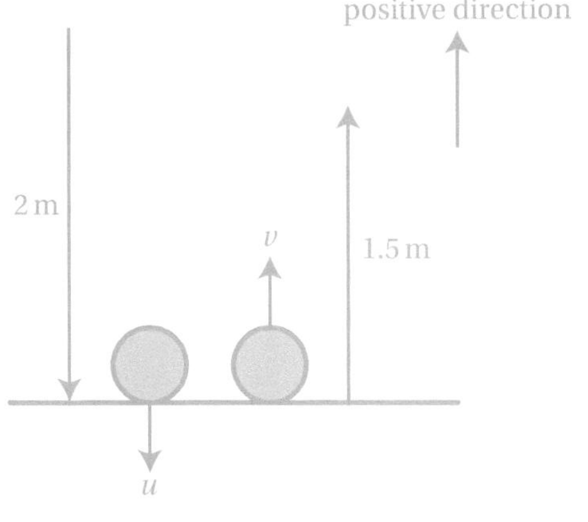

To find impulse you either need to know force and time or change in momentum. Momentum depends on velocity so you need to find the velocity at which the ball hits the ground and then the velocity at which the ball leaves the ground. To find the velocities you can either use energy equations or the equations for motion with constant acceleration.

a As the ball falls:

Loss in PE $= mgh = 0.4 \times 10 \times 2 = 8$ — First you need to find the velocity, u, at which the ball hits the ground. This example uses the work-energy principle.

Continues on next page ...

Gain in KE $= \frac{1}{2}mu^2 = 0.2u^2$

$0.2u^2 = 8$

$u = -\sqrt{40}$

By equating gain in kinetic energy (KE) to loss in potential energy (PE) you can find the value of u.

u is negative as it is in the downward direction.

As the ball bounces up:

You can use energy equations again to find the velocity v at which the ball leaves the ground.

Gain in PE $= mgh = 0.4 \times 10 \times 1.5 = 6$

Loss in KE $= \frac{1}{2}mv^2 = 0.2v^2$

$0.2v^2 = 6$

$v = \sqrt{30}$

By equating the loss in KE to the gain in PE, you can find the value of v.

Impulse on the ball is $mv - mu$

$= 0.4\left(\sqrt{30} - \left(-\sqrt{40}\right)\right)$ N s vertically up

Knowing the values of u and v, you can use the relationship between impulse and momentum to find the impulse of the ground on the ball.

The impulse of the ball on the ground is therefore $0.4\left(\sqrt{30} + \sqrt{40}\right)$ N s vertically down.

This is equal and opposite to the impulse of the ground on the ball.

b $v = -eu$

State the formula.

$-e = \frac{v}{u} = \frac{\sqrt{30}}{-\sqrt{40}}$

Substitute the values and simplify.

$\therefore e = \frac{\sqrt{3}}{2}$

Range of values of *e*

The value of *e* determines the final velocities of the colliding bodies and enables you to calculate whether further collisions will occur.

Tip

If two objects moving in the same straight line are going to collide, then there are two possibilities: either they are moving towards each other from opposite directions, or one is following the other and the follower is travelling faster than the object it is following.

Rewind

You learned about gravitational potential energy, mechanical energy and the principle of conservation of mechanical energy in Chapter 1.

WORKED EXAMPLE 3.17

A sphere, P, of mass $2m$ kg, moving at a velocity of 6 m s^{-1}, hits a sphere, Q, of mass $4m$ kg, which is at rest on a smooth horizontal surface. The coefficient of restitution between P and Q is 0.8. Q then hits a smooth vertical wall at right angles and rebounds. The coefficient of restitution between Q and the wall is e. Find the range of values of e for which there is a further collision between Q and P.

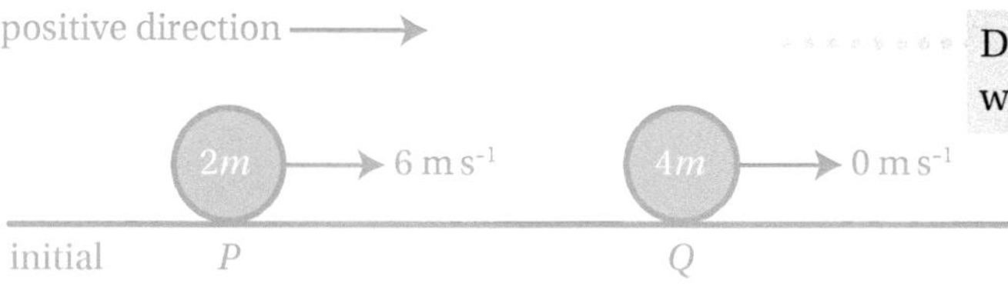

Draw a diagram for the first collision with the positive direction labelled.

2m → v_1 m s^{-1} 4m → v_2 m s^{-1}

final

$m_1u_1 + m_2u_2 = m_1v_1 + m_2v_2$

$(6 \times 2) + (4 \times 0) = 2v_1 + 4v_2$

Use the principle of conservation of linear momentum.

$2v_1 + 4v_2 = 12$ (1)

Simplify the equation.

$\frac{v_1 - v_2}{u_1 - u_2} = -e$

Use Newton's experimental law.

$v_1 - v_2 = -0.8(6 - 0)$

$v_1 - v_2 = -4.8$ (2)

Simplify the equation.

$v_1 = -1.2$ m s^{-1} and $v_2 = 3.6$ m s^{-1}

Solve (1) and (2) simultaneously and check your answers in equation (1).

The speed of Q after the collision with the wall $= -3.6e$

Use Newton's experimental law for the collision between Q and the wall.

Q is following P. The speed of P is 1.2 m s^{-1} away from the wall and the speed of Q is $3.6e$ m s^{-1} away from the wall. If Q collides with P then:

$3.6e > 1.2$

$e > \frac{1}{3}$

Now consider what is actually happening. If there is to be another collision then Q must be moving in the same direction as P and it must be moving faster than P.

Impulses transmitted through strings

If two particles, A and B, on a smooth horizontal surface, are joined by a light inextensible string that is initially not under tension, and A is projected horizontally, the string will become taut. There will be an instantaneous impulse transmitted through the string that will pull B into movement. When this situation is modelled mathematically an assumption is made that B starts to move in the direction of the string and that the component of the velocity of A along the string equals the velocity of B.

The impulse is equal to the magnitude of the change in momentum of each of the particles along the string.

WORKED EXAMPLE 3.18

Two particles, A, of mass 2 kg, and B, of mass 4 kg, are initially at rest on a smooth horizontal plane. A and B are joined by a light, non-elastic string that is initially slack. B is projected horizontally, away from A, with a speed of 12 m s^{-1}. After the string becomes taut, A and B move at the same velocity. Calculate:

a the speed of A and B immediately after the string becomes taut

b the impulse on A and B.

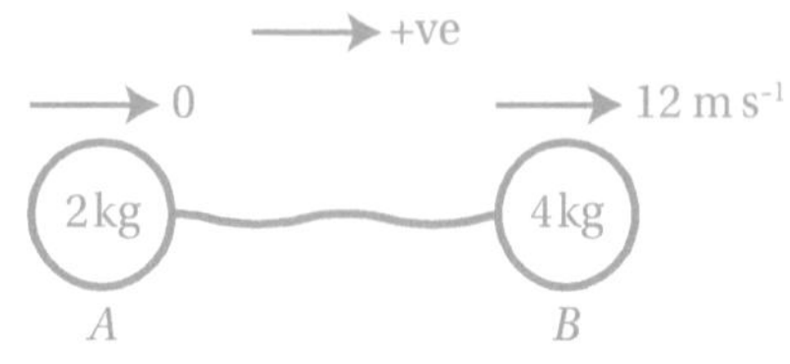

Draw a clear diagram and show the direction you have chosen to be positive.

a Conservation of linear momentum:

$(2\times 0)+(4\times 12)=2v+4v$

As soon as the string becomes taut,you can apply the principle of conservation of momentum to the whole system to find the common velocity of A and B.

$6v=48$

$v=8\text{ m s}^{-1}$

b Impulse = change in momentum

Apply the impulse-momentum principle for just one of the particles. The magnitude of the impulse will be equal in magnitude but in opposite directions for A and B.

$\text{Impulse}=2v-0$

$=16\text{ N s}$

It is easier to use A for the impulse calculation.

$\text{Impulse}=4v-(4\times 12)$

$=32-48$

$=-16\text{ N s}$

You can check your answer by also calculating the change in momentum of B.

EXERCISE 3C

1 A small sphere, of mass m, moving on a smooth horizontal plane with speed u hits a vertical wall at right angles and rebounds. The coefficient of restitution between the sphere and the wall is e. Find:

a the speed of the sphere after the collision

b the magnitude of the impulse of the wall on the sphere c the loss in kinetic energy of the sphere if:

i $u = 4$ m s^{-1} and $e = 0.3$ ii $u = 10$ m s^{-1} and $e = 1.0$ iii $u = 60$ m s^{-1} and $e = 0$

iv $u = 40$ m s^{-1} and $e = 0.8$ v $u = 10$ m s^{-1} and $e = 0.6$.

2 A 3 kg mass, *P*, moving at 4 m s^{-1} collides with a second mass of 2 kg, *Q*, moving towards it on the same straight line with speed 5 m s^{-1}. The coefficient of restitution between the two masses is 0.5. Find the speeds and directions of *P* and *Q* after the collision.

3 A particle *A*, of mass 0.5 kg, moving at 5 m s^{-1}, collides with a particle *B*, of mass 1 kg, moving towards it at a speed of 3 m s^{-1} on the same straight line. After the collision, *A* moves in the opposite direction with a speed of 0.6 m s^{-1}. Find:

a the speed and direction of *B* after the collision

b the coefficient of restitution between *A* and *B*.

4 A small, smooth sphere of mass 1.5 kg, at rest on a smooth horizontal floor, is hit with a blow of impulse 24 N s and immediately hits a vertical wall at right angles. If it rebounds with velocity –12 m s^{-1}, find:

a the coefficient of restitution between the wall and the sphere

b the magnitude of the impulse of the wall on the sphere

c the loss in kinetic energy of the sphere.

5 A small, smooth sphere of mass *m* kg, at rest on a smooth horizontal floor, is hit with a blow of impulse *J* N s and immediately hits a vertical wall at right angles. If it rebounds with velocity *V* m s^{-1}, find expressions, in terms of *J*, *m* and *v*, for:

a the coefficient of restitution between the wall and the sphere

b the magnitude of the impulse of the wall on the sphere

c the loss in kinetic energy of the sphere.

6 A small smooth ball-bearing, *A*, of mass 4 kg and moving with velocity *v* m s^{-1}, collides with another small, smooth ball-bearing, *B*, of mass 2.5 kg, moving in the same direction with velocity 10 m s^{-1}. After the collision, *A* and *B* are moving in the same direction, *A* with velocity 13.75 m s^{-1} and *B* with velocity *v* m s^{-1}.

a Find the value of *v*.

b Find the value of *e*, the coefficient of restitution between *A* and *B*.

c What is the total loss of kinetic energy in the collision?

7 A particle, *A*, of mass 200 grams, is moving at 10 m s^{-1} when it hits a vertical wall, at right angles to the wall, and rebounds. The coefficient of restitution between the wall and the particle is 0.6. The particle then hits another smooth particle, *B*, of mass 400 grams, which is initially at rest. After the collision, *A* is at rest. What is the coefficient of restitution between *A* and *B*?

8 A small sphere, *A*, of mass 400 g, moving in a straight line with velocity 8 m s^{-1}, collides with another small sphere, *B*, of mass 600 g, which is moving directly towards *A*, along the same straight line, with velocity -6 m s^{-1}. The coefficient of restitution between the spheres is 0.8.

a Find the magnitude and direction of the velocities of the two spheres immediately after the collision.

b What is the magnitude of the impulse on *B*?

9 A particle of mass 400 g is dropped from a height of 2 m onto a smooth horizontal surface and bounces back vertically up to a height h. The coefficient of restitution between the ball and the surface is 0.6. Taking g as 9.8 m s^{-2}, find the value of h.

10 Two small spheres, A, of mass $4m$ kg and B, of mass m kg, are moving directly towards each other along a smooth horizontal surface, with velocities $2u$ m s^{-1} and $3u$ m s^{-1}, respectively. The coefficient of restitution between the two spheres is 0.75.

a Find the magnitude and direction of the velocities of the two spheres immediately after the collision.

b What is the total loss of kinetic energy in the collision?

11 Two particles, A and B, each of mass m, are moving on a smooth horizontal surface in the same direction, in the same straight line, with speeds 6 m s^{-1} and 3 m s^{-1}, respectively, when they collide. If the coefficient of restitution between the two particles is 0.8, find the speed and direction of the two particles immediately after the collision.

12 A ball of mass m kg is dropped from a height h_1 metres onto a smooth horizontal surface and bounces back vertically up to a height h_2 metres. The coefficient of restitution between the ball and the surface is e. Find the ratio of h_1 to h_2.

13 Two particles, A and B, each of mass 400 g, are moving on a smooth horizontal surface in the same direction, in the same straight line, with speeds 6 m s^{-1} and 3 m s^{-1}, respectively, when they collide. At the instant of collision, each particle receives an impulse of 0.96 N s.

a Find the magnitude and direction of the velocities of the particles immediately after the collision.

b Calculate the coefficient of restitution between the two particles.

14 Two smooth spheres, A and B, each of mass 40 grams, move towards each other along the same straight horizontal line and collide when they are moving with speeds 5 m s^{-1} and 3 m s^{-1}, respectively. Immediately after the collision A moves with velocity 2.2 m s^{-1} away from B.

a What is the velocity of B immediately after the collision?

b What is the coefficient of restitution between the two spheres?

c Find the magnitude of the impulse exerted on A in the collision.

15 A small ball of mass 500 g is dropped from rest at a height of 2.5 m onto a smooth horizontal surface. It instantly bounces vertically up and reaches a height of 2 m. What is the impulse of the ground on the ball at the instant of the collision? Take g as 9.8 m s^{-2}.

16 A ball bearing, A, of mass 450 g is thrown vertically down with a speed of 4 m s^{-1} from a height of 2 m. It bounces back and just reaches its original height. Find the coefficient of restitution between A and the ground. Take g as 10 m s^{-2}.

17 Two particles A, of mass $2m$ kg, and B, of mass $3m$ kg, are at rest on a smooth horizontal plane. A is hit with a blow of impulse $8m$ N s in the direction AB. A collides with B, which then hits a smooth vertical wall at right angles. The coefficient of restitution between A and B is 0.8 and the coefficient of restitution between B and the wall is e. Find the range of values of e for which there is at least one more collision between A and B. Give your answer as a fraction.

18 Three particles, P of mass m kg, Q of mass $2m$ kg and R of mass $7m$ kg, are at rest in the same horizontal line on a smooth horizontal surface. P is projected along the plane towards Q at a velocity of 6 m s^{-1} and the coefficient of restitution between P and Q is 0.7. Q then collides with R. The coefficient of restitution between Q and R is e. Find the range of values of e for which there is a further collision between Q and P. Give your answer as a fraction.

19 Two masses, A, of 3 kg, and B, of 5 kg, are initially at rest on a smooth horizontal plane. A and B are joined by a light, non-elastic string that is initially slack. B is projected horizontally, away from A, with a speed of 16 m s^{-1}. After the string becomes taut, A and B move at the same velocity. Find:

a the speed of A and B immediately after the string becomes taut

b the magnitude of the impulse on A and B.

Checklist of learning and understanding

- Momentum = mass × velocity or momentum = mv
- Impulse of a constant force = force × time = change in momentum
  $I = Ft = mv - mu$
  The units of impulse (N s) and momentum (kg m s^{-1}) are equivalent.
- In general terms, if two objects of mass m_1 and m_2 are moving with velocities u_1 and u_2 in a straight line and they collide, then, if their velocities after the collision are v_1 and v_2, the total momentum remains constant.

  total momentum before collision = total momentum after collision

  $$m_1u_1 + m_2u_2 = m_1v_1 + m_2v_2$$

  This is called the principle of conservation of linear momentum.
- Newton's experimental law of collisions states that:

  $$\frac{\text{speed of separation}}{\text{speed of approach}} = -e \quad \text{or} \quad \frac{v_1 - v_2}{u_1 - u_2} = -e$$

  where e is a constant called the coefficient of restitution and $0 \leqslant e \leqslant 1$. The value of e varies depending on the material properties of the objects involved in the collision.
- For a perfectly elastic collision, $e = 1$ and there is no loss of total kinetic energy.
- If the colliding objects coalesce, then $e = 0$, and there is loss of kinetic energy. This is sometimes called a perfectly inelastic collision.
- In all other collisions the total kinetic energy of the system decreases and $0 < e < 1$.
- If an object, P, moving with velocity u collides with a fixed object, which is at right angles to the plane of movement of P, then the object rebounds with velocity $-eu$ where e is the coefficient of restitution between P and the fixed object.
  $v = -eu$

Mixed practice 3

1 Two particles P and Q are projected directly towards each other on a smooth horizontal surface. P has mass 0.4 kg and initial speed 5 m s^{-1}, and Q has mass 0.8 kg and initial speed 2.5 m s^{-1}. After a collision between P and Q, the speed of P is 1.5 m s^{-1} and the direction of its motion is reversed. Calculate:

a the change in the momentum of P

b the speed of Q after the collision.

2 A particle P of mass 0.8 kg is travelling with speed 10 m s^{-1} on a smooth horizontal plane towards a stationary particle Q of mass m kg (see diagram). The particles collide, and immediately after the collision P has speed 2 m s^{-1} and Q has speed 4 m s^{-1}.

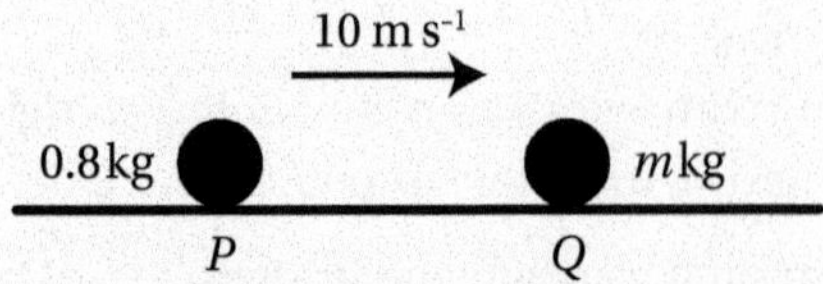

a Given that both particles are moving in the same direction after the collision, calculate m.

b Given instead that the particles are moving in opposite directions after the collision, calculate m.

3 A roller skater of mass 50 kg is moving in a straight line with speed 6 m s^{-1} when she collides with a roller skater of mass 75 kg moving in the opposite direction along the same straight line with speed 8 m s^{-1}. After the collision the roller skaters move together with a common speed in the same straight line. Calculate their common speed, and state their direction of motion.

4 A particle P of mass m kg is moving at 6 m s^{-1} when it collides with a particle Q, of mass $3m$ kg, moving in the same direction, in the same straight line at 2.5 m s^{-1}. The two particles coalesce to form a particle R moving in the same straight line. What is the velocity of R?

5

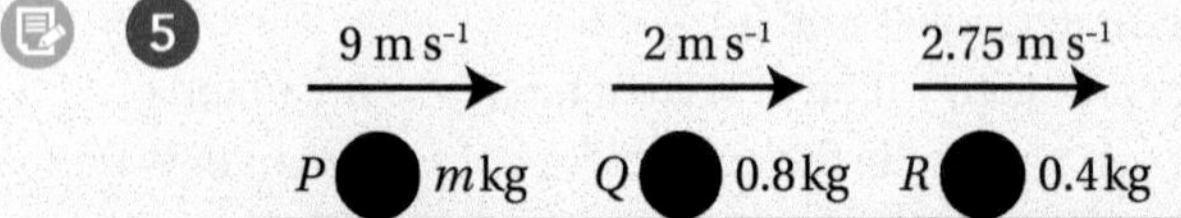

Three particles P, Q and R, are travelling in the same direction in the same straight line on a smooth horizontal surface. P has mass m kg and speed 9 m s^{-1}, Q has mass 0.8 kg and speed 2 m s^{-1} and R has mass 0.4 kg and speed 2.75 m s^{-1} (see diagram).

i A collision occurs between P and Q, after which P and Q move in opposite directions, each with speed 3.5 m s^{-1}. Calculate

a the value of m, **b** the change in the momentum of P.

ii When Q collides with R the two particles coalesce. Find their subsequent common speed.

6 Particles P and Q, of masses 0.3 kg and 0.5 kg respectively, are moving in the same direction along the same straight line on a smooth horizontal surface. P is moving with speed 2.2 m s^{-1} and Q is moving with speed 0.8 m s^{-1} immediately before they collide. In the collision, the speed of P is reduced by 50% and its direction of motion is unchanged.

i Calculate the speed of Q immediately after the collision.

ii Find the distance PQ at the instant 3 seconds after the collision.

© OCR, AS GCE Mathematics, Paper 4728, January 2012

7 Two particles P and Q are moving in opposite directions in the same straight line on a smooth horizontal surface when they collide. P has mass 0.4 kg and speed 3 m s^{-1}. Q has mass 0.6 kg and speed 1.5 m s^{-1}. Immediately after the collision, the speed of P is 0.1 m s^{-1}.

i Given that P and Q are moving in the same direction after the collision, find the speed of Q.

ii Given instead that P and Q are moving in opposite directions after the collision, find the distance between them 3 s after the collision.

© OCR, AS GCE Mathematics, Paper 4728, June 2010

8

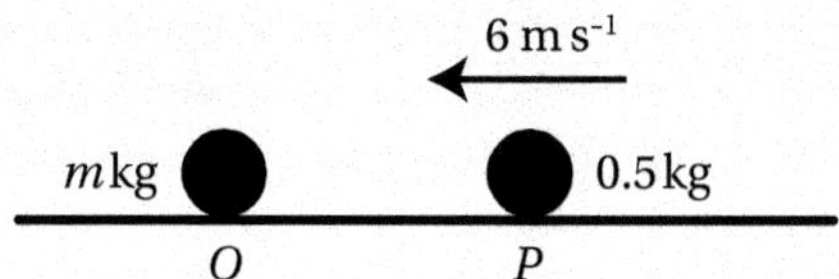

Fig. 1

i A particle P of mass 0.5 kg is projected with speed 6 m s^{-1} on a smooth horizontal surface towards a stationary particle Q of mass m kg (see Fig.1). After the particles collide, P has speed v m s^{-1} in its original direction of motion, and Q has speed 1 m s^{-1} more than P. Show that $v(m+0.5)=-m+3$.

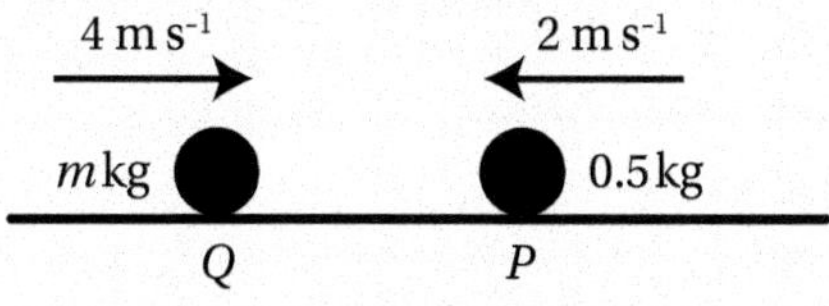

Fig. 2

ii Q and P are now projected towards each other with speeds 4 m s^{-1} and 2 m s^{-1}, respectively (see Fig.2). Immediately after the collision the speed of Q is v m s^{-1} with its direction of motion unchanged and P has speed 1 m s^{-1} more than Q. Find another relationship between m and v in the form $v(m+0.5)=am+b$, where a and b are constants.

iii By solving these two simultaneous equations show that $m=0.9$, and hence find v.

© OCR, AS GCE Mathematics, Paper 4728, June 2009

 **9** A railway wagon A of mass 2400 kg and moving with speed 5 m s^{-1} collides with railway wagon B which has mass 3600 kg and is moving towards A with speed 3 m s^{-1}. Immediately after the collision the speeds of A and B are equal.

i Given that the two wagons are moving in the same direction after the collision, find their common speed. State which wagon has changed its direction of motion.

ii Given instead that A and B are moving with equal speeds in opposite directions after the collision, calculate

a the speed of the wagons,

b the change in the momentum of A as a result of the collision.

 **10** Two uniform spheres, A and B, have the same radius. The mass of A is 0.4 kg and the mass of B is 0.2 kg. The spheres A and B are travelling in the same direction in a straight line on a smooth horizontal surface, A with speed 5 m s^{-1}, and B with speed v m s^{-1}, where $v < 5$. A collides directly with B and the impulse between them has magnitude 0.9 N s. Immediately after the collision, the speed of B is 6 m s^{-1}.

i Calculate v.

B subsequently collides directly with a stationary sphere C of mass 0.1 kg and the same radius as A and B. The coefficient of restitution between B and C is 0.6.

ii Determine whether there will be a further collision between A and B.

 **11** A small sphere of mass 0.2 kg is dropped from rest at a height of 3 m above horizontal ground. It falls vertically, hits the ground and rebounds vertically upwards, coming to instantaneous rest at a height of 1.8 m above the ground.

i Calculate the magnitude of the impulse which the ground exerts on the sphere.

ii Calculate the coefficient of restitution between the sphere and the ground.

  **12**

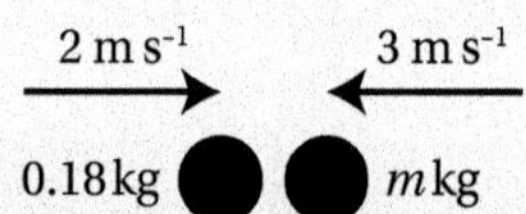

Two particles of masses 0.18 kg and m kg move on a smooth horizontal plane. They are moving towards each other in the same straight line when they collide. Immediately before the impact the speeds of the particles are 2 m s^{-1} and 3 m s^{-1} respectively (see diagram).

i Given that the particles are brought to rest by the impact, find m.

ii Given instead that the particles move with equal speeds of 1.5 m s^{-1} after the impact, find

a the value of m, assuming that the particles move in opposite directions after the impact,

b the two possible values of m, assuming that the particles coalesce.

 **13** Two spheres of the same radius with masses 2 kg and 3 kg are moving directly towards each other on a smooth horizontal plane with speeds 8 m s^{-1} and 4 m s^{-1} respectively. The spheres collide and the kinetic energy lost is 81 J. Calculate the speed and direction of motion of each sphere after the collision.

© OCR, GCE Mathematics, Paper 4729, January 2010

 **14** A particle A of mass $2m$ is moving with speed u on a smooth horizontal surface when it collides with a stationary particle B of mass m. After the collision the speed of A is v, the speed of B is $3v$ and the particles move in the same direction.

i Find v in terms of u.

ii Show that the coefficient of restitution between A and B is $\frac{4}{5}$.

B subsequently hits a vertical wall which is perpendicular to the direction of motion. As a result of the impact, B loses $\frac{3}{4}$ of its kinetic energy.

iii Show that the speed of B after hitting the wall is $\frac{3}{5}u$.

iv B then hits A. Calculate the speeds of A and B, in terms of u, after this collision and state their directions of motion.

© OCR, GCE Mathematics, Paper 4729, June 2010

4 Circular motion 1

In this chapter you will learn how to:

- model motion of a particle moving in a horizontal circular path at a constant speed
- link linear speed and angular speed of a particular moving in a horizontal circular path
- find the acceleration and forces acting on a particle moving in a horizontal circular path
- solve problems relating to motion in a horizontal circular path.

Before you start...

GCSE	You should know how to calculate arc length for a given proportion of a circle.	1 A circle has radius 5 cm. Calculate the length of the arc of a sector if the angle subtended at the centre is 120°.
GCSE **A Level Mathematics Student Book 1**	You should know how to write column vectors and what they mean.	2 Find the vector that translates (2, 3) to (−3, 10).
GCSE **A Level Mathematics Student Book 1**	You should be able to work with trigonometric ratios.	3 A point (3, 4) lies on a circle of radius 5 centred at the origin. Find the angle made with the positive x-axis of the straight line that goes through the origin and the point (3, 4).
A Level Mathematics Student Book 1	You should be able to work with simple rates of change related to speed, distance and time using calculus.	4 An object is accelerating with a constant acceleration of 3 m s^{-2}. Find an expression for its velocity and displacement given that the initial velocity is 2 m s^{-1} and the initial displacement is 3 m.
A Level Mathematics Student Book 2	You should be able to work in radians as an angular measure.	5 How many radians are the same as 150 degrees?

What is different about motion in a circle?

In your work on kinematics so far you have considered the velocity of a particle as a vector quantity with a magnitude (speed) and direction. When a particle moves in a circular path the direction of the velocity is constantly changing. You can consider a new way of measuring how the particle is moving over time. To do this you look at how the angle changes with respect to time.

Fast forward

AS Students studying only to AS Level should also see Chapter 9, Section 1, about motion in a vertical circle.

Section 1: Linear speed vs angular speed

> **Rewind**
>
> Kinematics is covered in Pure Core Student Book 1.

> **Rewind**
>
> Arc length is covered in A Level Mathematics Student Book 2.

WORKED EXAMPLE 4.1

A particle P is moving at a constant rate anticlockwise along a circle centre O of radius 5 cm. The particle takes 20 seconds to make one revolution of the circle.

a What angle (in radians) does the particle move through in 1 second?

b What is the arc length traced out by the particle every second?

a

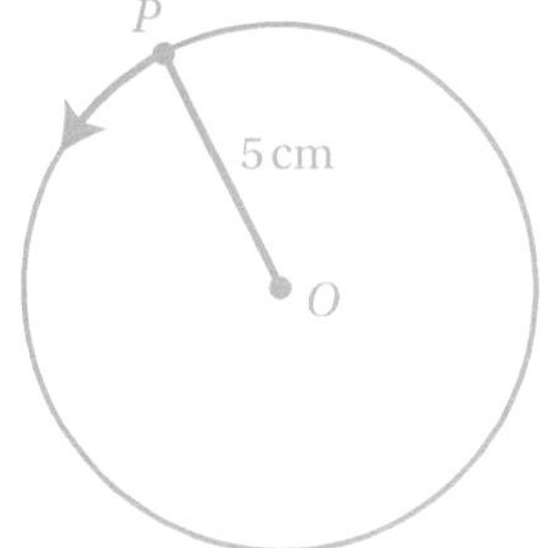

It is a good idea to draw a diagram first.

2π in 20 seconds

$\frac{\pi}{10}$ in 1 second

Hence angle turned though is

$\frac{\pi}{10} = 0.314$ rad (3 s.f.)

Write down the angle in a full turn and divide to find the angle turned through in 1 second.

b $l = r\theta$

$l = 5 \times \frac{\pi}{10}$

$= \frac{\pi}{2}$

$= 1.57$ cm (3 s.f.)

Start with the formula for arc length and then substitute the angle value found in part **a**.

Let O be the centre of a circle of radius r and let A be a fixed point on the circumference. At time t the particle P is at an angle of θ measured in radians anticlockwise from the radius OA. If the particle is travelling at a constant angular speed around the circle then the rate of change of the angle θ with respect to time t is a constant and is denoted by ω, i.e. $\frac{d\theta}{dt} = \omega$, where ω is measured in radians per second.

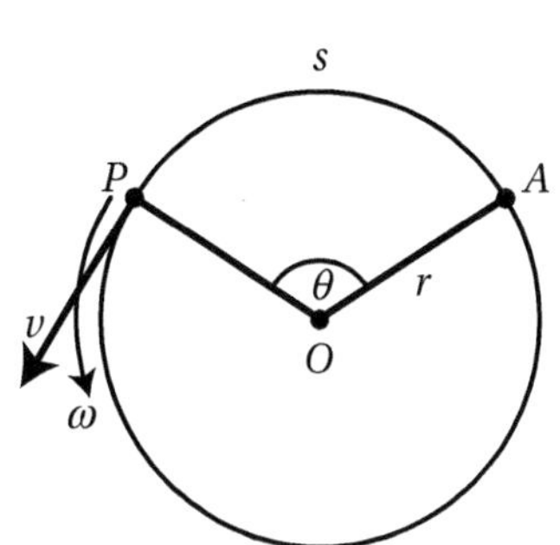

As it is equal to the arc length, the distance the particle P has travelled along the circumference is given by $s = r\theta$. Given that linear speed v (or tangential speed) is a change in distance s with respect to change in time t you can relate this to the angular speed by:

$$v = \frac{ds}{dt} = \frac{d(r\theta)}{dt} = r\frac{d\theta}{dt} = r\omega$$

You can remove r from the differentiation since it is a constant.

Key point 4.1

For a particle P moving in a circular path of radius r, centre O and with constant angular speed ω:

linear (tangential) speed $v = r\omega$

Tip

Sometimes ω is denoted by $\dot{\theta}$, which is $\frac{d\theta}{dt}$. This gives the formula for linear speed as $v = r\dot{\theta}$.

WORKED EXAMPLE 4.2

Two marbles are moving in two clockwise circles both centred at the origin O. One circle has radius 2 cm and the other has radius 5 cm. Both marbles have a constant angular speed of 3.5 rad s^{-1}. Calculate:

a the linear speed for each marble

b the time taken for each marble to complete one full circle.

a

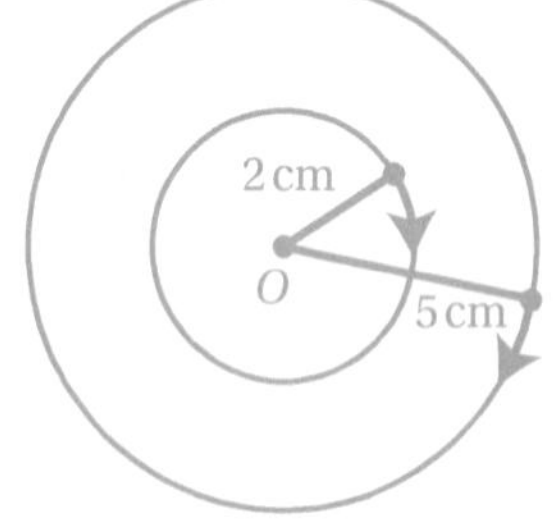

It is a good idea to draw a diagram first.

$v = r\omega$

For the circle radius 2 cm:

$v = 2 \times 3.5 = 7$ cm s^{-1}

You know that $v = r\omega$.

For the circle radius 5 cm:

$v = 5 \times 3.5 = 17.5$ cm s^{-1}

b $\omega = 3.5$ rad s^{-1}

You know that angular speed is the amount of turn with respect to time. Both particles have the same angular speed and, consequently, will take the same time to complete one full circle.

3.5 rad in 1 second = 1 rad in $\frac{2}{7}$ second

$= 2\pi$ rad in $\frac{4\pi}{7}$ seconds

Consider the angle in a full turn.

One full turn takes 1.80 seconds (3 s.f.)

WORKED EXAMPLE 4.3

A particle moves in a circular orbit of radius 2 m at a constant frequency of 0.6 revolutions per minute.

a How many revolutions does the particle complete in 1 second?

b What is the angular speed of the particle in radians per second?

c What is the linear speed of the particle?

a $0.6 \div 60 = 0.01$ revolutions in 1 second

You know that 1 minute = 60 seconds. The particle will travel through a smaller angle in 1 second than in 1 minute.

b $2\pi \times 0.01 = \frac{\pi}{50}$ radians turned in 1 second

$\omega = 0.0628$ rad s^{-1} (3 s.f.)

Angular speed is the angle turned through in 1 second so consider what proportion of a full turn has taken place in 1 second from part **a**.

c $v = r\omega = 2 \times \frac{\pi}{50} = \frac{\pi}{25}$

$= 0.126$ m s^{-1} (3 s.f.)

You know that $v = r\omega$.

Tip

It is important to make sure that you are using the right units for angular speed, linear speed, distance and time.

WORK IT OUT 4.1

Two particles A and B are moving in two clockwise circles, both centred at O, of radius 5 cm and 7 cm, respectively. Particle A moves at a linear speed of 2.5 m s^{-1} and particle B moves at an angular speed of 6 rad s^{-1}. Determine which particle has the greater angular speed.

Which is the correct solution? Can you identify the errors made in the incorrect solutions?

Solution 1	Solution 2	Solution 3
Angular speed: $\omega = \frac{v}{r}$ Particle A angular speed: $\omega = 2.5 \div 5 = 0.5$ rad s^{-1} Therefore, particle B has a greater angular speed.	Angular speed $\omega = rv$ $r = 5$ cm $= 0.05$ m Particle A angular speed: $\omega = 0.05 \times 2.5 = 0.125$ rad s^{-1} Therefore, particle B has a greater angular speed.	Angular speed: $\omega = \frac{v}{r}$ $r = 5$ cm $= 0.05$ m Particle A angular speed: $\omega = 2.5 \div 0.05 = 50$ rad s^{-1} Therefore, particle A has a greater angular speed.

EXERCISE 4A

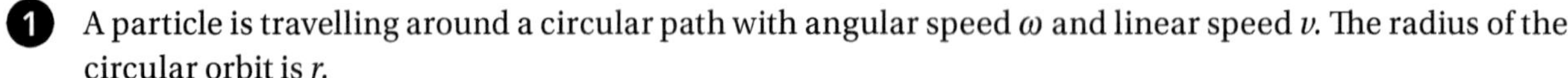

1 A particle is travelling around a circular path with angular speed ω and linear speed v. The radius of the circular orbit is r.

a i If $\omega = 3.4$ rad s^{-1} and $r = 3$ m, find v. ii If $\omega = 2.11$ rad s^{-1} and $r = 0.2$ m, find v.

b i If $v = 7$ m s^{-1} and $\omega = 4$ rad s^{-1}, find r. ii If $v = 3.2$ m s^{-1} and $\omega = 0.2$ rad s^{-1}, find r.

c i If the radius of the circular path is 30 cm and linear speed 3 m per min, find ω.

ii If the radius of the circular path is 124 mm and linear speed 10 km per hour, find ω.

d i If the particle makes 2 revolutions every second of a circular path of radius 2 cm, find v.

ii If the particle makes 10 revolutions every minute of a circular path of radius 3 m, find v.

2 a A particle takes 15 seconds to move around in a circle at a constant linear speed of 30 m s^{-1}. Find:

i the angular speed in rad s^{-1} ii the radius of the circle in m.

b A marble completes 20 revolutions every 30 seconds with a linear speed of 10 m s^{-1}. Find:

i the angular speed in rad s^{-1} ii the radius of the circle in m.

c A ball takes 1 minute to move round a circle at a constant linear speed of 5 m s^{-1}. Find:

i the angular speed in rad s^{-1} ii the radius of the circle in m.

3 A particle is travelling around a circular path of radius 30 cm at a constant linear speed of 3 m s^{-1}. Calculate the angular speed.

4 A cyclist rides clockwise around a circular track of radius 75 m at a linear speed of 8 m s^{-1}.

a Find the angular speed in rad s^{-1}. b How long does it take for one circuit?

5 A spinning disc of radius 10 cm completes one revolution every 45 seconds.

a What is the angular speed of the spinning disc in rad s^{-1}?

b What is the linear speed at the edge of the spinning disc?

c What radius would the spinning disc need to have a linear speed of 1 m s^{-1} at its edge?

6 Two gear wheels A and B, one of radius 5 cm and one of radius 10 cm, are connected. If the angular speed of wheel A is 0.5 rad s^{-1}, what is the angular speed of B?

7 An athlete runs at 7 m s^{-1} along the inside path of the track shown in the diagram.

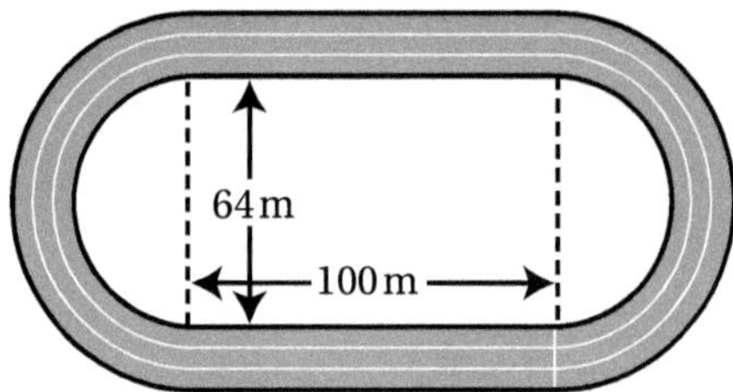

a How long does it take to complete one circuit?

b What is the angular speed of the athlete as he runs around the circular parts of the track?

8 Metis is a moon of Jupiter. It completes one orbit approximately every 7 hours. The orbit has an average distance from Jupiter of approximately 128 000 km.

a What assumptions do you need to make to be able to calculate the angular speed of Metis in its orbit?

b Making these modelling assumptions, determine:

i the angular speed of Metis in rad s^{-1}

ii the linear speed of the moon in km s^{-1}.

Section 2: Acceleration in horizontal circular motion

When a particle moves in a circular path there must be a resultant force that keeps the particle moving in a circle, otherwise the particle would stop turning and continue to move in a straight line.

If there is a force acting on the particle to keep it in a circular orbit, by Newton's second law, there must be an acceleration.

The diagram shows a particle P moving in a horizontal circle in the x–y plane.

The direction of the velocity is along the tangent to the circle.

The direction of the acceleration is towards the centre of the circle.

The formula for acceleration is given by $a = v\omega$ where v is the linear speed and ω the angular speed. (The proof of this result is beyond the scope of this section.)

Since $v = r\omega$, you can write $a = r\omega^2$ and, since $\omega = \frac{v}{r}$, you can write $a = \frac{v^2}{r}$. This means that you have a relationship between a and any two of the three variables v, ω and r.

Applying Newton's second law, $F = ma$, and resolving radially to a particle of mass m kg moving in a horizontal circular path, the force that gives rise to the circular motion is proportional to the acceleration, and is in the same direction. This force is often referred to as the **centripetal force**.

Key point 4.2

For a particle P moving in a circular path of radius r, centre O and with constant angular speed ω, the acceleration is given by $v\omega$, $r\omega^2$ or $\frac{v^2}{r}$, towards the centre of the circle.

This will appear in your formula book.

Rewind

Recall Newton's laws of motion, which you used in A Level Mathematics Student Book 1.

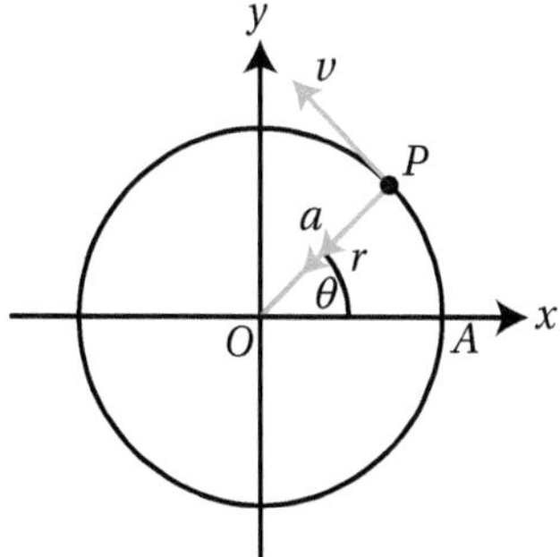

Tip

Sometimes acceleration is written as $a = r\ddot{\theta}$, where $\ddot{\theta}$ is $\frac{d^2\theta}{dt^2}$.

Focus on ...

In Focus on ... Proof 1, you will investigate the connection between the equations for linear motion with constant acceleration in a straight line and motion in a circle involving angular equivalents of s, u, v and a.

WORKED EXAMPLE 4.4

A ball of mass 200 g is attached to a light inextensible string of length 150 cm. One end of the string is fixed on a smooth horizontal table and the ball moves in a circular path with linear speed 4 m s^{-1}.

a What is the acceleration of the ball?

b What is the tension in the string?

a

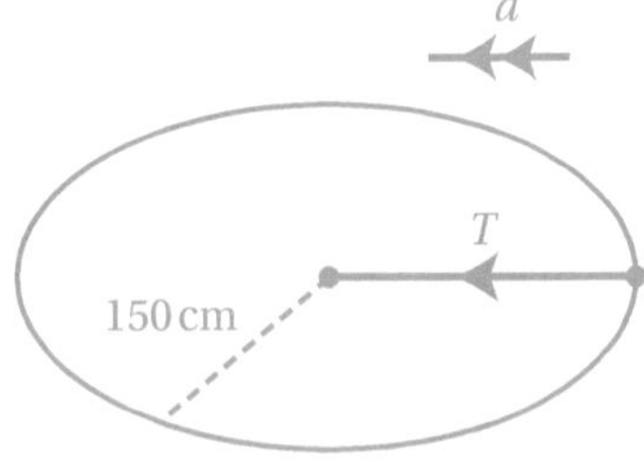

It is a good idea to draw a diagram first, labelling the direction of the acceleration.

$v = 4\text{ m s}^{-1}, r = 1.5\text{ m}$

Convert cm to m.

$a = \frac{v^2}{r} = \frac{4^2}{1.5} = 10.7\text{ m s}^{-2}$ (3 s.f.)

towards the centre of the circle

You know that $a = \frac{v^2}{r}$.

b $T = ma$

$m = 0.2$ kg

$T = 0.2 \times \frac{16}{1.5} = 2.13$ N (3 s.f.)

The resultant force directed towards the centre of the circular motion comes from the tension in the string and $F = ma$ using Newton's second law.

Rewind

When modelling with a rope, you can make the modelling assumptions that it is light and inextensible in order to produce a simple mathematical model of the situation, as you did in A Level Mathematics Student Book 1.

WORKED EXAMPLE 4.5

A toy car of mass 1 kg moves at an angular speed of $\frac{\pi}{30}$ rad s^{-1} around a circular path of radius 20 m. What is the centripetal force F required to keep the toy car travelling in this circular path?

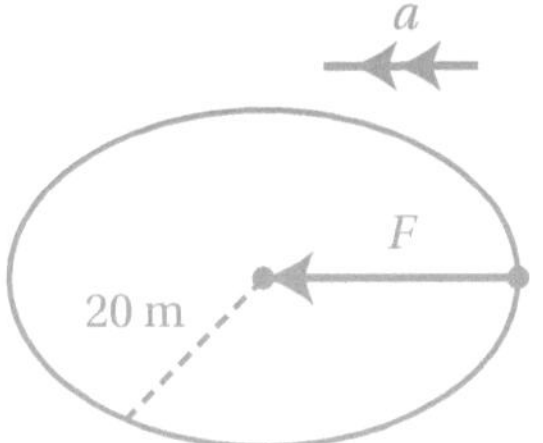

It is a good idea to draw a diagram first.

$F = ma = 1 \times a$

$a = r\omega^2 = 20 \times \left(\frac{\pi}{30}\right)^2 = 0.2193$

Hence $F = 1 \times 0.2193 = 0.219$ N (3 s.f.)

EXERCISE 4B

1 A particle of mass m kg is travelling around a circular path. ω is angular speed, v is linear speed, r is the radius of the circular orbit and a is the magnitude of the acceleration.

a **i** If $\omega = 4$ rad s^{-1}and $a = 5$ m s^{-2}, find r.

ii If $\omega = 2.33$ rad s^{-1}and $a = 7$ m s^{-2}, find r.

b **i** If $v = 5$ m s^{-1} and $a = 7$ m s^{-2}, find r.

ii If $v = 3.56$ m s^{-1} and $a = 9$ m s^{-2}, find r.

c **i** If $m = 20$ kg, $r = 0.3$ m and the force keeping the particle in a circular motion is 340 N, find v.

ii If $m = 35$ kg, $r = 0.5$ m and the force keeping the particle in a circular motion is 150 N, find v.

d **i** If $m = 5$ kg, $r = 2$ m and the force keeping the particle in a circular motion is 90 N, find ω.

ii If $m = 0.5$ kg, $r = 0.4$ m and the force keeping the particle in a circular motion is 30 N, find ω.

2 **a** A ball of mass 2 kg is attached to a light inextensible string of length 1 m. One end of the string is fixed on a smooth table and the ball moves in a circular path with linear speed 2 m s^{-1}.

i Find the acceleration due to the circular motion.

ii Find the magnitude of the resultant force acting on the ball.

b A car of mass 2900 kg is travelling in a circular path of diameter 50 m with a linear speed of 35 km h^{-1}.

i Find the acceleration due to the circular motion.

ii Find the magnitude of the resultant force acting on the car.

c A particle of mass 200 g is attached to a light inextensible string of length 15 cm that is fixed at the other end so that the particle is moving in a circular path on a smooth table at a constant rate of 1 revolution every 20 seconds.

i Find the acceleration due to the circular motion.

ii Find the magnitude of the resultant force acting on the particle.

3 A particle of mass 300 g is travelling around a circular path of radius 340 mm and makes 20 full circles every minute. Calculate the force keeping the particle in circular motion, to 3 significant figures.

4 A car of mass 1500 kg travels along a horizontal road that is an arc of a circle with radius 35 m. The maximum speed at which the car can travel on this circular bend without slipping outwards from the centre is 25 km h^{-1}. Calculate the acceleration and the maximal friction force on the car towards the centre of the arc of the circle.

5 Calculate the tension required in a light inextensible string of length 30 cm to keep a particle of mass 2 kg moving in a horizontal circular path if:

a the linear speed of the particle is 3 m s^{-1}

b the angular speed is 6 rad s^{-1}.

6 Emily sits on a roundabout, rotating at a constant angular speed ω, halfway between the centre and the edge. If Emily moves to a position that is $\frac{1}{3}$ of the radius from the edge, what effect does this have on the force that Emily experiences acting towards the centre of the roundabout? Provide calculations to support your argument.

A 7 A car travels at a constant speed along a bend in the road that is formed by an arc of a circle of radius 55 m.

a What is the greatest linear speed in km h^{-1} at which the car can travel around the bend without moving off at a tangent, if the coefficient of friction between the tyres of the car and the surface of the road is estimated as 0.1?

b Comment on whether this seems a sensible estimate for the value of the coefficient of friction.

Rewind

A You will have used the coefficient of friction in A Level Mathematics Student Book 2.

A 8 A marble is on a rough horizontal disc at a distance of 13 cm from its centre. When the disc is rotating at a constant speed of 12 rev min^{-1} the particle is on the point of moving tangentially outwards from the centre. Calculate the coefficient of friction between the marble and the disc.

A 9 Two particles A and B of mass 40 g and 30 g respectively are attached to opposite ends of a light inextensible string of length 30 cm. Particle A rests on a rough horizontal spinning table which has coefficient of friction 0.4 and the string passes through a smooth hole in the centre of the table. Particle B hangs freely below the table. Particle A is moving in a circular path with constant angular speed about the centre of the table. Find the linear speed of particle A, if the system is in equilibrium with particle A on the point of tangential displacement out from the centre of the spinning table, and particle B hanging 15 cm below the table.

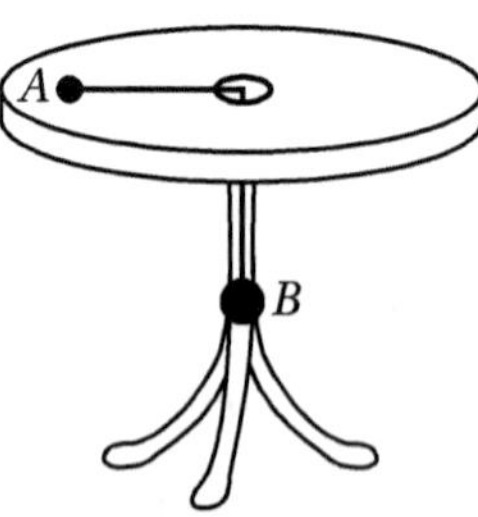

Tip

Remember that it is the resultant force acting horizontally towards the centre of the circular motion that you use for the force in $F = ma$.

A 10 Road surface conditions are being assessed for a horizontal bend in a road that is formed by an arc of a circle of radius 25 m. The road surface could be made of asphalt or concrete. The coefficient of friction between car tyres and asphalt is 0.72, and between car tyres and concrete 0.85.

a What assumptions need to be made?

b Calculate the maximum safe linear speed, in km h^{-1}, at which a car could travel around the bend without slipping for:

i a surface made from asphalt

ii a surface made from concrete.

c If the surface is wet, the coefficient of friction between the car tyres and asphalt is reduced to 0.25 and that between car tyres and concrete is reduced to 0.45. What are the maximum safe limits now?

d Given that concrete is more expensive than asphalt, which road surface would you use for the bend in the road?

 Let the position of a particle P in the diagram have coordinates $(r\cos\theta, r\sin\theta)$. Let ω be the constant angular speed of P so that the angle θ measured from the line OA anticlockwise at time t is ωt. Show that:

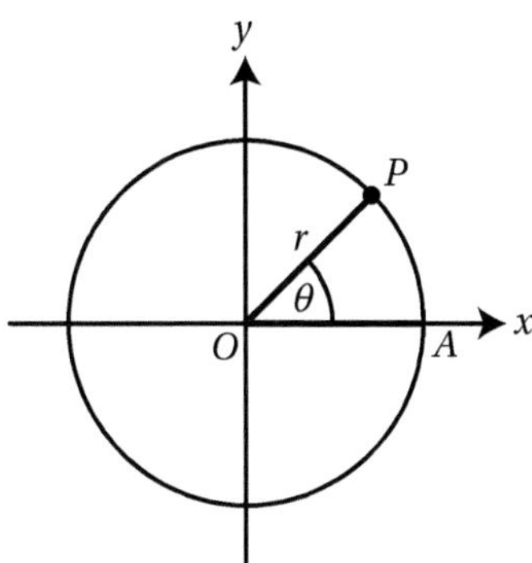

a the position vector of P is given by $\mathbf{r} = \begin{pmatrix} r\cos\omega t \\ r\sin\omega t \end{pmatrix}$

b the linear (tangential) velocity of P is $\mathbf{v} = \begin{pmatrix} -r\omega\sin\omega t \\ r\omega\cos\omega t \end{pmatrix}$

c the acceleration of P is given by $\mathbf{a} = \begin{pmatrix} -r\omega^2\cos\omega t \\ -r\omega^2\sin\omega t \end{pmatrix}$

d the acceleration is along a radius, directed towards the centre O, and of magnitude $r\omega^2$.

e Use the scalar product to show that the velocity vector is perpendicular to the radius.

 **Rewind**

Scalar product is covered in A Level Mathematics Student Book 1.

Explore

In A Level Mathematics, you may have seen various ways to convince yourself of how the trigonometric functions are differentiated. Using the following: www.cambridge.org/links/moscmec6001, you can start with your knowledge of motion in a circle to help you to understand the derivatives of sine and cosine.

Section 3: Solving problems involving motion in a horizontal circle

The examples you have seen so far in this chapter have all had a single horizontal force keeping a particle in a circular path. You are now going to consider situations where the forces are not necessarily acting horizontally but the particle is still moving in a horizontal circular path with a constant angular speed. This will require you to consider the components of a force.

One example of this type of motion is the **conical pendulum**, shown in the diagram. The particle is attached to a light inextensible string that makes an angle of θ with the downward vertical, and it is moving in a horizontal circle at a constant angular speed ω.

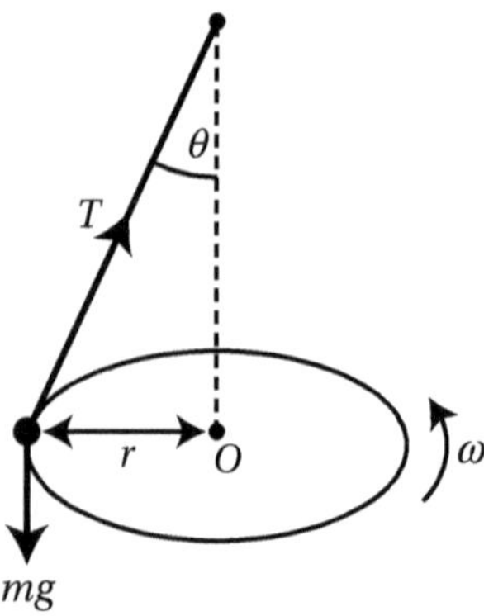

Focus on ...

You will learn about a simple pendulum in Focus on ... Modelling 2.

WORKED EXAMPLE 4.6

A particle, A, of mass 200 g is attached to the lower end of a light inextensible string with the upper end fixed at B. When the particle moves in a horizontal circular path, the string traces out the curved surface of a cone and makes an angle of 60° with the downward vertical. The centre of the circular path lies directly below the point B at a distance of 2 m.

a Find the tension in the string.

b Find the angular speed of the particle.

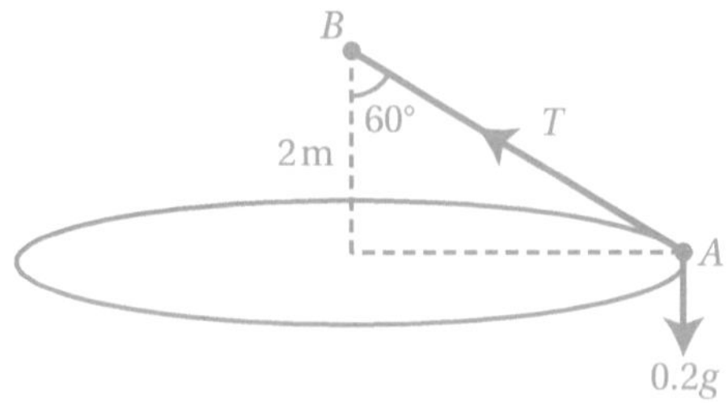

It is a good idea to draw a diagram first. Resolve forces vertically to form an equation involving T. Resolve forces horizontally and use Newton's second law to form an equation involving the centripetal acceleration, a. Use the value of acceleration with the equation for circular motion to calculate the angular speed.

a $T\cos 60 - mg = 0$

Therefore $T = \dfrac{mg}{\cos 60}$

$T = 0.2 \times 9.8 \div 0.5$

$= 3.92$ N

Resolve the forces vertically. The particle is not moving in the vertical direction.

b $T\sin 60 = ma$

so $3.92 \sin 60 = 0.2a$

Hence $a = 3.92 \times \sin 60° \div 0.2$

$= 16.97$

Resolve the forces horizontally in the direction of the acceleration.

$r = 2\tan 60$

Find the radius of the circular motion using trigonometry.

Use $a = r\omega^2$

where $\omega = \sqrt{\dfrac{a}{r}} = \sqrt{\dfrac{16.97}{2\tan 60}}$

≈ 2.21 rad s^{-1} (3 s.f.)

You can then substitute the values for r and a into the equation to find ω.

Rewind

Resolving forces is covered in A Level Mathematics Student Book 2, Chapter 21.

WORKED EXAMPLE 4.7

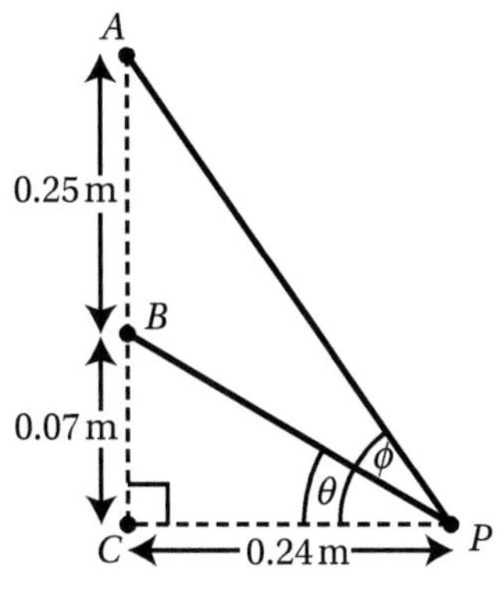

A particle, P, of mass 0.8 kg is attached to two light rods AP and BP, as shown in the diagram, where A, B, P and C all lie in the same vertical plane. The lengths of AB, BC and CP are 0.25, 0.07 and 0.24 metres respectively.

The particle is moving in a horizontal circle with linear speed 3 m s^{-1}.

a Calculate the tension in the rod BP.

b Calculate the magnitude of the force in the rod AP and determine if the rod is in tension or compression.

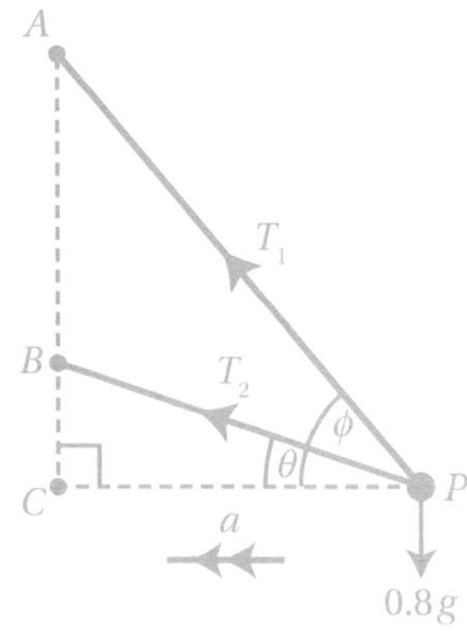

It is a good idea to draw a diagram first showing the forces acting on P.

a $T_1 \sin\phi + T_2 \sin\theta = 0.8g = 7.84$

Resolve the forces at P vertically.

$T_1 \cos\phi + T_2 \cos\theta = 0.8\frac{v^2}{r} = 30$

Resolve the forces horizontally in the direction of the acceleration. Use $a = \frac{v^2}{r}$.

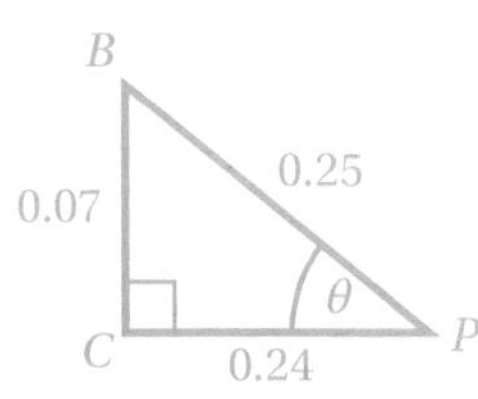

$\sin\theta = \frac{0.07}{0.25} = \frac{7}{25}$

$\cos\theta = \frac{0.24}{0.25} = \frac{24}{25}$

$\tan\theta = \frac{0.07}{0.24} = \frac{7}{24}$

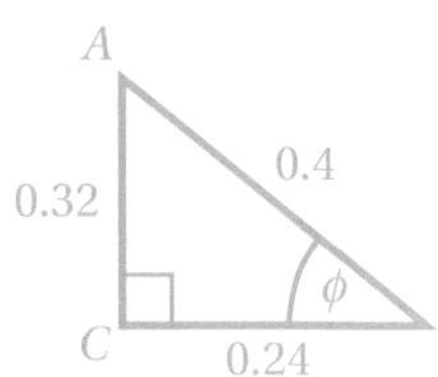

$\sin\phi = \frac{0.32}{0.4} = \frac{4}{5}$

$\cos\phi = \frac{0.24}{0.4} = \frac{3}{5}$

$\tan\phi = \frac{0.32}{0.24} = \frac{4}{3}$

It is a good idea to find the trigonometric ratios for the angles in the question.

$\frac{4}{5}T_1 + \frac{7}{25}T_2 = 7.84$

$\frac{3}{5}T_1 + \frac{24}{25}T_2 = 30$

$60T_1 + 21T_2 = 588$

$60T_1 + 96T_2 = 3000$

When the values are substituted you have a pair of simultaneous equations to solve.

$T_2 = 32.16 = 32.2$ N (3 s.f.)

You can find the tension T_2 by eliminating T_1.

Continues on next page ...

b $60T_1 + 21T_2 = 588$

$60T_1 = 588 - 21 \times 32.16$

$T_1 = -1.456 = -1.46$

Magnitude of the force in rod AP is 1.46 N.

You can substitute the value you found for T_2 into one of the equations to find T_1.

The force is directed towards P and rod AP is therefore in compression.

You initially assumed that T_1 was acting towards A. As the value of T_1 is negative it means that the direction must have been incorrect and the rod is in compression.

Rewind

Recall from A Level Mathematics Student Book 1 that a rod can be under tension or compression.

WORKED EXAMPLE 4.8

The fixed points A, B and C are in a vertical line with A above B, and B above C. A particle Q of mass 3 kg is joined to A, to B, and to a particle P of mass 2 kg, by three light rods where the length of rod AQ is 2 m and the length of rod QP is 1 m. Particle Q moves in a horizontal circle with centre B. Particle P moves in a horizontal circle with centre C, at the same constant angular speed ω as Q, in such a way that A, B, P and Q are coplanar. The rod AQ makes an angle of 30° with the downward vertical, rod QP makes an angle of 45° with the downward vertical and rod BQ is horizontal (see diagram).

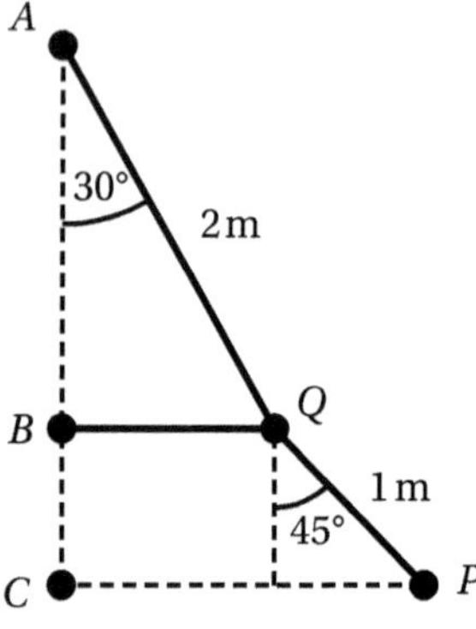

a Calculate the angular speed ω.

b Find the tension in the rod AQ.

c Find the force in the rod BQ and determine if the rod is in tension or compression.

a

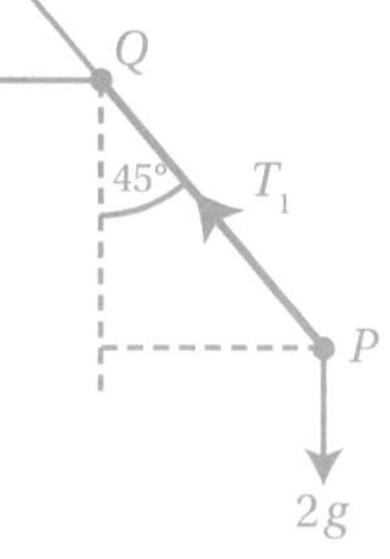

It is a good idea to draw a diagram first showing the forces acting on P.

$F = ma$

$T_1 \sin 45 = 2r\omega^2$

Resolve the forces horizontally in the direction of the acceleration to get an equation that involves the tension in the rod QP.

Continues on next page ...

$T_1 \cos 45 = 2g$

$T_1 = 27.72$

$r = |AQ|\sin 30 + |QP|\sin 45$

$r = 2\sin 30 + 1\sin 45$

$r = 2\sin 30 + \sin 45$

You can find the tension in the rod QP by resolving the forces vertically at P.

You need to find the radius of the circular motion for P. This will involve finding the horizontal distance CP, which is made up of two parts.

$$\omega = \sqrt{\frac{T_1 \sin 45}{2r}}$$

$$= \sqrt{\frac{27.72 \tan 45}{2(2\sin 30 + \sin 45)\cos 45}}$$

$\omega = 2.396 \text{ rad s}^{-1}$

You can then substitute the expression for T_1 and the radius r of the circular motion into a rearranged equation to find ω.

b

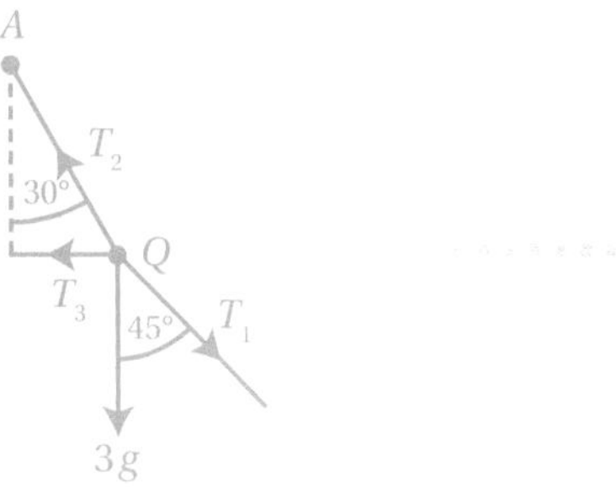

It is a good idea to draw a diagram first showing the forces acting on Q.

$T_2 \cos 30 = 3g + T_1 \cos 45$

$T_2 \cos 30 = 5g$

$T_2 = 56.6$ N (3 s.f.)

Resolving the forces at Q vertically allows you to find the tension in the rod AQ.

c $F = ma$

$T_3 + T_2 \sin 30 - T_1 \sin 45 = 3r\omega^2$

$T_3 = 3(2\sin 30)\omega^2 + T_1 \sin 45 - T_2 \sin 30$

$T_3 = 8.53$ N (3 s.f.)

Resolve the forces horizontally in the direction of the acceleration and use the values you found for ω, T_1 and T_2 to find T_3, the tension in BQ.

The rod is in tension.

Since the value of the tension is positive, the rod is in tension.

Banked tracks

Another example of horizontal circular motion is motion on a **banked track**. The two figures show an inward banked track, also known as camber.

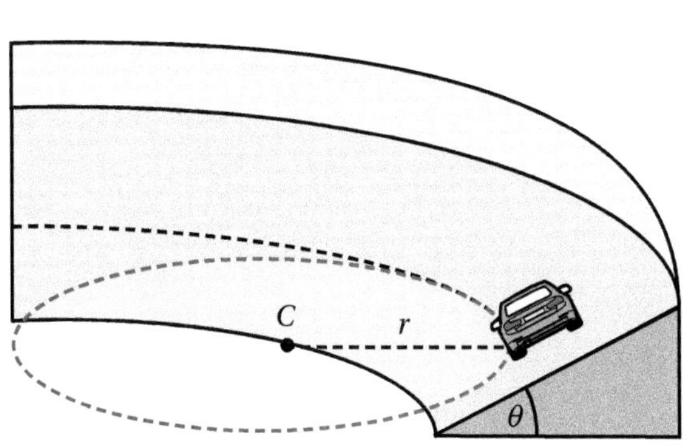

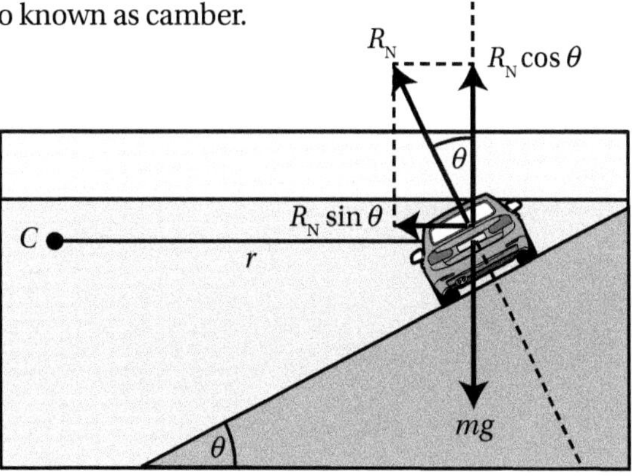

You can consider how cars move around bends that are banked at an angle θ to the horizontal, as shown in Worked examples 4.9 and 4.10.

Did you know?

The camber of a road or a cant of a railway track allows the vehicles to turn safely through a curve at higher speeds compared with a level surface.

WORKED EXAMPLE 4.9

A remote-control toy car travels around a bend of radius 14 m on a track which is banked at an angle of θ to the horizontal. If the car is travelling at 25 km h^{-1} and there is no friction between the car and the track, find the angle θ.

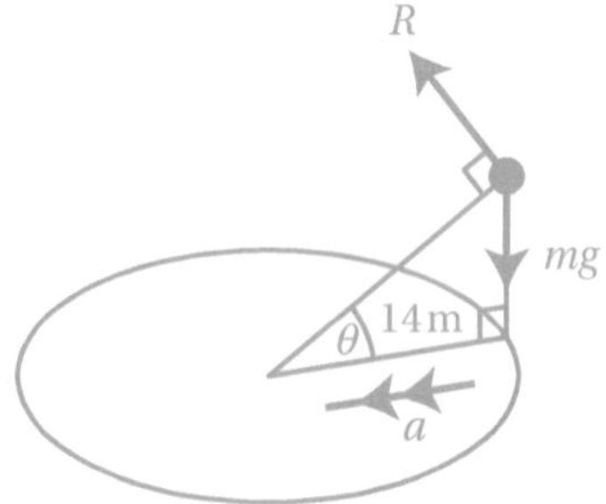

It is a good idea to draw a diagram first. Remember the reaction force (R) is always perpendicular to the road or track.

$R\sin\theta = ma$

Resolve the forces horizontally to form an equation involving a, m and R.

$R\cos\theta = mg$

Resolve the forces vertically to form an equation involving g, m and R.

Hence $\tan\theta = \dfrac{a}{g}$

Divide the first equation by the second to eliminate the unknowns R and m.

$a = \dfrac{v^2}{r}$

$v = 25\text{ km h}^{-1} = 6.944\text{ m s}^{-1}$ (3 s.f.)

$a = 6.944^2 \div 14 = 3.444\text{ m s}^{-2}$ (3 s.f.)

Hence $\tan\theta = 3.444 \div 9.8 = 0.3515$

Therefore $\theta = 19.4°$ (3 s.f.)

Use $a = \dfrac{v^2}{r}$ to write an expression for a. Make sure that all units are consistent.

Substitute and solve for θ.

WORKED EXAMPLE 4.10

A racing car travels at a constant speed around a bend in a road of radius 55 m. The road is banked at an angle θ to the horizontal with $\sin\theta = \frac{4}{5}$. If the coefficient of friction between the tyres of the car and the road is 0.45 find:

a the maximum linear speed at which the car can be driven around the bend

b the minimum linear speed at which the car can be driven around the bend.

a

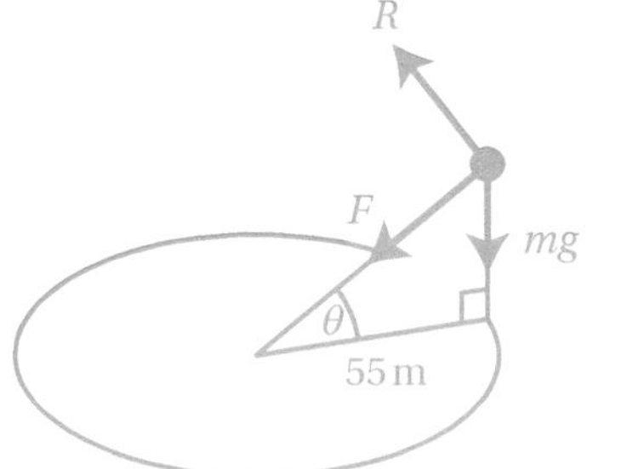

It is a good idea to draw a diagram first. Remember the reaction force (R) is always perpendicular to the road.

In this case, the greatest speed is the speed that is possible before slipping outwards from the centre, so friction acts towards the centre.

$F = 0.45R$

The maximum frictional force is proportional to the normal reaction force.

$R\cos\theta = mg + F\sin\theta$

$R\cos\theta = mg + 0.45R\sin\theta$

$0.6R = mg + 0.36R$

$0.24R = mg$

Resolve the forces vertically to form an equation involving g, m and R.

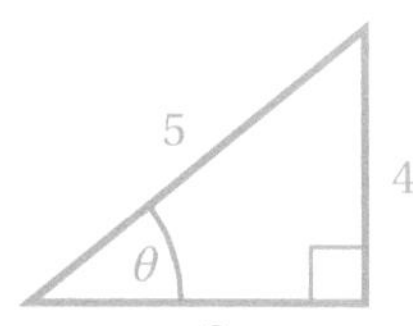

$\sin\theta = \frac{4}{5}$

$\cos\theta = \frac{3}{5}$

You are told that $\sin\theta = \frac{4}{5}$. Recall how to find exact values for sin, cos and tan using right-angled triangles.

$F\cos\theta + R\sin\theta = ma$

$0.45R\cos\theta + R\sin\theta = ma$

$0.27R + 0.8R = ma$

$1.07R = ma$

Resolve the forces horizontally to form an equation involving a, m and R.

Therefore $\frac{1.07R}{0.24R} = \frac{ma}{mg}$

$\frac{107}{24}g = a$

$v = \sqrt{ar} = \sqrt{\frac{107}{24} \times 9.8 \times 55}$

$= 49.0\ \text{m s}^{-1}$ (3 s.f.)

Using $a = \frac{v^2}{r}$, $v = \sqrt{ar}$.

b

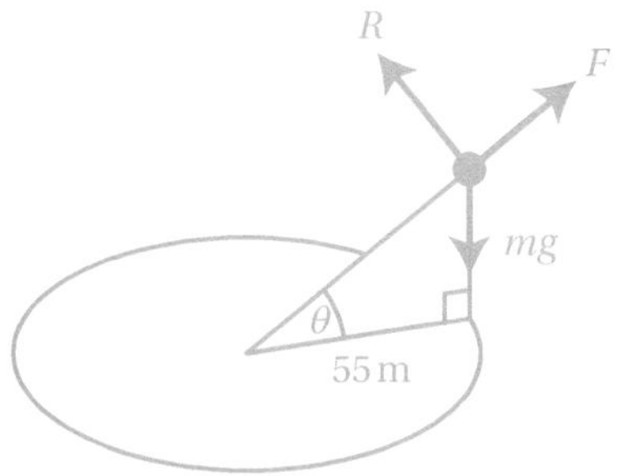

In this case, the least speed is the speed that is possible before slipping inwards towards the centre, so friction acts away from the centre.

Continues on next page ...

$F = 0.45R$

The maximum frictional force is proportional to the normal reaction force.

$R\cos\theta + F\sin\theta = mg$

$R\cos\theta + 0.45R\sin\theta = mg$

$0.6R + 0.36R = mg$

$0.96R = mg$

Resolve the forces vertically to form an equation involving g, m and R.

$R\sin\theta = ma + F\cos\theta$

$R\sin\theta = ma + 0.45R\cos\theta$

$0.8R = ma + 0.27R$

$R\,0.53R = ma$

Resolve the forces horizontally to form an equation involving a, m and R.

Therefore $\frac{0.53R}{0.96R} = \frac{ma}{mg}$

$\frac{53}{96}g = a$

$v = \sqrt{ar} = \sqrt{\frac{53}{96} \times 9.8 \times 55}$

$= 17.3\ \text{m s}^{-1}$ (3 s.f.)

Tip

If a particle is moving in a circular orbit on a rough inclined plane, then the direction of friction depends on the speed at which the particle is moving. A slowly moving particle will be on the point of slipping down the inclined plane and so friction will act up the inclined plane.

EXERCISE 4C

Unless otherwise instructed, when a numerical value for the acceleration due to gravity is needed, use $g = 9.8\ \text{m s}^{-2}$.

A particle of mass m kg is moving in a horizontal circle at a constant angular speed ω rad s^{-1} attached to a light inextensible string of length l m that makes an angle of θ with the downward vertical.

a **i** If $m = 2$ and $\theta = 20°$, find the tension in the string.

ii If $m = 3.5$ and $\theta = 35°$, find the tension in the string.

b **i** If $m = 2$, $\omega = 3$ and $l = 2$, find the tension in the string.

ii If $m = 3.5$, $\omega = 3$ and $l = 1.5$, find the tension in the string.

c **i** If $\theta = 30°$ and $l = 2.2$, find ω.

ii If $\theta = 60°$ and $l = 3.75$, find ω.

d **i** If $\omega = 3.25$ and $l = 1.2$, find the angle θ.

ii If $\omega = 5.2$ and $l = 3.2$, find the angle θ.

2 Here are incomplete force diagrams for some simple conical pendulums. Each consists of a light, inextensible string of length l suspended from a point A and a bob of mass m kg at point B. The bob moves in a horizontal circle centred vertically below A and the string forms an angle θ with the downward vertical. B moves with a constant angular speed ω rad s^{-1} and the tension in the string AB is T N.

a Find the angle θ.

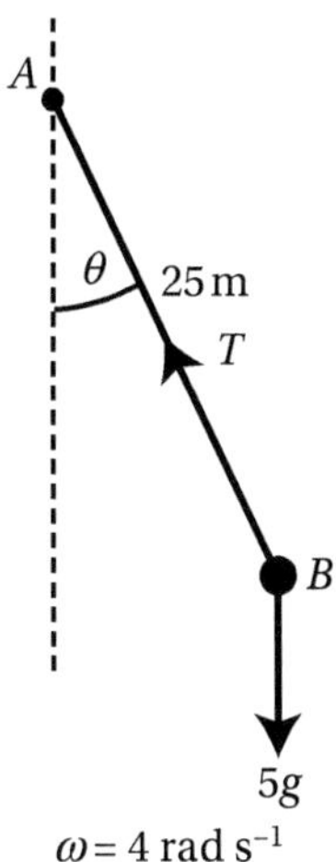

b Find the angular speed ω.

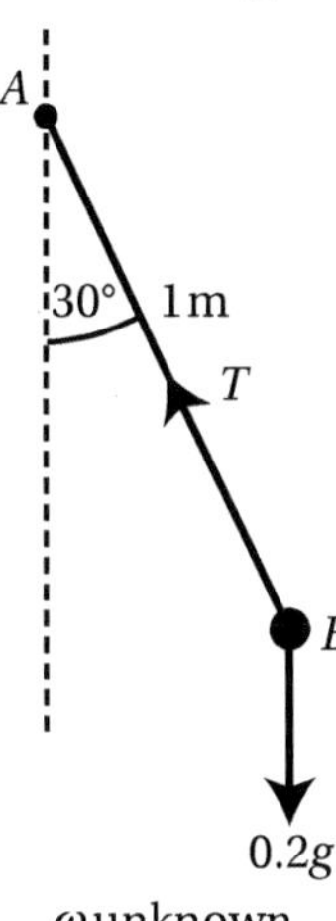

c Find the tension in the string.

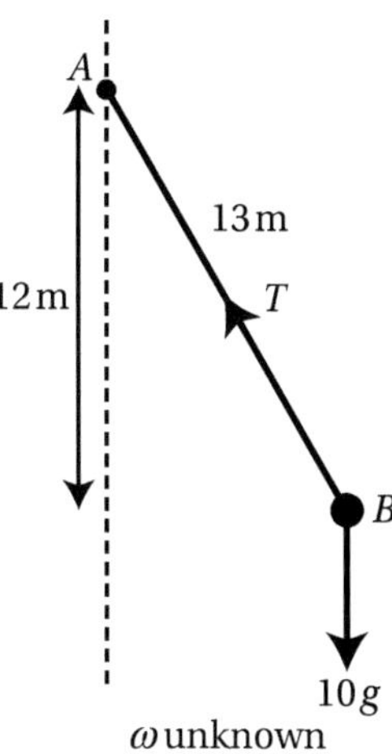

d Find the mass of the bob.

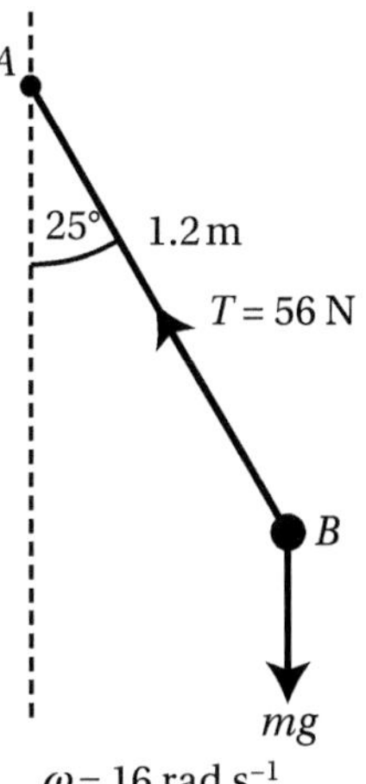

3 A particle is moving in a horizontal circle at a constant angular speed of 3.4 rad s^{-1}, attached to a light inextensible string of length 2 metres. Find the angle the string makes with the downward vertical to 3 significant figures.

4 A particle travels around a bend of radius 12 m, with the surface banked at an angle θ to the horizontal, where $\sin\theta = \frac{5}{13}$. Show that, if the surface is smooth, the particle will not slip if it travels with a linear speed of $\sqrt{5g}$.

Explore

Watch the video at www.cambridge.org/links/moscmec6002 and use the ideas introduced and explored in this chapter to create a mathematical model of this situation.

5 A smooth bead B of mass 500 g is threaded onto a light inextensible string. The two ends of the string are attached to fixed points X and Y, where X is vertically below Y. The string is taut and the bead rotates about the axis YX. The bead moves with a constant angular speed in a horizontal circular path of radius 0.8 m. Given that angle YXB is 60° and angle XYB is 30°, calculate:

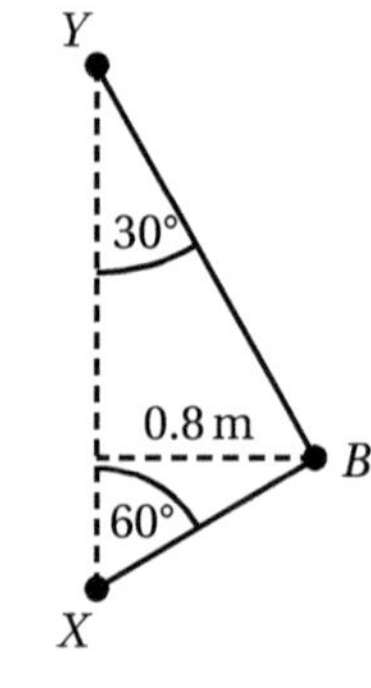

a the tension in the string **b** the angular speed.

6 A bend in a road is in the form of a horizontal circular arc of radius 10 m, with the road surface banked outward at an angle θ, where $\sin\theta = \frac{7}{25}$ to the horizontal. Show that, if there is a frictional force of 10 kN acting up the slope, a car of mass 1200 kg is moving at a linear speed of 7.63 m s^{-1} to 3 significant figures.

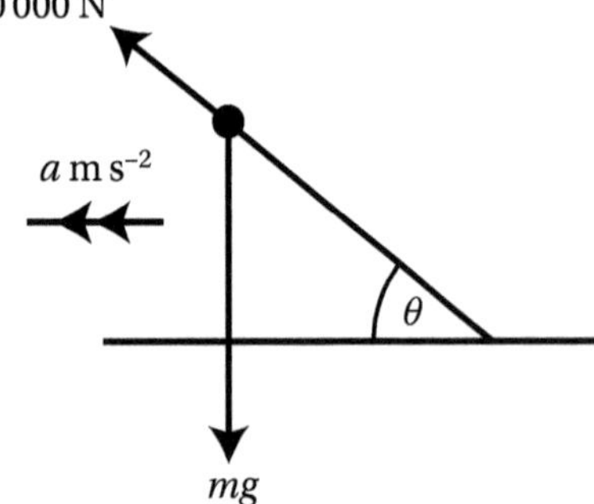

7 In the diagram the fixed points A and B are in a vertical line, with A above B at a distance of 1.80 m. A particle P of mass m kg is attached to two light inextensible strings, so that AP is 1.44 m and BP is 1.08 m. The particle P rotates at a constant angular speed of ω with both strings BP and AP taut.

a Find the tension in AP in terms of m, g and ω.

b Find the tension in BP in terms of m, g and ω.

c Calculate a lower bound for the angular speed ω given that BP remains taut.

8 Fixed points A, B and C are in a vertical line with A above B and B above C. A particle Q of mass 3 kg is joined to A, to B and to a particle P of mass 2 kg, by three light rods where the length of rod AQ is 2 m and the length of rod QP is 1 m. Particle Q moves in a horizontal circle with centre B. Particle P moves in a horizontal circle with centre C at the same constant angular speed ω as Q, in such a way that A, B, P and Q are coplanar. Rods AQ and QP both make an angle of 30° with the downward vertical and rod BQ is horizontal (see diagram).

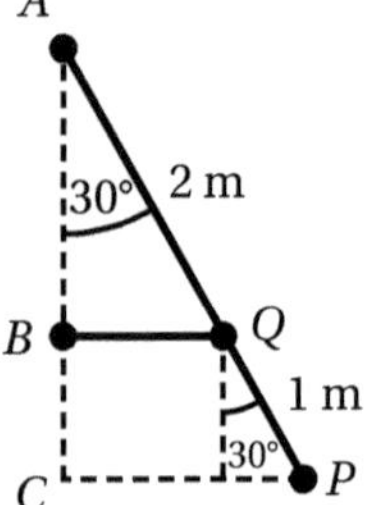

a Calculate the angular speed ω.

b Find the tension in the rod AQ.

c Find the magnitude of the force in the rod BQ and state whether the rod is in tension or compression.

9 A hemispherical bowl of radius r is fixed with its rim horizontal. A bead B of mass m kg is moving in a horizontal circle around the smooth inside surface of the bowl. The centre of the circle is $\frac{3}{5}r$ below the centre of the sphere of which the bowl forms a part.

a Find the magnitude of the reaction force between the bowl and the bead in terms of m and g.

b Find the linear speed of the bead in terms of g and r.

10 The fixed points A and B, B under A, lie in the same vertical plane. A particle P of mass 3 kg is joined to the point A by a light rod of length 1.3 m and to the point B by a light rod that is horizontal. The particle P moves in a horizontal circle with centre B at a constant angular speed ω.

a If the angle the rod AP makes with the downward vertical is 45°, calculate the tension in the rod AP.

b Calculate a lower bound for ω which would mean that the rod BP is in tension.

c If the angular speed of P is 2 rad s^{-1}, calculate the magnitude and direction of the force in the rod BP.

11 A conical pendulum consists of a light inextensible string AB of length 2 m, with the string fixed at A and a small ball of mass 3 kg at B. The ball moves in a horizontal circle, with centre vertically below the point A, with constant linear speed 3 m s^{-1}. Find the tension in the string and the radius of the circle.

A **12** A car moves in a horizontal circular path of radius 55 m, banked at 22° to the horizontal. The coefficient of friction between the car tyres and the track is 0.35. Find the maximum and minimum speeds at which the car can be driven around the circular path.

A **13** A car has a linear speed of v m s^{-1} and is on the verge of slipping when driven in a horizontal circular path of radius r that is banked to the horizontal at angle θ. Show that the coefficient of friction is

$$\frac{v^2 - rg\tan\theta}{rg + v^2\tan\theta}$$

Checklist of learning and understanding

- For a particle moving in a horizontal circular path of radius r m and at a constant angular speed ω rad s^{-1}:
  - linear speed is given by $v = r\omega$
  - acceleration is given by $v\omega$, $r\omega^2$ or $\frac{v^2}{r}$ and is directed towards the centre of the circular motion.

Mixed practice 4

Unless otherwise instructed, when a numerical value for the acceleration due to gravity is needed, use $g = 9.8\ \text{m s}^{-2}$.

1 A particle of mass 200 g moves in a circle of radius 5 m with constant speed $8\ \text{m s}^{-1}$.

a Find the angular speed of the particle.

b Find time it takes for one revolution.

c Find the force acting on the particle to keep it in a circular path.

A 2 A particle of mass m kg moves with a constant linear speed of $v\ \text{m s}^{-1}$ in a horizontal circle of radius r on a rough table with coefficient of friction 0.6. The particle is travelling at the maximum speed v that will keep it in a circular path.

a Draw a diagram to display the forces acting on the particle and its acceleration.

b If the radius of the horizontal circle is 30 cm, find the linear speed.

3 A particle of mass 0.5 kg is attached to a light inextensible string of length 350 cm. The string is fixed on a smooth horizontal table and the ball moves in a circular path with constant angular speed $1.96\ \text{rad s}^{-1}$.

a What is the acceleration of the ball?

b What is the tension in the string?

4 A car of mass 1.2 tonnes moves at a linear speed of $5.2\ \text{m s}^{-1}$ around a circular path of radius 25 m. What is the frictional force required to keep the car travelling in this circular path?

5 A light rod AB, of length l, has one particle of mass m attached at A and a second particle of mass $3m$ attached at B. The rod is held fixed at a point C and is free to rotate in a horizontal circle with a constant angular speed about the point C. Given that the tensions in parts AC and CB of the rod are equal, show that the length AC is $\frac{3}{4}l$.

6 Two particles, P and Q, are connected by a light inextensible string that passes through a smooth hole in a smooth horizontal table. Particle P, of mass m kg, moves on the table with constant angular speed in a circle of radius 0.25 m around the hole. Particle Q, of mass $4m$ kg, hangs vertically in equilibrium under the table, as shown in the diagram. Find the angular speed of P.

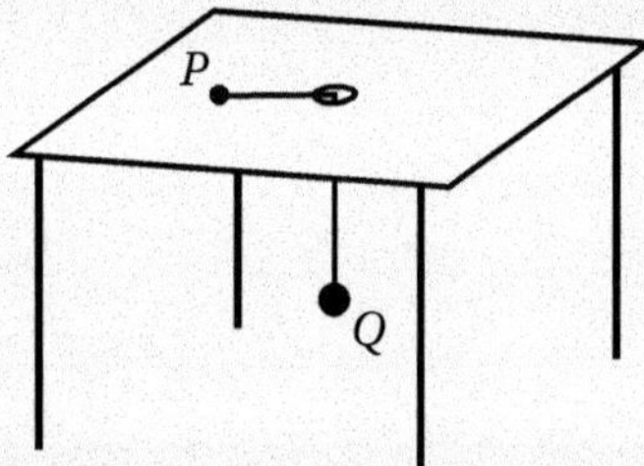

7 A small smooth ring R of mass m is threaded onto a light inextensible string of length $49L$. The two ends of the string are fixed at the points A and B, where B is vertically below A at a distance of $7L$. The ring is moving with constant linear speed in a horizontal circle with centre B and radius $24L$.

a Find the tension in the string in terms of m and g.

b Find the linear speed in terms of g and L.

c How did you use the assumption that the ring was smooth?

A **8** A car of mass m kg moves around a bend that is banked at a constant angle of 22° to the horizontal. The car is modelled as a particle moving in a horizontal circle of radius 10 m at a constant angular speed. Calculate the linear speed of the car in km h^{-1} if:

a there is no sideways frictional force on the car

b the coefficient of friction between the tyres and the surface is 0.25 and the car is on the point of

i slipping down the slope **ii** slipping up the slope.

 **9**

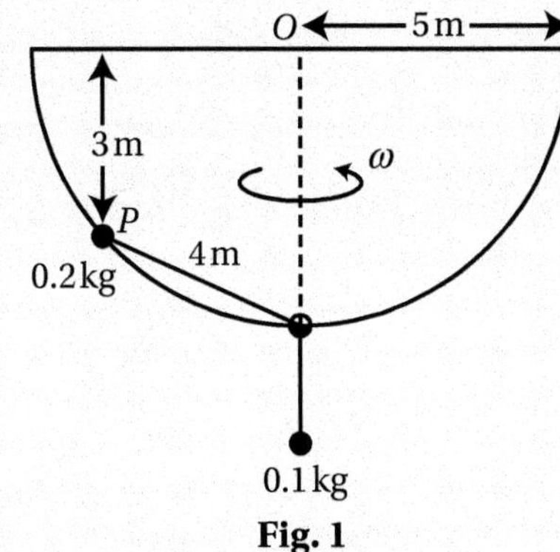

Fig. 1

A particle P of mass 0.2 kg is moving on the smooth inner surface of a fixed hollow hemisphere that has centre O and radius 5 m. P moves with constant angular speed ω in a horizontal circle at a vertical distance of 3 m below the level of O (see Fig. 1).

i Calculate the magnitude of the force exerted by the hemisphere on P.

ii Calculate ω.

A light inextensible string is now attached to P. The string passes through a small smooth hole at the lowest point of the hemisphere and a particle of mass 0.1 kg hangs in equilibrium at the end of the string. P moves in the same horizontal circle as before (see Fig. 2).

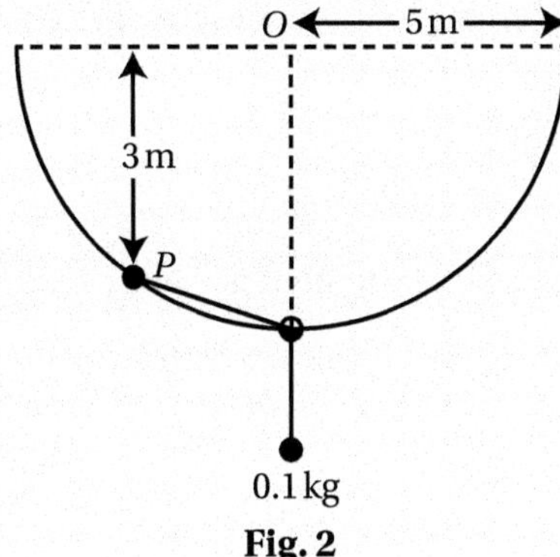

Fig. 2

iii Calculate the new angular speed of P.

10 A particle P of mass 0.5 kg is attached to points A and B on a fixed vertical axis by two light inextensible strings of equal length. Both strings are taut and each is inclined at 60° to the vertical (see diagram). The particle moves with constant speed 3 m s^{-1} in a horizontal circle of radius 0.4 m.

i Calculate the tensions in the two strings.

The particle now moves with constant angular speed ω rad s^{-1} and the string BP is on the point of becoming slack.

ii Calculate ω.

© OCR, GCE Mathematics, Paper 4729/01, June 2008

11 One end of a light inextensible string of length l is attached to the vertex of a smooth cone of semi-vertical angle 45°. The cone is fixed to the ground with its axis vertical. The other end of the string is attached to a particle of mass m which rotates in a horizontal circle in contact with the outer surface of the cone. The angular speed of the particle is ω (see diagram). The tension in the string is T and the contact force between the cone and the particle is R.

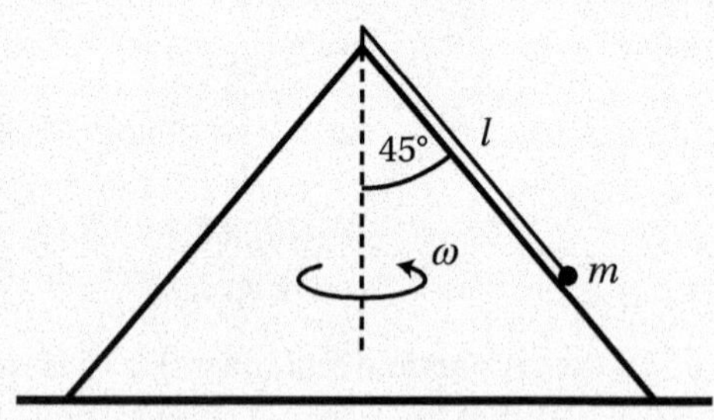

i By resolving horizontally and vertically, find two equations involving T and R and hence show that $T = \frac{1}{2}m\left(\sqrt{2}g + l\omega^2\right)$.

ii When the string has length 0.8 m, calculate the greatest value of ω for which the particle remains in contact with the cone.

© OCR, GCE Mathematics, Paper 4729, June 2010

12 A particle P, of mass 2 kg, is attached to fixed points A and B by light inextensible strings, each of length 2 m. A and B are 3.2 m apart with A vertically above B. The particle P moves in a horizontal circle with centre at the midpoint of AB.

i Find the tension in each string when the angular speed of P is 4 rad s^{-1}.

ii Find the least possible speed of P.

© OCR, GCE Mathematics, Paper 4729, June 2012

13 A circular cone is fixed so that the apex A of the cone is sitting on a horizontal surface and the axis of the cone is perpendicular to the horizontal surface. The angle the cone makes with the horizontal surface is θ. A particle P, of mass m kg, moves on the inner surface of the cone. The particle is joined to A by a light inextensible string AP, of length l. The particle moves in a horizontal circle with constant linear speed v and the string is taut. The inside of the cone is smooth.

a Show that the reaction force between the particle and the inner surface of the cone can be written in the form $mg\cos\theta + mv^2l^{-1}\tan\theta$.

b Find the tension in the string, in terms of m, l, v, g and $\sin\theta$.

c Show that the motion of the particle is only possible when $v^2 > gl\sin\theta$.

  **14** A vertical hollow cylinder of radius 0.4 m is rotating about its axis. A particle P is in contact with the rough inner surface of the cylinder. The cylinder and P rotate with the same constant angular speed. The coefficient of friction between P and the cylinder is μ.

i Given that the angular speed of the cylinder is 7 rad s^{-1} and P is on the point of moving downwards, find the value of μ.

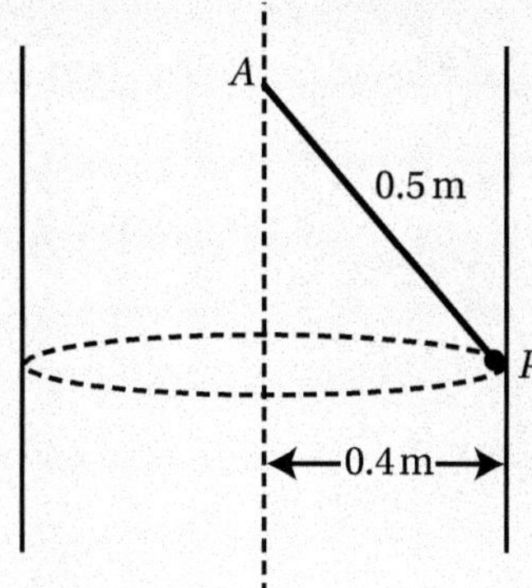

The particle is now attached to one end of a light inextensible string of length 0.5 m. The other end is fixed to a point A on the axis of the cylinder (see diagram).

ii Find the angular speed for which the contact force between P and the cylinder becomes zero.

Fast forward

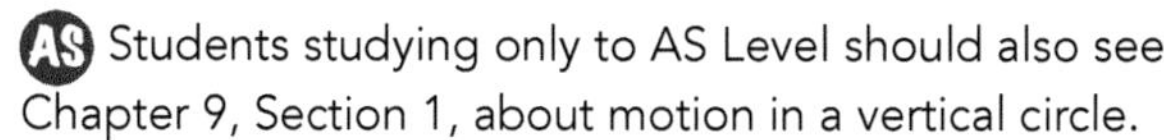

Students studying only to AS Level should also see Chapter 9, Section 1, about motion in a vertical circle.

5 Centres of mass 1

A This chapter is for A Level students only.
In this chapter you will learn how to:

- find the centre of mass of arrangements of particles, uniform rods and symmetrical uniform laminas
- find centres of mass of two- and three-dimensional objects of standard shape
- find centres of mass of composite bodies, including bent wires.

Before you start...

GCSE	You should be able to add and subtract vectors and to multiply a vector by a scalar.	1 Evaluate $=1.5\begin{pmatrix}-1\\3\\2\end{pmatrix}-3\begin{pmatrix}1\\0\\-1\end{pmatrix}$.

Where does mass act?

The particle model you have used in earlier chapters assumes that mass is all located at a single point with no volume. This approximation works well for small objects. More complex objects may consist of two or more particles located in different places, or a combination of one-, two- or three-dimensional objects. For example, mass may be spread along a rod, throughout a two-dimensional shape such as a circular disc, or throughout a solid object such as a cube. For many purposes, such as when modelling linear motion, a complex shape or rigid body can be modelled as though its mass is located at a single point, called the **centre of mass**. In this chapter, you will learn how to find the centre of mass of a range of different objects.

Fast forward

In Chapter 10 you will see that the location of the centre of mass of a complex object determines how it responds to forces that are applied to it, including its own weight. You will use your knowledge of the centre of mass, together with your knowledge of moments, to work out angles when objects are suspended in space. You will also work out whether objects placed on an inclined surface will rest in equilibrium, or topple over or slide.

Section 1: Centre of mass of a system of point masses

Centre of mass of two particles

The centre of mass of two identical particles lies at the midpoint of a straight line drawn between them.

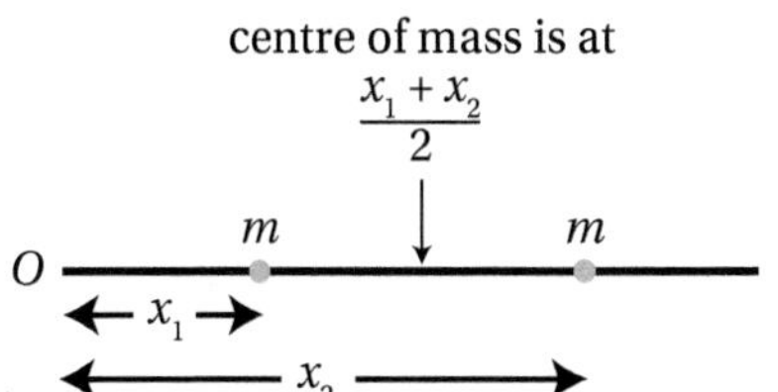

If the masses of the particles are different, then the centre of mass does not lie at the midpoint. It is closer to the larger mass. You find the position of the centre of mass, $\bar{x}$, by calculating a weighted average:

$$\bar{x} = \frac{m_1x_1 + m_2x_2}{m_1 + m_2}$$

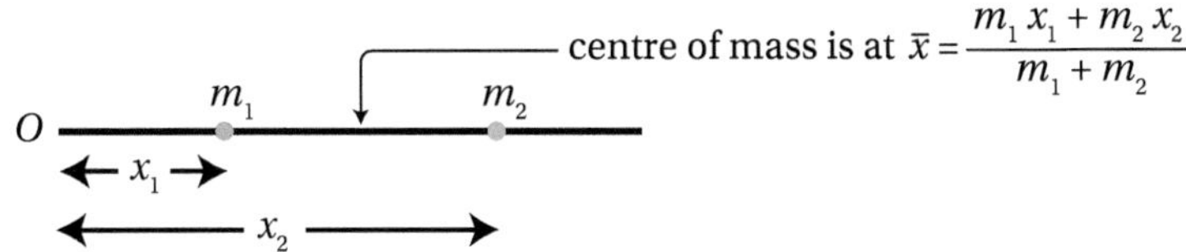

For example, if $m_1 = 2$ kg, $m_2 = 3$ kg$_1$, $x_1 = 0$ and $x_2 = l$, then $\bar{x} = \frac{2\times0+3\times l}{5} = \frac{3l}{5}$

The centre of mass divides the straight line joining the particles in the ratio $m_2 : m_1$.

Several particles arranged in a straight line

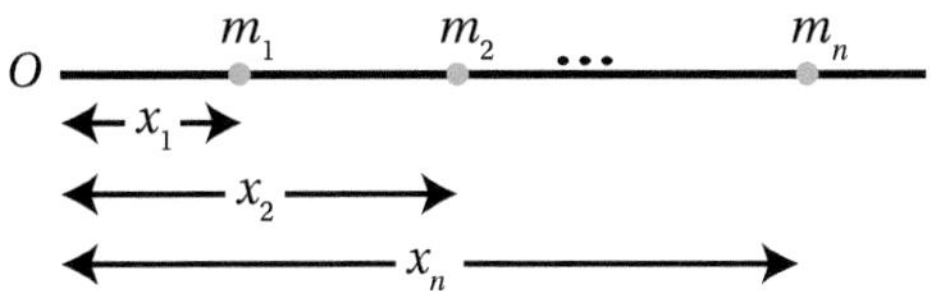

You now extend the formula for two masses to n masses:

$$\bar{x} = \frac{m_1x_1 + m_2x_2 + \ldots + m_nx_n}{m_1 + m_2 + \ldots + m_n}$$

If you write M instead of $m_1 + m_2 + \ldots + m_n$, the formula may alternatively be written:

$$M\bar{x} = m_1x_1 + m_2x_2 + \ldots + m_nx_n$$

Key point 5.1

A combination of n particles having masses $m_1, m_2, \ldots, m_n$ arranged in a straight line, at positions $x_1, x_2, \ldots, x_n$, can be modelled as a single object of mass M, with position $\bar{x}$ where:

$$M\bar{x} = m_1x_1 + m_2x_2 + \ldots m_nx_n$$

and:

$$M = m_1 + m_2 + \ldots + m_n$$

Rewind

You worked with moments in A Level Mathematics Student Book 2. The formula given in Key point 5.1 equates the sum of the moments of mass of n particles with the moment of mass of a combined particle acting at the centre of mass.

WORKED EXAMPLE 5.1

Three point masses are attached to a light bar AB of length 0.5 m. These have mass 150 g, 250 g and 350 g and are attached at the bar at A, the midpoint of the bar, and B, respectively. Find the distance of the centre of mass from A.

0.15 kg 0.25 kg 0.35 kg
A ———— B
0.25 m
0.5 m

Draw a diagram with masses and lengths from A in standard units.
The modelling assumption that the bar is 'light' means that you do not need to include its mass.

$M\bar{x}_A = 0.15 \times 0 + 0.25 \times 0.25 + 0.35 \times 0.5$

Use the formula for an arrangement of particles.
M is the total mass.
The distance of the 150 g mass from A is zero.

$0.75\bar{x}_A = 0.0625 + 0.175$

$0.75\bar{x}_A = 0.2375$

$\bar{x}_A = 0.317$ m (3 s.f.)

In Worked example 5.1 the centre of mass is 0.317 m from A. The system of three particles has the same moment of mass as a single particle of mass 750 g placed 0.317 m from A.

0.75 kg
A ———— B
0.317 m

WORKED EXAMPLE 5.2

A light rod AB of length 3.5 m has three masses attached to it. A 2 kg mass is attached 1 m from A. A 1.5 kg mass is attached 2 m from A, and an unknown mass, m kg, is attached at end B. Find the value of m given that the centre of mass of the system is 1.5 m from point A.

Total mass $= (2 + 1.5 + m)$ kg $= (3.5 + m)$ kg

Start by calculating the total mass.

$(3.5 + m) \times 1.5 = 2 \times 1 + 1.5 \times 2 + m \times 3.5$

$5.25 + 1.5m = 5 + 3.5m$

$\Rightarrow m = 0.125$ kg

Use the formula for point masses arranged in a straight line.
$M\bar{x} = m_1x_1 + m_2x_2 + \ldots + m_nx_n$

Particles arranged in a plane

If particles are arranged in a plane, you can find the position of the centre of mass separately for x and y. Vectors give you a nice way of combining these calculations.

Key point 5.2

If you have n particles with masses $m_1, m_2, \ldots, m_n$, at position vectors $\begin{pmatrix} x_1 \\ y_1 \end{pmatrix}, \begin{pmatrix} x_2 \\ y_2 \end{pmatrix}, \ldots,$ $\begin{pmatrix} x_n \\ y_n \end{pmatrix}$, you can model these as a single mass M, with position vector $\begin{pmatrix} \bar{x} \\ \bar{y} \end{pmatrix}$.

$$M\begin{pmatrix} \bar{x} \\ \bar{y} \end{pmatrix} = m_1\begin{pmatrix} x_1 \\ y_1 \end{pmatrix} + m_2\begin{pmatrix} x_2 \\ y_2 \end{pmatrix} + \ldots + m_n\begin{pmatrix} x_n \\ y_n \end{pmatrix}$$

WORKED EXAMPLE 5.3

Three particles are arranged in a plane. Particle A has mass 5 kg and is placed at (6, 2). Particle B has mass 3 kg and is placed at (7, 7). Particle C has mass 4 kg and is placed at (2, 6).

Find the x- and y-coordinates of the centre of mass.

Total mass = 12 kg — Start by calculating the total mass.

$$12\begin{pmatrix} \bar{x} \\ \bar{y} \end{pmatrix} = 4\begin{pmatrix} 2 \\ 6 \end{pmatrix} + 5\begin{pmatrix} 6 \\ 2 \end{pmatrix} + 3\begin{pmatrix} 7 \\ 7 \end{pmatrix}$$

Use the formula for point masses in a plane.
Multiply the position vector of each point mass by the mass placed there:

$$m_1\begin{pmatrix} x_1 \\ y_1 \end{pmatrix} + m_2\begin{pmatrix} x_2 \\ y_2 \end{pmatrix} + \ldots + m_n\begin{pmatrix} x_n \\ y_n \end{pmatrix}$$

$$\begin{pmatrix} \bar{x} \\ \bar{y} \end{pmatrix} = \frac{1}{12}\begin{pmatrix} 59 \\ 55 \end{pmatrix} = \begin{pmatrix} 4.92 \\ 4.58 \end{pmatrix} \text{ (3 s.f.)}$$

Divide the result by the total mass.

EXERCISE 5A

1. A light rod AB of length 2 m has a mass of 2 kg placed 40 cm from A and a mass of 4.5 kg placed at B. Find the distance of the centre of mass from A.

2. A light rod of length 1.5 m has a mass of 1.8 kg placed at one end A. A mass m kg is placed 30 cm from the other end B, and the centre of mass lies in the middle of the rod. Find m.

3. A light rod has masses 4 kg and 5 kg placed at each end, and the centre of mass lies 40 cm from the 4 kg mass. Find the length of the rod.

4. Masses m kg, $2m$ kg and $3m$ kg are placed $2x$ cm, $3x$ cm and $4x$ cm from one end, O, of a light rod. The centre of mass lies 25 cm from O. Find the value of x.

5 Three point masses have position vectors in the x–y plane as shown in the diagram. Find the centre of mass of the three masses combined.

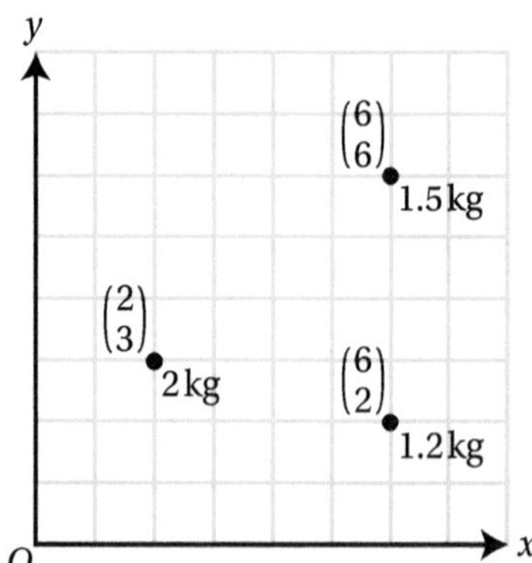

6 Four point masses have position vectors in the x–y plane as shown in the diagram. Find the centre of mass of the four masses combined.

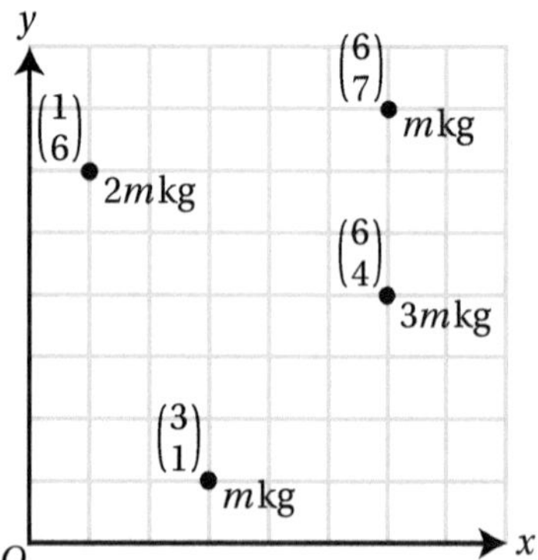

7 Four point masses have position vectors in the x–y plane as shown in the diagram. Find the centre of mass of the four masses combined.

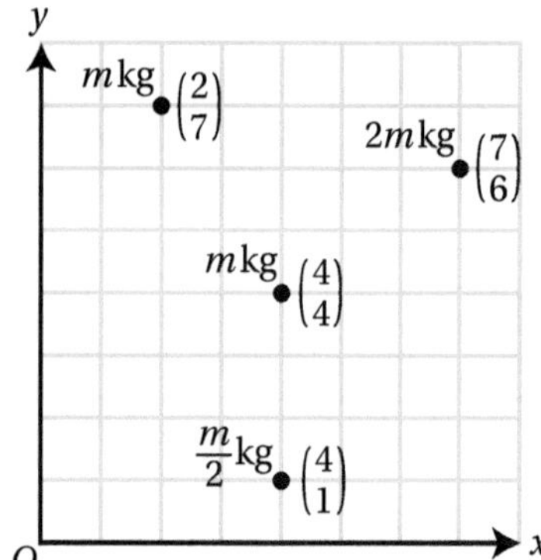

8 Three point masses, 1.5 kg, 2.5 kg and 2 kg are placed in a plane at $\begin{pmatrix}1\\2\end{pmatrix}$ cm, $\begin{pmatrix}-6\\5\end{pmatrix}$ cm, and $\begin{pmatrix}3\\-1\end{pmatrix}$ cm, respectively, from an origin at $\begin{pmatrix}0\\0\end{pmatrix}$ cm. Find the position vector of the centre of mass relative to $\begin{pmatrix}0\\0\end{pmatrix}$ cm.

9 Three point masses, 1.2 kg, 2.8 kg and 0.8 kg, are placed in a plane at $\begin{pmatrix}-1\\3\end{pmatrix}$ cm, at $\begin{pmatrix}2\\6\end{pmatrix}$ cm, and at $\begin{pmatrix}x\\y\end{pmatrix}$ cm, respectively, from an origin at $\begin{pmatrix}0\\0\end{pmatrix}$ cm. The centre of mass is at $\begin{pmatrix}1.75\\4.75\end{pmatrix}$ cm. Find the values of x and y.

Section 2: Centres of mass of standard shapes

Centre of mass of uniform rod

An inflexible body having its mass spread along a straight line is called a rod. Its shape is defined by its length; its cross-sectional area is zero. A uniform rod has constant mass per unit length (kg m^{-1} in standard units).

Rewind

You have learned to work with uniform rods in A Level Mathematics Student Book 2.

Key point 5.3

The centre of mass of a uniform rod lies at its midpoint.

Centre of mass of a uniform lamina of standard shape

A **lamina** is a two-dimensional object. An important modelling assumption used in calculations is that the lamina has zero thickness. A **uniform lamina** has constant mass per unit area (kg m^{-2} in standard units).

A compact disc is close in shape to what is meant by a lamina, as its cross-sectional area is much greater than its thickness.

Key point 5.4

The centre of mass of a symmetrical uniform lamina lies on any axis of symmetry.
If there is more than one axis of symmetry, then the centre of mass lies at the intersection of these.

The diagrams show the locations of the centre of mass of a uniform rectangular lamina and a uniform circular lamina, in relation to their axes of symmetry; (A circular lamina has an infinite number of lines of symmetry; only two are shown here.)

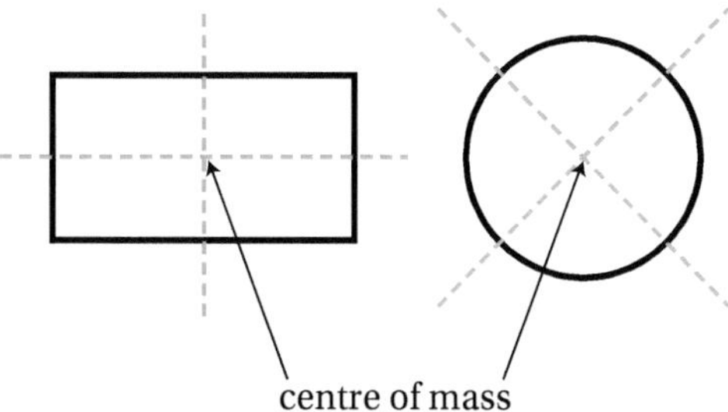

WORKED EXAMPLE 5.4

Calculate the coordinates of the centre of mass of the uniform rectangular lamina with vertices at (2, 3), (6, 1), (9, 7) and (5, 9).

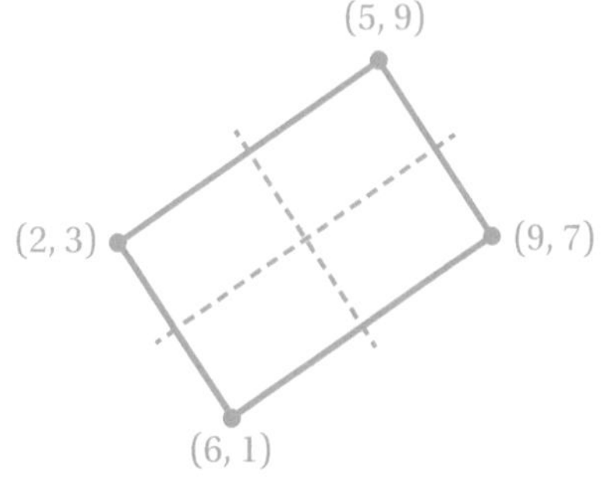

Draw a sketch.

The centre of mass lies at the intersection of the lines of symmetry shown.

$$\begin{pmatrix}\bar{x}\\ \bar{y}\end{pmatrix}=\begin{pmatrix}\frac{2+6+9+5}{4}\\ \frac{3+1+7+9}{4}\end{pmatrix}=\begin{pmatrix}5.5\\ 5\end{pmatrix}$$

Find the average of the x-coordinates and the average of the y-coordinates.

The centre of mass of a uniform triangular lamina lies at the intersections of the medians. A **median** of a triangle joins a vertex to the midpoint of the opposite side.

In the case of a lamina in the shape of an equilateral triangle, the medians are all axes of symmetry.

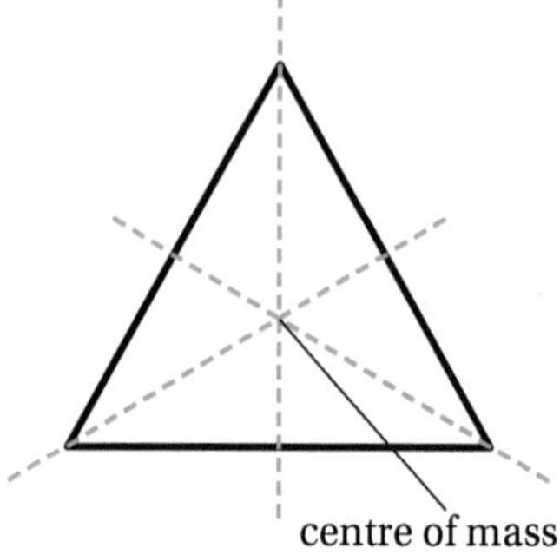

In any triangle, all three medians intersect at the same place, even when they are not axes of symmetry. The intersection of the medians divides each median in the ratio 1 : 2 (moving from side to apex). This intersection is the location of the centre of mass of a uniform triangular lamina.

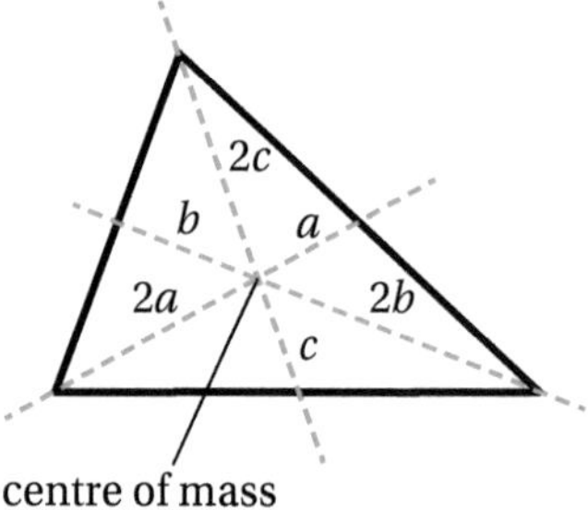

Key point 5.5

The medians of a triangle intersect at $\left(\frac{x_1+x_2+x_3}{3}, \frac{y_1+y_2+y_3}{3}\right)$, where (x_1, y_1), (x_2, y_2), (x_3, y_3) are the vertices of the triangle.

Focus on ...

You will prove the formula for the centre of mass of a uniform triangular lamina in Focus on ... Proof 2.

WORKED EXAMPLE 5.5

Find the distance of the centre of mass of the uniform triangular lamina from AB.

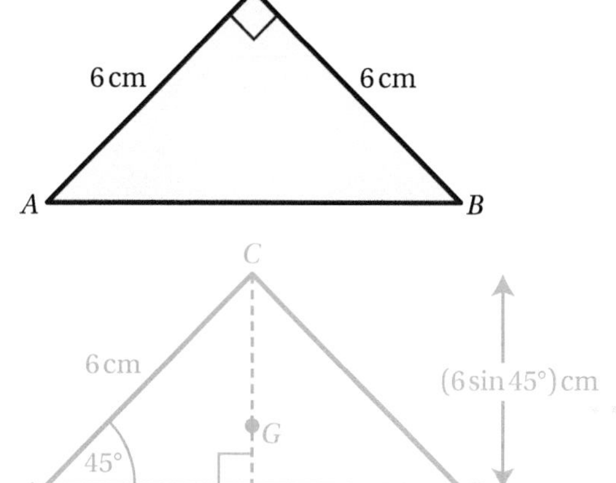

It is an isosceles triangle with angles 90°, 45°, 45°. Drop a perpendicular from C meeting AB at X.

$XC = 6\sin 45°$

Calculate the height of the triangle, XC.

The required distance is XG.

$XG = \frac{1}{3} \times 6\sin 45° = \sqrt{2} = 1.41$ cm (3 s.f.)

The centre of mass, G, divides the median XC in the ratio 1 : 2.

WORKED EXAMPLE 5.6

Calculate the coordinates of the centre of mass $\begin{pmatrix}\bar{x}\\ \bar{y}\end{pmatrix}$ of the uniform triangular lamina having vertices at (2, 5), (10, 3) and (7, 9).

$$\begin{pmatrix}\bar{x}\\ \bar{y}\end{pmatrix} = \begin{pmatrix}\frac{2+10+7}{3}\\ \frac{5+3+9}{3}\end{pmatrix} = \begin{pmatrix}6\frac{1}{3}\\ 5\frac{2}{3}\end{pmatrix}$$

Use the coordinates of the vertices.

WORKED EXAMPLE 5.7

Calculate the coordinates of the centre of mass $\begin{pmatrix}\bar{x}\\ \bar{y}\end{pmatrix}$ of this uniform triangular lamina.

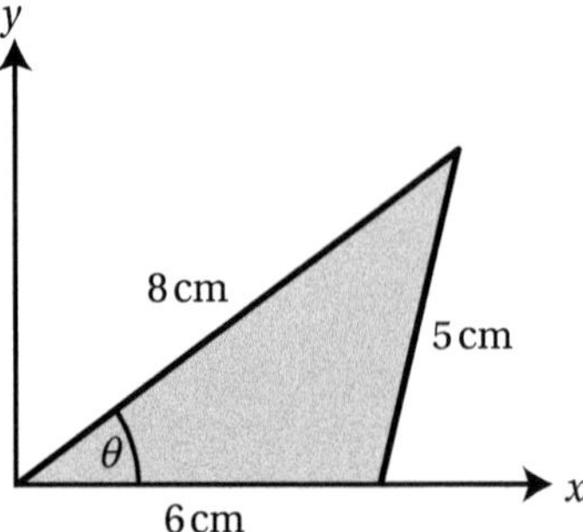

Vertices are at: (0, 0), (6, 0) and $(8\cos\theta, 8\sin\theta)$ — Use the coordinates of the vertices.

To find θ:

$$\theta = \cos^{-1}\left(\frac{8^2+6^2-5^2}{96}\right) \approx 38.62°$$

Use the cosine rule to find θ.

$(8\cos\theta, 8\sin\theta) \approx (6.250, 4.994)$ — Use the value of θ you found.

$$\begin{pmatrix}\bar{x}\\ \bar{y}\end{pmatrix} = \begin{pmatrix}\frac{0+6+6.250}{3}\\ \frac{0+0+4.994}{3}\end{pmatrix} = \begin{pmatrix}4.08\\ 1.66\end{pmatrix} \text{(3 s.f.)}$$

Give your values here to at least 4 significant figures so that you can give the final coordinates to 3 significant figures.

You can find the centre of mass of a lamina in the shape of a sector of a circle. This includes half and quarter discs. You are given the formula in the formula book.

Key point 5.6

The centre of mass of a sector of a circular disc, having radius r and angle 2α **radians** at the centre of the circle is $\frac{2r\sin\alpha}{3\alpha}$ from the centre of the sector, on the axis of symmetry.

This will appear in your formula book.

Rewind

Radian measure is introduced in A Level Mathematics Student Book 2, Chapter 7.

Tip

The angle that appears in the formula is α, which is *half* the angle at the centre of the sector. Make sure you know that the angle at the centre of the sector is 2α, so you remember to halve the angle at the centre of the sector before using the formula.

WORKED EXAMPLE 5.8

Find the centre of mass of a uniform quarter disc of radius 5 cm. Find the distance OG, where O is at the centre of the quadrant and G is the centre of mass.

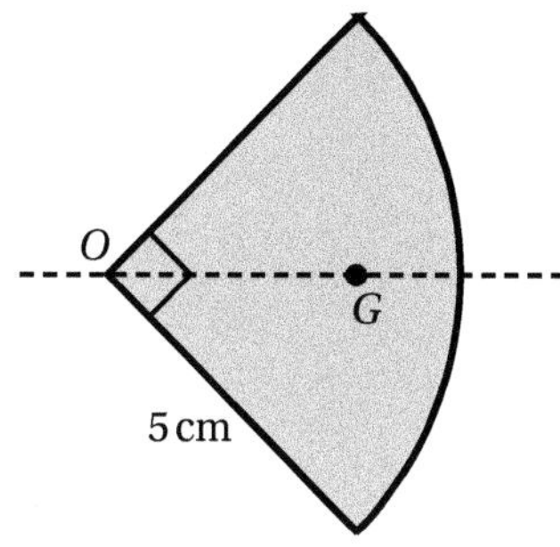

$2\alpha = \frac{\pi}{2} \Rightarrow \alpha = \frac{\pi}{4}$ — The angle at the centre of the sector is $\frac{\pi}{2}$ but the formula requires that the angle at the centre is 2α.

$OG = \frac{2r\sin\alpha}{3\alpha}$ — Use the standard formula: $\frac{2r\sin\alpha}{3\alpha}$

$OG = \frac{10\sin\frac{\pi}{4}}{\frac{3\pi}{4}}$ — Work in radians.

$OG = \frac{20\sqrt{2}}{3\pi} = 3.00 \text{ cm (3 s.f.)}$

Centre of mass of a uniform wire

A wire is a one-dimensional but flexible solid object. The centre of mass of a uniform straight wire lies at its midpoint.

A wire can be bent into several straight sections. You can combine the sections as though there are point masses at the centre of each section. Wires and rods can be combined together into a framework.

Key point 5.7

The centre of mass of a uniform wire bent to form an arc of a circle, having radius r and angle 2α radians at the centre of the circle, is $\frac{r\sin\alpha}{\alpha}$ from the centre of the sector.

This will appear in your formula book.

Tip

As with a sector of a circle, 2α is the angle at the centre, measured in radians, so you must halve this angle before making use of the formula.

WORKED EXAMPLE 5.9

A 5 cm length of uniform wire is bent to form an arc of a circle of radius 8 cm. Find the angle, θ, made by the arc at the centre of the circle, and the distance of the centre of mass G from O, the centre of the circle.

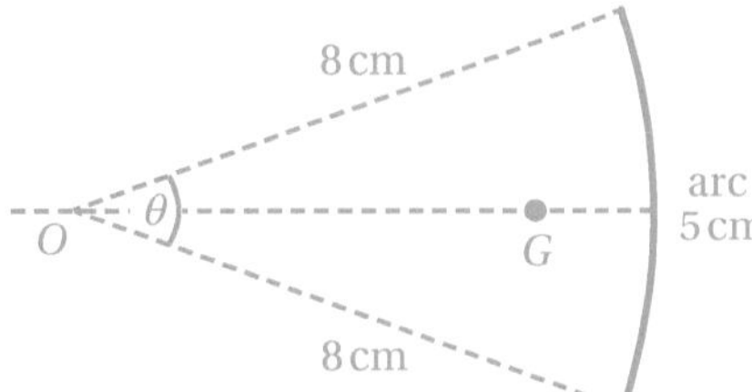

Draw a diagram.

Arc length = radius × θ

$5 = 8 \times \theta$

$\theta = 0.625$ rad

Use the formula for arc length to find θ.

$2\alpha = 0.625$

$\alpha = 0.3125$ rad

$$OG = \frac{r \sin \alpha}{\alpha}$$

$$= \frac{8 \sin 0.3125}{0.3125}$$

$= 7.87$ cm (3 s.f.)

Work in radians and use the formula.

EXERCISE 5B

1. A uniform rectangular lamina has vertices at (7, 2), (8, 4), (4, 6) and (3, 4). Find the coordinates of the centre of mass of the lamina.

2. A uniform square lamina has three of its vertices at (1, 3), (4, 1) and (6, 4). Determine the coordinates of the centre of mass.

3. A uniform lamina is in the shape of an equilateral triangle of side 3 cm. It is placed with one vertex at (0, 0) and one edge along the x-axis. Determine the coordinates of the centre of mass.

4. Find the centre of mass of a uniform triangular lamina with vertices as follows:

   a (1, 1), (6, 2) and (2, 3)
   b (–1, 3), (3, 7) and (4, 2)
   c (3, 2), (–5, –2) and (4, 5)
   d (–2, –6), (1, 4) and (0, 3)
   e (2, –4), (–8, 1) and (–3, 2)

5. A uniform semicircular lamina has radius 5 cm. Find the distance from the centre of the circle to the centre of mass.

6 Find the coordinates of the centre of mass of the following uniform triangular laminas by first finding the coordinates of the vertices.

a

b

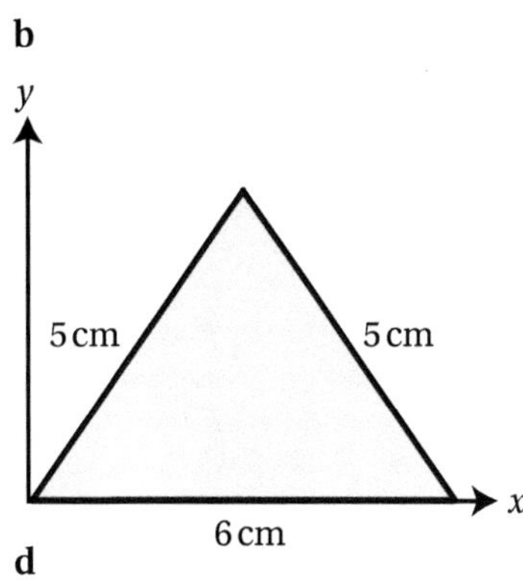

c

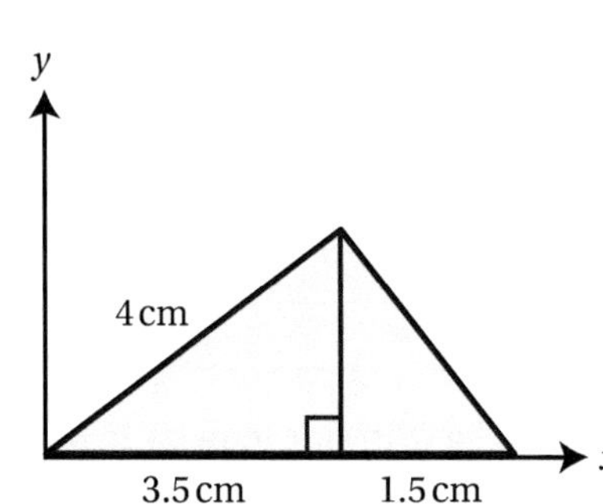

d

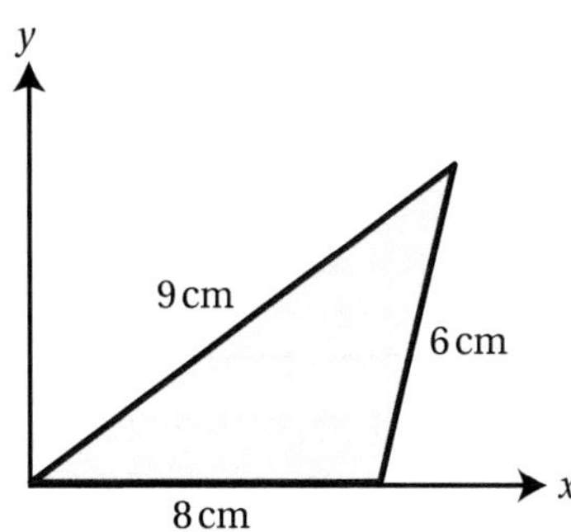

7 A length of uniform wire is bent to form an arc of a circle. The radius of the corresponding circle is 10 cm, and the arc makes an angle of $\frac{\pi}{4}$ at its centre. Find the distance of the centre of mass from the centre of the circle.

8 A length of uniform wire is bent to form an arc of a circle. The arc is of length 5 cm, and makes an angle at the centre of the corresponding circle of $\frac{\pi}{6}$. Find the distance of the centre of mass from the centre of the circle.

9 The centre of mass of a length of uniform wire bent to form an arc of a circle is $0.9r$ from the centre of the circle, where r is the radius of the circle. Find numerically the angle made by the arc at the centre of the circle, giving your answer in radians to 2 decimal places.

Section 3: Centres of mass of composite bodies

Key point 5.8

A **composite body** is one made from a combination of shapes.

For a composite body:

$$M\begin{pmatrix}\bar{x}\\ \bar{y}\end{pmatrix} = m_1\begin{pmatrix}\bar{x}_1\\ \bar{y}_1\end{pmatrix} + m_2\begin{pmatrix}\bar{x}_2\\ \bar{y}_2\end{pmatrix} + \ldots + m_n\begin{pmatrix}\bar{x}_n\\ \bar{y}_n\end{pmatrix}$$

Rewind

You met this formula in Section 1, Key point 5.2.

You have already used a similar formula to find an equivalent centre of mass of a system of particles.

The same approach can be applied to calculating the centre of mass of a composite body made from any combination of the shapes you have worked with so far. This time you work from the centres of mass of the component parts $\begin{pmatrix}\bar{x}_i\\ \bar{y}_i\end{pmatrix}$.

WORKED EXAMPLE 5.10

A uniform rod AB, of mass 5 kg and length 4 m, has three masses attached to it. A 3 kg mass is attached 0.5 m from A and a 4 kg mass is attached 0.5 m from B. A 2 kg mass is attached at point C. The centre of mass of the system is 2.2 m from A. Find the length AC.

For the uniform rod $\bar{x} = 2$ m

As the rod is uniform its centre of mass is at its midpoint.

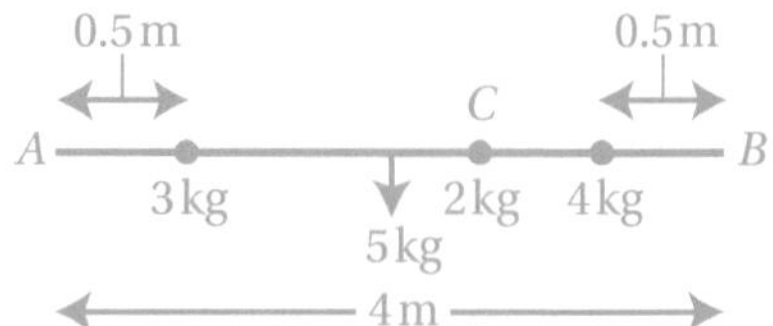

$14 \times 2.2 = 5 \times 2 + 3 \times 0.5 + 4 \times 3.5 + 2 \times AC$

$AC = 2.65$ m (3 s.f.)

Measure distances from A and use:

$M\bar{x} = m_1\bar{x}_1 + m_2\bar{x}_2 + \ldots + m_n\bar{x}_n$

WORKED EXAMPLE 5.11

A composite body is made from a uniform rectangular lamina of mass $2m$ kg with side lengths 25 cm and 40 cm placed with one vertex at (0, 0) and one of its longer sides along the y-axis. Point masses, m kg, $2m$ kg and $3m$ kg, are added at (20, 38), (10, 25) and (22, 8), respectively. Find the centre of mass of the composite body.

For the uniform rectangular lamina $\bar{x} = \begin{pmatrix} 12.5 \\ 20 \end{pmatrix}$

As the rectangular lamina is uniform its centre of mass is at its geometric centre.

Total mass $= 8m$ kg

Find the total mass.

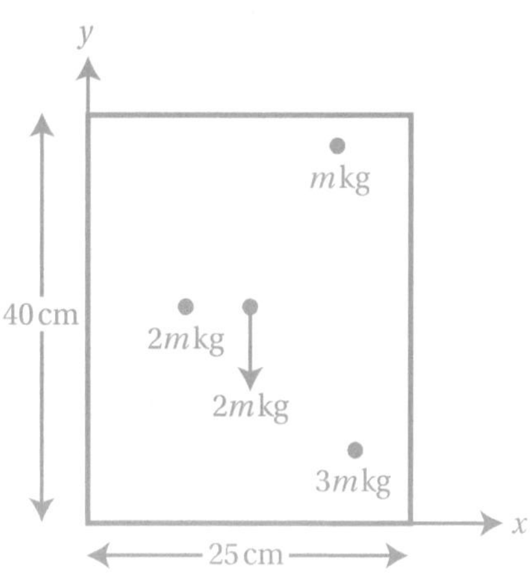

$$8m\begin{pmatrix} \bar{x} \\ \bar{y} \end{pmatrix} = 2m\begin{pmatrix} 12.5 \\ 20 \end{pmatrix} + m\begin{pmatrix} 20 \\ 38 \end{pmatrix} + 2m\begin{pmatrix} 10 \\ 25 \end{pmatrix} + 3m\begin{pmatrix} 22 \\ 8 \end{pmatrix}$$

$$\begin{pmatrix} \bar{x} \\ \bar{y} \end{pmatrix} = \begin{pmatrix} 16.4 \\ 19 \end{pmatrix} \text{cm}$$

Use:

$$M\begin{pmatrix} \bar{x} \\ \bar{y} \end{pmatrix} = m_1\begin{pmatrix} \bar{x}_1 \\ \bar{y}_1 \end{pmatrix} + m_2\begin{pmatrix} \bar{x}_2 \\ \bar{y}_2 \end{pmatrix} + \ldots + m_n\begin{pmatrix} \bar{x}_n \\ \bar{y}_n \end{pmatrix}$$

WORKED EXAMPLE 5.12

A composite body consists of a uniform rectangular lamina *ABCD* with dimensions 30 cm by 20 cm and a uniform circular lamina with diameter 20 cm joined on. A diameter of the circular lamina coincides with edge *BC* of the rectangle as shown. The mass density per unit area is the same for the rectangular and circular laminas. Find the distance of the centre of mass of the composite lamina from *AB* and *AD*.

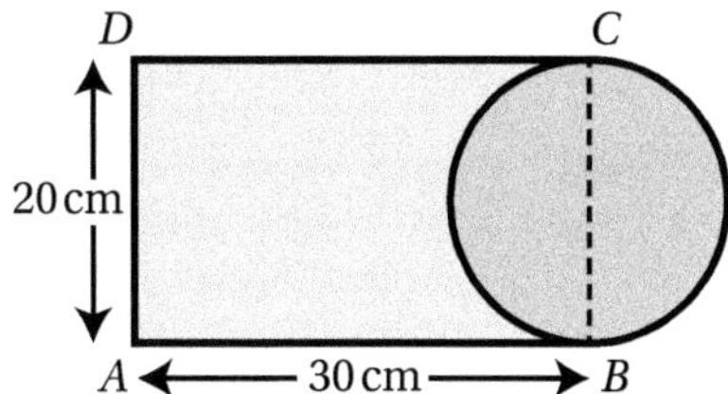

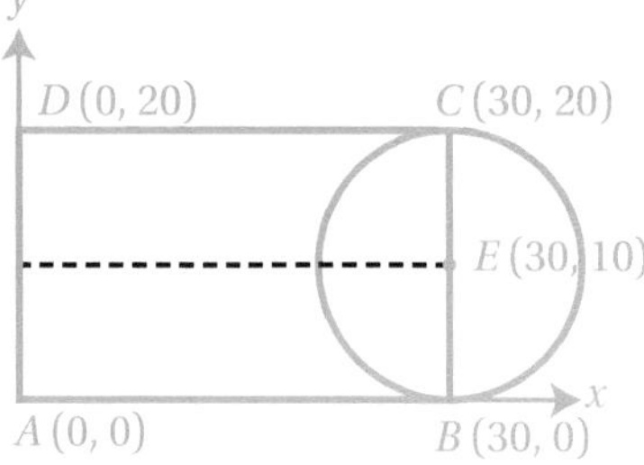

In this question you are not given the coordinates of the vertices. You can introduce the coordinate system with the origin at *A* and the axes along *AB* and *AD*.

E marks the position of the centre of the circle and the horizontal dashed line shows the axis of symmetry.

For the composite body, $\bar{y} = 10$ cm

The centre of mass lies on the axis of symmetry at $y = 10$ cm.

$M\bar{x} = m_1 \times \bar{x}_1 + m_2 \times \bar{x}_2$

Use the composite body formula.

Area of rectangle $= 600$ cm^2

Area of circle $= \pi \times 10^2$ cm^2

As the composite lamina is uniform, mass is directly proportional to area so you can work with areas.

$$(600 + 100\pi)\bar{x} = 600 \times 15 + 100\pi \times 30$$

$$914.2\bar{x} = 9000 + 9424.8$$

$$\bar{x} = 20.2 \text{ cm (3 s.f.)}$$

The centre of mass of the composite body is 10 cm from *AB* and 20.2 cm from *AD*.

Check that the *x*-coordinate of the centre of mass is sensible.

When part of a larger shape has been cut out, you can use the usual formula for a composite lamina. This time m_2 is the mass of the original lamina before removal of the part of mass m_1 and $M = m_2 - m_1$.

$$M\begin{pmatrix}\bar{x}\\ \bar{y}\end{pmatrix} = m_2\begin{pmatrix}\bar{x}_2\\ \bar{y}_2\end{pmatrix} - m_1\begin{pmatrix}\bar{x}_1\\ \bar{y}_1\end{pmatrix}, M = m_2 - m_1$$

WORKED EXAMPLE 5.13

The rectangular uniform lamina *ABCD* has had a 2 cm square cut out. Find the distance of the centre of mass of the composite lamina from *AB* and *AD*.

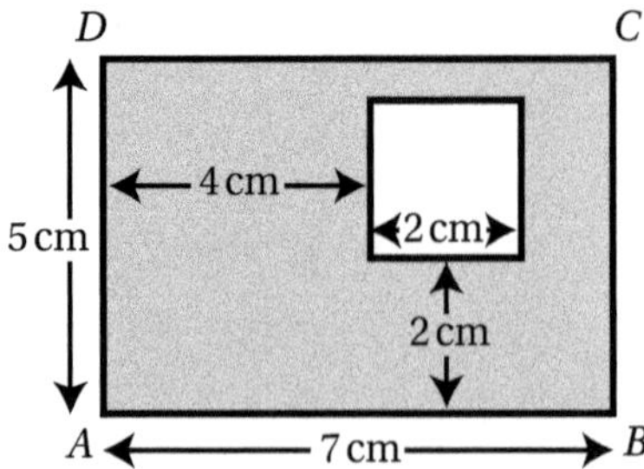

Let *AB* be the *x*-axis and *AD* be the *y*-axis.

Let *A* be (0, 0).

Area of lamina = area of rectangle *ABCD* − area of square

The mass of the lamina and the square cut out are directly proportional to area, so you can work with areas.

Area of lamina = (35 − 4) = 31 cm²

$$31\begin{pmatrix}\bar{x}\\ \bar{y}\end{pmatrix} = 35\times\begin{pmatrix}3.5\\ 2.5\end{pmatrix} - 4\times\begin{pmatrix}5\\ 3\end{pmatrix}$$

$$\begin{pmatrix}\bar{x}\\ \bar{y}\end{pmatrix} = \begin{pmatrix}3.31\\ 2.44\end{pmatrix}\text{ cm (to 3 s.f.)}$$

Check with the diagram to make sure that the centre of mass looks sensible.

A wire can be bent into several straight sections. You combine the sections as though there are point masses at the centre of each section.

WORKED EXAMPLE 5.14

A uniform wire of length 120 cm is bent to form three sides, *AB*, *BC* and *CD* of a rectangle as shown. Find the distance of the centre of mass from the straight line passing through *AD*.

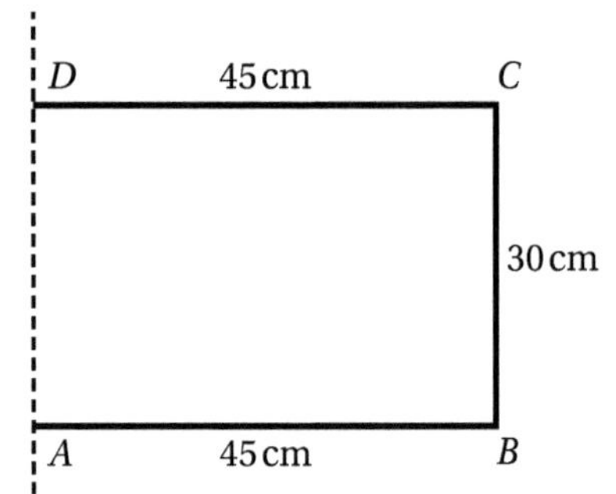

Let *AB* be the *x*-axis and *AD* be the *y*-axis.

Let *A* be (0, 0).

Continues on next page ...

The centres of mass of AB and DC are 22.5 cm from AD.

As the sections of wire are uniform, the centres of mass are at the midpoints.

$120\bar{x} = (45 \times 22.5) + (30 \times 45) + (45 \times 22.5)$

As the wire is uniform, its mass is directly proportional to length.

$\bar{x} = 28.1$ cm (3 s.f.)

The centre of mass is 28.1 cm from the straight line passing through AD.

The centre of mass of the wire does not lie on the wire itself.

WORKED EXAMPLE 5.15

A uniform wire is bent into a framework consisting of a semicircular arc AB of radius 3 cm together with the diameter joining AB. Find the distance of the centre of mass from AB.

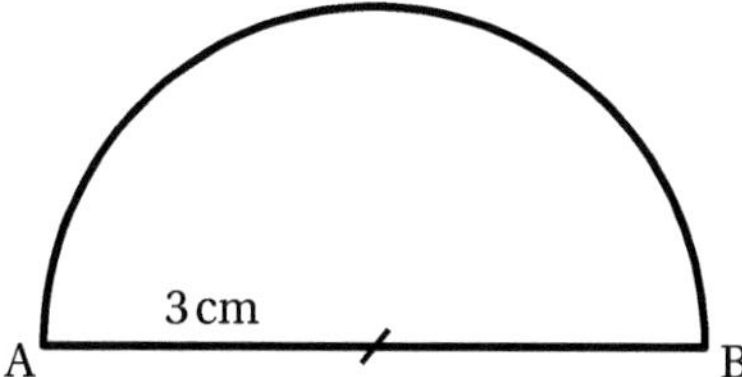

Let AB be the x-axis.

Let the y-axis pass through the midpoint of AB.

Total length of framework $= 6 + 3\pi$ cm

As the wire is uniform mass is proportional to length.

Use $\frac{r \sin \alpha}{\alpha}$, where $r = 3$ and $\alpha = \frac{\pi}{2}$

Use the formula for the centre of mass of a uniform arc of wire.

$$\frac{r \sin \alpha}{\alpha} = \frac{3 \sin \frac{\pi}{2}}{\frac{\pi}{2}} = \frac{6}{\pi}$$

The centre of mass of the arc is $\frac{6}{\pi}$ from AB

$(3\pi + 6)\bar{y} = 3\pi \times \frac{6}{\pi} + 6 \times 0$

Combine the straight edge and the arc.

$\therefore \bar{y} = 1.17$ cm (to 3 s.f.)

The centre of mass of the framework is 1.17 cm from AB.

Centres of mass of standard three-dimensional figures

You need to know how to use formulae for centres of mass of a solid hemisphere, hemispherical shell, solid right cone or pyramid and conical shell. **The formulae are all given in the formula book.**

Solid hemisphere, radius r	$\frac{3}{8}r$ from centre
Hemispherical shell, radius r	$\frac{1}{2}r$ from centre
Solid cone or pyramid of height h	$\frac{1}{4}h$ above the base on the line from centre of base to vertex
Conical shell of height h	$\frac{1}{3}h$ above the base on the line from centre of base to vertex

Did you know?

You may know about beds that can be folded up by hand into a wall cupboard when not in use. The design of the folding mechanism means that little lifting force is needed. This is remarkable when you consider the significant weight of the bed, including the mattress and bedding. How is it possible to achieve this? The answer lies in 'counter-weighting', which enables the bed to be fairly well balanced in all positions. Counter-weighting relies on an understanding of how mass is spread over the object to be lifted and a means of counteracting its weight in all positions. To start with, you would need to know the location of the centre of mass of the object to be lifted.

Fast forward

In Chapter 10 you will learn how to find the centre of mass of a solid hemisphere and a solid cone by integration.

WORKED EXAMPLE 5.16

A uniform conical shell of perpendicular height 24 cm and radius 10 cm is joined to a uniform disc of radius 10 cm. The mass per unit area of the shell and the circular base are the same.

Find the distance of the centre of mass of the composite shell from the base.

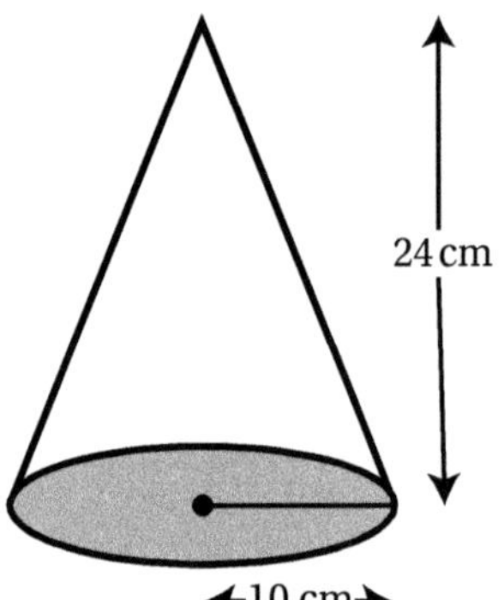

Let the centre of the circular base be (0, 0).

Let the main axis of the cone be the y-axis.

Continues on next page ...

Slant height of cone $= \sqrt{24^2 + 10^2}$
$= 26$ cm

Curved surface area $= \pi \times 10 \times 26$
$= 260\pi$

Curved surface area of cone $= \pi \times r \times l$

Area of base $= \pi \times 10^2 = 100\pi$

As the shell and base are uniform and have the same mass per unit area, mass is proportional to surface area.

$(260\pi + 100\pi)\,\bar{y} = (260\pi \times 8) + (100\pi \times 0)$

The centre of mass of a conical shell is $\frac{1}{3}h$ above the base on the line from centre of the base to vertex.

Cancel π and simplify:

$36\bar{y} = 26 \times 8 \Rightarrow \bar{y} = 5.78$ cm (3 s.f.)

Note: The centre of mass lies along the central line of symmetry for all of these standard solids.

WORKED EXAMPLE 5.17

A solid hemisphere of radius r is joined to a solid cone of radius r and height $3r$. Both solids are uniform with the same mass per unit volume. The base of the cone coincides with the base of the hemisphere. Show that the centre of mass is $\frac{27r}{10}$ from the vertex of the cone.

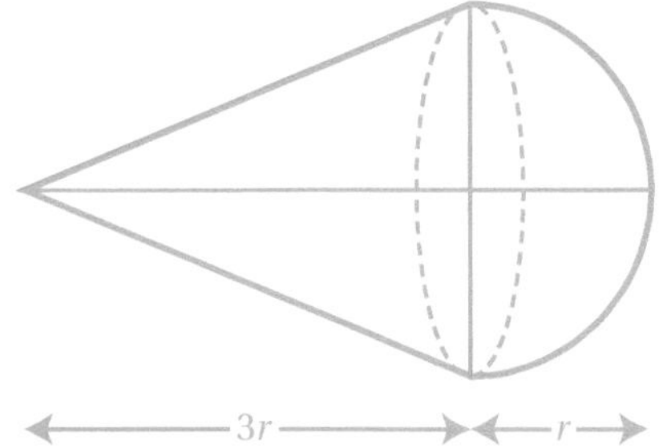

Draw a diagram.

Let the vertex of the cone be (0, 0).

Let the main axis of the cone be the x-axis.

Volume of cone $= \frac{1}{3} \times \pi \times r^2 \times 3r = \pi \times r^3$

Volume of hemisphere $= \frac{2}{3} \times \pi \times r^3$

Total volume of composite shape $= \frac{5}{3} \times \pi \times r^3$

As the solids are uniform, mass is proportional to volume.

For the cone, $\bar{x}_1 = \frac{3}{4} \times 3r = \frac{9r}{4}$

The centre of mass of a uniform solid cone is $\frac{h}{4}$ from the centre of its base.

For the hemisphere, $\bar{x}_2 = 3r + \frac{3r}{8} = \frac{27r}{8}$

The centre of mass of a uniform hemisphere is $\frac{3r}{8}$ from the centre.

Continues on next page ...

$$\frac{5}{3}\times\pi r^3\times\bar{x}=\left(\pi\times r^3\times\frac{9r}{4}\right)+\left(\frac{2}{3}\times\pi\times r^3\times\frac{27r}{8}\right)$$

$\bar{x}=\frac{27r}{20}+\frac{27r}{20}=\frac{27r}{10}$, as required. Cancel πr^3 and simplify.

WORK IT OUT 5.1

A brooch is modelled as a lamina in the shape of a sector of a circle, together with an arc of wire on the curved edge of the sector, as shown. The angle at the centre of the sector is $\frac{\pi}{3}$ radians, the mass of the sector is 200 g and the mass of the arc of wire is 300 g.

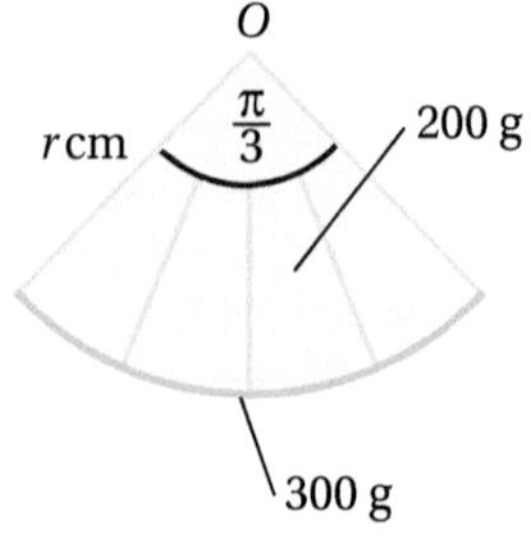

Form an equation that could be used to find the distance of the centre of mass of the brooch, $\bar{r}$, from O. Which solution is correct? Can you identify the errors made in the incorrect solutions?

Solution 1	Solution 2	Solution 3
$500\bar{r}=200\times\frac{2r\sin\frac{\pi}{6}}{3\times\frac{\pi}{6}}+300\times\frac{r\sin\frac{\pi}{6}}{\frac{\pi}{6}}$	$500\bar{r}=200\times\frac{2r\sin\frac{\pi}{3}}{3\times\frac{\pi}{3}}+300\times\frac{r\sin\frac{\pi}{3}}{\frac{\pi}{3}}$	$500\bar{r}=300\times\frac{2r\sin\frac{\pi}{6}}{3\times\frac{\pi}{6}}+200\times\frac{r\sin\frac{\pi}{6}}{\frac{\pi}{6}}$

Did you know?

You can see the Moon moving across the night sky as it revolves around the Earth, but the Earth and Moon together revolve around the Sun. In order to calculate the orbit of the Earth around the Sun, astronomers sometimes calculate the position of centre of mass not just of the Earth, but of the Earth and Moon taken together. The centre of mass of the Earth and Moon taken together actually lies within the Earth, about 1700 km below the surface. This centre of mass moves as the Moon rotates. This moving centre of mass causes deviation in the path of the Earth from a smooth curve around the Sun. The Earth wobbles in its orbit.

EXERCISE 5C

1 Find the centres of mass of the uniform laminas in the following diagrams.

a

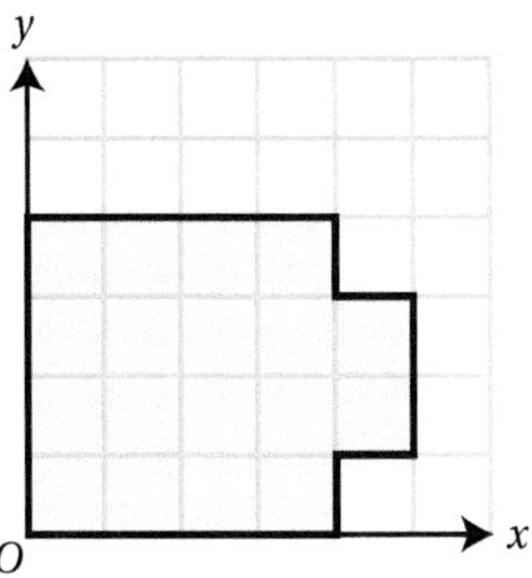

b

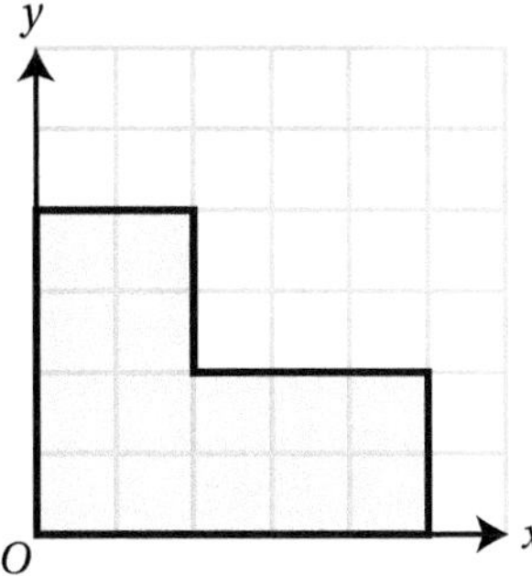

c

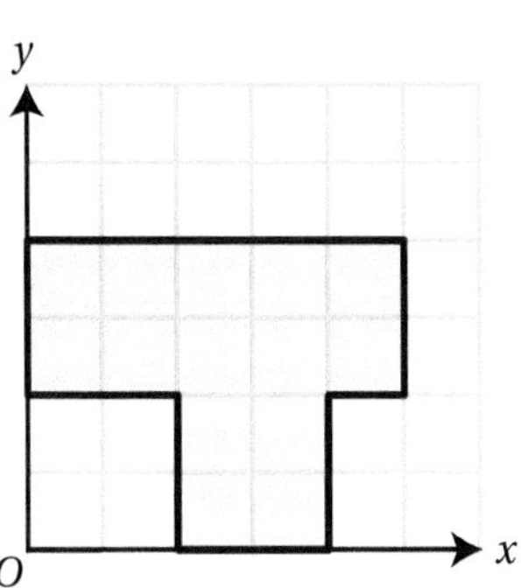

d

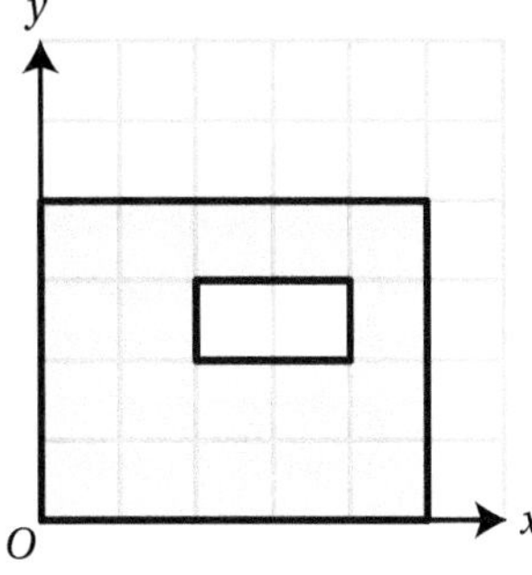

e

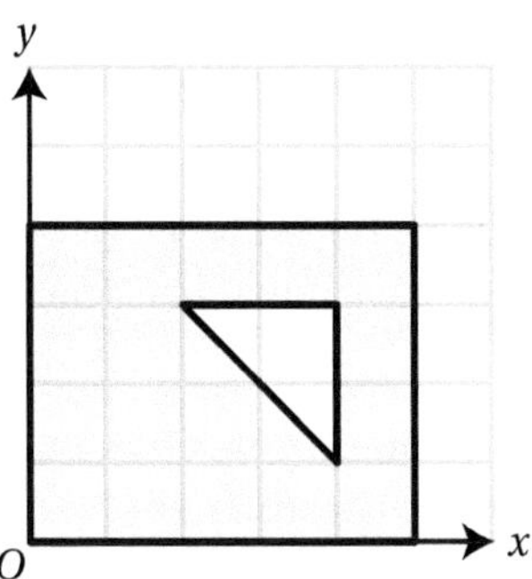

f

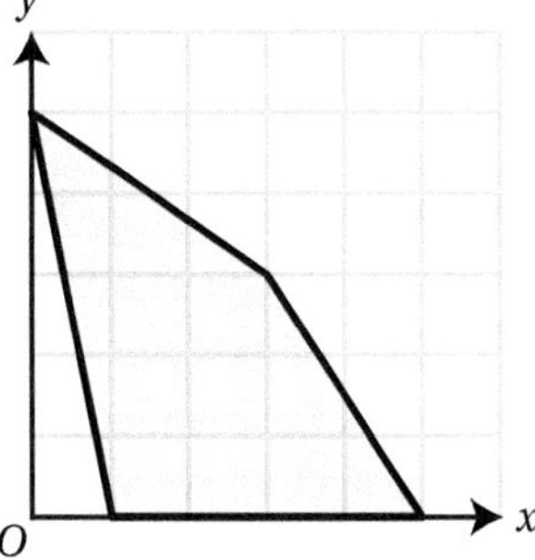

g

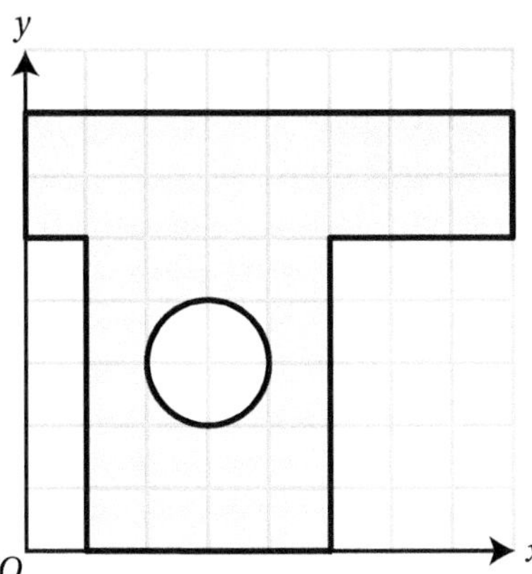

h

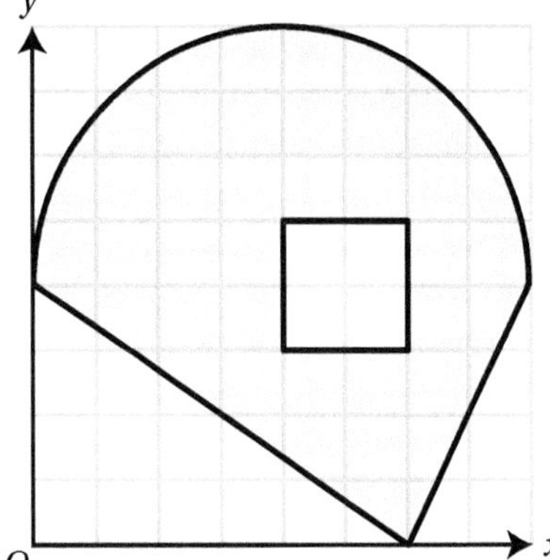

2 A composite body is made from a uniform rod AB of mass 2.5 kg and length 1.2 m with three point masses, X, Y and Z attached to it. X has mass 1.2 kg and AX is 0.2 m. Y has mass 0.8 kg and AY is 1.1 m. Z has mass 1.8 kg and AZ is 0.7 m. Find the distance of the centre of mass of the composite body from A.

3 A composite body is made from a rectangular lamina $ABCD$ of mass 1 kg with side lengths 30 cm and 20 cm together with point masses, 2.5 kg each, added at X and Y, as shown. Find the distance of the centre of mass of the composite body from AB and AD.

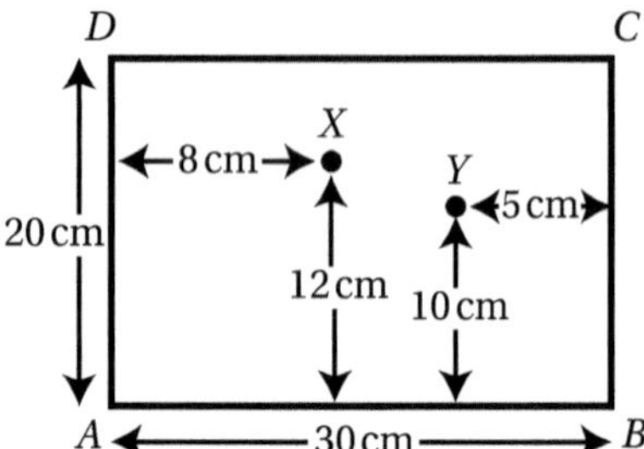

4 When a point mass of 1 kg is added to a uniform rod XY of mass 2.5 kg and length a metres, it moves the position of the centre of mass. Find where the additional mass must be added to move the centre of mass to $\frac{5a}{12}$ metres from X.

5 A composite body is made from a rod AB of length 80 cm and mass 2.5 kg that has a disc of mass 1 kg attached to end B, with its centre placed at the end of the rod. A point mass of m kg is attached to end A of the rod. Find the value of m if the centre of mass is to be 20 cm from A.

6 A length of uniform wire is bent to form three sides of a rectangle $ABCD$, $AB = CD = 10$ cm and $BC = 8$ cm. AB is the base of the rectangle and the rectangle is open at AD. Find the distance of the centre of mass from AD.

7 Three uniform rods are joined together to make a right-angled triangular framework. Edge AB is of length 12 cm, edge BC is of length 13 cm and edge AC is of length 5 cm. The rods have equal mass density per unit length. Calculate the distance of the centre of mass from AB and AC.

8 A uniform triangular lamina of mass 2.5 kg has vertices at $A(0, 0)$, $B(7, 2)$ and $C(4, 6)$. A 3 kg mass is attached to the lamina at (4, 5) and a 2 kg mass is attached at (4, 2). Find the coordinates of the centre of mass of the composite body.

9 A uniform composite lamina consists of a rectangle $ABCD$ and a semicircular lamina. AB is of length 30 cm and AD is of length 20 cm. The rectangular lamina and the semicircular lamina have the same mass per unit area. The semicircular lamina has diameter 20 cm and is joined on so its diameter coincides with BC (see diagram). Find the distance of the centre of mass from AD.

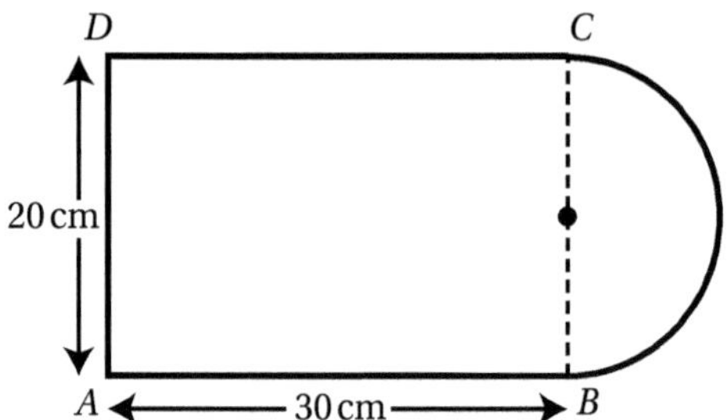

10 A shop sign consists of a uniform horizontal rod AB together with a lamina in the shape of a trapezium, as shown in the diagram. The rod is 1.5 m in length and has a mass of 4.5 kg. The lamina has a mass of 3 kg and hangs with BC vertical. Find the distance of the centre of mass of the shop sign from edges AB and BC.

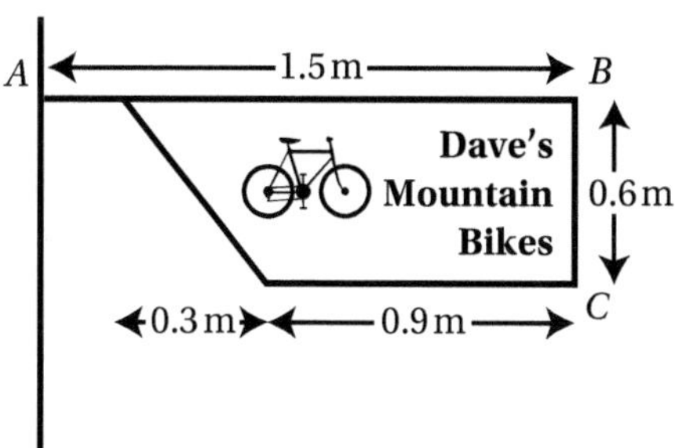

11 A garden ornament is made from a solid cylinder with a solid hemisphere placed on top. The radius of the cylinder is 5 cm, its height is 20 cm, and it mass is 4 kg. The hemisphere has radius 8 cm and mass 2 kg. The main axis of the cylinder passes through the centre of the hemisphere. The ornament is placed on level ground with the hemispherical part uppermost. Find the height of the centre of mass of the ornament above the ground.

12 A solid uniform frustum of a cone has been made from a solid cone of base radius 15 cm and height 50 cm. A cone of height 30 cm has been removed from the vertex end, as shown in the diagram. Calculate the distance of the centre of mass of the frustum from the base.

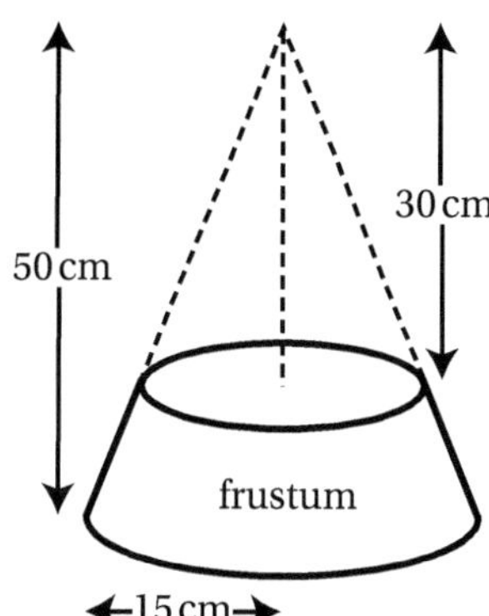

13 A hat is modelled as a conical shell together with a brim, both made of the same uniform fabric. The conical shell has a radius of 9.45 cm and a slant height of 33.75 cm. The brim is an annulus (a plane figure made by cutting out a concentric disc from a larger disc) with inner radius 9.45 cm and outer radius 14.5 cm. The diagram shows the shape of the hat. Find the vertical distance of the centre of mass of the hat above its brim.

14 A uniform solid is made from a solid hemisphere and a solid cone. The hemisphere and cone have the same base radius and the centre of the circular plane face of the hemisphere coincides with the centre of the circular base of the cone. The centre of mass of the composite solid lies in the plane of the join. Show that the height of the cone is given by $h = \sqrt{3}\,r$.

Checklist of learning and understanding

- A combination of n point masses $m_1, m_2, \ldots m_n$ etc. arranged on a straight line at $x_1, x_2, \ldots x_n$, can be modelled as a single mass $M = m_1 + m_2 + \ldots + m_n$, with position $\bar{x}$, where $M\bar{x} = m_1x_1 + m_2x_2 + \ldots + x_nm_n$.
- A combination of n point masses $m_1, m_2, \ldots m_n$ etc. arranged in a plane at positions $\begin{pmatrix} x_1 \\ y_1 \end{pmatrix}, \begin{pmatrix} x_2 \\ y_2 \end{pmatrix}, \ldots \begin{pmatrix} x_n \\ y_n \end{pmatrix}$ can be modelled as a single mass $M = m_1 + m_2 + \ldots + m_n$, with position vector:

$$M\begin{pmatrix} \bar{x} \\ \bar{y} \end{pmatrix} = m_1\begin{pmatrix} x_1 \\ y_1 \end{pmatrix} + m_2\begin{pmatrix} x_2 \\ y_2 \end{pmatrix} + \ldots + m_n\begin{pmatrix} x_n \\ y_n \end{pmatrix}$$

- The centre of mass of a uniform rod lies at its midpoint.
- The centre of mass of a symmetrical uniform lamina lies on any axis of symmetry. If there is more than one axis of symmetry the centre of mass lies at the intersection of these.
- The centre of mass of a uniform triangular lamina lies at the intersection of its medians. The medians intersect at $\left(\dfrac{x_1 + x_2 + x_3}{3}, \dfrac{y_1 + y_2 + y_3}{3}\right)$ where (x_1, y_1), (x_2, y_2) and (x_3, y_3) are the vertices of the triangle.
- The centre of mass of a uniform sector of a circle, having radius r and angle 2α radians at the centre of the circle, is $\dfrac{2r\sin\alpha}{3\alpha}$ from the centre of the sector.
- The centre of mass of a uniform wire bent to form an arc of a circle, having radius r and angle 2α radians at the centre of the circle, is $\dfrac{r\sin\alpha}{\alpha}$ from the centre of the circle.
- The rule for combination of point masses may be extended to composite bodies comprising point masses, wires, and laminas. $M\begin{pmatrix} \bar{x} \\ \bar{y} \end{pmatrix} = m_1\begin{pmatrix} \bar{x}_1 \\ \bar{y}_1 \end{pmatrix} + m_2\begin{pmatrix} \bar{x}_2 \\ \bar{y}_2 \end{pmatrix} + \ldots m_n\begin{pmatrix} \bar{x}_n \\ \bar{y}_n \end{pmatrix}$, where $M = m_1 + m_2 + \ldots + m_n$
- The centre of mass of a solid hemisphere radius r lies $\frac{3}{8}r$ from the centre.
- The centre of mass of a hemispherical shell radius r lies $\frac{1}{2}r$ from the centre.
- The centre of mass of a solid right cone or pyramid of height h lies $\frac{1}{4}h$ above the base on the line from the centre of the base to the vertex.
- The centre of mass of a conical shell of height h lies $\frac{1}{3}h$ above the base on the line from the centre of the base to the vertex.

Mixed practice 5

1 A uniform rod AB, of mass 3 kg and length 4.5 m, has three masses attached to it. A 4.5 kg mass is attached at the end A and 7.5 kg mass is attached at the end B. A 5 kg mass is attached at a point C on the rod.

Find the distance AC if the centre of mass of the system is 2.5 m from point A.

2 Three particles are attached to a light rectangular lamina $OABC$. Take OA as the x-axis and OC as the y-axis, as shown.

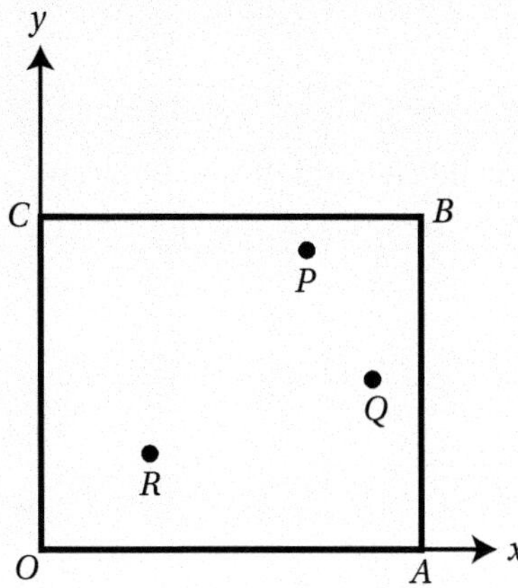

Particle P has mass 1.5 kg and is attached at (10, 12).

Particle Q has mass 3.5 kg and is attached at (14, 8).

Particle R has mass 2 kg and is attached at (5, 4).

Find the coordinates of the centre of mass of the system.

3 Four tools are attached to a board. The board is to be modelled as a uniform lamina and the four tools as four particles. The diagram shows the lamina, the four particles A, B, C and D, and the x- and y-axes.

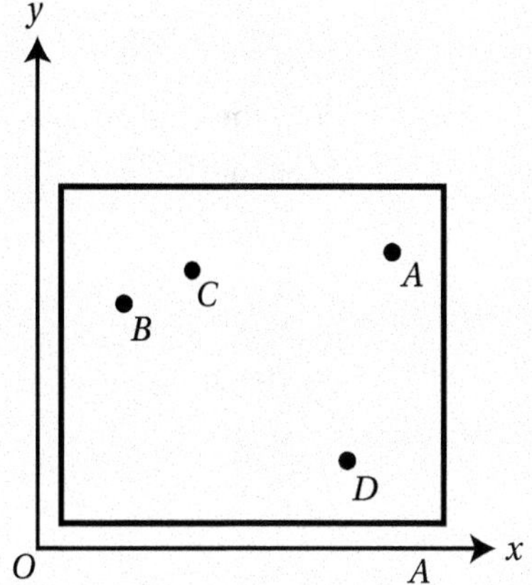

The board has mass 4 kg and its centre of mass is at the point (6, 4).

Particle A has mass 3 kg and is at the point (10, 7).

Particle B has mass 2 kg and is at the point (1, 5).

Particle C has mass 1 kg and is at the point (4, 6).

Particle D has mass 5 kg and is at the point (8, 1).

Find the coordinates of the centre of mass of the system of board and tools.

4 A uniform lamina $ABCDE$ consists of a rectangular lamina $ABCE$ and a lamina in the shape of an isosceles triangle CDE joined together along CE, as shown. $AE = BC = 4$ cm, $AB = EC = 6$ cm and $ED = CD = 5$ cm. Find the distance of the centre of mass of the lamina from AB.

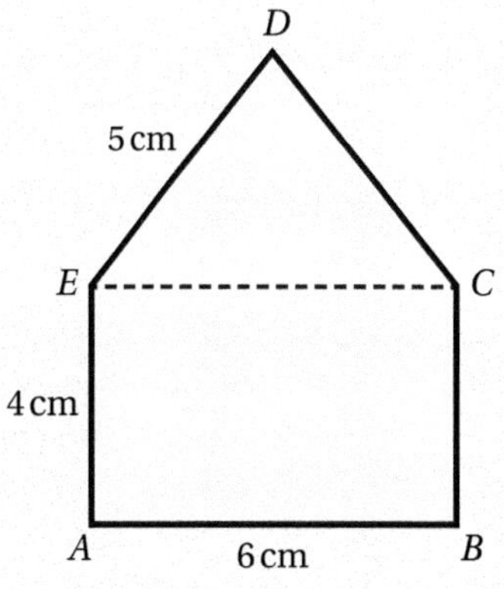

5 A uniform square lamina $ABCD$ of side 8 cm has a half disc, with AB as diameter, cut out. Find the distance of the centre of mass of the remaining lamina from CD.

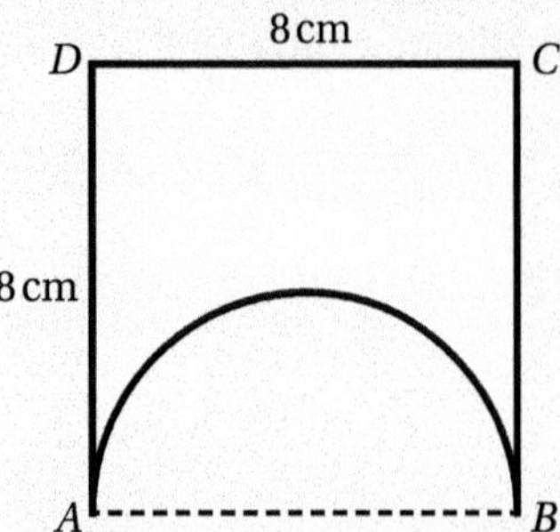

6 A lamina is made from a uniform rectangular lamina, with side lengths 18 cm and 9 cm, together with a uniform lamina in the shape of a quarter disc of radius 9 cm, as shown.

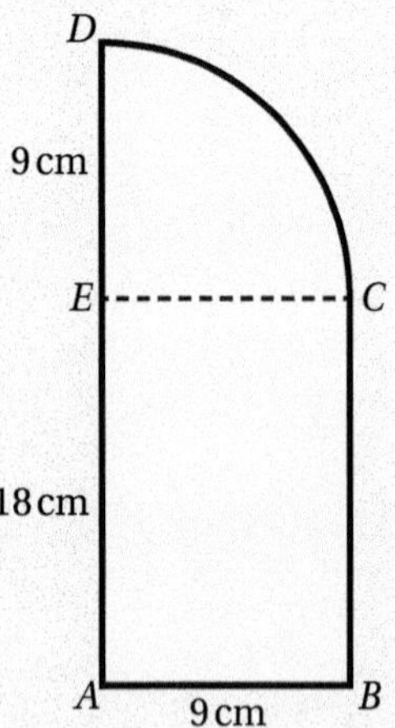

Find the coordinates of the centre of mass of the lamina, taking A as (0, 0), AB as $y = 0$ and AD as $x = 0$.

7 A composite body is made from a uniform rod, of length 0.5 m and mass 0.8 kg, together with a semicircular arc of wire of diameter 0.5 m, its ends fixed to the ends of the rod, of mass 0.5 kg. Find the distance of the centre of mass from the rod, giving your answer to 3 significant figures.

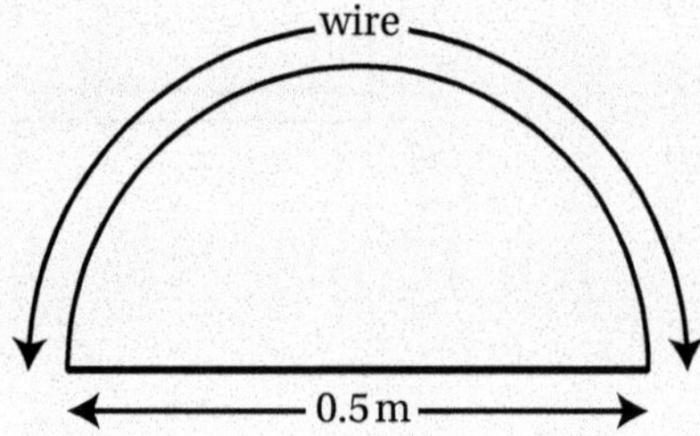

8 A composite body is made from two uniform rods, of length 1.2 m, joined together at right angles. Rod OX has mass 3.5 kg and rod OY has mass 4.5 kg. A length of wire of mass 1 kg, is bent to form a quarter circle of radius 1.2 m and is joined to the rods at X and Y. Find the distance of the centre of mass from O, giving your answer to 3 significant figures.

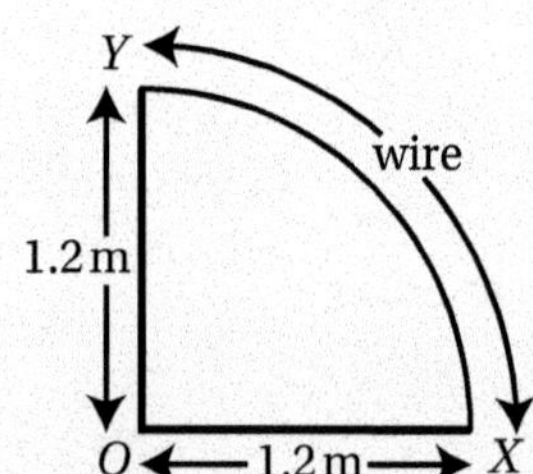

9 Two uniform right-angled triangular laminas are joined together to form one shape *ACD*, as shown. $AB = 12$ cm, $BD = 6$ cm and $BC = 9$ cm. Find the distance of the centre of mass of the combined shape from *AC* and *BD*, giving your answers to 3 significant figures.

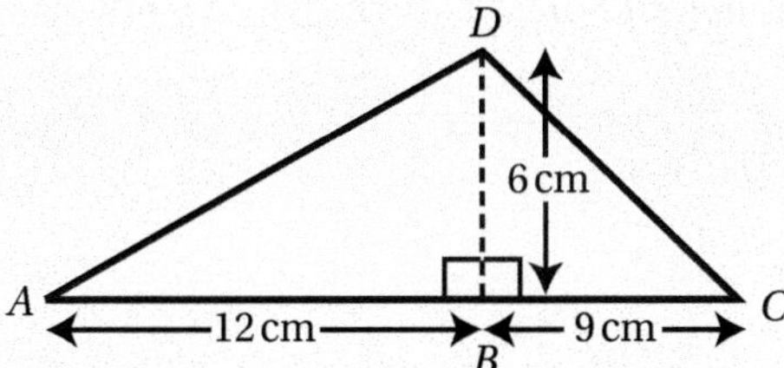

10 A child's toy is a uniform solid consisting of a hemisphere of radius 5 cm joined to a cone of base radius 5 cm. The curved surface of the cone makes an angle of 65° with its base. The two shapes are joined at the plane faces with their circumferences coinciding (see diagram). The distance of the centre of mass of the toy above the common circular plane face is x cm. Calculate the value of x.

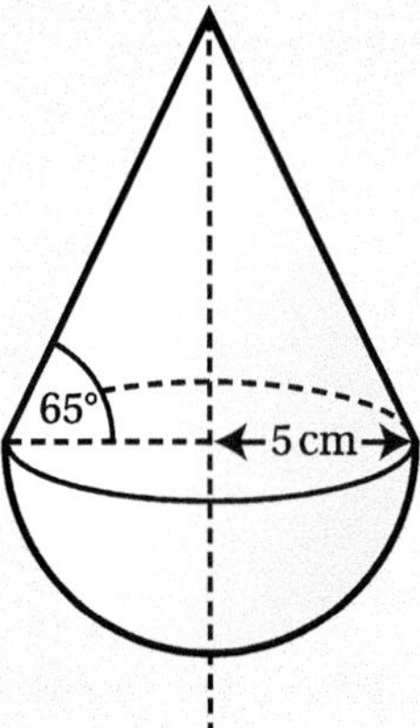

[The volume of a sphere is $\frac{4}{3}\pi r^3$ and the volume of a cone is $\frac{1}{3}\pi r^2 h$.]

11 A uniform conical shell has mass 0.5 kg, height 0.6 m and base diameter 1.6 m. A uniform hollow cylinder has mass 0.75 kg, length 1.4 m and diameter 1.6 m. The conical shell is attached to the cylinder, with the circumference of its base coinciding with one end of the cylinder (see diagram). Calculate the distance of the centre of mass of the combined object from the vertex of the conical shell.

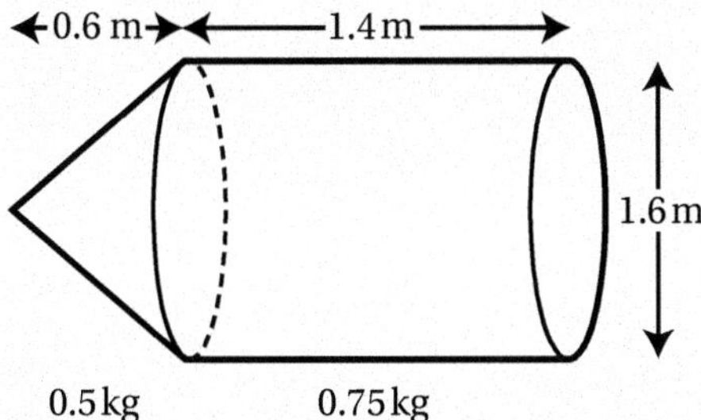

FOCUS ON ... PROOF 1

Is there a connection between the equations for linear motion with constant acceleration in a straight line and for motion in a circle involving angular equivalents of s, u, v and a? Can you prove an equivalent set of equations for constant angular acceleration?

The linear equations, sometimes known as the SUVAT equations, are:

$$v = u + at \qquad (1)$$

$$v^2 - u^2 = 2as \qquad (2)$$

$$s_0 = ut + \frac{1}{2}at^2 \qquad (3)$$

$$s_0 = vt - \frac{1}{2}at^2 \qquad (4)$$

$$s = \frac{1}{2}(u + v)t \qquad (5)$$

where u is the initial velocity, v is the final velocity, a is the acceleration, s is the displacement and t is the time taken.

You obtain equation (1) by applying calculus to basic definitions.

$$a = \frac{dv}{dt}$$

$$\int_0^t a\,dt = \int_0^t \frac{dv}{dt}dt = \int_u^v dv$$

$$[at]_0^t = [v]_u^v$$

$$at - (a \times 0) = v - u$$

$$v = u + at$$

Angular displacement is usually represented by the symbol θ. Angular velocity is the rate of change of angle and is denoted by the symbol ω or $\dot{\theta}$; angular acceleration, which is the rate of change of angular velocity, is denoted by $\ddot{\theta}$ or α (to distinguish it from linear acceleration a).

Again, you use the basic definition to obtain the equation. You use ω_0 for the initial angular velocity and ω_1 for the final angular velocity after the constant acceleration has been acting for time t.

$$\ddot{\theta} = \alpha = \frac{d\omega}{dt}$$

$$\int_0^t \alpha\,dt = \int_0^t \frac{d\omega}{dt}dt = \int_{\omega_0}^{\omega_1} d\omega$$

$$\alpha t = [\omega]_{\omega_0}^{\omega_1}$$

$$\omega_1 - \omega_0 = \alpha t$$

$$\omega_1 = \omega_0 + \omega t$$

Questions

1. Show, by integration, that the equivalent of equation (3) for motion in a circle with constant acceleration is:

$$\theta = \omega_0 t + \frac{1}{2}\alpha t^2$$

2. Find the angular equivalents of equations (2), (4) and (5).

 A particle P is moving with constant acceleration of 4 rad s^{-2}. Initially its angular velocity is 10 rad s^{-1}. What is its angular velocity after 10 seconds?

Although there is a distinction between a velocity vector and its magnitude, which is called speed, there is not an appropriate word to make the same distinction between an acceleration vector and its magnitude. You call them both acceleration and allow the context to tell you whether you are referring to a scalar or a vector quantity.

When you are dealing with Cartesian coordinates, the directions with which you relate the acceleration are obvious (x, y and z or **i**, **j** and **k**). When you refer to a particle moving in a circle with constant acceleration, you are referring to a scalar quantity because the direction of the acceleration is changing so cannot be a constant vector relative to Cartesian coordinates.

FOCUS ON ... PROBLEM SOLVING 1

It is very easy to think of Mechanics in separate blocks, rather like the chapters in this book, but sometimes you have to use more than one principle to solve a problem in Mechanics. The best way to solve a Mechanics problem is to split the problem up into a series of logical steps. In this Focus on ... section, you are going to look at problems involving more than one principle.

Consider this problem:

A small, smooth sphere of mass 400 g is free to move in a smooth vertical groove, which is in the shape of a circle of radius 1 m. At $t = 0$ the sphere is at rest at a point A at the lowest point of the groove when it is hit with a blow of impulse 3 N s in a direction that is a tangent to the circular groove at A. What is the speed of the sphere when it reaches the highest point of the groove? Take g as 10 m s^{-2}.

Visualising

You need to have a clear picture in your mind of what is happening - not the maths but the actual physical situation. Without this picture you cannot represent what is happening on a diagram. You need to put as much relevant information as you can on the diagram so that it makes sense to you. You may need more than one diagram.

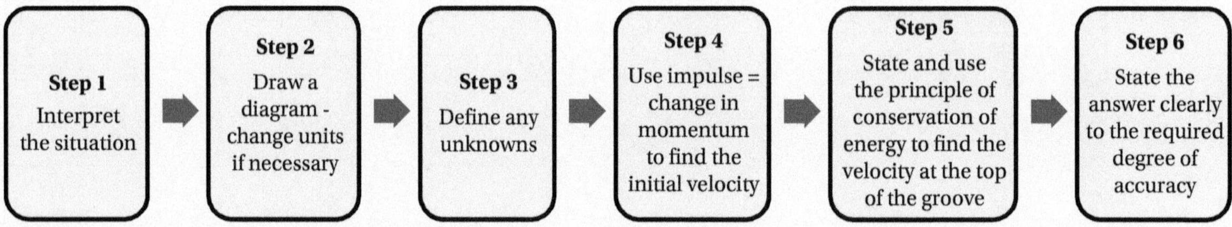

Step 1

Consider the connections to find the principles needed. You need to work out the connection between impulse, height and velocity. Impulse produces momentum and velocity so you need to use the impulse-momentum principle to find initial velocity. As the sphere rises, it slows down and the principle of conservation of energy will give us the relationship between velocity and height.

Step 2

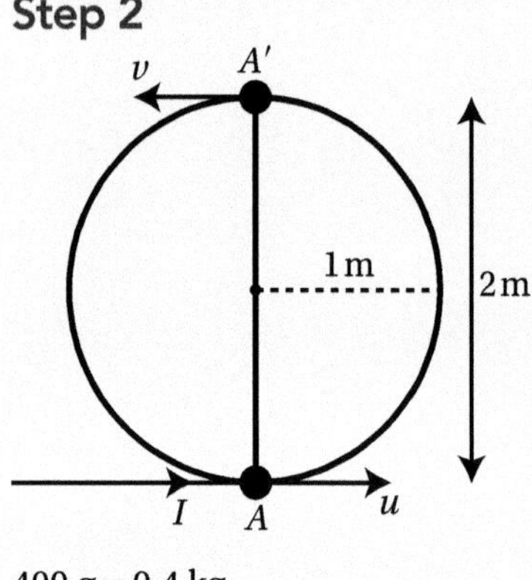

400 g = 0.4 kg

Step 3

Let u be the initial velocity of the particle.

Let v be the velocity of the particle at the highest point.

Step 4

Impulse = change in momentum

$$= mu - 0$$

$3 = 0.4u$

$u = 7.5 \text{ m s}^{-1}$

Step 5

KE loss = PE gain

$$\frac{1}{2}mu^2 - \frac{1}{2}mv^2 = mgh$$

$$\frac{1}{2}mv^2 = \frac{1}{2}mu^2 - mgh$$

$$\frac{1}{2}\times 0.4v^2 = \frac{1}{2}\times 0.4\times 7.5^2 - 0.4\times 10\times 2$$

$$v^2 = 16.25$$

Step 6

The speed of the sphere at the top of the groove (A') is 4.031 m s^{-1} (3 d.p.)

So look at the problem and make a plan. Remember that you may need to use more than one principle to solve a Mechanics problem.

Questions

1. A particle of mass 2 kg is at rest on the edge of a smooth horizontal table which is 1 m high. It is hit with an impulse of 10 N in a horizontal direction away from the table and at right angles to the edge of the table. How far from the edge of the table does the particle land?

2. A particle of mass 600 g is at rest at a point A in a smooth, horizontal groove when it is hit with a blow of impulse 2 N. The groove is in the shape of a circle of radius 1.5 m. In how many seconds does the particle return to A?

3. A particle of mass 2 kg is dropped from rest and falls a vertical distance of 4 m to the horizontal ground. The constant air resistance acting on the particle during the fall is 0.2 N. When it hits the ground, it rebounds with velocity $v \text{ m s}^{-1}$. Given that the coefficient of restitution between the particle and the ground is 0.6, find the magnitude of v. Use $g = 9.8 \text{ m s}^{-2}$ and give your answer to an appropriate degree of accuracy.

FOCUS ON ... MODELLING 1

A fairground game of 'test your strength' involves a competitor using a hammer to hit one side of a platform, which is balanced on a pivot. As the force of the hammer sends one side of the platform down, the other side rises up and sends a ball up a vertical tube towards a bell. If the ball hits the bell, then you win a prize.

In this Focus on ... section we are going to look at how we can model this situation and how we can then improve the model to make it more realistic.

Model 1

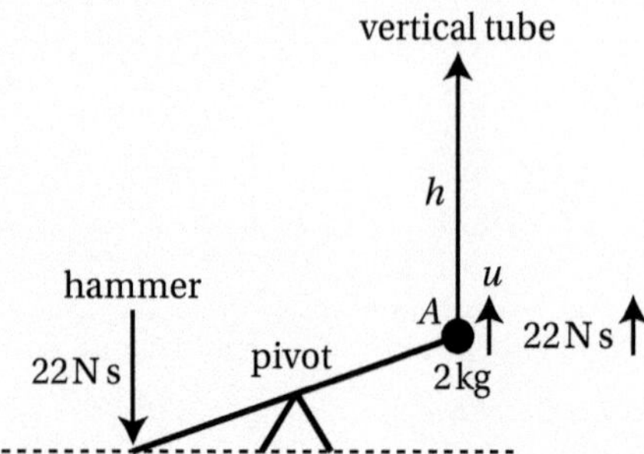

In this model, the ball is assumed to be a particle, i.e. its mass acts at one point.

The impulse generated by the hammer is instantaneous and is 22 N s. All of the impulse is transmitted via the pivot to a ball which is of mass 2 kg. The vertical tube is smooth and the bell is 3 m above the ground. Does the ball reach the bell?

Let u be the initial velocity of the particle. (Take $g = 10$ m s^{-2})

We need to use the impulse-momentum principle to find u and then energy equations to find h.

$22 = 2u$

$u = 11$ m s^{-1}

The final velocity of the particle is 0 (taking $g = 10$ m s^{-2}):

Loss in KE = Gain in PE

$\frac{1}{2} \times 2 \times 11^2 = 2 \times 10 \times h$

$h = 6\,\text{m} (1\,\text{s.f.})$

The ball hits the bell.

How do we make a better model?

How realistic is Model 1? What assumptions have we made? Which physical details have we left out?

We have assumed that:

- the contact of the hammer is instant
- it takes no time for the platform to reach the ground
- the vertical tube is smooth
- the initial direction of the ball would be vertical if it were free to move.

We have left out:

- the length of the platform
- the height of the ball above the ground when it leaves the platform
- the radius of the ball.

Let's do the calculation again with the following changes.

Model 2

The platform is of length 1 m and is supported at its centre by a pivot of height 40 cm. The impulse transmitted to the ball is 22 N s and is at right angles to the platform. The ball is at the end of the platform at the base of the tube. The radius of the ball is 7.5 cm.

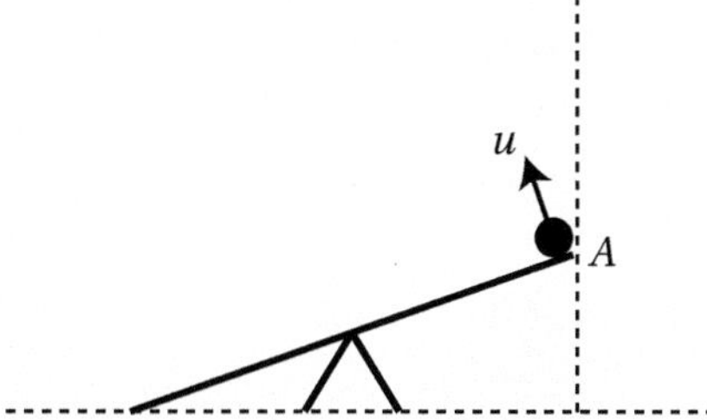

Questions

1. Find the component of the initial velocity of A in the vertical direction.
2. Work out the total height it now needs to rise through to reach the bell.
3. Does the ball still reach the bell?

Model 3

To improve the model further, we need to look at the possibility of friction between the ball and the tube that it moves through. Frictional forces exist between most surfaces in contact and should be included to make this model more realistic.

Question

4. A constant frictional force of 1 N acts on the ball whilst it is in the tube. Calculate the height to which the ball now rises.

CROSS-TOPIC REVIEW EXERCISE 1

1 The terminal velocity of a falling object is reached when the upward force on the object (the drag) is equal to the weight of the object. The formula for the drag force is of the form:

drag force $= \frac{C}{2}\rho^{\alpha} v^{\beta} A^{\gamma}$

where C is a dimensionless constant, ρ is the density of the atmosphere, v is the terminal velocity and A is the exposed area of the falling object. Use dimensional analysis to find the values of α, β and γ and hence find a formula for the drag force.

2 A small toy boat of mass 2 kg is sailing in a straight line with initial velocity 1 m s^{-1}. It is acted on by a constant wind with force 3 N for 10 seconds.

a What is the total impulse on the boat in these 10 seconds?

b Hence, what is its final velocity?

3 A group of children are playing on a playground roundabout that is spinning at a constant rate of 15 revolutions per minute. A small parcel of mass 4 kg is at rest on the roundabout at a distance of 1 m from the centre. If the parcel is at rest, what is the frictonal force acting on the parcel? You can model the roundabout as a horizontal disc and the parcel as a point mass.

4 A particle, A, of mass 500 g is attached to one end of a light inextensible string of length 1 m. The other end of the string is attached to a fixed point B, vertically above A.

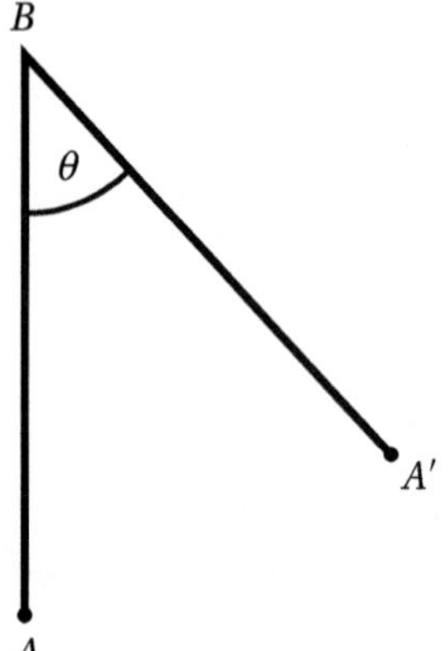

A is hit with a blow of impulse 1.5 N in a horizontal direction. Find the angle that the string makes with the vertical when the particle first comes to rest.

5 A car of mass 1500 kg is going up a hill at an angle θ to the horizontal where $\sin\theta = 0.1$. The car is travelling against a constant frictional force of 300 N with a constant speed of 20 m s^{-1}. What is the power output of the car's engine as it goes up the hill? (Take $g = 10$ m s^{-2})

6 Prove by induction that $\left[\frac{d^n x}{dt^n}\right] = \mathbf{LT}^{-n}$

7 Two smooth spheres, A and B, both of mass 2 kg, are at rest on a smooth horizontal table that is 1.4 m high. The line joining A and B is at right angles to the edge of the table. A is 1.5 m from the edge of the table and B is 0.5 m from the edge of the table. A is projected towards B at 4 m s^{-1}. A is brought to rest by the collision and B subsequently moves to the edge of table and falls off it. What is the time from the collision to the moment that B hits the ground? (Take $g = 10$ m s^{-2})

8 Two particles, P of mass 1 kg and Q of mass 3 kg, are on a smooth horizontal plane. A is moving at $4\ \text{m s}^{-1}$ and B at $2\ \text{m s}^{-1}$. The particles collide and coalesce to form a new particle C, which then hits a vertical wall at right angles. The coefficient of restitution between C and the wall is 0.8. What is the velocity of C as it leaves the wall?

A 9 A uniform circular lamina C, with equation $x^2 + y^2 = 49$, has the circle $(x - 3)^2 + y^2 = 9$ removed from it. What are the coordinates of the centre of mass of the new shape?

10 Brinell's test evaluates the hardness of a material using a Brinell hardness number (BHN). The test involves forcing a steel or tungsten carbide sphere into the material being tested and measuring the diameter of the indentation. The formula is:

$$\text{BHN} = \frac{2P}{\pi D\left(D - \sqrt{D^2 - d^2}\right)}$$

where P is the applied force, D is the diameter of the sphere and d is the diameter of the indentation.

a What are the dimensions of force?

b What are the dimensions of BHN?

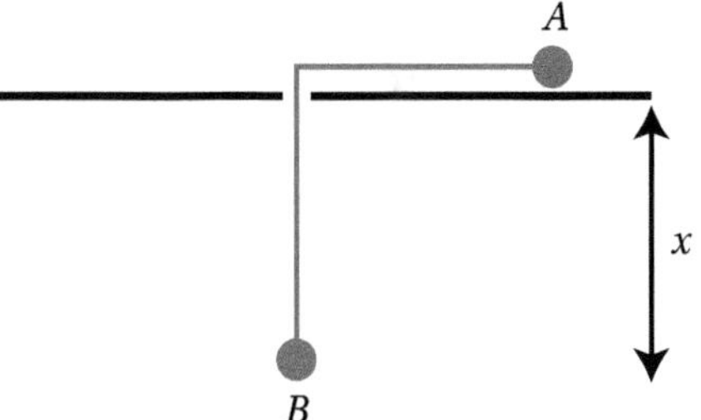

11 Particles A and B, both of mass 3 kg, are joined by a light inextensible string of length 2 m. A is moving in a circle on a smooth horizontal surface at a constant speed of $3.5\ \text{m s}^{-1}$. The string goes through a small, smooth hole in the surface and B hangs at rest at a distance x below it. Find the value of x. (Take $g = 10\ \text{m s}^{-2}$)

12 A conical pendulum consists of a particle A, of mass 2 kg, attached by a light inextensible string, of length 1.5 m, to a point B. The particle moves in a horizontal circle at a constant speed of $5\ \text{m s}^{-1}$ so that the string describes a cone. What is the volume of the cone?

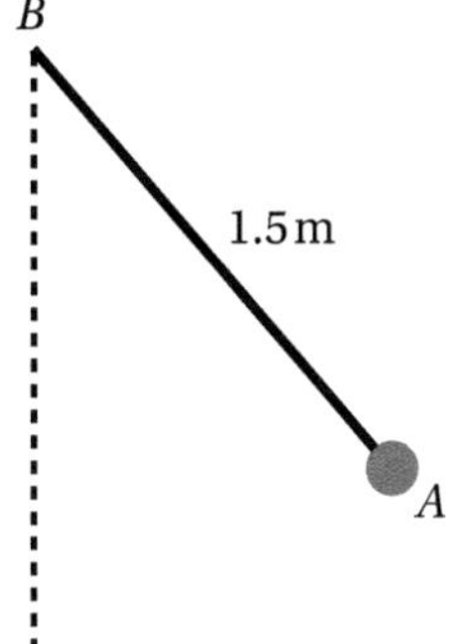

A 13 A square lamina with vertices at coordinates (0, 0), (0, 4), (4, 4) and (4, 0) has a smaller square lamina, made of material of double the mass per unit area of the first lamina, added to it. The coordinates of the vertices of the second square are (2, 2), (4, 2), (4, 4) and (2, 4). What are the coordinates of the centre of mass of the combined shape?

6 Work, energy and power 2

A This chapter is for A Level students only.
In this chapter you will learn how to:

- calculate the work done by a variable force $f(x)$ when displacement is along the x-axis
- understand and use Hooke's law for elastic strings **and** springs
- calculate the work done extending an elastic string
- calculate the work done extending or compressing an elastic spring
- include elastic potential energy in problems involving conservation of energy
- use vectors to calculate work done, kinetic energy and power.

Before you start...

Chapter 1	You should know that work done is the product of force and displacement in the direction of motion and that work done is measured in joules.	1 Calculate the work done by gravity when a stone of mass 2 kg falls vertically 10 m.
Chapter 1	You should know that kinetic energy is defined as $\frac{1}{2}mv^2$ and is measured in joules.	2 Calculate the change in kinetic energy when a boy of mass 72 kg increases his running speed from 4.2 m s^{-1} to 6 m s^{-1}.
Chapter 1	You should know that the work done by a force acting on an object causes a change in its kinetic energy. This is the work–energy principle.	3 Find the horizontal resistive force that causes an ice hockey puck of mass 150 g to reduce speed from 2.1 m s^{-1} to 0.65 m s^{-1} over 25 m.
A Level Mathematics Student Book 2	You should be able to integrate a function between limits, x_1 and x_2, to find a quantity: $\int_{x_1}^{x_2} f(x)dx$	4 Find $\int_0^{\pi} \sin x \, dx$.

Extending your knowledge of work and energy

The weight of an object is approximately constant close to the Earth's surface and the change in gravitational potential energy caused by a change in height can be accurately modelled as the work done by or against constant weight. When a rocket is fired into space its weight reduces as its distance from the centre of the Earth increases. Weight is an example of a force that varies with distance.

Other forces can vary. In this chapter, you are going to learn how to work with forces that vary with distance. A particularly important example is the force in an elastic spring or string, which increases with extension (Hooke's law). As a spring is extended, you do work

Rewind

You learned about the work done by a constant force and the work–energy principle in Chapter 1. You also learned about conservation of mechanical energy. These ideas are crucial to understanding how energy is converted to useful work.

against an increasing tension. The work is stored as elastic potential energy. Springs have many practical uses. In mountain bikes springs called shock absorbers are used to help smooth out the effects of unevenness in the road surface. When your bike hits a bump, the spring compresses. The compression absorbs some of the energy that would otherwise pass straight through to the rider. There is elastic potential energy in the spring. If you hit a bump too hard you can break your shock absorber - you have gone beyond its elastic limit.

Force, displacement and velocity can all be expressed as vector quantities. Work done, the product of force and distance, can be defined more precisely as the scalar product of vector force and vector displacement. Power can likewise be determined from the scalar product of vector velocity and vector force.

Fast forward

You will learn about Hooke's law in Section 2. You will learn to work with the scalar product in Section 4.

Section 1: Work done by a variable force f(*x*)

You know that for a constant driving force acting in the direction of motion:

$$\text{work done} = \text{force} \times \text{distance}$$

If the force is always parallel to the motion but the magnitude of the force is changing you need to use integration to find the work done.

Key point 6.1

If an object is moved in a straight line from a position x_1 to a position x_2 by the action of a variable force f(x) that depends on displacement, x, work done is defined as:

$$\text{work done} = \int_{x_1}^{x_2} f(x)\,dx$$

WORKED EXAMPLE 6.1

Find the work done by a force $8x + 15$ N that displaces an object from $x = 2$ m to $x = 5$ m.

$\text{Work done} = \int_2^5 (8x+15)\,dx$

Work done $= \int_{x_1}^{x_2} f(x)\,dx$

$= \left[4x^2+15x\right]_2^5$

Let $x_1 = 2$ and $x_2 = 5$.

Integrate and substitute the limits of integration.

$= (4\times5^2+15\times5)-(4\times2^2+15\times2)$

$= 175 - 46$

$= 129$ J

WORKED EXAMPLE 6.2

A car of mass 1020 kg moves from rest at A on a horizontal surface. The driving force is constant at 1800 N and resistance to motion is modelled as $\frac{x^2}{8}$ N. The car moves 120 m to B.

a Find the work done by the driving force and the work done against resistance as the car travels from A to B.

b Find the speed of the car at B.

a The work done by the driving force $= 1800 \times 120$

$= 216\,000$ J

As the driving force is constant, you can use the definition of the work done by a constant force.

The work done against resistance $= \int_0^{120} \frac{x^2}{8} dx$

Use integration to find the work done against the variable resistive force.

$= \left[\frac{x^3}{24}\right]_0^{120}$

$= \frac{120^3}{24}$

$= 72\,000$ J

Let $x_1 = 0$ and $x_2 = 120$.

Integrate and substitute the limits of integration.

b Work done by driving force − work done against resistance = increase in kinetic energy

Use the work-energy principle.

$216\,000 - 72\,000 = \frac{1}{2} \times 1020 \times v^2$

Car moves from rest $\Rightarrow u = 0$.

$\therefore v^2 = \frac{144000 \times 2}{1020}$

Rearrange to find the car's final speed.

$v = 16.8$ m s^{-1} (3 s.f.)

WORKED EXAMPLE 6.3

An object is moving in a horizontal straight line against a resistive force that is directly proportional to its distance from its starting point, $f(x) = kx$. If the work done against resistance as the object travels from the origin, $x = 0$ m, to a point 15 m away, $x = 15$ m, is 337.5 kJ:

a find the magnitude of k

b state the units of k.

a Work done $= \int_{x_1}^{x_2} f(x) dx$

Use the definition of work done by a force that depends on displacement.

$= \int_0^{15} kx\, dx$

Integrate between the given limits to find an expression for work done in terms of k.

$= \left[\frac{kx^2}{2}\right]_0^{15}$

$= \frac{225k}{2}$

Continues on next page ...

But work done = 337 500 J

$\therefore \frac{225k}{2} = 337\,500$

so $k = 3000$

Use the given value for work done to calculate k.

b Since f is a force (unit N), k must have units N m^{-1}.

EXERCISE 6A

For questions 1 to 4, calculate the work done by force f(x) N moving an object along the x-axis from x_1 m to x_2 m. Use the formula:

$$\text{work done} = \int_{x_1}^{x_2} f(x)\mathrm{d}x$$

	f(x)	x_1	x_2
1	$2\sqrt{x}$	5	7.5
2	$5 \cos x$	0	$\frac{\pi}{2}$
3	$10 \sin^2 x$	π	2π
4	$200 - 10x$	5	10

5 The work done by a force kx^2 moving an object from $x = 1$ m to $x = 2$ m is 210 J. Find the value of k.

6 The work done by a force $\frac{1}{2x}$ moving an object from $x = 4$ m to $x = a$ m is ln 4. Find an exact value for a.

7 A particle moves along the x-axis under the action of a force $\frac{75}{0.04 + x^2}$ newtons, where x is measured in m from O. Find the work done by the force moving the particle from $x = 20$ cm to $x = 30$ cm.

8 A vehicle of mass 850 kg moves along a horizontal road with driving force 500 N. It starts from rest at $x = 0$ m and experiences a resistance to motion of $2x$ N. Find the speed of the vehicle when it reaches $x = 100$ m.

9 A particle of mass 3.5 kg moves along a horizontal axis with driving force 50 N. The particle starts from rest at $x = 0$ m and experiences a resistance to motion of $\sqrt{x}$ N. Find the speed of the particle when it reaches $x = 256$ m.

10 A piston of mass 1.2 kg moves in a straight line inside a cylinder against a resistance of $Re^{-1.25x}$ N, where x is measured in metres. When $x = 0$ cm the speed of the piston is 25 m s^{-1}, and when $x = 8$ cm the speed of the piston is 5 m s^{-1}. Find the value of R.

11 A truck of mass 30 tonnes experiences a resistance to motion of $2500x$ N, where x is the distance travelled after the brakes are applied. The truck is travelling at 45 km h^{-1} when the driver applies the brakes with a constant braking force of 10 000 N. Find how far the truck travels before coming to rest.

 A vehicle of mass 960 kg starts from rest at $x = 0$ m and moves in a straight line parallel to the x-axis. There is a driving force of $5 + 2x^2$ N and a resistive force of $8x$ N. Derive an expression to represent work done after the vehicle has travelled x m. Numerically find the value of x when the vehicle is travelling at $25\ \text{m s}^{-1}$.

Section 2: Hooke's law, work done against elasticity and elastic potential energy

Robert Hooke was an English experimental scientist, born in 1635. He found that the extension caused when stretching an **elastic string** obeyed a simple rule. The same rule applied to the extension or compression (reduction in length) of an **elastic spring**. The rule is known as Hooke's law. Hooke measured the force required and found that, providing the object was not deformed past its **elastic limit**:

- when stretching: force $\propto$ extension
- when compressing: force $\propto$ compression.

Elastic strings may be extended but not compressed. Elastic springs may be extended and compressed. Extension or compression must occur within the elastic limit of the string or spring.

When an elastic string is stretched beyond its elastic limit it does not return to its original length when the force is removed.

As you stretch or compress an elastic object, you do work against elasticity and this work is stored as **elastic potential energy**:

Total mechanical energy = kinetic energy (KE)
+ gravitational potential energy (GPE)
+ elastic potential energy (EPE)

You can use this extended definition of mechanical energy to solve problems about the motion of objects attached to elastic strings or springs.

 **Rewind**

In Chapter 1 you learned that when gravity is the only force acting on an object:

total mechanical energy = kinetic energy + gravitational potential energy

Hooke's law for elastic strings and springs

When an elastic string or spring is extended from its natural length, there is a **tension** in the string or spring in the opposite direction to the extending force.

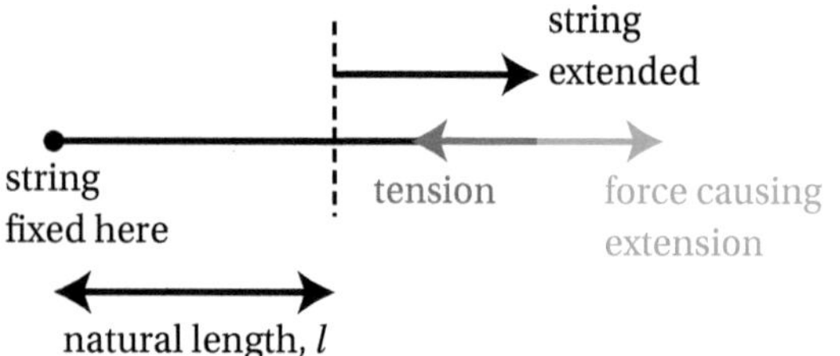

When an elastic spring is compressed from its natural length, there is a **thrust** in the spring in the opposite direction to the compressing force.

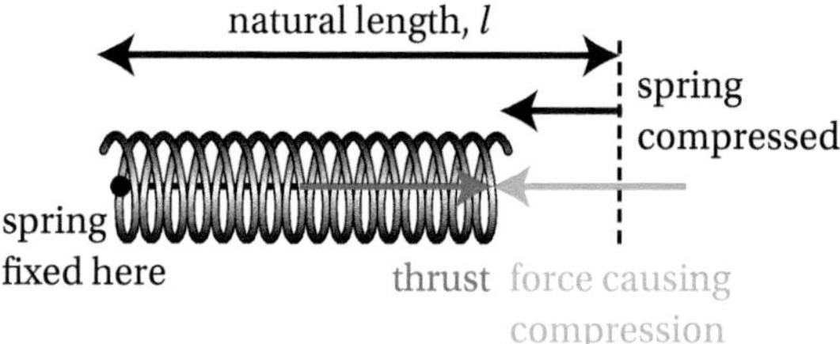

You can relate the extension or compression of an elastic spring, x, to the tension or thrust in the spring, T, by the formula:

$$T = \frac{\lambda x}{l}$$

where l is the natural length of the spring. The **modulus of elasticity**, λ, is the force required to double the length of the spring, assuming that such an extension does not cause the spring to exceed its elastic limit. If a spring does exceed its elastic limit, then Hooke's law no longer applies. The same formula applies to the extension of an elastic string. The modulus of elasticity, λ, is measured in N.

Did you know?

In A Level Physics you may see an alternative formula for Hooke's law, $T = kx$, with k being the stiffness of the object being compressed or extended.

Key point 6.2

Hooke's law for an elastic string or spring is:

$$T = \frac{\lambda x}{l}$$

- A low value for λ means that the string or spring is quite flexible and easy to extend or compress.
- A high value for λ means the string or spring is quite stiff and difficult to extend or compress.

An important assumption is that the elastic string or spring is 'light', that is, its mass can be ignored. If the string were not 'light' then the tension or thrust through the string or spring could vary along its length.

WORKED EXAMPLE 6.4

A light elastic spring, which has modulus of elasticity 85 N and natural length 1.8 m, has one end attached at a fixed point A. A horizontal force, of magnitude 40 N, is applied to the spring causing a compression. The spring rests in equilibrium. Find the distance that the spring is compressed from its natural length.

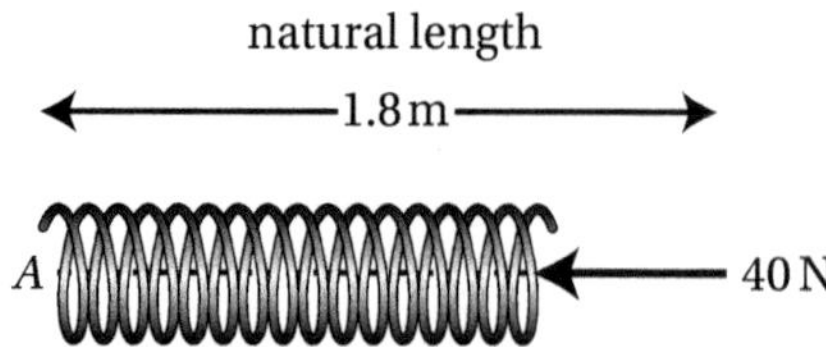

$T - 40 = 0$

$\Rightarrow T = 40$

Since the spring is in equilibrium there is zero resultant force.

$x = \frac{Tl}{\lambda}$

Rearrange the formula for Hooke's law to make extension the subject.

$x = \frac{40 \times 1.8}{85} \Rightarrow x = 0.847$

The compression of the spring is 0.847 m (3 s.f.)

The compression of the spring is less than its natural length. This is a simple check of validity.

WORKED EXAMPLE 6.5

A light elastic string is attached to a fixed point and hangs vertically, in equilibrium, with an object of mass 400 g attached to its lower end. The string has natural length 0.8 m and the object is resting 1.3 m below the point of suspension. Find the modulus of elasticity of the string.

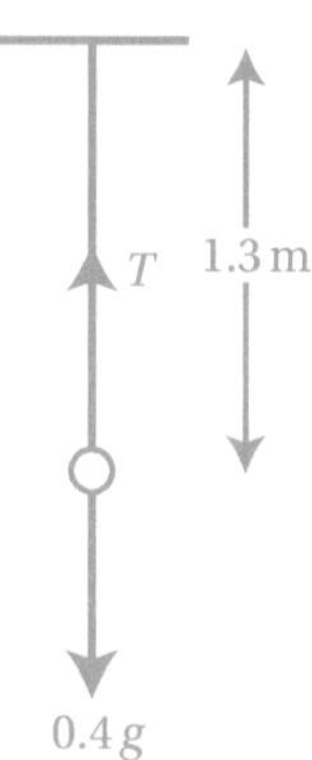

Draw a diagram showing the forces acting on the particle.

$400\text{g} = 0.4 \text{ kg}$

Convert grams to kilograms.

$T - 0.4g = 0 \Rightarrow T = 0.4g$

Since the string is in equilibrium there is zero resultant force.

$T = \frac{\lambda x}{l} \Rightarrow \lambda = \frac{Tl}{x}$

Rearrange the formula for Hooke's law to make λ the subject.

$\lambda = \frac{0.4g \times 0.8}{0.5} = 6.272 \text{ N}$

WORKED EXAMPLE 6.6

An object of mass 1.5 kg is attached to the end of a light elastic string of length 1.5 m. The other end of the string is fixed to point A. The object is held at A and released. The modulus of elasticity of the string is 50 N. Find the extension of the string when the object reaches its maximum speed, and hence its distance below A at this time.

Using $F = ma$

$1.5g = 1.5a$ — To start with the object falls under gravity for 1.5 m. There is no tension in the string.

$1.5g - T = 1.5a$ — As the string extends beyond its natural length the increasing tension in the string reduces the acceleration.

When $a = 0$ — Speed reaches its maximum value when $a = 0$.

$1.5g = T$

$1.5g = \frac{\lambda x}{l} \Rightarrow 1.5g = \frac{50x}{1.5}$ — Use Hooke's law for T.

$x = \frac{2.25g}{50} = 0.441$ m (3 s.f.) — Rearrange to find the extension.

So the object is 1.94 m below A when it reaches maximum velocity. — Find the total distance fallen.

WORKED EXAMPLE 6.7

An object P of mass 10 kg is attached to the lower ends of two light elastic strings. One string is of natural length 0.5 m with modulus of elasticity 25 N. The other string is of natural length 0.4 m with modulus of elasticity 30 N. The free ends of the strings are attached to a point A and P hangs in equilibrium vertically below A. Find the distance AP.

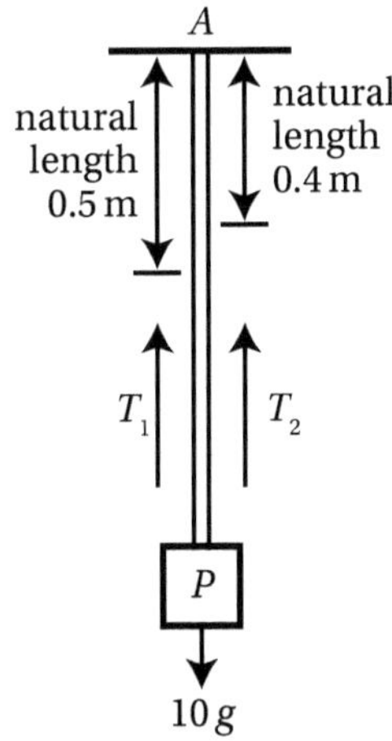

Continues on next page ...

Let the tensions in the strings be T_1 and T_2

$T_1 + T_2 - 10g = 0$ — The mass hangs in equilibrium so there is zero resultant force on P.

Let distance AP be D metres.

$T_1 = \frac{25(D-0.5)}{0.5}$ and $T_2 = \frac{30(D-0.4)}{0.4}$ — Use $\frac{\lambda x}{l}$ for the tensions in the strings. Extension $= D - l$ in each case.

$50(D-0.5) + 75(D-0.4) = 10g$ — Substitute your expressions for tension.

$125D = 55 + 10g \Rightarrow D = 1.22$ m — Rearrange to find the value of D.

Work done extending an elastic string

The force required to extend an elastic string or spring varies with the extension of the string. This means that you cannot find the work done by multiplying force and distance. You need to integrate to find the work done against a variable force.

Key point 6.3

Work done extending an elastic string from extension x_1 to x_2 is given by:

$$\frac{\lambda}{2l}\left(x_2^2 - x_1^2\right)$$

The same formula is used to calculate the work done compressing an elastic spring from compression x_1 to compression x_2.

PROOF 1

An elastic string has modulus of elasticity λ and natural length l. Prove that the work done extending from extension x_1 to extension x_2 is $\frac{\lambda}{2l}\left(x_2^2 - x_1^2\right)$.

Work done $= \int_{x_1}^{x_2} T \, dx = \int_{x_1}^{x_2} \frac{\lambda x}{l} dx$ — The string is extended from x_1 to x_2. Integrate your expression for T from x_1 to x_2.

Work done $= \frac{\lambda}{l}\left[\frac{x^2}{2}\right]_{x_1}^{x_2}$ — Take the constants out of the integration.

Work done $= \frac{\lambda}{2l}\left(x_2^2 - x_1^2\right)$ — Substitute the limits.

Tip

When calculating the work done against elasticity, make sure you take the difference of the squares of the extensions, not the square of the difference:

$$x_2^2 - x_1^2 \neq (x_2 - x_1)^2$$

WORKED EXAMPLE 6.8

Find the work done when a light elastic string of natural length 1.2 m and modulus of elasticity 80 N is stretched from a length of 1.5 m to 1.8 m.

$x_1 = 0.3$ and $x_2 = 0.6$ — Work out the starting and ending extensions.

$\text{Work done} = \frac{\lambda}{2l}(x_2^2 - x_1^2)$ — Use the formula for work done against elasticity.

$\text{Work done} = \frac{80}{2 \times 1.2}(0.6^2 - 0.3^2) = 9\text{ J}$ — Substitute in the values.

Elastic potential energy

The work done extending a light elastic string or spring is stored as elastic potential energy. When the string or spring is released, it will contract towards its natural length and elastic potential energy is converted to kinetic energy.

Similarly, the work done compressing a spring is stored as elastic potential energy. When the spring is released it will expand towards its natural length, converting elastic potential energy to kinetic energy.

Key point 6.4

Elastic potential energy (EPE) is the energy stored in a string or spring extended by x, or in a spring compressed by x.

$$\text{EPE} = \frac{\lambda x^2}{2l}$$

Key point 6.5

Using the principle of conservation of energy, when an object is acted on only by its weight and the force in an elastic string or spring:

$$\text{GPE} + \text{EPE} + \text{KE} = \text{constant}$$

where GPE is gravitational potential energy, EPE is elastic potential energy and KE is kinetic energy.

Rewind

In Chapter 1 you learned that work done against gravity is stored as gravitational potential energy and that when the only force acting on an object is its weight, the sum of kinetic and gravitational potential energy is conserved.

WORKED EXAMPLE 6.9

A light elastic spring with natural length 15 cm rests on a smooth horizontal table. One end is attached to a fixed point A and a 250 g mass is attached at the other end B, held 10 cm from A. The modulus of elasticity of the spring is 600 N.

a Find the elastic potential energy in the spring.

The spring is released and B moves horizontally away from A.

b Find how fast the mass is travelling when the spring reaches its natural length.

a $\text{EPE} = \dfrac{\lambda x^2}{2l}$

$\lambda = 600\text{ N}$

$x = 0.15 - 0.10 = 0.05\text{ m}$ — Convert centimetres to metres.

$l = 0.15\text{ m}$

$\text{EPE} = \dfrac{600 \times 0.05^2}{2 \times 0.15} = 5\text{ J}$

b $\text{EPE}_1 + \text{KE}_1 = \text{EPE}_2 + \text{KE}_2$ — When the spring reaches its natural length, all its EPE has been converted to KE. $\text{KE}_1 = 0$ and $\text{EPE}_2 = 0$.

$5 = \dfrac{1}{2} \times 0.25 \times v^2$

$v^2 = 40$

$v = 6.32\text{ m s}^{-1}$ (3 s.f.)

WORKED EXAMPLE 6.10

One end of a light elastic string of natural length 0.8 m and modulus of elasticity 50 N is attached to a fixed point O. A particle P of mass 1.5 kg is attached to the other end of the string. P is released from rest at O and falls vertically. Assuming there is no air resistance, find:

a the extension of the string when P is at its lowest position

b the acceleration of P at its lowest position.

a $mgh = \text{final EPE}$

Use the principle of conservation of energy:
$GPE_1 + EPE_1 + KE_1 = GPE_2 + EPE_2 + KE_2$
Let the lowest point be the zero level for GPE.
Then $GPE_2 = 0$.
$GPE_1 = mgh$, where h is the height fallen.
P is stationary at O and at its lowest position:
$KE_1 = KE_2 = 0$
At O the string is not extended, so $EPE_1 = 0$.

$$mg(l+x) = \frac{\lambda x^2}{2l}$$

Take x to represent extension, as usual.

$$1.5g(0.8+x) = \frac{50x^2}{2\times 0.8}$$
$$\Rightarrow 11.76 + 14.7x = 31.25x^2$$
$$\Rightarrow 31.25x^2 - 14.7x - 11.76 = 0$$

Substitute in the given values and rearrange the quadratic equation.

$$x = \frac{14.7 \pm \sqrt{14.7^2 - 4\times 31.25 \times -11.76}}{2\times 31.25}$$
$$x = 0.8922 = 0.892 \text{ m (3 s.f.)}$$

Solve the quadratic, taking the positive solution for x. This is the maximum extension of the string.

b $T - mg = ma$

At the maximum extension of the string, take upwards as positive, and use $F = ma$.

$$\frac{\lambda x}{l} - mg = ma$$

Use Hooke's law $T = \frac{\lambda x}{l}$ for the tension.

When $x = 0.8922$

$$\frac{50\times 0.8922}{0.8} - 1.5g = 1.5a$$

Use the value for the maximum extension found in part **a**.

$$a = \frac{50\times 0.8922}{0.8\times 1.5} - g$$
$$a = 27.4 \text{ m s}^{-2} \text{ (3 s.f.)}$$

WORKED EXAMPLE 6.11

A light elastic spring, of natural length 20 cm, has one end fixed to a horizontal surface with the other end vertically above. A sphere of mass 0.8 kg rests on the top of the spring, which is in equilibrium, 12 cm above the surface.

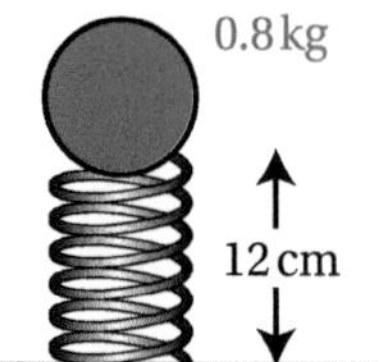

a Show that modulus of elasticity of the spring is $2g$ N.

The spring is compressed a further 3 cm.

b Find the maximum speed of the sphere in the subsequent vertical motion.

a $T - mg = 0$ — The sphere rests in equilibrium so the resultant force is zero.

$\frac{\lambda x}{l} - mg = 0$ — Use Hooke's law $T = \frac{\lambda x}{l}$.

$\frac{\lambda \times 0.08}{0.2} = 0.8g$ — Compression = 8 cm = 0.08 m

$\lambda = 2g$ N, as required

b KE + GPE + EPE = constant — Use the principle of conservation of mechanical energy for the upward movement.

Let x be the final compression of the spring:

$mgh = 0.8g\,(0.11 - x)$ — Let the GPE at the start of the upward movement be zero $\Rightarrow$ $\text{GPE}_1 = 0$.
$\text{GPE}_2 = mgh$, where h is the distance moved:
h = starting compression − final compression

$\frac{2g \times 0.11^2}{2 \times 0.2} = \frac{1}{2} \times 0.8\,v^2 + 0.8g\,(0.11 - x) + \frac{2g \times x^2}{2 \times 0.2}$ — $\text{EPE}_1 = \text{KE}_2 + \text{GPE}_2 + \text{EPE}_2$

$0.4v^2 + 0.8624 - 7.84x + 49\,x^2 = 0.5929$ — Simplify, substituting $g = 9.8$.

$v^2 = -122.5\,(x^2 - 0.16x) - 0.67375$ — Rearrange to express v^2 in terms of a quadratic in x.

$v^2 = 0.11025 - 122.5\,(x - 0.08)^2$ — Complete the square to find the stationary point for v^2.

Maximum speed $= 0.332$ m s^{-1} when $x = 8$ cm — The maximum speed arises at the equilibrium compression of the spring.

Focus on ...

You will use an alternative method of finding the maximum speed in Focus on ... Problem solving 2.

WORK IT OUT 6.1

A light elastic string has one end attached to a fixed point O and the free end attached to a particle P of mass m kg. Particle P is released from rest at O and falls a distance $(l+x)$ metres, where l m is the natural length of the string and x is its extension. David wants to work out an expression for P's kinetic energy. Which of the following energy equations should he use?

Which solution is correct? Can you identify the errors in the incorrect solutions?

Solution 1	Solution 2	Solution 3
$\frac{1}{2}mv^2 = mg(l+x)+\frac{\lambda x^2}{2l}$	$mg(l+x)=\frac{1}{2}mv^2+\frac{\lambda x^2}{2l}$	$\frac{1}{2}mv^2+mg(l+x)=\frac{\lambda x^2}{2l}$

EXERCISE 6B

1 Calculate the tension in a light elastic string when it is extended from a natural length of 0.8 m by 0.25 m. The modulus of elasticity is 85 N.

2 Calculate the thrust in a light elastic spring that is compressed from its natural length of 0.35 m to 0.25 m. The modulus of elasticity is 150 N.

3 A light elastic string of natural length 60 cm is extended by 15 cm. The tension in the string is 55 N. Find the modulus of elasticity.

4 A light elastic spring is compressed from its natural length of 40 cm. The thrust in the spring is 45 N and the modulus of elasticity is 145 N. Find the compression of the spring.

5 A light elastic string is attached to a fixed point and hangs vertically, in equilibrium, with an object of mass 1.5 kg attached to its lower end. The string has natural length 0.85 m and the modulus of elasticity is 120 N. Find the extension of the string.

6 A light elastic string is attached to a fixed point and hangs vertically, in equilibrium, with an object of mass 1250 g attached to its lower end. The string has natural length 1.1 m and the object is resting 1.5 m below the point of suspension. Find the modulus of elasticity of the string.

7 A light elastic spring of natural length 0.75 m has one end attached to a fixed point on a smooth horizontal surface. A horizontal force is applied to the other end of the spring causing a compression of 20 cm. The modulus of elasticity of the spring is 125 N. Find the magnitude of the force causing the compression.

8 A light elastic spring of natural length 85 cm has one end attached to a fixed point on a smooth horizontal surface. The spring is extended by a horizontal force of magnitude 105 N. The modulus of elasticity is 200 N. Find the extension of the spring.

9 Find the elastic potential energy stored in a light elastic spring of natural length 1.2 m and modulus of elasticity 250 N when it is compressed to a length of 1.02 m.

10 Find the increase of elastic potential energy when a light elastic string of natural length 1.8 m and modulus of elasticity 125 N is extended from 2.05 m to 2.8 m.

11 A light elastic string of natural length 1.4 m is extended from 1.5 m to 1.75 m. The work done against elasticity extending the string is 21 J. Find the modulus of elasticity of the string.

12 A light elastic spring having modulus of elasticity 360 N and natural length 1.2 m is compressed from its natural length. The elastic potential energy stored within the spring is 65 J. Find the length of the compressed spring.

13 An object P of mass 1.2 kg is attached to one end of a light elastic string of natural length 1.25 m with its other end attached to a fixed point, O. The modulus of elasticity of the string is 65 N. P is dropped from O. Find the extension of the string when the object reaches its maximum velocity.

14 One end of a light elastic string of natural length 95 cm and modulus of elasticity 75 N is attached to a fixed point O. A particle P of mass 1.75 kg is attached to the other end of the string. P is released from rest at O and falls vertically. Assuming there is no air resistance, find:

a the extension of the string when P is at its lowest position

b the acceleration of P at its lowest position, stating the direction.

15 A light elastic string has natural length l, modulus of elasticity λ and extension x. Show that the work done extending from $(l+x_1)$ to $(l+x_2)$ can be expressed as the change in string tension multiplied by the mean extension of the string.

16 A particle of mass 1.6 kg is attached to the free end of an elastic string of natural length 1.5 m. The other end is attached to a fixed point, O. The particle is held 1.8 m below O and released. Given the modulus of elasticity of the string is 158 N, find how far the particle is from O when it comes to instantaneous rest.

17 An object Q of mass 8 kg is attached to the lower ends of two parallel light elastic strings. One string is of natural length 0.4 m with modulus of elasticity 35 N. The other string is of natural length 0.6 m with modulus of elasticity 42 N. The free ends of the strings are attached to a point O, and Q hangs in equilibrium vertically below O. Find the distance OQ.

18 A light elastic spring with natural length 18 cm rests on a smooth horizontal table. One end is attached to a fixed point A and a 280 g mass is attached at the other end B, held 12 cm from A. The modulus of elasticity of the spring is 550 N.

a Find the elastic potential energy in the spring.

The spring is released and B moves horizontally away from A.

b Find how fast the mass is travelling when it is 16 cm from A.

Section 3: Problem solving involving work, energy and power

More complex problems may combine the work-energy principle and the principle of conservation of energy. You may be working with any of the propulsive or resistive forces you have met in Chapter 1, Sections 1 and 2.

WORKED EXAMPLE 6.12

An object, P, of mass 2 kg, is attached to the ends of two light elastic strings with the same natural length, 0.75 m, but different modulus of elasticity. One of the strings is attached to a point A and the other is attached to point B on the same horizontal level as A, such that the distance AB is 2 m. P hangs in equilibrium. The distance AP is 1.5 m and BP is 0.9 m. Calculate the modulus of elasticity of each of the strings.

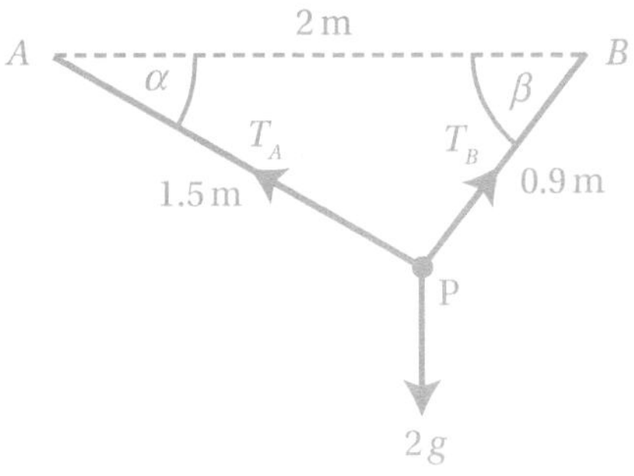

Draw a clearly labelled diagram.

$$\alpha = \cos^{-1}\frac{1.5^2+2^2-0.9^2}{2\times2\times1.5} \approx 24.95°$$

$$\beta = \cos^{-1}\frac{0.9^2+2^2-1.5^2}{2\times0.9\times2} \approx 44.67°$$

Use the cosine rule to find angles PAB, α, and PBA, β. Keep 4 significant figures at this stage.

$$(\leftarrow)\ T_A\cos\alpha - T_B\cos\beta = 0$$

$$\therefore T_A\cos\alpha = T_B\cos\beta$$

$$T_A = \frac{\cos\beta}{\cos\alpha}\times T_B$$

Resolve horizontally and get an expression for T_A in terms of T_B.

$$(\uparrow)\ T_A\sin\alpha + T_B\sin\beta - 2g = 0$$

Resolve vertically and then substitute for T_A.

$$\frac{\cos\beta}{\cos\alpha}\times T_B\sin\alpha + T_B\sin\beta - 2g = 0$$

$$T_B = \frac{2g}{\cos\beta\tan\alpha+\sin\beta} \Rightarrow T_B \approx 18.96\text{ N}$$

Rearrange to make T_B the subject and calculate T_B.

$$\text{But } T_A = \frac{\cos\beta}{\cos\alpha}\times T_B \Rightarrow T_A \approx 14.87\text{ N}$$

Now calculate T_A.

$$\lambda = \frac{Tl}{x}$$

Use Hooke's law.

$$\lambda_A = \frac{14.87\times0.75}{(1.5-0.75)} = 14.9\text{ N (3 s.f.)}$$

$$\lambda_B = \frac{18.96\times0.75}{(0.9-0.75)} = 94.8\text{ N (3 s.f.)}$$

Use Hooke's law for each string to find each modulus of elasticity.

WORKED EXAMPLE 6.13

A light elastic string, of natural length 0.8 m, has one end fixed to point A on a rough plane inclined at 30° to the horizontal. The string has modulus of elasticity 150 N. A particle P of mass 2.1 kg is attached to the free end of the string. P is released from rest at A and descends the plane to B, where it comes to rest. Given that the coefficient of friction between P and the plane is 0.35:

a find the distance AB

b determine whether the particle remains stationary at B or starts to travel back up the plane.

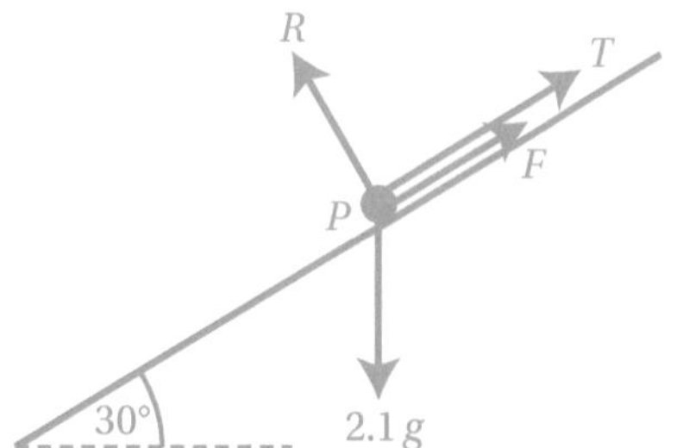

Draw a diagram showing the forces acting on P as it slides down the plane from A to B.

a Work done by gravity − work done against tension − work done against friction = increase in kinetic energy

Use the work-energy principle: net work done = change in kinetic energy

Work done by gravity − work done against tension − work done against friction = 0

The particle is at rest at A and at B so the increase in kinetic energy is zero.

Work done by gravity = mgh

$= 2.1g \sin 30° (0.8 + x)$

The distance travelled down the slope by P is the natural length, 0.8 m, plus the extension in the string x m.

Work done against friction = $F(0.8 + x)$

Let F be the frictional force.

Work done against tension = $\frac{\lambda x^2}{2l}$

$$2.1g \sin 30° (0.8 + x) - F(0.8 + x) - \frac{\lambda x^2}{2l} = 0$$

$F = 2.1g \cos 30° \times \mu$

While P is moving, $F = \mu R$, where $R = 2.1g \cos 30°$.

$$\left(2.1g \times \frac{1}{2} - 2.1g \frac{\sqrt{3}}{2} \times 0.35\right)(0.8 + x) - \frac{150x^2}{1.6} = 0$$

Substitute for F in the work-energy equation.

Continues on next page ...

$4.052(0.8+x) - 93.75x^2 = 0$

$93.75x^2 - 4.052x - 3.242 = 0$

$x = 0.2088$

$x \approx 0.209$ m (3 s.f.)

Simplify to get a quadratic equation and take the positive value for the extension.

b At $x \approx 0.2088$ m

$T = \frac{\lambda x}{l} = 39.2$ N

Find the tension in the string when it is at its maximum extension.

$T - 2.1g\sin 30° = 28.9$ N (3 s.f.) (towards A)

Calculate the total force parallel to the plane without friction.

$F = 2.1g\frac{\sqrt{3}}{2} \times 0.35 = 6.24$ N (3 s.f.) (away from A)

Using the expression for F from part **a**.

$T - 2.1g\sin 30° > F$

$28.9 > 6.24$

Consider the resultant force up the plane.

∴ the particle will start to travel back up the plane.

WORKED EXAMPLE 6.14

One end of a light elastic string, of natural length 0.8 m and modulus of elasticity $0.75mg$ N, is attached to a fixed point O on a smooth plane inclined at an angle α to the horizontal, where $\sin\alpha = \frac{3}{8}$.

A particle P, of mass m kg, is attached to the other end of the string. P is released from rest at O and travels down the plane without reaching the bottom. Find the maximum speed of P as it travels down the plane.

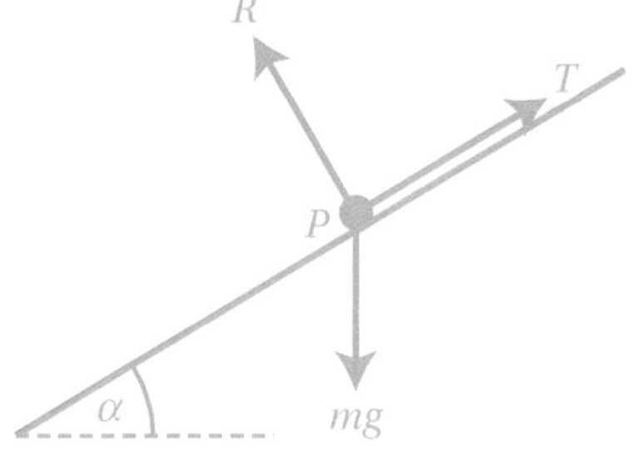

Draw a diagram showing the forces acting on P as it slides down the plane from O.

Let the extension of the elastic string be x m.

Component of weight of P parallel to the plane is $mg\sin\alpha$.

At maximum speed:

$mg\sin\alpha - T = 0$

P has maximum speed when acceleration is zero because there is no resultant force parallel to the plane.

Continues on next page ...

and $T = \frac{\lambda x}{l} = \frac{0.75mgx}{0.8}$ — Use Hooke's law.

$mg \times \frac{3}{8} = \frac{15}{16}mgx$ — x is the extension of the string.

$x = 0.4$

P has travelled 1.2 m from O when it reaches its maximum speed. — Distance from O is natural length plus extension.

$GPE_1 + KE_1 + EPE_1 = GPE_2 + KE_2 + EPE_2$ — GPE + EPE + KE is constant.

$GPE_1 = KE_2 + EPE_2$ — Let $GPE_2 = 0$ (when P is travelling at its maximum speed)

$KE_1 = 0$ (P moves from rest)

$EPE_1 = 0$

$mg \times \frac{3}{8} \times 1.2 = \frac{1}{2}mv^2 + \frac{0.75mg \times 0.4^2}{2 \times 0.8}$ — Substitute and rearrange to find v.

$4.41 = 0.5v^2 + 0.735$

$v = 2.71\ \text{m s}^{-1}$ (3 s.f.)

WORKED EXAMPLE 6.15

a A car of mass 1150 kg moves along a straight horizontal road. The resistance to motion is 580 N; the engine is working at 14.5 kW and the car is moving with constant speed. Find the constant speed of the car in km h^{-1}.

b The same car now moves up a hill inclined at 4° to the horizontal. The car's engine continues working at 14.5 kW and the resistance to motion is unchanged. Find the new, constant, speed of the car up the hill, in km h^{-1}.

a

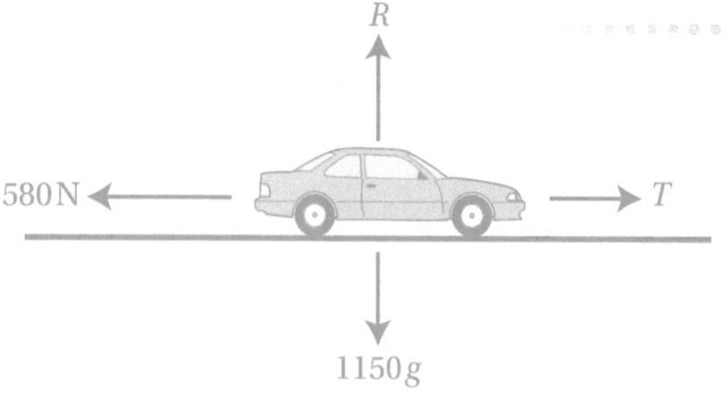

Draw a clearly labelled diagram.

T is the constant tractive force.

(→) Tractive force − resistive force = 0 — Constant speed ⇒ resultant force = 0

$T - 580 = 0$

$\therefore T = 580$ N

14.5 kW = 14 500 W — Convert kilowatts to watts.

Continues on next page ...

$14\,500 = 580 \times \text{speed}$	Use power = tractive force × speed.
$\Rightarrow \text{speed} = \frac{14\,500}{580}\ \text{m s}^{-1} = 25\ \text{m s}^{-1}$	Rearrange the formula to find the speed.
$25\ \text{m s}^{-1} = 90\ \text{km h}^{-1}$	Convert m s^{-1} to km h^{-1}.
b When travelling uphill:	Draw a clearly labelled diagram. Use T' to represent new tractive force.

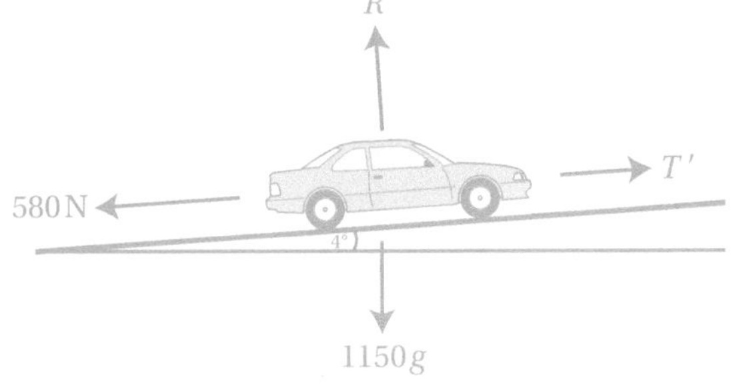

Tractive force − resistive force − component of weight acting parallel to road surface = 0	Constant speed ⇒ resultant force = 0
$T' - 580 - 1150g \sin 4 = 0$	The component of the car's weight acting parallel to the road surface is $1150g \sin 4$, as the road surface is inclined at 4° to the horizontal.
$\therefore T' = 580 + 1150g \sin 4$	Rearrange to find the tractive force.
$T' = 1366\ \text{N}$	
Power = tractive force × speed	Use power = tractive force × speed.
$14\,500 \approx 1366 \times \text{speed}$	
$\Rightarrow \text{Speed} = \frac{14\,500}{1366}\ \text{m s}^{-1} = 10.6\ \text{m s}^{-1}$ (3 s.f.)	Rearrange to find speed.
$10.6\ \text{m s}^{-1} = 38.2\ \text{km h}^{-1}$ (3 s.f.)	Convert m s^{-1} to km h^{-1}.

WORKED EXAMPLE 6.16

A car and driver of combined mass 1150 kg accelerate from rest up a road inclined at 5° to the horizontal, with average resistance to motion of 850 N. The car engine is working at a constant rate of 32 kW. The car reaches a speed of 15 m s^{-1} after it has travelled 80 m. Calculate the time taken.

To find the time taken when the vehicle engine is operating at constant power you can find the total work done and use the definition:

$$\text{power} = \frac{\text{work done}}{\text{time}} \Rightarrow \text{time} = \frac{\text{work done}}{\text{power}}$$

Continues on next page ...

Work done by engine – work done against resistance + KE_1 + GPE_1 = KE_2 + GPE_2

Mechanical energy is increased because the car is accelerating up a hill. This increase in mechanical energy comes from the car engine. But some of the work done by the engine is expended on resistance to motion.

Work done by engine = work done against resistance + KE_2 + GPE_2

Calculate the total work done by the car's engine.

$KE_1 = 0$ (car moves from rest)

Let $GPE_1 = 0$ (at the start of the travel)

Work done against resistance = 850×80 J

$KE_2 = \frac{1}{2} \times 1150 \times 15^2$ J

$PE_2 = 1150g \times \sin 5^\circ \times 80$ J

$\Rightarrow$ Work done by engine

$= 850 \times 80 + \frac{1}{2} \times 1150 \times 15^2 + 1150g \times 80 \sin 5^\circ$

$= 275\,954.61\ldots$

32 kW = 32 000 W

Convert kilowatts to watts.

Time taken $= \frac{275\,954.61\ldots}{32\,000}$ s

Time taken = 8.62 s (3 s.f.)

Divide the work done by the engine's constant power output.

EXERCISE 6C

1 A block of mass 2 kg is being pushed in a straight line along horizontal ground by a force of 16 N inclined at 12° above the horizontal. The block moves a distance of 6.5 m in 7 seconds. Find:

a the work done by the force

b the power with which the force is working.

2 Darius is pulling a wheeled suitcase of mass 2.5 kg up a plane inclined at 10° to the horizontal. The strap he is holding is taut, with tension 7.5 N, and angled at 30° to the horizontal. The resistance to motion is 2.5 N.

a Calculate the increase in the suitcase's kinetic energy as it moves 10 m up the slope.

Darius trips slightly and releases the strap. The suitcase comes to rest before rolling back down the slope against the same resistance to motion.

b Find the speed of the suitcase after it has travelled 5 m down the slope from rest.

3 A block of mass 1.25 kg is projected up an inclined plane at 1.5 m s^{-1} and comes to rest after travelling 75 cm up the plane. Given that the resistance to motion up the plane is constant at 0.5 N, find the inclination of the plane, to the nearest degree.

4 A parcel of mass 250 g is projected up a smooth plane inclined at 15° to the horizontal with a speed 2.5 m s^{-1}. Find:

a the speed of the parcel after it has travelled 50 cm up the plane

b how far the parcel travels up the plane before it stops moving.

5 A car and driver of combined mass 1025 kg accelerate from rest down a road inclined at 3° to the horizontal, with average resistance to motion of 850 N. The car engine is working at a constant rate of 8.5 kW. The car reaches a speed of 15 m s^{-1} after it has travelled 65 m; calculate the time taken.

6 A package of mass 800 g is projected up a rough plane inclined at 20° to the horizontal. The speed of projection is 3.2 m s^{-1} and the resistance to motion is constant at 2.2 N. Calculate the speed of the package when it returns to its starting point.

7 An object of mass 1.8 kg is attached to the ends of two light elastic strings having the same modulus of elasticity. One of the strings has natural length 0.8 m and the other has a natural length of 1.1 m. The longer string is attached at A and the shorter string is attached at B on the same horizontal level. The object hangs 0.85 m below O, a point on the same level as A and B, 1.4 m from A and 0.8 m from B. Find the modulus of elasticity of the strings.

8 A light elastic string AB, of natural length 1.2 m, is fixed at point A on a rough plane inclined at 30° to the horizontal. The string has modulus of elasticity 115 N. A particle of mass 2 kg is attached to end B and the particle is released from rest to descend the plane from A to C. The particle descends 1.45 m from A.

a Show that the coefficient of friction between the particle and the inclined plane is 0.456.

b Find the acceleration of the particle at C.

9 A car of mass 1500 kg moves along a straight horizontal road. The resistance to motion is constant, 750 N, and the car's engine is working at a constant rate of 19.5 kW.

a Find the acceleration of the car when the car's speed is 21.5 m s^{-1}.

The road now ascends a constant slope inclined at 5° to the horizontal. The car's engine continues working at 19.5 kW and the resistance to motion remains 750 N.

b Find the greatest steady speed of the car as it ascends the hill.

10 A car of mass 710 kg is ascending a hill inclined at 6° to the horizontal. The power exerted by the engine is 14 kW and the car has a constant speed of 18 m s^{-1}. It is assumed that resistance to motion is kv N, where v is the car's speed and k is a constant value.

a Show that $k \approx 2.8$.

The power of the engine is now increased to 17.5 kW.

b Calculate the maximum speed of the car while ascending the hill.

Section 4: Using vectors to calculate work done, kinetic energy and power

Force, displacement and velocity are all vector quantities. This means that you can use your ability to manipulate vectors to solve problems connected with work and energy.

> **Rewind**
>
> In Chapter 1 you learned about work, kinetic energy and the work–energy principle.

Using the scalar product to calculate work done by a constant force

If a constant force is directed at an angle θ to the direction of motion then:

work done = force $\times \cos\theta \times$ distance

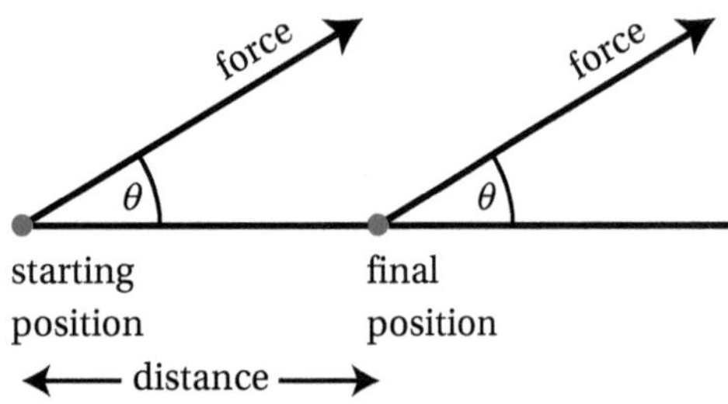

> **Tip**
>
> The work done by a force is a scalar quantity.

You can use the scalar product to find the work done by a force.

> **Key point 6.6**
>
> The work done by a constant force **F** that causes a displacement **x** is given by the formula:
>
> $$\text{work done} = \mathbf{F}\,.\,\mathbf{x} = (|\mathbf{F}|\cos\theta)(|\text{displacement}|)$$
>
> This is the scalar product of the force and displacement vectors.

> **Rewind**
>
> Remember the definition of the scalar product that you learned in Pure Core Student Book 1:
>
> $\mathbf{a}\,.\,\mathbf{b} = |\mathbf{a}|\,|\mathbf{b}|\cos\theta$, where θ is the angle between vectors **a** and **b**.

WORKED EXAMPLE 6.17

A force $(2\mathbf{i}+\mathbf{j})$ N is acting on an object that moves from A, with position vector $(3\mathbf{i}+\mathbf{j})$ m, to B with position vector $(4\mathbf{i}+2\mathbf{j})$ m. Find the work done by the force.

$\overrightarrow{AB} = (4\mathbf{i}+2\mathbf{j}) - (3\mathbf{i}+\mathbf{j}) = \mathbf{i}+\mathbf{j}$ m — Displacement = final position − starting position

Work done = force vector . displacement vector — Calculate the scalar product of force and displacement.

$= (2\mathbf{i}+\mathbf{j})\,.\,(\mathbf{i}+\mathbf{j})$

$= 2\times 1 + 1\times 1$ — Work done is a scalar quantity.

$= 3$ J

WORKED EXAMPLE 6.18

An object, of mass 2 kg, is at rest at A when a constant force $(2\mathbf{i} - \mathbf{j})$ N causes the object to move to B. A has position vector $(\mathbf{i} - 2\mathbf{j})$ m and B has position vector $(2\mathbf{i} - 6\mathbf{j})$ m. Given that no other forces act on the object, use the work-energy principle to find the speed of the object at B.

$\overrightarrow{AB} = \underline{i} - 4\underline{j}$ m — Displacement = final position – starting position

Work done = force vector . displacement vector — Calculate the work done by the force.

$= (2\underline{i} - \underline{j}) \cdot (\underline{i} - 4\underline{j})$

$= 2 \times 1 + (-1) \times (-4)$

$= 6$ J

Work done = increase in kinetic energy — The work-energy principle states that the work done by a propulsive force is equivalent to the increase in kinetic energy.

$6 = \frac{1}{2} \times 2 \times v^2$

$v^2 = 6$

$v = 2.45$ m s^{-1} (3 s.f.)

Tip

Work done on an object *by* a *propulsive* force is positive in sign.

Work done on an object *by* a *resistive* force is negative in sign.

WORKED EXAMPLE 6.19

A force $-3\mathbf{i} + 2\mathbf{j}$ N is acting on an object that moves from A, with position vector $\mathbf{i} - \mathbf{j}$ m, to B with position vector $5\mathbf{i} + 4\mathbf{j}$ m. Find the work done by the force and state whether the force is propulsive or resistive.

$\overrightarrow{AB} = (5\underline{i} + 4\underline{j}) - (\underline{i} - \underline{j}) = 4\underline{i} + 5\underline{j}$ m — Displacement = final position – starting position

Work done = force vector . displacement vector — Calculate the scalar product of force and displacement.

$= (-3\underline{i} + 2\underline{j}) \cdot (4\underline{i} + 5\underline{j})$

$= -3 \times 4 + 2 \times 5$ — Work done is negative in sign so the applied force is resistive.

$= -2$ J

Using the scalar product to calculate kinetic energy

You have previously learned how to calculate the kinetic energy of a moving body in terms of its speed. If instead of working with speed (a scalar quantity) you are working with a velocity (a vector quantity), you can calculate v^2 by using the scalar product.

$v^2 = \mathbf{v}.\mathbf{v}$ where **v** is the velocity vector.

This means that a velocity vector, rather than speed, can be used to calculate the kinetic energy of a moving object.

Rewind

In Chapter 1, Section 2, kinetic energy is defined as $\frac{1}{2}mv^2$, where m is mass and v is speed.

If mass is measured in kg and speed in m s^{-1} then kinetic energy is measured in joules (J).

Key point 6.7

The kinetic energy of an object of mass m kg moving with velocity **v** m s^{-1} is defined as

$$\text{kinetic energy} = \frac{1}{2}m(\mathbf{v}.\mathbf{v})$$

where **v**.**v** is the scalar product of velocity with itself.

Tip

Remember that we use bold letters to represent vectors and italic letters to represent their magnitudes; so v is the magnitude of **v**.

WORKED EXAMPLE 6.20

A rocket of mass 2 tonnes is moving with velocity $(2\mathbf{i} + 5\mathbf{j})\ \text{m s}^{-1}$. Find the kinetic energy of the rocket, giving your answer in kJ.

$v^2 = \underline{v}.\underline{v} = (2\underline{i} + 5\underline{j}).(2\underline{i} + 5\underline{j})$ — Find v^2 using the scalar product.

$v^2 = 2\times2 + 5\times5$

$= 29$

$\text{Kinetic energy} = \frac{1}{2}mv^2$ — 2 tonnes is 2000 kg.

$= \frac{1}{2}\times2000\times29$

$= 29\,000$ J or 29 kJ

Equations of motion can also be written in vector form, using scalar products.

Rewind

In A Level Mathematics Student Book 1, Chapter 20, you learned to use the formula for motion in a straight line with constant acceleration: $v^2 = u^2 + 2as$; where u and v represent starting and final velocity, a is constant acceleration and s is displacement.

Key point 6.8

If an object is moving with constant acceleration, **a**, then:

$$\mathbf{v}.\mathbf{v} = \mathbf{u}.\mathbf{u} + 2\,\mathbf{a}.\mathbf{s}$$

v, **u** and **s** represent final velocity, starting velocity and displacement, respectively, in vector form.

The formula can also be written: $v^2 = u^2 + 2\,\mathbf{a}.\mathbf{s}$

WORKED EXAMPLE 6.21

A small object of mass 500 g accelerates across a horizontal surface due to the action of a force that is acting at an angle to the resulting displacement. The driving force is $5\mathbf{i} + 3\mathbf{j}$ N, and the displacement is $65\mathbf{i} + 80\mathbf{j}$ m. Given that the starting speed is 4.5 m s^{-1}, find the final speed of the object.

$\begin{pmatrix} 5 \\ 3 \end{pmatrix} = 0.5 \times \underline{a}$ — Use $\mathbf{F} = m\mathbf{a}$ to find the acceleration vector.

$\underline{a} = \begin{pmatrix} 10 \\ 6 \end{pmatrix} \text{m s}^{-2}$

$v^2 = 4.5^2 + 2\begin{pmatrix} 10 \\ 6 \end{pmatrix} . \begin{pmatrix} 65 \\ 80 \end{pmatrix}$ — Substitute in the formula $v^2 = u^2 + 2\,\mathbf{a}\,.\,\mathbf{s}$

$v^2 = 20.25 + 2(10 \times 65 + 6 \times 80)$

$v^2 = 2280.25$

$v = 47.8 \text{ m s}^{-1}$ (3 s.f.)

Using the scalar product to calculate the power of a driving force

If driving force and velocity are both given in vector form, then power is the scalar product of the driving force and velocity vectors.

Rewind

In Chapter 1 you learned that power can be expressed as driving force × speed, given that the driving force is acting in the direction of motion.

Key point 6.9

The power of an engine producing a driving force **F** N on a vehicle moving with velocity **v** m s^{-1} can be calculated from the formula:

$$\text{power} = \mathbf{F}\,.\,\mathbf{v}$$

Tip

The power of a propulsive force acting on an object is positive in sign.

The power of a resistive force acting on an object is negative in sign.

WORKED EXAMPLE 6.22

A vehicle is moving under the action of a driving force $35\mathbf{i} - 60\mathbf{j}$ N in a horizontal plane with velocity $5\mathbf{i} - 7\mathbf{j}$ m s^{-1}. Given that no other forces are acting on the vehicle, find the power of the vehicle engine.

Power $= \underline{F} . \underline{v}$ — Use the formula for power using the scalar product **F** . **v**.

Power $= \begin{pmatrix} 35 \\ -60 \end{pmatrix} . \begin{pmatrix} 5 \\ -7 \end{pmatrix}$ — Evaluate the scalar product to find the power of the vehicle engine.

Power $= 35 \times 5 + (-60) \times (-7)$

$\Rightarrow$ Power $= 595$ W

WORKED EXAMPLE 6.23

A vehicle of mass 850 kg is moving in a horizontal plane, at time t seconds, $t \geqslant 0.5$, with velocity

$$3t\mathbf{i} - \sqrt{2t-1}\,\mathbf{j}\ \mathrm{m\,s^{-1}}$$

a Find the power, in kW, of the vehicle engine when $t = 5$.

b Find the work done, in kJ, by the vehicle engine between $t = 0.5$ and $t = 5$ seconds.

a $\underline{v} = 3t\underline{i} - \sqrt{2t-1}\,\underline{j}$

When $t = 5$, $\underline{v} = 15\underline{i} - 3\underline{j}$

Find the velocity of the vehicle when $t = 5$.

$\underline{a} = \dfrac{dv}{dt} = 3\underline{i} - \dfrac{1}{\sqrt{2t-1}}\underline{j}$

Differentiate v to find the acceleration vector.

$\underline{F} = m\underline{a}$

When $t = 5$, $\underline{F} = 850 \times 3\underline{i} + 850 \times \left(-\dfrac{1}{3}\right)\underline{j}$

$\Rightarrow \underline{F} = 2550\underline{i} - 283\dfrac{1}{3}\underline{j}$

Use $\mathbf{F} = m\mathbf{a}$ to find the tractive force of the vehicle engine when $t = 5$.

Power $= \underline{F}\,.\,\underline{v}$

Power $= \begin{pmatrix} 2550 \\ -283\frac{1}{3} \end{pmatrix} \cdot \begin{pmatrix} 15 \\ -3 \end{pmatrix}$

$\Rightarrow$ Power $= 39\,100$ W or 39.1 kW

Evaluate the scalar product to find the power of the vehicle engine.

b Net work done by propulsive force = increase in kinetic energy

The driving force is variable but the total work done can be calculated using the work-energy principle.

When $t = 0.5$ s, $\underline{v} = 1.5\underline{i}$

When $t = 5$ s, $\underline{v} = 15\underline{i} - 3\underline{j}$

Calculate the starting and final velocities.

Increase in KE $= 0.5m\,\underline{v}\,.\,\underline{v}$

$\Rightarrow$ Work done $= 0.5 \times 850 \times ((15^2 + 3^2) - (1.5^2))$

$= 98493.75$ J

$= 98.5$ kJ (3 s.f.)

EXERCISE 6D

1 **a** Calculate the work done when:

i a force $6\mathbf{i} + 8\mathbf{j}$ N causes a displacement of $50\mathbf{i} + 64\mathbf{j}$ m

ii a force $5\mathbf{i} - 2\mathbf{j}$ N causes a displacement of $10\mathbf{i} - 6\mathbf{j}$ m

iii a force $-6\mathbf{i} + 2\mathbf{j}$ N causes an object to move from A, with position vector $2\mathbf{i} + 8\mathbf{j}$ m, to B with position vector $-5\mathbf{i} + 12\mathbf{j}$ m.

b The work done by a force $a\mathbf{i} + 2a\mathbf{j}$ N causing a displacement $10\mathbf{i} + 15\mathbf{j}$ m is 220 J. Calculate a.

c The work done by a force $3\mathbf{i} + 4\mathbf{j}$ N causing a displacement $x\mathbf{i} - \mathbf{j}$ m is 56 J. Calculate x.

2 **a** Calculate the kinetic energy when:

i an object of mass 2.2 kg is moving with a velocity $-3\mathbf{i} + 2.5\mathbf{j}\ \text{m s}^{-1}$

ii an object of mass 1.5 kg is moving with velocity $5\mathbf{i} - 6\mathbf{j}\ \text{m s}^{-1}$.

b Use work and energy to calculate the final speed when:

i a particle having mass 0.8 kg and starting velocity $1.5\mathbf{i} + 2\mathbf{j}\ \text{m s}^{-1}$ is acted on by a force of $2\mathbf{i} - \mathbf{j}$ N causing a displacement of $2.5\mathbf{i} - 2\mathbf{j}$ m

ii a particle having mass 1.2 kg and starting velocity $0.8\mathbf{i} - 0.6\mathbf{j}\ \text{m s}^{-1}$ is acted on by a force of $3.5\mathbf{i} + 2\mathbf{j}$ N causing a displacement of $2\mathbf{i} + 0.9\mathbf{j}$ m.

c An object of mass 0.6 kg is moving with speed $3.5\ \text{m}^{-1}$ after being acted upon by a force of $0.5\mathbf{i} + 0.8\mathbf{j}$ N causing a displacement of $2\mathbf{i} + 2.5\mathbf{j}$ m. Find the starting speed of the object.

3 **a** Calculate the power when:

i an object acted on by a driving force of $2\mathbf{i} + 4\mathbf{j}$ N is travelling with velocity $3\mathbf{i} + 4\,\mathbf{j}\ \text{m s}^{-1}$

ii an object acted on by a driving force of $-1.5\mathbf{i} + 2.5\mathbf{j}$ N is travelling with velocity $1.5\mathbf{i} + 1.2\mathbf{j}\ \text{m s}^{-1}$.

b A particle acted on by a driving force of $x\mathbf{i} + 2.5\mathbf{j}$ N is moving with velocity $6\mathbf{i} - 3\mathbf{j}\ \text{m s}^{-1}$. Find the value of x, given the power is 4.5 W.

c A particle acted on by a driving force of $x\mathbf{i} + 3\mathbf{j}$ N is moving with velocity $x\mathbf{i} + 2x\mathbf{j}\ \text{m s}^{-1}$. Find possible values of x, given the power is 16 W.

4 An object is acted on by a force $2\mathbf{i} + 3\mathbf{j}$ N and is moving parallel to the vector $\mathbf{i} + 2\mathbf{j}$ m. Given the work done is 320 J, find the displacement vector.

5 A particle of mass 2 kg is displaced $50\mathbf{i} - 120\mathbf{j}$ m while moving with acceleration $3\mathbf{i} - 5\mathbf{j}\ \text{m s}^{-2}$. Find the change in kinetic energy due to action of the force.

6 A particle is displaced $-35\mathbf{i} + 85\mathbf{j}$ m while moving with acceleration $-7.5\mathbf{i} + 8.5\mathbf{j}\ \text{m s}^{-2}$. The starting velocity is $2\mathbf{i} + 7\mathbf{j}\ \text{m s}^{-1}$. Find the final speed of the particle.

7 A vehicle engine is providing a driving force of $300\mathbf{i} + 450\mathbf{j}$ N as the vehicle travels with velocity $9\mathbf{i} + 12\mathbf{j}\ \text{m s}^{-1}$. Find the power of the vehicle engine at this time.

8 A vehicle engine is providing a driving force of $500\mathbf{i} + 750\mathbf{j}$ N as the vehicle travels parallel to $\mathbf{i} + 2\mathbf{j}\ \text{m s}^{-1}$ with engine power 30.5 kW. Find the velocity of the vehicle.

9 A particle of mass 500 g is moving with velocity $2t\mathbf{i} + t^2\mathbf{j}$.

a Find the force acting on the particle when $t = 5$ s.

b Find the power exerted by the force when $t = 5$ s.

c Find the work done by the force between $t = 2$ and $t = 5$ s.

10 A particle of mass 2.5 kg at rest at $t = 0$ seconds is acted on by a force $(100t - 50)\mathbf{i} + 200\sqrt{t}\,\mathbf{j}$ N.

a Find the velocity of the particle when $t = 4$ seconds.

b Find the power exerted by the force when $t = 4$ seconds.

c Find the work done by the force between $t = 1$ and $t = 4$ seconds.

Checklist of learning and understanding

- For a variable force f(x) that depends on displacement, x, work done is defined as: $\int_{x_1}^{x_2} \mathrm{f}(x)\,\mathrm{d}x$
- Hooke's law for an elastic string or spring is: $T = \frac{\lambda x}{l}$ where λ is the modulus of elasticity
- Work done against elasticity is: $\frac{\lambda}{2l}\left(x_2^2 - x_1^2\right)$
- Elastic potential energy is: $\frac{\lambda x^2}{2l}$
- KE + GPE + EPE = constant
- Work done = $\mathbf{F}\,.\,\mathbf{x} = (|\mathbf{F}|\,|\mathbf{x}|\cos\theta)$, which is the scalar product of the force and displacement vectors
- Kinetic energy $= \frac{1}{2}m(\mathbf{v}\,.\,\mathbf{v})$ joules, where $\mathbf{v}\,.\,\mathbf{v}$ is the scalar product of velocity with itself
- When an object moves with constant acceleration: $\mathbf{v}\,.\,\mathbf{v} = \mathbf{u}\,.\,\mathbf{u} + 2\,\mathbf{a}\,.\,\mathbf{s}$
- Power = $\mathbf{F}\,.\,\mathbf{v}$, the scalar product of vector force and vector velocity

Mixed practice 6

1. An object, O, moves under the action of a force, $\mathbf{F} = 2\mathbf{i} + 5\mathbf{j}$ N. O is displaced from A, having position vector $-2\mathbf{i} + 2\mathbf{j}$ m, to B, having position vector $4\mathbf{i} + 9\mathbf{j}$ m. Calculate the change in kinetic energy of O as it moves from A to B.

2. A body, M, of mass 2.5 kg moves under the action of a force $\mathbf{F}$. At time t seconds, the velocity of M is $\mathbf{v}$ m s^{-1}, where $\mathbf{v} = 2t\mathbf{i} + t^2\mathbf{j}$, $t \geqslant 0$.

   a Find $\mathbf{F}$ in terms of t.

   b Calculate the rate at which the force is working when $t = 2$.

   c By considering the change in kinetic energy of M, calculate the work done by the force $\mathbf{F}$ during the time interval $0 \leqslant t \leqslant 2$.

3. A body P, of mass 5 kg, moves under the action of a force $\frac{4}{t}\mathbf{i} + 2t\mathbf{j}$ N, at time t seconds where $t \geqslant 1$. When $t = 1$, P's velocity is $0.2\mathbf{j}$ m s^{-1}.

   a Determine the acceleration of P.

   b Determine the velocity of P when $t = 2$.

   c Calculate the rate at which the force is working when $t = 2$, giving your answer to 1 decimal place.

4. A small object W of weight 100 N is attached to one end of each of two parallel light elastic strings. One string is of natural length 0.4 m and has modulus of elasticity 20 N; the other string is of natural length 0.6 m and has modulus of elasticity 30 N. The upper ends of both strings are attached to a horizontal ceiling and W hangs in equilibrium at a distance d m below the ceiling (see diagram). Find d.

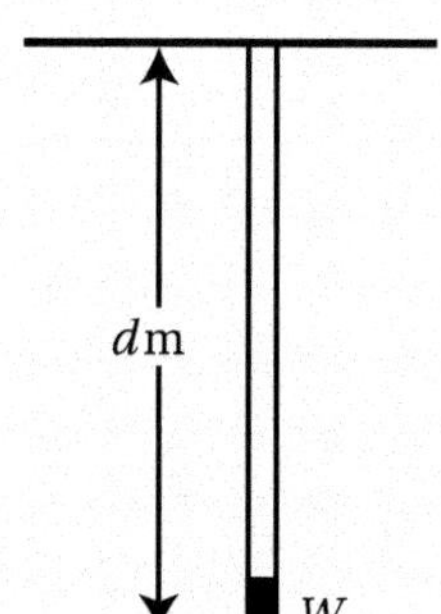

5. A particle of mass 2.5 kg moves in the x–y plane with acceleration $7e^{-t}\mathbf{i} + 2t\mathbf{j}$ m s^{-2}.

   a Find the force $\mathbf{F}$ acting on the particle when $t = 1.5$ seconds, giving your answer to 3 significant figures.

   When $t = 0$ the particle has velocity $3\mathbf{j}$ m s^{-1}.

   b Find the power of force $\mathbf{F}$ when $t = 1.5$ seconds, giving your answer to 3 significant figures.

6. A particle P of mass m kg is attached to one end of a light elastic string of natural length 1.8 m and modulus of elasticity $1.35mg$ N. The other end of the string is attached to a fixed point O on a smooth horizontal surface. P is held at rest at a point on the surface 3 m from O. The particle is then released. Find

   i the initial acceleration of P,

   ii the speed of P at the instant the string becomes slack.

7 One end of a light elastic string, of natural length 0.6 m and modulus of elasticity 30 N, is attached to a fixed point O. A particle P of weight 48 N is attached to the other end of the string. P is released from rest at a point d m vertically below O. Subsequently P just reaches O.

i Find d.

ii Find the magnitude and direction of the acceleration of P when it has travelled 1.3 m from its point of release.

8 One end of a light elastic string, of natural length 0.75 m and modulus of elasticity 44.1 N, is attached to a fixed point O. A particle P of mass 1.8 kg is attached to the other end of the string. P is released from rest at O and falls vertically. Assuming there is no air resistance, find

i the extension of the string when P is at its lowest position,

ii the acceleration of P at its lowest position.

9 One end of a light elastic string, of natural length 0.78 m and modulus of elasticity 0.8 mg N, is attached to a fixed point O on a smooth plane inclined at an angle α to the horizontal, where $\sin\alpha = \frac{5}{13}$. A particle P of mass m kg is attached to the other end of the string. P is released from rest at O and moves down the plane without reaching the bottom. Find

i the maximum speed of P in the subsequent motion,

ii the distance of P from O when it is at its lowest point.

10 A particle P, of mass 2.5 kg, is in equilibrium suspended from a fixed point A by a light elastic string of natural length 3 m and modulus of elasticity 36.75 N. Another particle Q, of mass 1 kg, is released from rest at A and falls freely until it reaches P and becomes attached to it.

i Show that the speed of the combined particles, immediately after Q becomes attached to P, is $2\sqrt{2}$ m s^{-1}.

The combined particles fall a further distance X m before coming to instantaneous rest.

ii Find a quadratic equation satisfied by X, and show that it simplifies to $35X^2 - 56X - 80 = 0$.

11 A light elastic string of natural length 1.6 m has modulus of elasticity 120 N. One end of the string is attached to a fixed point O and the other end is attached to a particle P of weight 1.5 N. The particle is released from rest at the point A, which is 2.1 m vertically below O. It comes instantaneously to rest at B, which is vertically above O.

i Verify that the distance AB is 4 m.

ii Find the maximum speed of P during its upward motion from A to B.

12 A vehicle of mass 750 kg is supplied with a constant power of 8 kW to move it along a straight horizontal road against a variable force that may be approximated as $\frac{8500}{x}$ N, where x represents the distance from a fixed point O on the road and $x \geqslant 50$ m. Initially the vehicle is at A, 50 m from O, travelling with speed 6.5 m s^{-1}. After T seconds, the vehicle is at B, 80 m from O, travelling with speed 9.5 m s^{-1}. Find the value of T.

13 A vehicle of mass 950 kg moves along a horizontal road with driving force 525 N. It starts from rest and experiences a resistance to motion of $2.1x$ N. Find the speed of the vehicle after it has travelled 100 m.

14 A truck of mass 32 tonnes experiences a resistance to motion of $2400x$ N, where x is the distance travelled after the brakes are applied. The truck is travelling at 45 km h^{-1} when the driver applies the brakes with a constant braking force of 9800 N. Find how far the truck travels before coming to rest.

 15

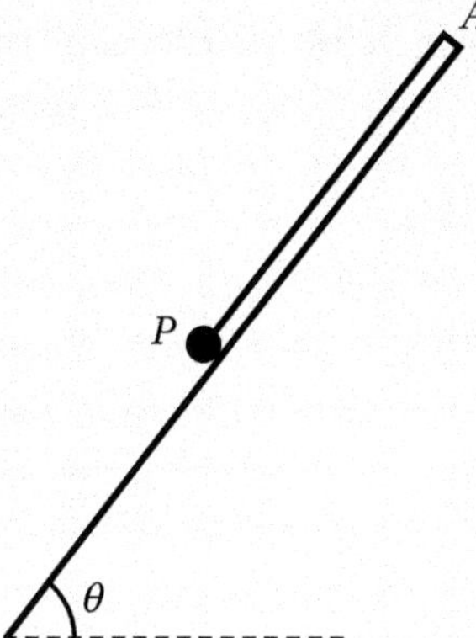

A particle P, of mass 3.5 kg, is in equilibrium suspended from the top A of a smooth slope inclined at an angle θ to the horizontal, where $\sin\theta = \frac{40}{49}$, by an elastic rope of natural length 4 m and modulus of elasticity 112 N (see diagram). Another particle Q, of mass 0.5 kg, is released from rest at A and slides freely downwards until it reaches P and becomes attached to it.

i Find the value of V^2, where V m s^{-1} is the speed of Q immediately before it becomes attached to P, and show that the speed of the combined particles, immediately after Q becomes attached to P, is $\frac{1}{2}\sqrt{5}$ m s^{-1}.

The combined particles slide downwards for a distance of X m, before coming instantaneously to rest at B.

ii Show that $28X^2 - 8X - 5 = 0$.

16 A bungee jumper of weight W N is joined to a fixed point O by a light elastic rope of natural length 20 m and modulus of elasticity 32 000 N. The jumper starts from rest at O and falls vertically. The jumper is modelled as a particle and air resistance is ignored.

i Given that the jumper just reaches a point 25 m below O, find the value of W.

ii Find the maximum speed reached by the jumper.

iii Find the maximum value of the deceleration of the jumper during the downward motion.

  A particle of mass 0.8 kg is attached to one end of a light elastic string of natural length 2 m and modulus of elasticity 20 N. The other end of the string is attached to a fixed point O. The particle is held at rest at O and then released. When the extension of the string is x m, the particle is moving with speed v m s^{-1}.

i By considering energy show that $v^2 = 39.2 + 19.6x - 12.5x^2$.

ii Hence find

a the maximum extension of the string,

b the maximum speed of the particle,

c the maximum magnitude of the acceleration of the particle.

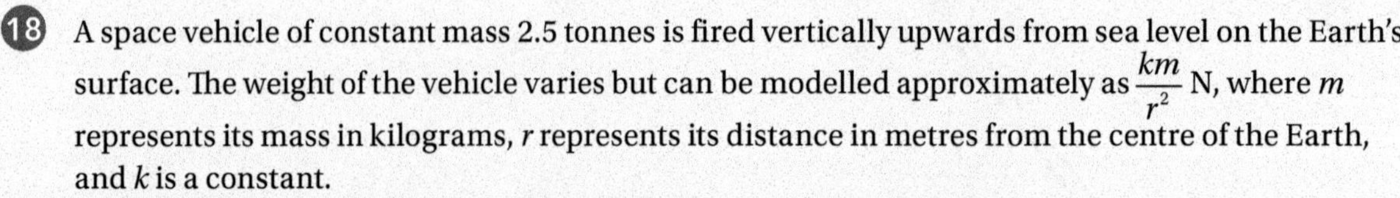

18 A space vehicle of constant mass 2.5 tonnes is fired vertically upwards from sea level on the Earth's surface. The weight of the vehicle varies but can be modelled approximately as $\frac{km}{r^2}$ N, where m represents its mass in kilograms, r represents its distance in metres from the centre of the Earth, and k is a constant.

a Explain why $mg = \frac{km}{r^2}$, where R is the radius of the Earth in metres.

b Given that the radius of the Earth is approximately 6.37×10^6 m, find an approximate value for k.

c Find an approximation for the work done against gravity by the rocket in propelling the space vehicle as it climbs from sea level to a height of 100 km above sea level.

19 A particle P of mass m kg has the following displacement vector relative to an origin O given by:

$r \cos \omega t\ \mathbf{i} + r \sin \omega t\ \mathbf{j}$ m

a Derive an expression for **F**, the force acting on particle P.

b Find an expression for the magnitude of **F**.

c Use the scalar product $\mathbf{v} \cdot \mathbf{v}$ to find the kinetic energy of particle P.

d Show that the power of force **F** is zero for all values of t.

7 Linear motion under variable force

A This chapter is for A Level students only.

In this chapter you will learn how to:

- solve equations of motion of a particle when the **velocity** is given as a function of **displacement**
- solve equations of motion of a particle when the **acceleration** is a function of **velocity** or **displacement**
- use connected rates of change to solve linear motion problems
- set up and solve problems which can be modelled as linear motion of a particle acting under a variable force.

Before you start…

A Level Mathematics Student Book 1	You should be able to calculate the force acting on a particle moving in a straight line.	1 A particle of mass 3 kg is moving in a straight line along a smooth plane with constant acceleration $4\ \text{m s}^{-2}$. Calculate the force acting on the particle.
A Level Mathematics Student Book 2	You should know the relationship between acceleration (a), velocity (v) and displacement (x) for variable acceleration as a function of time.	2 A particle P is moving along the x-axis in the positive x-direction. At time t seconds the particle is x metres from the origin and its velocity is given by $v = 5e^{-0.5t}$ for $t \geqslant 0$. When $t = 0$, P is 3 m from the origin. a Find the magnitude and direction of the acceleration when $t = 2$. b Find the displacement of P when $t = 10$.
A Level Mathematics Student Book 2	You should be able to separate variables to solve differential equations.	3 Solve the differential equation $\frac{dy}{dx} = \frac{\sin x}{y^2}$.
Chapter 3	You should be able to use the impulse and conservation of linear momentum formulae for two particles colliding.	4 A particle of mass 10 kg is moving with a constant speed of $3\ \text{m s}^{-1}$ when it hits a stationary particle of mass 3 kg. After impact both particles move in the same direction with speed $v\ \text{m s}^{-1}$. a Find speed of each particle after impact. b Find the magnitude of the impulse given to the stationary particle.
Pure Core Student Book 2	You should be able to use an integrating factor to solve linear differential equations.	5 Find the particular solution, given that when $x = 0$, $y = 5$, for $\frac{dy}{dx} + 8y = x^2$

Why do we need to study variable force?

In A Level Mathematics you extended your work on linear motion of particles to include variable acceleration, where acceleration, velocity and displacement all vary with time. This enabled you to solve problems using connections in the rates of change, as shown here.

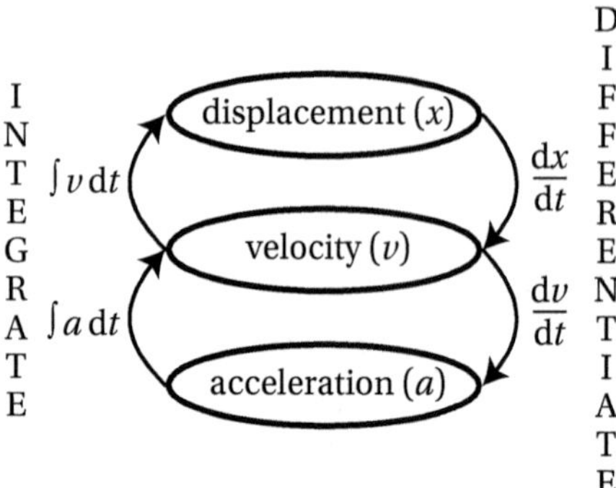

By Newton's second law of motion you know that $F = ma$, and consequently, if acceleration varies with time, then force also varies with time. This enables you to work with force as a function of time in linear motion.

Acceleration, velocity, displacement and force are not always defined as a function of time. For example, the force of gravity acting on a rocket as it leaves the Earth decreases with displacement, the force between two charged particles varies with their distance apart, and the force in a stretched string or compressed spring depends on the displacement. This means that you will need to revisit a mathematical model given for a particular situation and apply your knowledge of connected rates of change for problems that can be modelled as linear motion under variable force.

Section 1 extends the work on variable acceleration that you have completed at A Level.

Section 2 uses all the processes developed in Section 1 and brings in Newton's second law.

Section 1: Working with acceleration, velocity and displacement

When acceleration, $a(t)$, velocity, $v(t)$, and displacement, $x(t)$, are given as functions of time you can use the following formulae to solve problems:

$$v = \frac{\mathrm{d}x}{\mathrm{d}t}$$

$$a = \frac{\mathrm{d}v}{\mathrm{d}t} = \frac{\mathrm{d}^2x}{\mathrm{d}t^2}$$

$$v = \int a\,\mathrm{d}t$$

$$x = \int v\,\mathrm{d}t$$

However, sometimes acceleration and velocity are functions of displacement, for example when using Hooke's law. This means that these relationships cannot be applied in the same way.

 **Rewind**

You worked with Hooke's law in Chapter 6.

Velocity as a function of displacement

When velocity is given as a function of displacement, $v(x)$, you can find the associated acceleration function by differentiating with respect to t. You can use the chain rule to derive a relationship for a:

$$a=\frac{\mathrm{d}}{\mathrm{d}t}[v(x)]=\frac{\mathrm{d}v}{\mathrm{d}x}\times\frac{\mathrm{d}x}{\mathrm{d}t}$$

and given that $v=\frac{\mathrm{d}x}{\mathrm{d}t}$, $a=v\frac{\mathrm{d}v}{\mathrm{d}x}$.

Related rates of change are dealt with in A Level Mathematics Student Book 2.

 **Key point 7.1**

When velocity is given as a function of displacement, you can use the relationship:

$$a=v\frac{\mathrm{d}v}{\mathrm{d}x}$$

to find an expression for acceleration.

WORKED EXAMPLE 7.1

A particle P is travelling along the x-axis in the positive x-direction with velocity $v=5\mathrm{e}^{-0.5x}$. Given that x measures the displacement from the origin, find:

a the velocity when $x=5$ m

b the magnitude and direction of the acceleration when $x=0$ m

c the displacement when $v=3$ m s^{-1}.

a $v=5e^{-0.5\times5}$

$v=0.410$ m s^{-1} (3 s.f.)

b $a=v\frac{dv}{dx}$

Velocity is given in terms of displacement, so you can use the formula in Key point 7.1 to find a.

$\frac{dv}{dx}=-2.5e^{-0.5x}$

To use the formula you need to find $\frac{\mathrm{d}v}{\mathrm{d}x}$.

$a=5e^{-0.5x}\times-2.5e^{-0.5x}=-12.5e^{-x}$

When $x=0$, $a=-12.5$

Hence the magnitude of a is 12.5 m s^{-2}.

Acceleration is in the negative x-direction.

c $3=5e^{-0.5x}$

$\ln\frac{3}{5}=-0.5x$

$x=2\ln\frac{5}{3}$

$x=1.02$ m (3 s.f.)

Given that velocity is a function of displacement $v(x)$ and that $v=\frac{\mathrm{d}x}{\mathrm{d}t}$, we can use these to find a relationship between time and displacement, via velocity:

$$v(x)=\frac{\mathrm{d}x}{\mathrm{d}t}$$

Separating variables gives $\int 1\,\mathrm{d}t=\int \frac{1}{v(x)}\mathrm{d}x$.

Hence $t=\int \frac{1}{v(x)}\mathrm{d}x$.

Rewind

Separation of variables is dealt with in A Level Mathematics Student Book 2.

Key point 7.2

If velocity is a function of displacement then:

$$t=\int \frac{1}{v(x)}\mathrm{d}x$$

WORKED EXAMPLE 7.2

A particle P is moving along the x-axis in the positive x-direction. Initially the particle is 4 m from the origin. The velocity of P is given by $v=x^2-3x$ where x is the displacement in metres from the origin.

a Find the time at which P is 10 m from the origin.
b Find x as a function of t.

a $t=\int \frac{1}{v(x)}\mathrm{d}x$

The velocity is given as a function of displacement and we wish to find a time so we can use the formula given in Key point 7.2.

$t=\int \frac{1}{x^2-3x}\mathrm{d}x$

Integrals of this form require the use of partial fractions.

$\frac{1}{x^2-3x}=\frac{A}{x}+\frac{B}{x-3}$

Equating the numerators:

$1=A(x-3)+B(x)$

$x=3$ gives $B=\frac{1}{3}$

$x=0$ gives $A=-\frac{1}{3}$

Hence $\frac{1}{x^2-3x}=\frac{1}{3}\left(-\frac{1}{x}+\frac{1}{x-3}\right)$

$t=\frac{1}{3}\int -\frac{1}{x}+\frac{1}{x-3}\mathrm{d}x$

$t=\frac{1}{3}(-\ln|x|+\ln|x-3|)+c$

Continues on next page ...

When $t=0, x=4$

Hence:

$0=\frac{1}{3}(-\ln 4+\ln(4-3))+c$

$0=-\frac{1}{3}\ln 4+c$

$c=\frac{1}{3}\ln 4$

Substitute in the boundary condition to find the value of the constant. Since $x=4$ at $t=0$, we will choose the modulus in the logarithm functions to be $\ln(x-3)$ and $\ln x$. However, this does mean our solution is only valid for $x>3$.

$t=\frac{1}{3}(-\ln x+\ln(x-3)+\ln 4)$

$t=\frac{1}{3}(-\ln 10+\ln(10-3)+\ln 4)$

We can use the laws of logarithms to help simplify the right-hand side.

$t=\frac{1}{3}\ln\frac{28}{10}$

$t=0.343$ s (3 s.f.)

b $3t=\ln\left|\frac{4(x-3)}{x}\right|$

We can use inverse function for natural logarithm to rearrange to make x the subject.

$e^{3t}=\frac{4(x-3)}{x}$

$xe^{3t}=4x-12$

$4x-xe^{3t}=12$

$x=\frac{12}{4-e^{3t}}$

This solution is only valid for $0 \leqslant t < \frac{(\ln 4)}{3}$. As t increases (remembering that we are talking about motion) the velocity tends to infinity as t tends to $\frac{(\ln 4)}{3}$.

Tip

When working with the logarithm functions as the result of an integral, we need to correctly identify the branch of the result we need. This then gives conditions on when the solution we have found is valid.

Acceleration as a function of displacement

When acceleration is given as a function of displacement, $a(x)$, you can use the relationship from Key point 7.1, $a=v\frac{dv}{dx}$, to find velocity as a function of displacement.

Starting with $a(x)=v\frac{dv}{dx}$ you can separate variables to give:

$$\int v\,dv=\int a(x)\,dx$$

Hence $\frac{1}{2}v^2=\int a(x)\,dx$.

You can then rearrange to make v the subject.

Key point 7.3

If acceleration is given as a function of displacement then:

$$\frac{1}{2}v^2=\int a(x)\,dx$$

WORKED EXAMPLE 7.3

The acceleration of a particle moving in a straight line is given by $a = 2x + 12$. The particle is travelling along the x-axis in the positive x-direction and initially $x = 4$ and $v = 10\sqrt{2}$.

a Find an expression for v as a function of x.
b Find an expression for t as a function of x.

a $\frac{1}{2}v^2 = \int 2x + 12\,dx$

The acceleration is given as a function of displacement and you want to find the velocity, so you can use the formula given in Key point 7.3.

$\frac{1}{2}v^2 = x^2 + 12x + c$

$\frac{1}{2}(10\sqrt{2})^2 = 4^2 + 12 \times 4 + c$

$c = 36$

In order to find an expression for v as a function of x you need to substitute in the boundary condition to find the value of c.

$\frac{1}{2}v^2 = x^2 + 12x + 36$

$\frac{1}{2}v^2 = (x+6)^2$

In order to rearrange to make v the subject you need to square root the function in x. However, you can see it is a perfect square.

$v^2 = 2(x+6)^2$

$v = \sqrt{2}(x+6)$

Only the positive solution is required because the particle is moving in the positive x-direction.

b $\frac{dx}{dt} = \sqrt{2}(x+6)$

Recall that $v = \frac{dx}{dt}$.

$\int \frac{1}{x+6}\,dx = \int \sqrt{2}\,dt$

In order to perform this integration, you need to separate variables.

$\sqrt{2}t = \ln|x+6| + c$

$t = \frac{1}{\sqrt{2}}\ln|x+6| + b$

$0 = \frac{1}{\sqrt{2}}\ln|10| + b$

$b = -\frac{1}{\sqrt{2}}\ln 10$

In order to find an expression for t as a function of x you need to substitute in the boundary condition to find the value of b.

$t = \frac{1}{\sqrt{2}}\ln|x+6| - \frac{1}{\sqrt{2}}\ln 10$

$t = \frac{1}{\sqrt{2}}\ln\left|\frac{x+6}{10}\right|$

Acceleration as a function of velocity

When acceleration is given as a function of velocity, $a(v)$, you can use $a(v) = \frac{dv}{dt}$ to find t in terms of v by separating variables: $\int 1\,dt = \int \frac{1}{a(v)}\,dv$

Key point 7.4

If acceleration is given as a function of velocity then:

$$t = \int \frac{1}{a(v)} \, dv$$

WORKED EXAMPLE 7.4

A particle starts moving from $x = 3$ m along the x-axis in the positive x-direction. At $t = 10$ s it is travelling at 6 m s^{-1}. Given that its acceleration is $a = \frac{9}{v^2}$ with a direction towards the origin and $t < 36$:

a find the initial velocity of the particle

b express its displacement as a function of time.

a $t = \int \frac{1}{a(v)} \, dv$

The acceleration is given as a function of velocity and you wish to find the initial velocity. So, you can relate the acceleration to time by using the formula given in Key point 7.4.

$t = -\frac{1}{9} \int v^2 \, dv$

$t = -\frac{1}{9}\left(\frac{1}{3}v^3\right) + c$

You are told that the direction of acceleration is towards the origin so $a = -\frac{9}{v^2}$.

$t = -\frac{v^3}{27} + c$

$10 = -\frac{1}{27}(6)^3 + c$

$c = 18$

Substitute in the boundary condition to evaluate c.

Hence $t = 18 - \frac{v^3}{27}$

$0 = 18 - \frac{v^3}{27}$

$18 = \frac{v^3}{27}$

$v = 7.86$ m s^{-1} (3 s.f.)

Substitute in $t = 0$ and solve to find the initial velocity.

b $t = 18 - \frac{v^3}{27}$

$-27(t - 18) = v^3$

$v = 3\sqrt[3]{18 - t} = 3(18 - t)^{\frac{1}{3}}$

You want to find displacement as a function of time, so you can use $v = \frac{dx}{dt}$ to relate the function you have found to displacement.

$\frac{dx}{dt} = 3(18 - t)^{\frac{1}{3}}$

$x = 3\int (18 - t)^{\frac{1}{3}} \, dt$

You can integrate with respect to t to find an expression for x.

$x = 3\frac{-1(18 - t)^{\frac{4}{3}}}{\frac{4}{3}} + c$

$x = \frac{-9(18 - t)^{\frac{4}{3}}}{4} + c$

$3 = \frac{-9(18)^{\frac{4}{3}}}{4} + c$

To find c, substitute the boundary conditions, $t = 0$ and $x = 3$.

$c = 3 + \frac{9}{4}(18)^{\frac{4}{3}}$

$x = 3 + \frac{9}{4}\left(18^{\frac{4}{3}} - (18 - t)^{\frac{4}{3}}\right)$

Substitute for c and simplify to express displacement as a function of time.

An alternative approach when acceleration is given as a function of velocity is to use $a(v)=v\frac{dv}{dx}$ from Key point 7.1.
After separating variables:

$$\int 1\,dx=\int\frac{v}{a(v)}\,dv$$

You can then find x in terms of v.

Key point 7.5

If acceleration is given as a function of velocity then:

$$x=\int\frac{v}{a(v)}\,dv$$

WORKED EXAMPLE 7.5

A particle P is travels along the x-axis in the positive x-direction after starting at the origin at rest. Its acceleration is given by $a=4-v^2$ m s^{-2}.

a Find the displacement from the x-axis when P is travelling at 1 m s^{-1}.
b Find the velocity of P as x tends to infinity.

a $x=\int\frac{v}{a(v)}dv$

The acceleration is given as a function of velocity and you wish to find the displacement. You can use the formula given in Key point 7.5.

$x=\int\frac{v}{4-v^2}dv+c$

$x=-\frac{1}{2}\ln|4-v^2|+c$

Recognise that this integral is of the form $\int\frac{f'(x)}{f(x)}dx$ and hence find by inspection.

When $x=0$, $v=0$

Hence $0=-\frac{1}{2}\ln|4-0^2|+c$

$c=\frac{1}{2}\ln 4=\ln 2$

Substitute in the boundary conditions to find the unknown value c.

$x=\ln 2-\frac{1}{2}\ln|4-v^2|$

$x=\ln 2-\frac{1}{2}\ln|4-1^2|$

$x=\ln 2-\frac{1}{2}\ln|3|$

$x=0.144$ m (3 s.f.)

Substitute $v=1$ to calculate displacement from the origin.

b $x=\ln\left|\frac{2}{\sqrt{4-v^2}}\right|$

$e^x=\frac{2}{\sqrt{4-v^2}}$

$e^{2x}=\frac{4}{4-v^2}$

$4-v^2=4e^{-2x}$

Rearrange to make v the subject.

Continues on next page ...

$v^2 = 4(1 - e^{-2x})$

$v = 2\sqrt{1 - e^{-2x}}$

Only the positive solution is required.

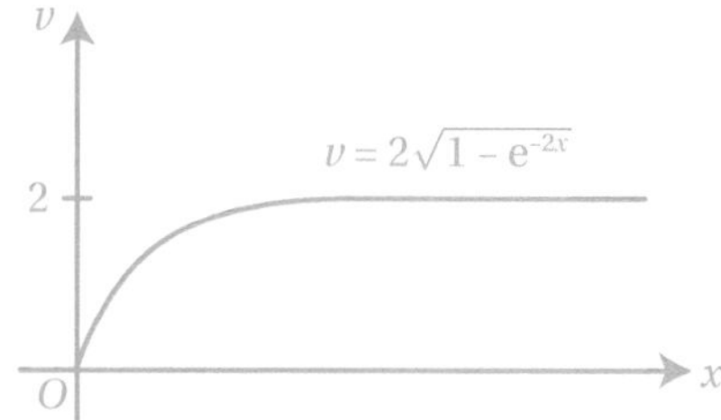

As x tends to infinity, the velocity tends to 2 m s^{-1}.

This is because as $x \to \infty$, $e^{-2x} \to 0$

Hence $v \to 2\sqrt{1} = 2$

EXERCISE 7A

Q1–11 all involve a particle moving along the x-axis in the positive x-direction. Assume that all units are SI units.

1 Given $v = f(x)$, find a general expression for t in terms of x when:

a $f(x) = \frac{1}{x^2}$ **b** $f(x) = \frac{1}{2 + \sin^2 x}$

2 Given $a = f(x)$, find a general expression for v^2 in terms of x when:

a $f(x) = 20 - 4x$ **b** $f(x) = x\,e^x$

3 Given $a = f(v)$, find a general expression for t in terms of v when:

a $f(v) = 4v - v^3$ **b** $f(v) = \sqrt{1 - v^2}$

4 Given $a = f(v)$, find a general expression for x in terms of v when:

a $f(v) = \frac{1}{v^2 - 4}$ **b** $f(v) = \sec v$

5 Given $v = f(x)$, find a general expression for a in terms of x when:

a $f(x) = 6x - \frac{1}{x^3}$ **b** $f(x) = e^{x^2 - 1}$

6 Given $v = \frac{3}{2}x - 5$, what is a when $x = 5$ m?

7 Given $a = \frac{1}{2v - 3}$ and when $t = 2$ s, $v = 0\text{ m s}^{-1}$, what is t when $v = 4\text{ m s}^{-1}$?

8 Given $a = e^{2x}$, and when $x = 0$ m, then $v = 1\text{ m s}^{-1}$, what is the velocity when $x = 2$ m?

9 Given $a = v$, and when $t = 5$ s, $v = 1$ m s^{-1}, what is v when $t = 1$ s?

10 Given $v = \operatorname{cosec} x$ and when $t = 5$ s, $x = 0$ m, find t when $x = \frac{\pi}{2}$ m.

11 Given $a = x^2 + 5$ and $v = 2$ m s^{-1} when $x = 0$ m, find v when $x = 10$ m.

12 A particle P is moving along the x-axis in the positive x-direction. The particle is initially at the origin and at time t seconds the particle is x m from the origin. The particle is accelerating in the positive x-direction with $a = 25 - \frac{1}{5}x$ m s^{-2}.

a State, giving a reason for your answer, the value of x at which the maximum speed of P occurs.

b Given that the maximum speed of P is 8 m s^{-1}, find an expression for v^2 in terms of x.

13 A particle is moving along the x-axis in the positive x-direction. After 5 seconds the particle passes through the origin and its velocity is given by $v = \frac{4}{x^2}$ m s^{-1}.

a Find the distance and direction of the particle from the origin when the particle is accelerating at 1 m s^{-2}.

b Find the time taken for the particle to travel from the origin to 10 m in the positive x-direction.

Tip

Recall that expressions involving products can often be integrated using integration by parts.

14 A particle P is moving along the x-axis in the positive x-direction. At $x = 5$ m, the particle is travelling at 2 m s^{-1}. Acceleration is given by $a = 2v$. Find the displacement of P when it is travelling at 5 m s^{-1}.

15 A particle P is travelling in a straight line away from a fixed point O. At time t the particle is x m from O and travelling with velocity given by $v = 20 - x - x^2$. After 5 seconds P is -0.5 m from the fixed point O.

a State the magnitude and direction of the acceleration for P when it is 2 m away from O.

b Express x as a function of t.

c State a bound on the distance P travels from O, giving reasons for your answer.

Tip

Recall that integrals with a factorisable polynomial denominator require splitting into partial fractions in order to integrate.

16 A particle P moves right and left along the x-axis periodically with maximum displacement 5 m from the origin. Its velocity changes based on its displacement. Suggest a function that could model this movement and hence find general expressions for its acceleration with respect to x and velocity with respect to time.

Explore

Underground Mathematics has reproduced some examples of exam questions from the Cambridge Assessment Group Archives. Have a go at this question from 1966: www.cambridge.org/links/moscmec6003

Section 2: Variable force

In Section 1 you worked with variable acceleration to solve kinematic problems. This was an extension to the work you completed in A Level Mathematics on variable acceleration. In this section, you will use the relationships found in Section 1 to solve problems involving forces using Newton's second law.

Since the mass of an object will be assumed constant in this section, the theory of variable acceleration extends naturally to an object moving under a variable force.

Force as a function of time

For a particle of mass m travelling in a horizontal line acting under a force, $F(t)$, you can use Newton's second law $F = ma$ and knowledge of connected rates of change to form a differential equation.

$F = ma$ and $a = \frac{\mathrm{d}v}{\mathrm{d}t}$

$$F(t) = m\frac{\mathrm{d}v}{\mathrm{d}t}$$

Separating variables gives $\int F(t)\,\mathrm{d}t = \int m\,\mathrm{d}v$

Hence $mv = \int F(t)\,\mathrm{d}t$

Fast forward

Integrating a force over a time period gives rise to a change in momentum, which is equal to an impulse. You will study this in Chapter 8.

Key point 7.6

If force is given as a function of time, using Newton's second law and $a = \frac{\mathrm{d}v}{\mathrm{d}t}$ you can find the velocity of the particle using:

$$v = \frac{1}{m}\int F(t)\,\mathrm{d}t$$

WORKED EXAMPLE 7.6

A particle P of mass 2 kg starts at the origin and travels along the x-axis in the positive x-direction with initial speed $v = 2\text{ m s}^{-1}$. At time t seconds the particle is x m from the origin, and for $0 \leqslant t \leqslant 5$ a single force acts against the direction of motion magnitude $F = \mathrm{e}^{-2t}$ N.

a Find the velocity of P when $t = 5$ s.

b Find the displacement of P when $t = 4$ s.

Continues on next page ...

a $v = \frac{1}{2}\int -e^{-2t}\,dt$

$v = \frac{1}{4}e^{-2t} + c$

You have the force given as a function of time, so you can use Key point 7.6, noting that the force is acting in the opposite direction.

When $t = 0$, $v = 2$

Hence $2 = \frac{1}{4} + c$

Substitute in the boundary condition to evaluate c.

$c = \frac{7}{4}$

$v = \frac{1}{4}e^{-2t} + \frac{7}{4}$

You now have the equation for v as a function of t.

$v = \frac{1}{4}e^{-10} + \frac{7}{4}$

Substitute $t = 5$.

$v = 1.75\ \text{m s}^{-1}$ (3 s.f.)

b $\frac{dx}{dt} = \frac{1}{4}e^{-2t} + \frac{7}{4}$

You want to find the displacement and your function from part **a** relates velocity to time. Use $v = \frac{dx}{dt}$ to relate displacement to time.

$\int dx = \int \frac{1}{4}e^{-2t} + \frac{7}{4}\,dt$

Integrate.

$x = -\frac{1}{8}e^{-2t} + \frac{7}{4}t + d$

When $t = 0$, $x = 0$

Hence $0 = -\frac{1}{8} + d$

Substitute in the boundary condition to evaluate d.

$d = \frac{1}{8}$

$x = -\frac{1}{8}e^{-2t} + \frac{7}{4}t + \frac{1}{8}$

You now have the equation for x as a function of t.

$x = -\frac{1}{8}e^{-8} + 7 + \frac{1}{8}$

Substitute $t = 4$.

$x = 7.12$ m (3 s.f.)

Force as a function of displacement

Using $F = ma$ and $a = v\frac{dv}{dx}$ you get $F(x) = mv\frac{dv}{dx}$.

Separating variables gives $\int F(x)\,dx = \int mv\,dv = \frac{1}{2}mv^2$.

Key point 7.7

$$\tfrac{1}{2}mv^2 = \int F(x)\,dx$$

To find velocity as a function of displacement, rearrange to make v the subject.

Rewind

This links the change in kinetic energy to the work done by or against a variable force, as seen in Chapter 6.

WORKED EXAMPLE 7.7

A particle P of mass 500 g is initially at rest at the origin and then moves along the x-axis in the positive x-direction under the action of a single force. When OP is x m the force is given by $F = \sin x$ N.

a Show that $v^2 = 4(1 - \cos x)$.

b Calculate the maximum speed reached by P.

a $m = 0.5$ kg

$\frac{1}{2}mv^2 = \int F(x)\,dx$

$0.25v^2 = \int \sin x\,dx$

Make sure units are the correct standard units.

Since you are given the force as a function of displacement you can use Key point 7.7.

$0.25v^2 = -\cos x + c$

When $v = 0, x = 0$

Hence $0 = -1 + c$

$c = 1$

Integrate and substitute in the boundary condition to evaluate c.

$0.25v^2 = 1 - \cos x$

$v^2 = 4(1 - \cos x)$

You now need to rearrange to get the format given in the question.

b $v^2_{MAX} = 4(1 - -1) = 8$

Hence $v = 2\sqrt{2} = 2.83$ m s^{-1} (3 s.f.)

Maximum speed occurs when v^2 is maximised. This happens when $\cos x = -1$.

Force as a function of velocity

When force is given as a function of velocity, there are two alternative differential equations you can form, depending on how the acceleration is written.

Using $a = \frac{dv}{dt}$, $F(v) = m\frac{dv}{dt}$

Separating variables gives $\int dt = \int \frac{m}{F(v)}dv$

Hence $t = \int \frac{m}{F(v)}dv$

Using $a = v\frac{dv}{dx}$, $F(v) = mv\frac{dv}{dx}$

Separating variables gives $\int dx = \int \frac{mv}{F(v)}dv$.

Hence $x = \int \frac{mv}{F(v)}dv$

The choice of form for acceleration depends on the demands of the problem being solved.

Key point 7.8

If force is given as a function of displacement, using Newton's second law either $a=\frac{dv}{dt}$ or $a=v\frac{dv}{dx}$ can be used to find $t(v)$ or $x(v)$:

$$t=\int\frac{m}{F(v)}dv \quad \text{and} \quad x=\int\frac{mv}{F(v)}dv$$

WORKED EXAMPLE 7.8

A particle P of mass 5 kg is travelling along the x-axis in the positive x-direction. Initially the particle is at rest at the origin, until acted upon by a single force F in the positive x-direction, where $F=16-v^2$ N.

a Find v in terms of t and calculate the velocity when $t=5$ s.

b Calculate the displacement of P when $v=2\text{ m s}^{-1}$.

a $t=\int\frac{5}{16-v^2}dv$

Given that you have force as a function of velocity and you require velocity in terms of time, you can use the first formula from Key point 7.8.

$$\frac{1}{(4-v)(4+v)}=\frac{A}{4-v}+\frac{B}{4+v}$$

$$1=A(4+v)+B(4-v)$$

Recall that integrals of this form require partial fractions.

When $v=-4$, $1=8B$, hence $B=\frac{1}{8}$

When $v=4$, $1=8A$, hence $A=\frac{1}{8}$

Therefore $t=\frac{5}{8}\int\frac{1}{4-v}+\frac{1}{4+v}dv$

$$t=\frac{5}{8}\left(-\ln|4-v|+\ln|4+v|\right)+c$$

When $t=0$, $v=0$

$0=\frac{5}{8}\left(-\ln|4|+\ln|4|\right)+c$

Hence $c=0$

Substitute in the boundary condition to evaluate c.

$$t=\frac{5}{8}\left(-\ln|4-v|+\ln|4+v|\right)$$

Rearrange to make v the subject.

$$\frac{8}{5}t=\ln\left|\frac{4+v}{4-v}\right|$$

$$e^{\frac{8}{5}t}=\frac{4+v}{4-v}$$

$$(4-v)e^{\frac{8}{5}t}=4+v$$

$$4(e^{\frac{8}{5}t}-1)=v(1+e^{\frac{8}{5}t})$$

$$v=\frac{4(e^{\frac{8}{5}t}-1)}{(1+e^{\frac{8}{5}t})}$$

When $t=5$

$v=\frac{4(e^8-1)}{(1+e^8)}$

$v=4.00\text{ m s}^{-1}$

Continues on next page ...

b $x=\int \frac{mv}{F(v)}\mathrm{d}v$

Given that you have force as a function of velocity and you require velocity in terms of displacement, you can use the second formula from Key point 7.8.

$x=\int \frac{5v}{16-v^2}\mathrm{d}v$

$x=-\frac{5}{2}\ln|16-v^2|+c$

You should recognise that this integral is of the form $\int \frac{f'(x)}{f(x)}\mathrm{d}x$ and hence find by inspection the integral.

When $v=0$, $x=0$

Hence $0=-\frac{5}{2}\ln|16|+c$

$c=\frac{5}{2}\ln|16|$

Substitute in the boundary condition to evaluate c.

$x=\frac{5}{2}\ln|16|-\frac{5}{2}\ln|16-v^2|$

When $v=2$

$x=\frac{5}{2}\ln|16|-\frac{5}{2}\ln|16-2^2|$

$x=0.719$ m (3 s.f.)

Substitute in v to calculate x.

Note: it is also possible to use your answer to part **a** and $v=\frac{\mathrm{d}x}{\mathrm{d}t}$ to find x. However, this would give $\frac{\mathrm{d}x}{\mathrm{d}t}=\frac{4(e^{\frac{8}{5}t}-1)}{(1+e^{\frac{8}{5}t})}$, which is a far more involved function to integrate.

Vertical motion

If a particle is moving in a vertical straight line then its weight must also be taken into account when using Newton's second law.

WORKED EXAMPLE 7.9

A ball of mass m kg is released from rest and falls vertically downwards. The ball experiences a single resistive force against its motion that is proportional to the speed of the object.

a Find an expression of the velocity v at time t for the ball.
b What is the long-term behaviour of the velocity of the ball?
c Find the distance the object falls after t seconds.

a R = resistive force

$R\propto v$

$R=kv$

where k is a constant of proportionality.

If the resistive force is proportional to the speed, you need a constant of proportionality to make this relationship into an equation.

Continues on next page ...

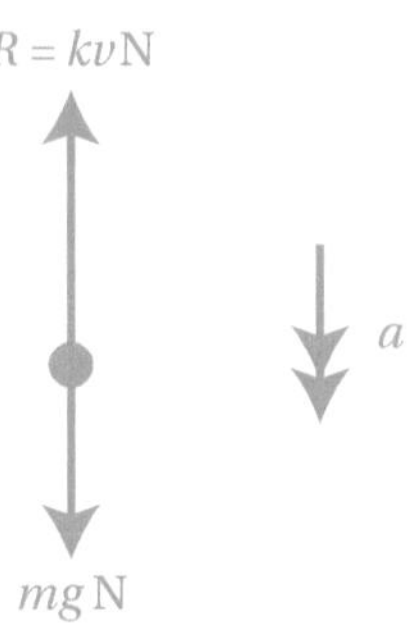

$F = ma$

Use Newton's second law with mg the weight of the particle and R the resistive force.

$mg - R = m\frac{dv}{dt}$

$mg - kv = m\frac{dv}{dt}$

$g - \frac{kv}{m} = \frac{dv}{dt}$

$\frac{dv}{dt} + \frac{kv}{m} = g$

You require velocity as a function of t so you need to use $a = \frac{dv}{dt}$.

Manipulate the differential equation into a form that you can integrate.

The integrating factor is $e^{\int \frac{k}{m} dt} = e^{\frac{k}{m}t}$

You now have

$ve^{\frac{k}{m}t} = \int ge^{\frac{k}{m}t}\,dt$

$ve^{\frac{k}{m}t} = \frac{mg}{k}e^{\frac{k}{m}t} + c$

where c is a constant of integration.

Since k, m and g are all constant, you can solve this differential equation by separating the variables, but notice that it is also in the form $\frac{dy}{dx} + P(x)y = Q(x)$. This type of differential equation can be solved using an integrating factor.

Once you have found the integrating factor you can then find a general solution for the differential equation.

At $t = 0$, $v = 0$ so:

$0 = \frac{mg}{k} + c$

and hence

$c = -\frac{mg}{k}$

Use the initial conditions in the question to find the constant of integration.

Therefore

$v = e^{-\frac{k}{m}t}\left(\frac{mg}{k}e^{\frac{k}{m}t} - \frac{mg}{k}\right)$

$v = \frac{mg}{k}\left(1 - e^{-\frac{k}{m}t}\right)$

where k is a constant of proportionality.

After some manipulation, you have found v as a function of t.

Continues on next page ...

Rewind

The integrating factor method for solving differential equations is dealt with in A Level Mathematics Student Book 2.

b As $t \to \infty$, you have $v \to \dfrac{mg}{k}$.

In the long term you need to look at what happens to $e^{-\frac{k}{m}t}$ as $t \to \infty$.

c To find distance fallen x as a function of time t:

$$\frac{dx}{dt} = \frac{mg}{k}\left(1 - e^{-\frac{k}{m}t}\right)$$

$$\int 1\,dx = \int \frac{mg}{k}\left(1 - e^{-\frac{k}{m}t}\right)dt$$

$$x = \frac{mgt}{k} + \frac{m^2 g}{k^2}e^{-\frac{k}{m}t} + A$$

where A is a constant of integration.

To find the distance as a function of time you need to use the relationship $v = \dfrac{dx}{dt}$ and integrate to derive a function of x in terms of t.

At $t = 0$, $x = 0$ so:

$$0 = \frac{m^2 g}{k^2} + A$$

$$A = -\frac{m^2 g}{k^2}$$

Once integrated, you again have to find the constant of integration using the initial conditions.

Therefore

$$x = \frac{mgt}{k} + \frac{m^2 g}{k^2}e^{-\frac{k}{m}t} - \frac{m^2 g}{k^2}$$

Finally, you can write the distance the ball has fallen as a function of t.

Explore

In Worked example 7.9, you looked at a model of an object under a resistive force proportional to its speed. Explore a model of a falling object where the resistive forces are proportional to v^2.

You might like to experiment by dropping from a height various objects that have different cross-sectional areas from their plan view.

Can you find out the same information about the falling object as you did in Worked example 7.9?

WORKED EXAMPLE 7.10

A parachutist falls from a plane and moves in a vertical straight line towards the ground. The parachutist is acted upon by a single resistive force of magnitude $R = \dfrac{5mv}{t+1}$ where m is the mass, v is the speed and t is the time since falling of the parachutist. Calculate the velocity of the parachutist after 1 second. Give your answer to 2 significant figures.

$$R = \frac{5mv}{t+1}$$

The resistive force is equal to a function involving mass, speed and time.

Continues on next page ...

$R = \frac{5mv}{t+1}$ N

a

mg N

$$mg - R = m\frac{dv}{dt}$$

$$mg - \frac{5mv}{t+1} = m\frac{dv}{dt}$$

$$g - \frac{5v}{t+1} = \frac{dv}{dt}$$

$$\frac{dv}{dt} + \frac{5v}{t+1} = g$$

The weight of the particle mg and the resistive force R act vertically. Use Newton's second law to form the equation of motion.

You require velocity as a function of time t so need $a = \frac{dv}{dt}$.

You can manipulate the differential equation into a form that you can integrate.

The integrating factor is:

$$e^{\int \frac{5}{t+1} dt} = e^{5\ln(t+1)} = e^{\ln(t+1)^5} = (t+1)^5$$

You now have

$$v(t+1)^5 = \int g(t+1)^5 dt$$

$$v(t+1)^5 = \frac{g}{6}(t+1)^6 + c$$

where c is a constant of integration.

You have formed a differential equation of the form $\frac{dy}{dx} + P(x)y = Q(x)$. This type of differential equation requires an integrating factor to solve it.

Once you have found the integrating factor, you can then find a general solution for the differential equation.

At $t = 0$, $v = 0$, so

$$0 = \frac{g}{6} + c$$

$$c = -\frac{g}{6}$$

You can use the initial conditions in the question to find the constant of integration.

Therefore

$$v = \frac{g}{6}(t+1) - \frac{g}{6(t+1)^5}$$

At $t = 1$:

$$v = \frac{g}{6}(2) - \frac{g}{6(2)^5}$$

$$v = 3.2 \text{ m s}^{-1}$$

You can then substitute $t = 1$ into the equation you have found to calculate the velocity to 2 significant figures.

Power under a variable force

Rewind

Recall that power is measured in watts and defined as $P = Fv$. You used this in Chapter 1.

WORKED EXAMPLE 7.11

A car of mass 1500 kg is travelling in a straight horizontal line. It has a power output of 120 W and resistance to motion magnitude $0.15v^2$. When the car passes point A it is travelling at 28.8 km h^{-1}. Calculate the speed of the car when it has travelled a further 0.25 km.

$28.8 \text{ km h}^{-1} = 8 \text{ m s}^{-1}$ — Convert km h^{-1} to m s^{-1}.

$0.25 \text{ km} = 250 \text{ m}$

$P = Fv$ — Recall the formula for power from Chapter 1. Use this to find an expression for the driving force F.

$120 = Fv$

Hence $F = \frac{120}{v}$

Draw and label a diagram to show all forces acting on the car.

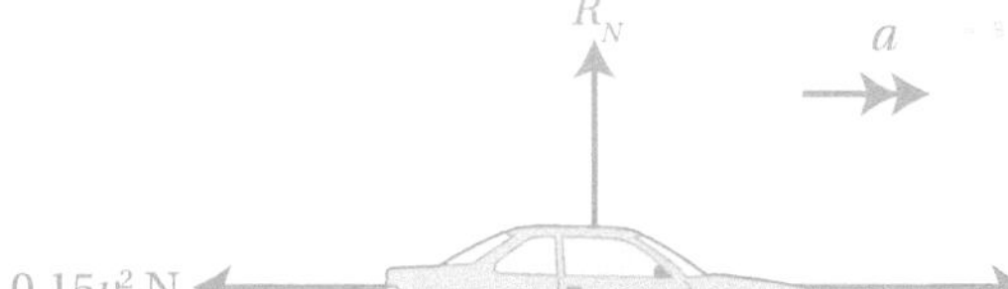

$(\rightarrow)$ Resultant force $= ma$ — Use Newton's second law to form the equation of motion.

$\frac{120}{v} - 0.15v^2 = 1500v\frac{dv}{dx}$ — Use $a = v\frac{dv}{dx}$ to form a differential equation.

$\frac{120 - 0.15v^3}{v} = 1500v\frac{dv}{dx}$

$\int dx = \int \frac{1500v^2}{120 - 0.15v^3} dv$ — Recognise that this integral is of the form $\int \frac{f'(x)}{f(x)} dx$ and hence find by inspection.

$x = \int \frac{10000v^2}{800 - v^3} dv$

$x = -\frac{10000}{3} \ln|800 - v^3| + c$

When $x = 0$ m, $v = 8$ m s^{-1} — Substitute in the boundary conditions and evaluate c.

Hence $0 = -\frac{10000}{3} \ln|800 - 8^3| + c$

$c = \frac{10000}{3} \ln 288$

$x = \frac{10000}{3} \ln 288 - \frac{10000}{3} \ln|800 - v^3|$

Continues on next page ...

When $x = 250$ m:

Substitute $x = 250$ m and solve to find v.

$$250 = \frac{10000}{3}\ln 288 - \frac{10000}{3}\ln\left|800 - v^3\right|$$

$$0.075 = \ln 288 - \ln\left|800 - v^3\right|$$

$$0.075 = \ln\left|\frac{288}{800 - v^3}\right|$$

$$e^{0.075} = \frac{288}{800 - v^3}$$

$$800 - v^3 = \frac{288}{e^{0.075}}$$

$$v^3 = 800 - \frac{288}{e^{0.075}}$$

$v = 8.11\ \mathrm{m\,s^{-1}}$ (3 s.f.) $= 29.2\ \mathrm{km\,h^{-1}}$ (3 s.f.)

EXERCISE 7B

1. A particle P of mass 2 kg moves along the x-axis in the positive x-direction. A single horizontal force acts on the particle away from the origin such that $F = 2\cos(3t)$ N. Given that the particle starts at rest at the origin and that $0 \leqslant t \leqslant \frac{\pi}{6}$, find velocity as a function of time.

2. A particle P of mass 5 kg moves horizontally from a fixed point O on a smooth horizontal plane. At time t, OP is x metres and a single force $F = v^2 - 5$ N acts on the particle in the direction of motion. Given that when the particle is 5 m from the origin the speed of the particle is 6 m s^{-1}, find its displacement as a function of velocity.

3. A particle P of mass 2 kg is travelling along the x-axis in the positive x-direction. At time t seconds the particle is x metres away from the origin, from where it starts with velocity 10 m s^{-1}. The particle moves under a single force $F = e^{-3x}$ N against the direction of motion. Find the speed and direction of the particle when $x = 15$ m.

4. A particle P of mass 300 g is travelling in a horizontal line across a smooth horizontal plane away from a fixed point A. At time t seconds the particle is x metres from A with velocity v m s^{-1}. Given the particle starts $\frac{\pi}{3}$ m from A with velocity 4 m s^{-1} and moves under the act of a single force $F = \sin(x)$ N in the direction of motion, find the speed of P when $x = 10$ m.

5 A particle P of mass 5 kg moves along the x-axis in the positive x-direction under the motion of a single force $F = 4 - t$ N against the direction of motion. Given the particle starts at rest at the origin and after t seconds the particle has a displacement of x metres from the origin with velocity v m s^{-1}, what is the speed and direction of P when $t = 1.5$ s?

6 A particle P of mass 3500 g is travelling along the x-axis in the negative x-direction. It has velocity 6 m s^{-1} at a displacement of 10 m from the origin when it is acted upon by a single force $F = 2 - v^2$ N in the positive x-direction. Find the displacement and direction of P from the origin when $v = 10$ m s^{-1}.

7 A particle P of mass 5 kg is travelling along the x-axis in the positive x-direction. Initially, the particle is at the origin with speed 2 m s^{-1} and moves under the act of a single force $F = 3 - v$ N in the positive x-direction such that at time t seconds it is x metres from the origin. Find the displacement of P as a function of velocity.

8 A particle P of mass 10 kg travels in a horizontal straight line away from a fixed point O. At time t seconds, the particle is x metres from O. The particle moves under the act of a single force in the direction of motion, $F = x\,e^{-x^2}$ N. Given that the particle starts at O with velocity 2 m s^{-1}, show that $v^2 = \frac{1}{10}\left(41 - e^{-x^2}\right)$.

9 A single force $F = e^{-v^2}$ N acts on a particle P of mass 500 g in the direction of motion. At time t seconds P is x metres from a fixed point A after initially starting at A with velocity $v = 0$ m s^{-1}. Find velocity as a function of displacement.

10 A particle P of mass 6 kg travels along the x-axis in the positive x-direction under the action of a force $F = 0.25v$ N in the direction of motion and with resistance to motion magnitude $R = 0.5t^2$ N. The particle starts at the origin with velocity $v = 0$ m s^{-1} and after time t seconds the particle is x metres from the origin. Find the velocity of P as a function of time.

Tip

If it is not possible to separate the variables, try the integrating factor method for solving differential equations that is given in Pure Core Student Book 2.

11 A stone of mass 2 kg is released from rest and falls freely under gravity with resistance to motion $F = 0.25t^2$ N. After t seconds the stone has fallen x metres and has velocity v m s^{-1}.

a Find the stone's velocity as a function of time.

b Find its displacement as a function of time.

The stone falls 27 m until it hits the ground.

c How long is the stone falling before it hits the ground?

d What is the velocity of the stone when it hits the ground?

Checklist of learning and understanding

For a particle moving in a straight line with variable acceleration:

- if velocity is a function of displacement, then $a = v\frac{\mathrm{d}v}{\mathrm{d}x}$
- if velocity is a function of displacement, then $t = \int \frac{1}{v(x)}\mathrm{d}x$
- if acceleration is a function of displacement, then $\frac{1}{2}v^2 = \int a(x)\,\mathrm{d}x$
- if acceleration is a function of velocity, then $t = \int \frac{1}{a(v)}\mathrm{d}v$
- if acceleration is given as a function of velocity, then $x = \int \frac{v}{a(v)}\mathrm{d}v$.

For a particle moving in a straight line under a variable force:

- if force is given as a function of time, then from Newton's second law you can find the velocity of the particle using $v = \frac{1}{m}\int F(t)\,\mathrm{d}t$.
- if force is given as a function of displacement, then from Newton's second law you can find the velocity of the particle using $\frac{1}{2}mv^2 = \int F(x)\,\mathrm{d}x$ and rearranging to make v the subject
- if force is given as a function of velocity, then from Newton's second law you can use either $a = \frac{\mathrm{d}v}{\mathrm{d}t}$ or $a = v\frac{\mathrm{d}v}{\mathrm{d}x}$ to find $t(v)$ or $x(v)$.
  Then $t = \int \frac{m}{F(v)}\mathrm{d}v$ and $x = \int \frac{mv}{F(v)}\mathrm{d}v$
- if the linear motion of the particle is vertical, then its weight has to be taken into account when using Newton's second law to form the equation of motion.

Mixed practice 7

1 A particle P is moving in a straight, horizontal line such that at time t seconds it is x metres away from a fixed point A. Velocity is given by $v = e^{-x}$ m s^{-1} and the particle starts from the point A.

a Find an expression for the acceleration of P in terms of displacement.

b Hence calculate the acceleration of P when it is 4 m from A.

c Find an expression for the displacement of P in terms of time.

d Hence calculate the displacement of P from A after 10 s.

2 A particle P is moving along the positive x-axis in the positive x-direction with acceleration given by $a = \cos(3x)$ m s^{-2}. At time t seconds the particle is x metres from the origin and when P passed through the origin it had speed $v = 3$ m s^{-1}. Show that $v^2 = \frac{2}{3}\sin(3x) + 9$.

3 A particle P is travelling in a horizontal straight line away from a fixed point A. At time t seconds it is x metres from A, moving with velocity v m s^{-1}. Acceleration is given by $a = 2x - 4.5$ m s^{-2} and the particle started at the origin with velocity $v = 2$ m s^{-1}. Calculate the displacement and direction of acceleration of P from the origin when it is instantaneously at rest.

4 A particle P is travelling along the x-axis in the positive x-direction. At time t seconds the particle is x metres from the origin with velocity v m s^{-1}. The particle P passes through the origin at time $t = 3$ s. Given that $v = \frac{1}{2x-6}$ m s^{-1} find:

a an expression for time in terms of displacement

b an expression for displacement in terms of time and hence the displacement of P when $t = 10$ s

c an expression for the acceleration of P

d the magnitude and direction of the acceleration when $t = 19$ s.

5 A particle P of mass 0.2 kg is projected horizontally with speed u m s^{-1} from a fixed point O on a smooth horizontal surface. P moves in a straight line and, at time t s after projection, P has speed v m s^{-1} and is x m from O. The only force acting on P has magnitude $0.4v^2$ N and is directed towards O.

i Show that $\frac{1}{v}\frac{dv}{dx} = -2$.

ii Hence show that $v = ue^{-2x}$.

iii Find u, given that $x = 2$ when $t = 4$.

© OCR, GCE Mathematics, Paper 4730/01, June 2007

6 O is a fixed point on a horizontal plane. A particle P of mass 0.25 kg is released from rest at O and moves in a straight line on the plane. At time t s after release the only horizontal force acting on P has magnitude:

$$\frac{1}{2400}(144 - t^2)\text{N} \qquad \text{for } 0 \leqslant t \leqslant 12 \text{ s}$$

and

$$\frac{1}{2400}(t^2 - 144)\text{N} \qquad \text{for } t \geqslant 12 \text{ s.}$$

The force acts in the direction of P's motion. P's velocity at time t s is v m s^{-1}.

i Find an expression for v in terms of t, valid for $t \geqslant 12$ s, and hence show that v is three times greater when $t = 24$ s than it is when $t = 12$ s.

ii Sketch the (t, v) graph for $0 \leqslant t \leqslant 24$ s.

© OCR, GCE Mathematics, Paper 4730, June 2010

7 A duck of mass 2 kg is travelling with horizontal speed 4 m s^{-1} when it lands on a lake. The duck is brought to rest by the action of resistive forces, acting in the direction opposite to the duck's motion and having total magnitude $(2v + 3v^2)$ N, where v m s^{-1} is the speed of the duck. Show that the duck comes to rest after travelling approximately 1.30 m from the point of its initial contact with the surface of the lake.

© OCR, GCE Mathematics, Paper 4730, June 2006

8 A stone of mass 0.125 kg falls freely under gravity, from rest, until it has travelled a distance of 10 m. The stone then continues to fall in a medium which exerts an upward resisting force of $0.025v$ N, where v m s^{-1} is the speed of the stone t s after the instant that it enters the resisting medium.

i Show by integration that $v = 49 - 35\,e^{-0.2t}$.

ii Find how far the stone travels during the first 3 seconds in the medium.

© OCR, GCE Mathematics, Paper 4730, January 2009

9 A motor-cycle, whose mass including the rider is 120 kg, is decelerating on a horizontal straight road. The motor-cycle passes a point A with speed 40 m s^{-1} and when it has travelled a distance of x m beyond A its speed is v m s^{-1}. The engine develops a constant power of 8 kW and resistances are modelled by a force of $0.25v^2$ N opposing the motion.

i Show that $\dfrac{480v^2}{v^3 - 32000}\dfrac{dv}{dx} = -1$.

ii Find the speed of the motor-cycle when it has travelled 500 m beyond A.

© OCR, GCE Mathematics, Paper 4730, June 2009

10 A particle of mass m kg is released from rest at a fixed point O and falls vertically. The particle is subject to an upward resisting force of magnitude of $0.49mv$ N where v m s^{-1} is the velocity of the particle when it has fallen a distance of x m from O.

i Write down a differential equation for the motion of the particle, and show that the equation can be written as $\left(\dfrac{20}{20-v} - 1\right)\dfrac{dv}{dx} = 0.49$.

ii Hence find an expression for x in terms of v.

© OCR, GCE Mathematics, Paper 4730/01, January 2008

8 Momentum and collisions 2

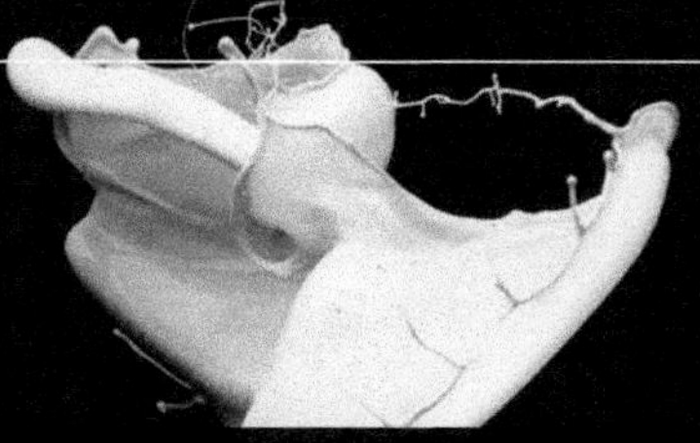

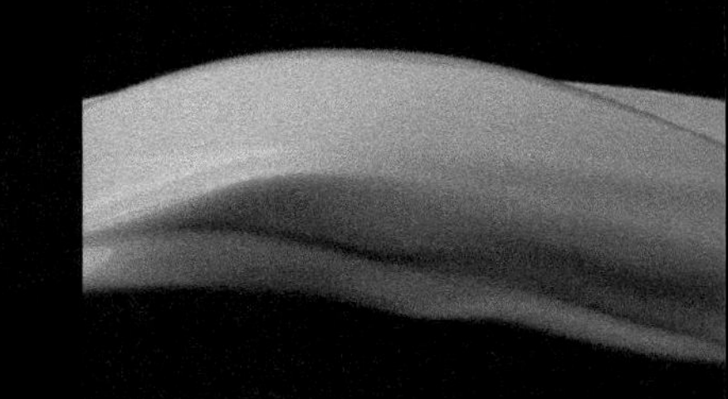

A This chapter is for A level students only.
In this chapter you will learn how to:

- find the impulse of a variable force
- apply the principles of impulse, conservation of momentum and Newton's experimental law in two dimensions using vector notation
- calculate the result of oblique impacts.

Before you start…

Chapter 3	You should know the relationship between force, impulse and momentum.	1 A force of 3 N acts on a mass m kg for 3 seconds. What is the change in momentum of the mass during those 3 seconds?
Chapter 3	You should know the principle of conservation of momentum and Newton's experimental law.	2 A particle of mass m kg travelling in a straight line on a horizontal surface hits a vertical wall with speed u and rebounds with speed v. What is the coefficient of restitution between the wall and the particle?
A Level Mathematics Student Book 1	You should understand how to combine vectors, including drawing triangles to find the sum of two vectors.	3 Draw a sketch of a triangle to show the sum of two vectors **a** and **b**.
A Level Mathematics Student Book 2	You should be able to resolve a vector into two perpendicular components and be able to find the magnitude of a vector from its components.	4 The force F acts at 60° to the horizontal. What are the horizontal and vertical components of F?
A Level Mathematics Student Book 1	You should be able to integrate simple functions and apply limits.	5 Find $\int_0^3 (3t^2 - 4t)\,\mathrm{d}t$.

Variable forces and oblique impacts

In Chapter 3 you learned about momentum and impulse involving constant forces and direct collisions. Collisions are not restricted to situations where two objects are moving in the same straight line; collisions can also occur when the objects are moving at an angle to each other. These are called oblique collisions. You see this in tennis matches when the racket head does not meet the tennis ball straight on but sends it in a completely different direction. In this chapter, you will analyse more realistic situations such as those involving variable forces or oblique impacts.

Section 1: Variable force and vector notation

For a constant force F acting for time t, the impulse of the force is force × time and this is equal to the change in momentum.

Key point 8.1

For a constant force, F,

$$\text{impulse} = Ft = mv - mu$$

Rewind

You learned about impulse and momentum in Chapter 3.

A graph of force against time for a constant force will be a horizontal line and the impulse is given by the area between the force line and the time axis.

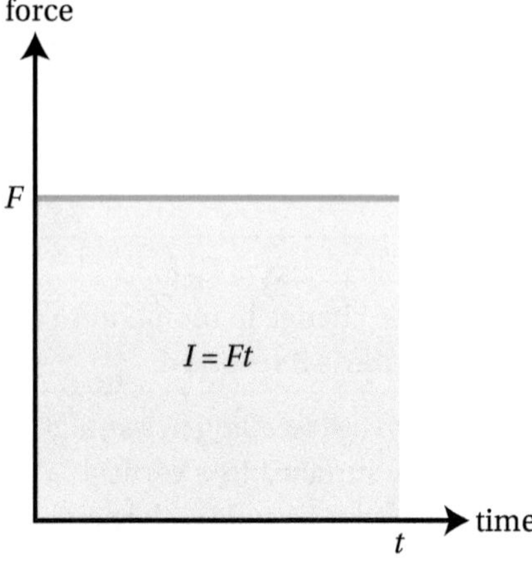

Not all forces are constant. The more you stretch an elastic band, the greater the force trying to pull it back. The force increases with the extension of the band.

If the force is not constant, you may need to find the impulse using integration.

Key point 8.2

The impulse, I, of a variable force F acting for a time $t_1 \leqslant t \leqslant t_2$ is:

$$I = \int_{t_1}^{t_2} F \, \mathrm{d}t$$

WORKED EXAMPLE 8.1

The force-time graph for the force F acting on a mass of 2 kg is shown.

The mass, A, is initially moving in a straight line with velocity 5 m s^{-1} and the force is acting along the same straight line in the direction of motion.

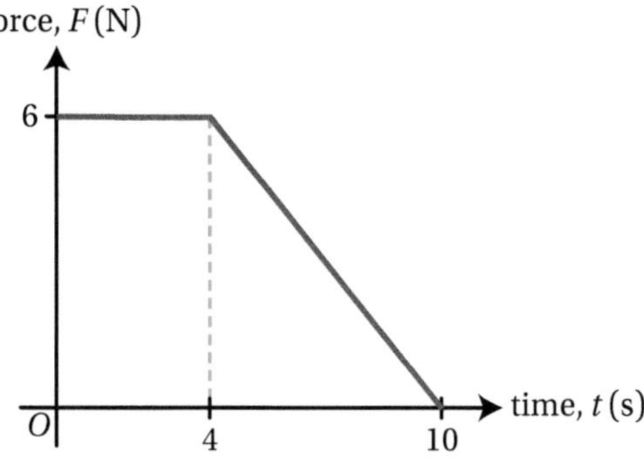

Calculate the speed of A after:

a 4 seconds

b 10 seconds.

a Let v be the speed of A after 4 seconds. — First define the unknown quantity.

$I = Ft = mv - mu$ — Use impulse = change in momentum

Total impulse in the first 4 seconds $= 6 \times 4 = 24$ — The impulse in the first 4 seconds is the area under the graph between $t = 0$ and $t = 4$.

Change in momentum $= mv - mu$
$= 2v - 2 \times 5$
$= 2v - 10$ — Use change in momentum = final momentum − initial momentum

$24 = 2v - 10$ — Use $I = mv - mu$

Therefore $v = 17$ m s^{-1}

You could use this result to help you to calculate the answer for part **b** but it is safer to start again in case you have made an error.

b Let w be the speed of A after 10 seconds. — Define the unknown.

Total impulse in the first 10 seconds is:

$\frac{1}{2}h(a+b) = \frac{1}{2}6(4+10) = 42$ — The impulse in the first 10 seconds is the area under the graph between $t = 0$ and $t = 10$, which is a trapezium of height 6 and sides 4 and 10.

Change in momentum $= mw - mu$
$= 2w - 2 \times 5$
$42 = 2w - 10$ — Use $I = mv - mu$ and solve for w.

Therefore $w = 26$ m s^{-1}

WORKED EXAMPLE 8.2

A smooth sphere of mass 2 kg is acted on by a variable force $F = (t^2 - 6t + 8)$ N in the direction of motion of the sphere.

a Find the magnitude of the impulse between $t = 0$ and $t = 4$.

b When $t = 0$ the speed of the sphere is 2 m s^{-1}. What is the speed of the sphere after 4 seconds?

a Impulse $I = \int F\,dt$ — To find the change in momentum you need to integrate F from $t = 0$ to $t = 4$.

$$I = \int_0^4 (3t^2 - 6t + 8)\,dt = \left[\frac{3t^3}{3} - \frac{6t^2}{2} + 8t\right]_0^4$$

$$= \left[\frac{3\times64}{3} - \frac{6\times16}{2} + 32\right] - [0]$$

$$= 64 - 48 + 32 = 48 \text{ Ns}$$

Integrate F between $t = 0$ and $t = 4$.

Substitute in the limits and calculate I.

b Let the speed of the sphere after 4 s be v. — Define the unknown quantity.

Change in momentum $= mv - mu$ — Write an expression for the change in momentum.

$$2v - 2\times2 = 2v - 4$$

$$2v - 4 = 48$$

Equate to the impulse and work out v.

Therefore $v = 26$ m s^{-1}

WORKED EXAMPLE 8.3

A particle, A, of mass 500 g, is acted on by a variable force F N, which is defined as:

$$F = 0.3t^2 + 0.5t \quad \text{for } 0 \leqslant t \leqslant 3\text{ s}$$

$$F = t + 1.2 \quad \text{for } 3 < t \leqslant 5\text{ s}$$

Find the speed of A after 4 seconds if the speed is 2 m s^{-1} when $t = 0$.

To find the increase in momentum of A you need to know the total impulse on A during the 4 seconds.

500 g = 0.5 kg — Change g to kg.

Let the speed of A after 4 seconds be v. — Define the unknown.

$$I = \int_0^3 (0.3t^2 + 0.5t)\,dt + \int_3^4 (t + 1.2)\,dt$$

$$= \left[0.3\frac{t^3}{3} + 0.5\frac{t^2}{2}\right]_0^3 + \left[\frac{t^2}{2} + 1.2t\right]_3^4$$

$$= [(2.7 + 2.25) - (0)] + [(8 + 4.8) - (4.5 + 3.6)]$$

$$= 4.95 + 4.7 = 9.65 \text{ Ns}$$

Integrate the force between $t = 0$ and $t = 4$ to find the total impulse on A in that time.

$9.65 = 0.5v - (0.5\times2)$

$v = 21.3$ m s^{-1}

Use $I = mv - mu$

Solve for v.

Vector notation

The same principles and equations that you learned in Chapter 3 can be applied when velocity and impulse are given in vector format.

Explore

Rockets are an example of a momentum–impulse problem where there is a constantly changing situation because fuel is expelled from the back of the rocket, so the mass of the rocket decreases. Look up the Tsiolkovsky rocket equation on the internet.

WORKED EXAMPLE 8.4

A toy sailing boat of mass 800 g is blown along by a constant wind, which produces a force $(\mathbf{i} + 2\mathbf{j})$ N on the boat. If the boat is initially at rest, find its velocity after 10 seconds.

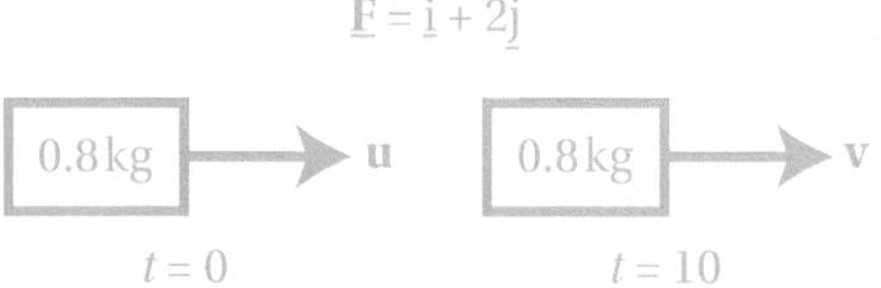

Draw a diagram with arrows to show the direction of motion.

$\underline{u} = 0$

$m = 800\text{ g} = 0.8\text{ kg}$ — Convert to g to kg.

$\underline{F} = \underline{i} + 2\underline{j}$

$t = 10$

Let final velocity be $\underline{v} = a\underline{i} + b\underline{j}$ — Write an expression for the final velocity vector.

$\text{Impulse} = \underline{F}t = m\underline{v} - m\underline{u}$ — The formula for impulse can be written with **F**, **u** and **v** as vectors.

$10(\underline{i} + 2\underline{j}) = 0.8(a\underline{i} + b\underline{j}) - 0.8(0\underline{i} + 0\underline{j})$ — Substitute in the values.

$10 = 0.8a - 0 \quad \text{so} \quad a = 12.5$

$20 = 0.8b - 0 \quad \text{so} \quad b = 25$

Equate the **i** values of both sides of the equation and the **j** values of both sides of the equation to form two scalar equations. You should not write **i** and **j** in these equations.

Solve to find the components of **v**.

$\underline{v} = (12.5\underline{i} + 25\underline{j})\text{ m s}^{-1}$ — State the value of **v** in vector format.

Continues on next page ...

Alternative method: — You may find it easier to work with column vectors.

$\underline{u} = 0$

$m = 800\text{ g} = 0.8\text{ kg}$ — Convert g to kg.

$\underline{F} = \begin{pmatrix} 1 \\ 2 \end{pmatrix}$

$t = 10$

Let final velocity $\underline{v} = \begin{pmatrix} a \\ b \end{pmatrix}$ — Write an expression for the final velocity vector.

$\text{Impulse} = \underline{F}t = m\underline{v} - m\underline{u}$ — The formula for impulse can be written with **F**, **u** and **v** as vectors.

$10\begin{pmatrix} 1 \\ 2 \end{pmatrix} = 0.8\begin{pmatrix} a \\ b \end{pmatrix} - 0.8\begin{pmatrix} 0 \\ 0 \end{pmatrix}$ — Substitute in the values.

$10 = 0.8a - 0 \quad \text{so} \quad a = 12.5$

$20 = 0.8b - 0 \quad \text{so} \quad b = 25$

Equate the **i** values (top line) and the **j** values (bottom line) of both sides of the equation.

You should not write **i** and **j** in these equations.

Solve to find the components of **v**.

$\underline{v} = (12.5\underline{i} + 25\underline{j})\text{ m s}^{-1}$ — State the value of the velocity vector in the format of the question.

WORKED EXAMPLE 8.5

A particle A, of mass 2 kg, is moving with velocity $(2\mathbf{i} + 3\mathbf{j})\text{ m s}^{-1}$ when it collides with particle B, of mass 1.5 kg, which is moving with velocity $(\mathbf{i} + 2\mathbf{j})\text{ m s}^{-1}$. If the particles coalesce during the collision:

a find the velocity of the combined particle after the collision

b find the total loss in kinetic energy as a result of the collision.

a $m_1\underline{u}_1 + m_2\underline{u}_2 = m_1\underline{v}_1 + m_2\underline{v}_2$ — Use the principle of conservation of linear momentum in vector format.

Let the final velocity of the combined particle be $a\underline{i} + b\underline{j}$

$2\begin{pmatrix} 2 \\ 3 \end{pmatrix} + 1.5\begin{pmatrix} 1 \\ 2 \end{pmatrix} = 3.5\begin{pmatrix} a \\ b \end{pmatrix}$ — Substitute in the values. It is easier to work with column vectors.

$\begin{pmatrix} 4 \\ 6 \end{pmatrix} + \begin{pmatrix} 1.5 \\ 3 \end{pmatrix} = \begin{pmatrix} 3.5a \\ 3.5b \end{pmatrix}$

Continues on next page ...

$4+1.5=3.5a$	Equate the **i** components to find *a*.
$a=\frac{5.5}{3.5}=\frac{11}{7}$	
$6+3=3.5b$	Equate the **j** components to find *b*.
$b=\frac{9}{3.5}=\frac{18}{7}$	
$\underset{\sim}{v}=\frac{11}{7}\underset{\sim}{i}+\frac{18}{7}\underset{\sim}{j}\,\text{m s}^{-1}$	Give the answer in the original format.
b $\text{KE}=\frac{1}{2}mv^2$	You need to be able to find v^2, which is a scalar quantity.
$(\text{Initial velocity of } A)^2=\lvert 2\underset{\sim}{i}+3\underset{\sim}{j}\rvert^2=2^2+3^2=13$	Find the square of the magnitude of the velocity of *A* (i.e. the square of the speed of *A*) ...
$(\text{Initial velocity of } B)^2=\lvert \underset{\sim}{i}+2\underset{\sim}{j}\rvert^2=1^2+2^2=5$	... and the square of the magnitude of the velocity of *B* (i.e. the square of the speed of *B*).
$\text{Initial KE}=\left(\frac{1}{2}\times2\times13\right)+\left(\frac{1}{2}\times1.5\times5\right)=16.75$	The initial KE is the sum KE_A+KE_B.
$\lvert\text{Velocity of combined particle}\rvert^2=\left(\frac{11}{7}\right)^2+\left(\frac{18}{7}\right)^2=\frac{445}{49}$	Find the square of the magnitude of the velocity of the combined particle ...
$\text{Final KE}=\left(\frac{1}{2}\times3.5\times\frac{445}{49}\right)=\frac{445}{28}$	... and use this to find the final KE of the combined particle.
$\text{Loss in KE}=16.75-\frac{445}{28}=0.857\text{ J}$	Loss in KE = initial KE – final KE.

EXERCISE 8A

1 Find the impulse generated by the forces shown by the solid lines between $t = 0$ and $t = 10$.

a force (N)

6

O 5 10 time (s)

b

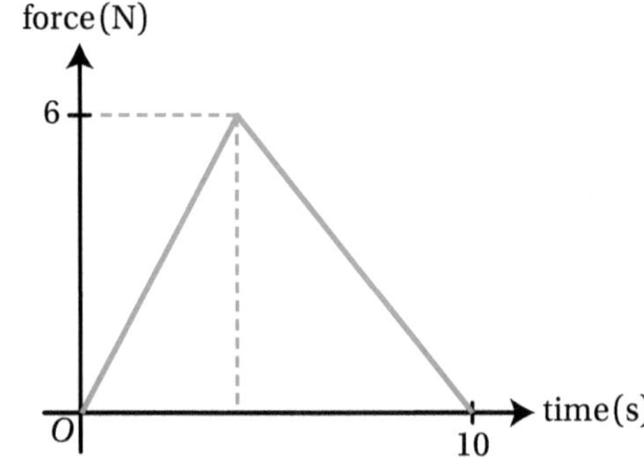

c

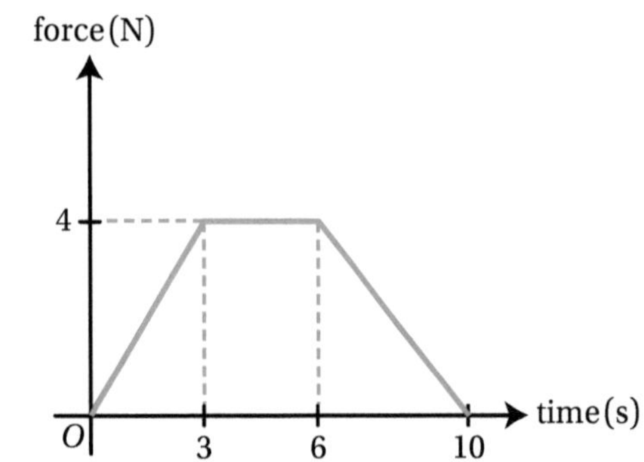

d

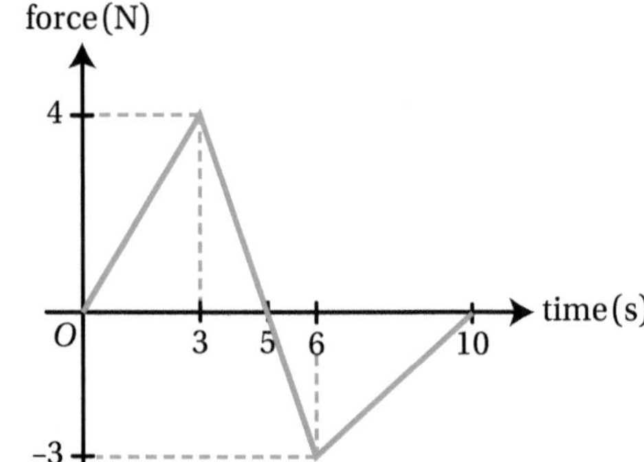

2 A particle of mass 4 kg is moving in a straight line on a smooth horizontal plane, when it is acted on by a force F in the same straight line. If the speed of the particle is $6\ \text{m s}^{-1}$ when $t = 0$, find the speed of the particle after 10 seconds for each of the forces shown in the diagrams in Question 1.

3 Fill in the gaps in this table.

Mass (kg)	Initial velocity (m s^{-1})	Final velocity (m s^{-1})	Constant force (N)	Time (s)
2	0	$8\mathbf{i} + 10\mathbf{j}$		5
1	$2\mathbf{i} - \mathbf{j}$	$14\mathbf{i} + 15\mathbf{j}$	$3\mathbf{i} + 4\mathbf{j}$	
	$-3\mathbf{i} + 5\mathbf{j}$	$-7\mathbf{i} + 11\mathbf{j}$	$-2\mathbf{i} + 3\mathbf{j}$	4
0.5	$2\mathbf{i} + 7\mathbf{j}$		$-\mathbf{i} + \mathbf{j}$	6
4		$1.5\mathbf{i} + 8\mathbf{j}$	$-2\mathbf{i} - 4\mathbf{j}$	5

4 A particle A, of mass 2 kg, is moving with velocity $(2\mathbf{i} + 3\mathbf{j})\ \text{m s}^{-1}$ when it collides with particle B, of mass 3 kg, which is moving with velocity $(\mathbf{i} + 2\mathbf{j})\ \text{m s}^{-1}$. If the particles coalesce during the collision, find the velocity of the combined particle after the collision.

5 A particle A, of mass 2 kg, is moving with velocity $(2\mathbf{i} + 3\mathbf{j})\ \text{m s}^{-1}$ when it collides with particle B, of mass 3 kg, which is moving with velocity $(\mathbf{i} + 2\mathbf{j})\ \text{m s}^{-1}$. If the velocity of B after the collision is $(1.6\mathbf{i} + 2.6\mathbf{j})\ \text{m s}^{-1}$, find the velocity of A after the collision.

6 A particle P, of mass 2.5 kg, moving in a straight line on a smooth horizontal plane, is acted on in the same straight line by a force F for 6 seconds, such that $F = 2t$ N.

a Find the total impulse of the force on P between $t = 0$ and $t = 6$.

b If the speed of P is $4\ \text{m s}^{-1}$ when $t = 0$, find the speed of P when $t = 6$.

7 A particle A, of mass 3 kg, is moving with velocity $(2\mathbf{i} - 3\mathbf{j})$ m s^{-1} when it collides with particle B, also of mass 3 kg, which is moving with velocity $(\mathbf{i} + 4\mathbf{j})$ m s^{-1}. The two particles coalesce.

a Find the velocity of the combined particle after the collision.

b What is the loss in kinetic energy as a result of the collision?

8 A mass, A, of 10 kg, moving in a straight line on a smooth horizontal plane at 5 m s^{-1}, is acted on by a force F along its line of motion. F is defined as:

$F = 3t^2 + 1 \quad 0 \leqslant t \leqslant 2$ s

$F = 6t + 1 \quad t > 2$ s

a Find the magnitude of the total impulse on A:

i between $t = 0$ and $t = 2$ s **ii** between $t = 0$ and $t = 6$ s.

b Hence find the speed of A when $t = 6$ s.

9 At time $t = 0$, a particle P, of mass 5 kg, is moving in a straight line at a constant speed of 4 m s^{-1} on a smooth horizontal plane when it is acted on by a force $F = (t^3 - 6t^2 + 8t)$ N in the same straight line.

a Find the total impulse on P:

i between $t = 0$ and $t = 2$ s **ii** between $t = 2$ and $t = 4$ s.

b What is the speed of P when $t = 4$ s?

10 At time $t = 0$, a particle P, of mass 4 kg, is moving in a straight line at a constant velocity of 4 m s^{-1} on a smooth horizontal plane P when it is acted on by a force $F = (4t - 6)$ N acting in the same straight line. At time T seconds later, the particle is moving with velocity 6 m s^{-1}. Find the value of T.

Section 2: Oblique impacts and the impulse–momentum triangle

So far, you have considered direct impacts with objects moving along their line of centres or hitting walls at right angles. You are now going to look at **oblique impacts**.

Consider a football, of mass m kg, kicked along the ground so that it hits a wall at an angle of magnitude θ. If the wall is smooth and has a coefficient of restitution equal to 1, the ball will bounce back at the same angle at which it hit the wall, as shown in the diagram.

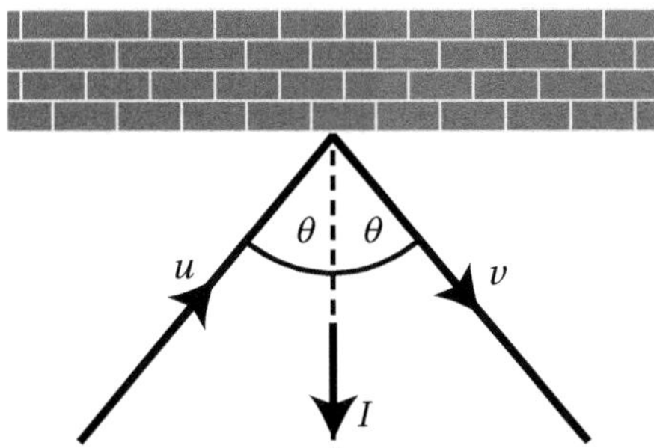

The impulse that the smooth wall exerts on the ball will be perpendicular to the wall. The vector diagram shows what happens when $e = 1$. The component of the velocity parallel to the wall, **a**, is unchanged by the impact. The velocity perpendicular to the wall, **b**, has the same magnitude after the collision, but is in the opposite direction, **–b**. The velocity of approach **u** and the velocity of rebound **v** therefore have the same magnitude of $\sqrt{a^2 + b^2}$, but are in different directions.

Rewind

You looked at coefficient of restitution in Chapter 3.

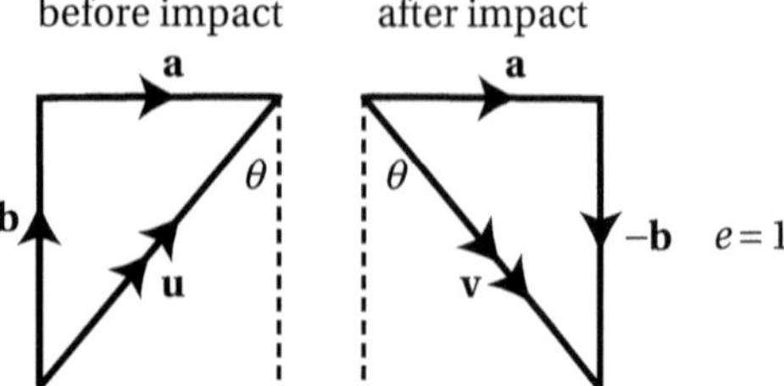

If the coefficient of restitution is not equal to 1 but the wall is still smooth:

- the impulse is again perpendicular to the wall so has no effect on the component of the velocity parallel to the wall
- the impulse changes the magnitude of the component of the velocity perpendicular to the wall.

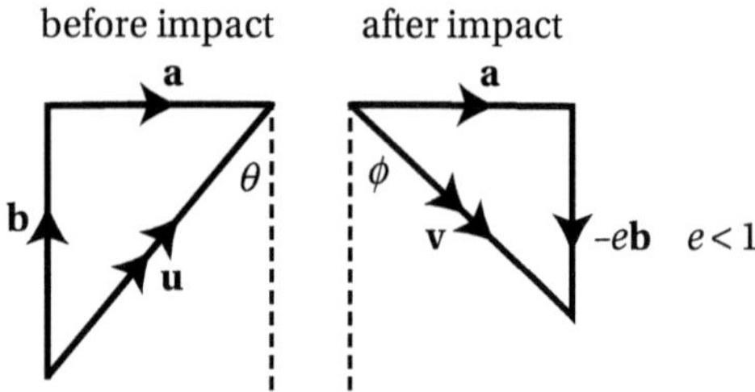

The velocity, **b**, perpendicular to the wall is changed by the impact with the wall to –*e***b**. The magnitude of the angle that the direction of motion of the football makes with the perpendicular to the wall will change.

Rewind

You learned about collisions at right angles to walls in Chapter 3.

Before the impact the football is travelling towards the wall with speed $u = \sqrt{a^2 + b^2}$ at an angle θ to the perpendicular with the wall where $\tan\theta = \frac{a}{b}$.

After the collision the football is travelling away from the wall with speed $v = \sqrt{a^2 + (eb^2)}$ at an angle ϕ to the perpendicular with the wall where $\tan\phi = \frac{a}{eb}$.

If we compare these two we can see that $\tan\theta = e\tan\phi$.

The impulse acting on the football is perpendicular to the wall and is equal to the change in momentum in that direction. In this case, taking the direction away from the wall as positive:

$$I = meb - (-mb) = meb + mb$$

We can apply this principle to all impacts of spheres with smooth surfaces.

Key point 8.3

When an object moving at velocity u collides at an angle θ with a smooth, flat surface and rebounds:

- The impulse acts at right angles to the surface and is equal to the change in momentum in that direction.
- The component of the velocity parallel to the surface remains unchanged.
- The component of the velocity perpendicular to the surface is multiplied by $-e$, where e is the coefficient of restitution between the object and the surface.

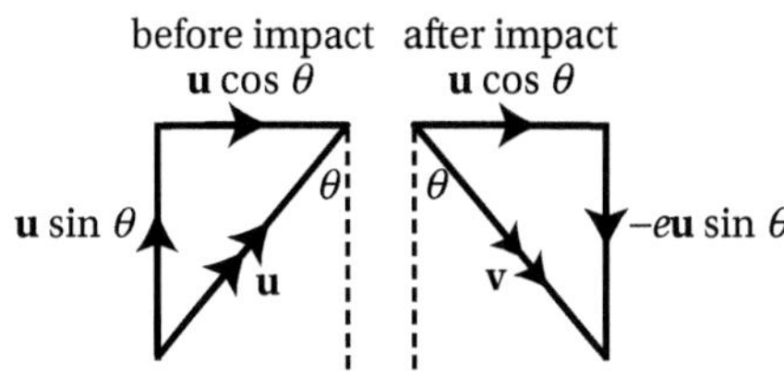

WORKED EXAMPLE 8.6

An exercise ball, A, of mass 2 kg, is moving in a straight line at 5 m s^{-1} on a smooth horizontal surface when it collides with a smooth wall. The line of motion of the ball makes an angle of 40° with the wall. If the coefficient of restitution between the wall and the ball is 0.6, find the speed and direction of the ball when it rebounds from the wall. Give your speed correct to 2 decimal places and the angle correct to 1 decimal place.

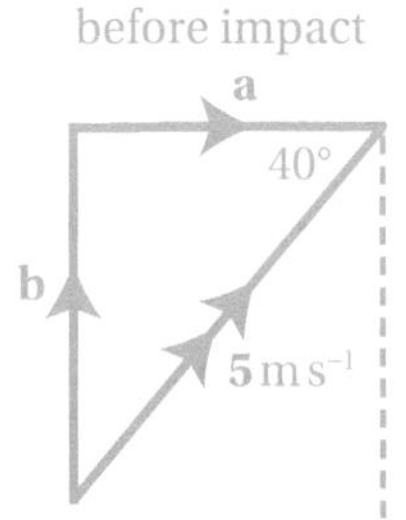

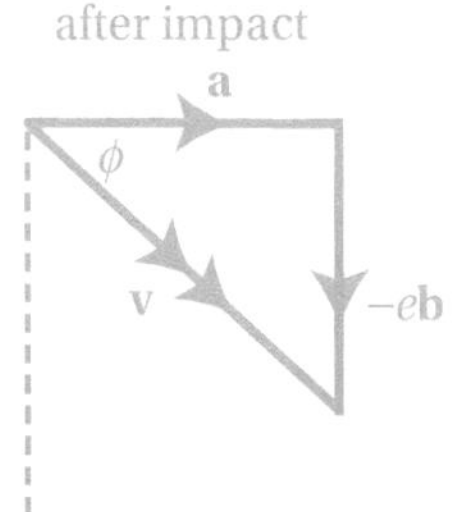

Draw a clear diagram showing the component of velocity parallel to the wall unchanged and the component of velocity perpendicular to the wall changed to $-eb$. You can write the components in as a and b or 5 cos 40 and 5 sin 40.

$a = 5\cos 40$

$b = 5\sin 40$

$eb = 0.6 \times 5\sin 40$

Resolve u (= 5 m s^{-1}) to find the values of a and b and work out eb.

$v = \sqrt{(5\cos 40)^2 + (0.6 \times 5\sin 40)^2}$

$v = 4.29\text{ m s}^{-1}$

Use Pythagoras' theorem to find v.

$\tan\phi = \frac{eb}{a} = \frac{0.6 \times 5\sin 40}{5\cos 40}$

$\phi = 26.7°$

Use trigonometry to find the angle.

WORKED EXAMPLE 8.7

A smooth vertical wall is parallel to the **i** direction. A smooth sphere of mass 3 kg moving with velocity $(3\mathbf{i}+5\mathbf{j})$ m s^{-1} on a smooth horizontal plane collides with the wall and rebounds with velocity $(a\mathbf{i}+b\mathbf{j})$ m s^{-1}. If the coefficient of restitution between the wall and the sphere is 0.75, find the values of a and b.

Working	Explanation
Velocity before collision $= 3\underset{\sim}{i}+5\underset{\sim}{j}$ Rebound velocity $= a\underset{\sim}{i}+b\underset{\sim}{j}$	As the velocity is given as a vector, you know the components of the velocity so there is no need to resolve.
$a=3$	There is no impulse parallel to the wall so there is no change of speed parallel to the wall.
$b=-e\times 5=-0.75\times 5$ $=-3.75$	Perpendicular to the wall, use the relationship $v=-eu$. Note that here you include the minus sign in $v=-eu$ since you are modelling the motion in the positive **j** direction. A negative answer tells you the sphere is now moving in the negative **j** direction.
$a=3, b=-3.75$	You were asked for the values of a and b so you do not need to write the answer as a vector.

Finding the impulse

In Worked example 8.6, the impulse on the 2 kg ball was acting perpendicular to the wall, as in the diagram.

Taking the direction away from the wall as the positive direction, the perpendicular component of impulse is the change in momentum perpendicular to the wall, which equals $meb-(-mb)=meb+mb$.

$mb=2\times 5\sin 40$

$meb=2\times 0.6\times 5\sin 40$

$I=meb+mb=6\sin 40+10\sin 40=10.3$ N s (to 3 s.f.)

There is no component of impulse parallel to the wall.

An alternative approach is to use vectors to find **I** from an impulse-momentum vector triangle. The vector triangle needs to show the final momentum $m\mathbf{v}$ as the resultant of $m\mathbf{u}$ and **I**. In vectors $m\mathbf{v}=m\mathbf{u}+\mathbf{I}$ or $\mathbf{I}=m\mathbf{v}-m\mathbf{u}$ or $\mathbf{I}=-m\mathbf{u}+m\mathbf{v}$ as shown in the diagram. The easiest way to get the sides in the correct order is to draw the initial and final momentum from the same point.

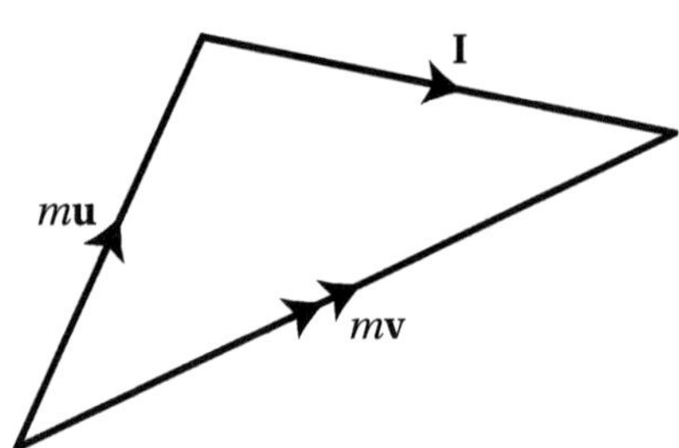

The double arrows on the $m\mathbf{v}$ side of the triangle indicate that it is the resultant of $m\mathbf{u}$ and **I**, as you would expect.

In Worked example 8.6, the mass of the ball was 2 kg and $|u|$ was 5 m s^{-1} and you found that $|v| = 4.29$ m s^{-1} and $\phi = 26.7°$.

Therefore $m|u| = 2 \times 5 = 10$ kg m s^{-1} and $m|v| = 2 \times 4.29 = 8.58$ kg m s^{-1}. Using these values, the triangle would look like this:

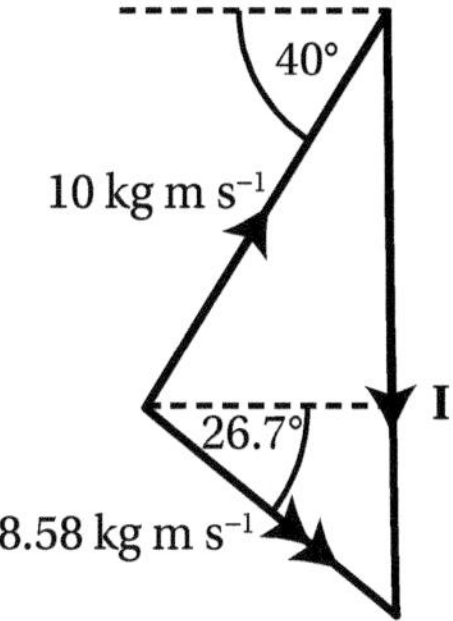

and $\mathbf{I} = 10 \sin 40 + 8.58 \sin 26.7 = 10.3$ N s (to 3 s.f.).

Tip

In a problem involving a simple impact with a wall, when the impulse acts at right angles to the wall, then the method of splitting into components works best but in some problems drawing the impulse–momentum triangle can save pages of calculation. These are usually problems with a single moving object being hit so that it is deflected through a given angle, or collisions with a rough wall when you are specifically told that the impulse is not perpendicular to the wall.

WORKED EXAMPLE 8.8

A small smooth sphere of mass 600 g is moving in a horizontal plane at 60° to a smooth vertical wall when it collides with the wall. The speed of the sphere immediately before the collision is 10 m s^{-1}. The coefficient of restitution between the sphere and the wall is 0.7.

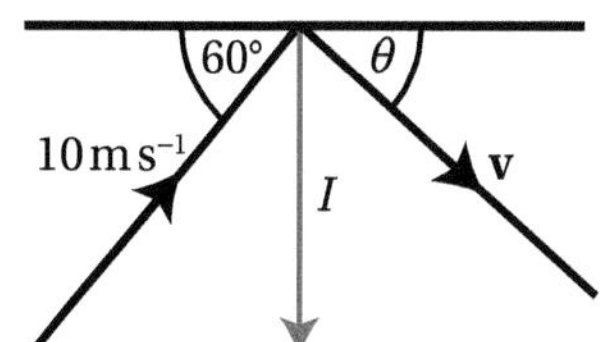

a Find the magnitude and direction of the sphere's velocity immediately after the collision.

b Find the impulse of the wall on the sphere.

a

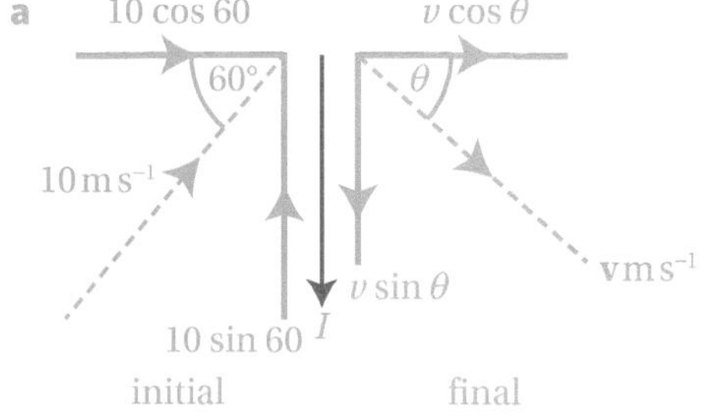

This is an oblique collision between a sphere moving horizontally and a vertical wall so can you solve it by resolving parallel and perpendicular to the wall.

Draw clear diagrams with arrows showing the direction and values of the velocities before and after the collision, split into the components of their speeds parallel and perpendicular to the wall.

Let the speed of the sphere after the collision be v m s^{-1} at angle θ to the wall.

Define any unknown values.

Continues on next page ...

$v\cos\theta = 10\cos 60 = 10 \times 0.5 = 5$

The component of the initial velocity parallel to the wall remains unchanged in the collision, as there is no impulse in that direction.

$v\sin\theta = e \times 10\sin 60$

$= 0.7 \times 10 \times \frac{\sqrt{3}}{2} = 3.5\sqrt{3}$

Find the component of the velocity perpendicular to the wall using $v = -eu$.

$v^2 = 5^2 + (3.5\sqrt{3})^2 = 61.75$

Calculate the value of v from its components.

$v = 7.86\ \text{m s}^{-1}$ (3 s.f.)

$\frac{v\sin\theta}{v\cos\theta} = \tan\theta$

$= \frac{3.5\sqrt{3}}{5}$

$\theta = 50.5°$

Find $\tan\theta$ and hence θ.

b $600\ \text{g} = 0.6\ \text{kg}$

Convert g to kg.

$I = mv\sin\theta - (-m10\sin 60)$

$= 0.6 \times 3.5 \times \sqrt{3} - (-0.6 \times 5 \times \sqrt{3})$

$= 8.83$ N s (3 s.f.) away from the wall

Use impulse = change in momentum $= mv - mu$.

Decide on a direction to be positive - it is usually best to take away from the wall as positive - and substitute in the values.

WORKED EXAMPLE 8.9

A cricket ball of mass 160 g is travelling horizontally at speed of 30 m s^{-1} when it is hit by a cricket bat. It leaves the bat, horizontally, at a speed of 40 m s^{-1} travelling at 40° to the line of its original path as shown in the diagram. What is the magnitude of the impulse of the bat on the ball?

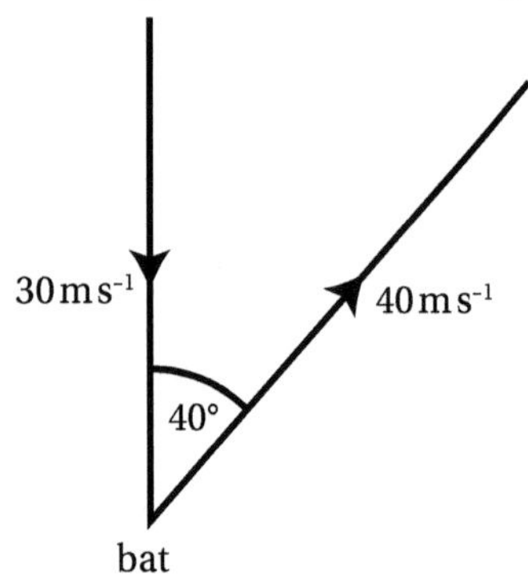

$160\ \text{g} = 0.16\ \text{kg}$

Convert g to kg.

$|mu| = 4.8\ \text{kg m s}^{-1}$ and $|mv| = 6.4\ \text{kg m s}^{-1}$

Calculate $|mu|$ and $|mv|$.

Continues on next page ...

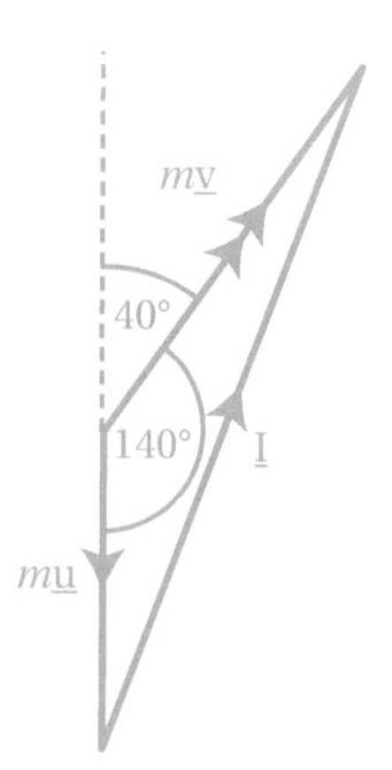

Draw a momentum-impulse triangle, remembering to keep the directions of the two velocities and to draw $m\mathbf{u}$ and $m\mathbf{v}$ coming away from the same point. You need to find the obtuse angle in the triangle.

$I^2 = 6.4^2 + 4.8^2 - (2 \times 6.4 \times 4.8 \times \cos 140)$

$I^2 = 40.96 + 23.04 - (61.44 \times (-0.766)) = 111.066$

$I = 10.5$ N (to 3 s.f.)

Use the cosine rule to find I.

WORKED EXAMPLE 8.10

A sphere of mass 5 kg is moving with velocity 4 m s^{-1} in the positive **i** direction when it is hit with a blow of impulse 15 N s in the positive **j** direction. What is the speed and direction of the sphere immediately after the impulse?

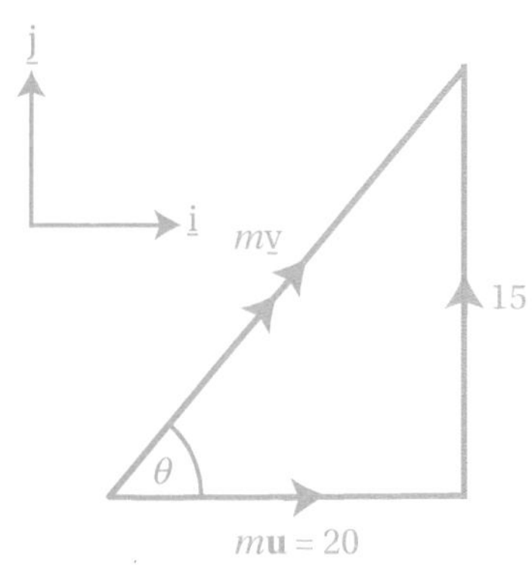

Draw the impulse-momentum triangle, remembering to multiply the velocity by the mass to get the momentum. You are given the magnitude and direction of the impulse and the magnitude and direction of $m\mathbf{u}$. Remember to show $m\mathbf{v}$ and $m\mathbf{u}$ coming away from the same point.

$(mv)^2 = 15^2 + 20^2$

Use Pythagoras' theorem to find mv.

$mv = 25$

$v = \frac{25}{5}$

$= 5$ m s^{-1}

Divide by m to find the speed.

$\theta = \tan^{-1}\left(\frac{15}{20}\right) = 36.9°$

Use trigonometry to find the angle.

Immediately after the collision the sphere moves with speed 5 m s^{-1} at 36.9° to the positive i direction.

State the final speed and direction of the sphere.

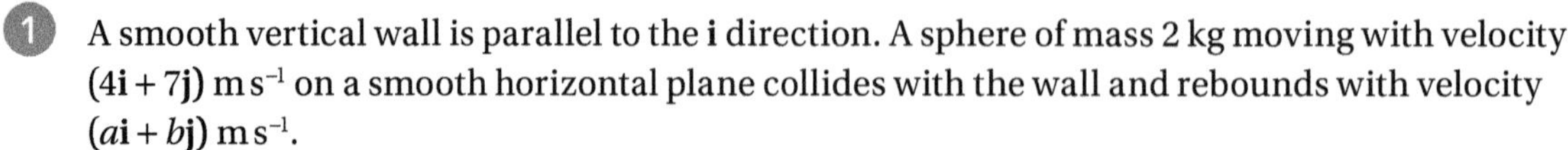

Focus on ...

You will use an impulse–momentum triangle to solve a problem involving conservation of energy in Focus on ... Problem solving 2.

EXERCISE 8B

1 A smooth vertical wall is parallel to the **i** direction. A sphere of mass 2 kg moving with velocity $(4\mathbf{i}+7\mathbf{j})\ \mathrm{m\,s^{-1}}$ on a smooth horizontal plane collides with the wall and rebounds with velocity $(a\mathbf{i}+b\mathbf{j})\ \mathrm{m\,s^{-1}}$.

a If the coefficient of restitution between the wall and the sphere is 0.6, find the values of a and b.

b What is the magnitude of the velocity of the sphere when it rebounds from the wall?

2 A smooth vertical wall is parallel to the **i** direction. A sphere of mass 4 kg moving with velocity $(\mathbf{i}+6\mathbf{j})\ \mathrm{m\,s^{-1}}$ on a smooth horizontal plane collides with the wall and rebounds with velocity $(a\mathbf{i}+b\mathbf{j})\ \mathrm{m\,s^{-1}}$.

a If the coefficient of restitution between the wall and the sphere is 0.8, find the values of a and b.

b What is the loss of kinetic energy of the sphere as a result of its collision with the wall?

3 A particle, A, of mass 4 kg is moving in a straight line at $5\ \mathrm{m\,s^{-1}}$ on a smooth horizontal surface when it collides with a smooth vertical wall. The line of motion of the particle makes an angle of $60°$ with the wall.

a What is the component of the speed of the particle parallel to the wall?

b What is the component of the speed of the particle perpendicular to the wall before the collision?

c If the coefficient of restitution between the wall and the particle is 0.5, find the component of the speed perpendicular to the wall immediately after the collision.

d Find the speed and direction of the particle when it rebounds from the wall. Give your speed correct to 2 decimal places and the angle correct to 1 decimal place.

4 A sphere of mass 3 kg is moving in a straight line at $5\ \mathrm{m\,s^{-1}}$ on a smooth horizontal surface when it collides with a smooth vertical wall. The line of motion of the sphere makes an angle of $30°$ with the wall. If the coefficient of restitution between the wall and the sphere is 0.4, find the speed and direction of the sphere when it rebounds from the wall. Give your speed correct to 2 decimal places and the angle correct to 1 decimal place.

5 A particle, of mass m kg, is moving in a straight line at $v\ \mathrm{m\,s^{-1}}$ on a smooth horizontal surface when it collides with a smooth vertical wall. The line of motion of the sphere makes an angle of θ with the wall.

a What is the component of the velocity of the particle parallel to the wall, immediately before the collision?

b What is the component of the velocity of the particle parallel to the wall, immediately after the collision?

c What is the component of the velocity of the particle perpendicular to the wall, immediately before the collision?

d If the coefficient of restitution between the wall and the sphere is e, what is the component of the velocity of the particle perpendicular to the wall, immediately after the collision?

e Find the magnitude of the velocity of the particle immediately after the collision.

f Show that the loss in kinetic energy as a result of the collision is $\frac{1}{2}mv^2\sin^2\theta\left(1-e^2\right)$.

6 A small smooth ball of mass 800 g is moving in a straight line at 4 m s^{-1} on a smooth horizontal surface when it collides with a smooth vertical wall. The line of motion of the ball makes an angle of 45° with the wall. If the coefficient of restitution between the wall and the sphere is 0.6:

a find the speed and direction of the ball when it rebounds from the wall

b find the impulse of the wall on the ball.

7 A sphere of mass 2 kg is moving in the positive **i** direction with speed 4 m s^{-1} when it receives a blow of impulse 6 N s acting in the negative **j** direction. Find the magnitude and direction of the velocity of the sphere immediately after the impact.

8 A sphere of mass 6 kg is moving in the positive **i** direction with speed 8 m s^{-1} when it receives a blow of impulse 10 N s acting in the **j** direction. Find the change in kinetic energy of the sphere as a result of the impulse.

9 A football of mass 400 g is travelling horizontally at speed of 20 m s^{-1}. The football is then kicked, and it immediately moves horizontally, at a speed of 25 m s^{-1}, travelling at 30° to the line of its original path, as shown in the diagram. What is the magnitude of the impulse of the kick?

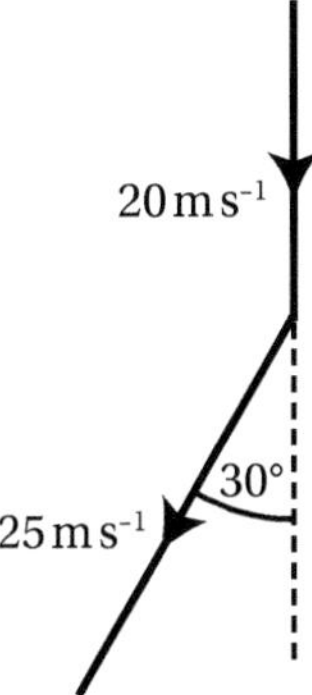

10 A snooker ball of mass 160 g hits a vertical side cushion of a snooker table at a speed of 5 m s^{-1} at an angle of 35° to the cushion, as shown in the diagram. The impulse of the cushion on the ball is perpendicular to the side of the table and the coefficient of restitution between the ball and the side cushion is 0.8.

a At what speed and angle to the side of the table does the ball leave the side cushion of the table?

b What is the kinetic energy lost by the snooker ball as a result of the collision?

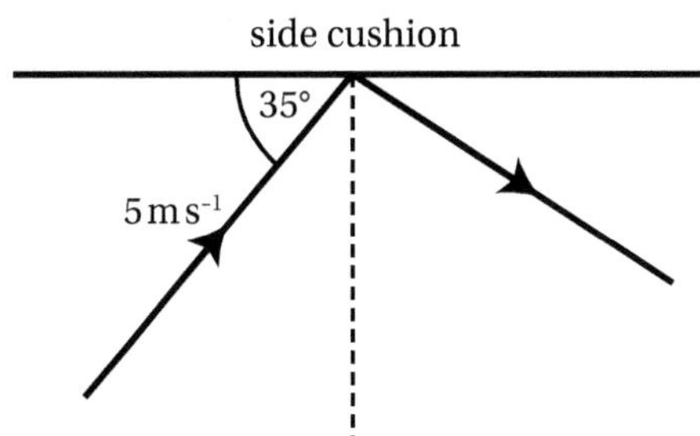

11 A snooker ball of mass 160 g hits a vertical side cushion of a snooker table at a speed of u m s^{-1} at an angle of θ to the cushion as shown in the diagram. The impulse of the cushion on the ball is perpendicular to the side of the table and the coefficient of restitution between the ball and the side cushion is 0.8. The ball then hits the side cushion that is at right angles to the original cushion. The coefficient of restitution between the ball and this side cushion is also 0.8. At what speed and angle to the side of the table does the ball leave the second side cushion?

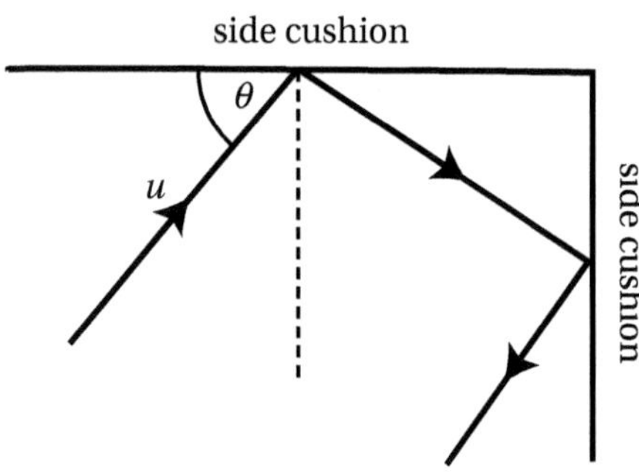

Section 3: Oblique collisions of two spheres and impulsive tensions in strings

You are now going to consider the oblique impact of two moving spheres.

When two smooth spheres collide, the force of the collision will act along the line joining the centre of the spheres - at right angles to the tangent at the point where they meet, as shown in the diagram.

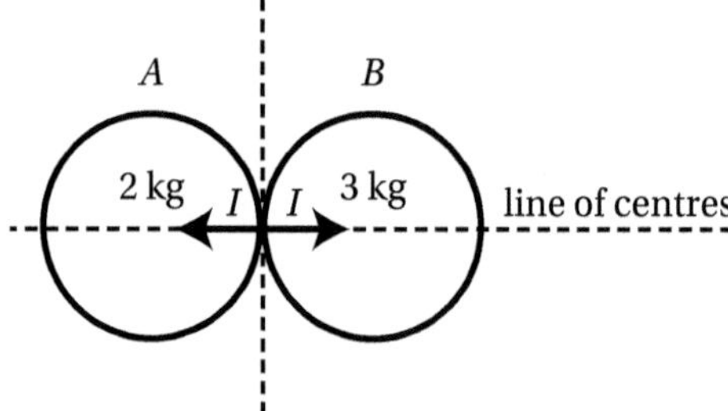

Key point 8.4

When two smooth spheres collide, the impulse is along the line of centres of the spheres.

You can apply the principle of conservation of momentum and Newton's experimental law to the components of velocity along the line of centres.

There is no change in the components of velocity perpendicular to the line of centres as there is no impulse in that direction.

Did you know?

In a standard game of snooker all the balls are the same size and weight, but in coin-operated pool and bar-billiards machines the white cue ball is a different weight and size from the rest of the colours. This is so that the machine can detect if it goes down a pocket and can return it.

WORKED EXAMPLE 8.11

A sphere, A, of mass 2 kg, is moving on a smooth horizontal surface with velocity $(4\mathbf{i}+5\mathbf{j})$ m s^{-1} when it collides with a second sphere, B, of equal size and mass 3 kg, moving on the same surface with velocity $(3\mathbf{i}+\mathbf{j})$ m s^{-1}. The line of centres of the two spheres at the moment of collision is parallel to the **i** direction and the coefficient of restitution between the two spheres is 0.8. Find the velocities of A and B immediately after the collision.

Let the velocity of A after the collision be $a\underset{\sim}{i}+b\underset{\sim}{j}$ and let the velocity of B after the collision be $c\underset{\sim}{i}+d\underset{\sim}{j}$.

Define any unknowns. Put both A and B in component form so you have four unknowns.

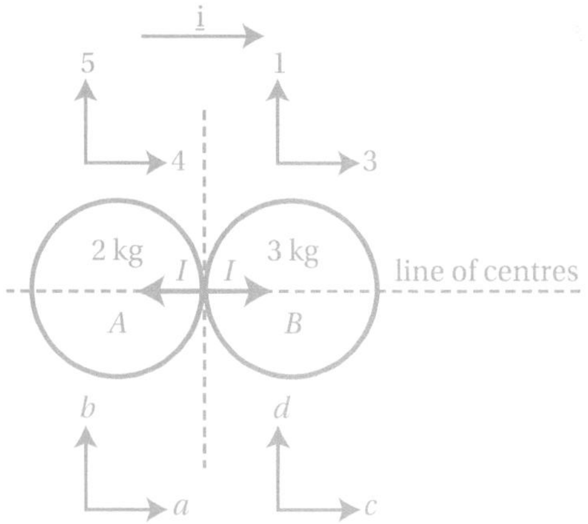

Draw a clear diagram.

$b=5$ and $d=1$

Deal with the components of the velocity perpendicular to the line of centres first. These components remain unchanged.

$$m_1u_1+m_2u_2=m_1v_1+m_2v_2$$

$$(2\times4)+(3\times3)=2a+3c$$

$$\text{so } 2a+3c=17 \qquad (1)$$

Apply the principle of conservation of linear momentum to the components along the line of centres. State the equation and substitute the values you know.

$$e=\frac{c-a}{4-3}$$

$$0.8(4-3)=c-a$$

$$\text{so } c-a=0.8 \qquad (2)$$

Apply Newton's experimental law. State the equation and substitute the values you know.

$a=2.92$ and $c=3.72$

Solve (1) and (2) simultaneously to find a and b.

Velocity of $A=2.92\underset{\sim}{i}+5\underset{\sim}{j}$

Velocity of $B=3.72\underset{\sim}{i}+\underset{\sim}{j}$

Give the velocities of A and B in vector format.

If you are not given the velocities in component form, then you have to resolve the velocities parallel and perpendicular to the line of centres before you start the calculation.

You learned how to resolve a force into components in A Level Mathematics Student Book 2.

WORKED EXAMPLE 8.12

Two smooth spheres, A and B, of masses 4 kg and 1 kg, respectively, collide. Immediately before the collision, A is moving at 4 m s^{-1} at an angle θ above the line of centres, where $\sin\theta = \frac{4}{5}$. B is moving at 3 m s^{-1} towards A, at an angle ϕ below the line of centres, where $\sin\phi = \frac{3}{5}$, as shown in the diagram. The coefficient of restitution between the two spheres is 0.4.

a What are the magnitudes and directions of the velocities of the two spheres immediately after the collision?

b What is the magnitude of the impulse on B?

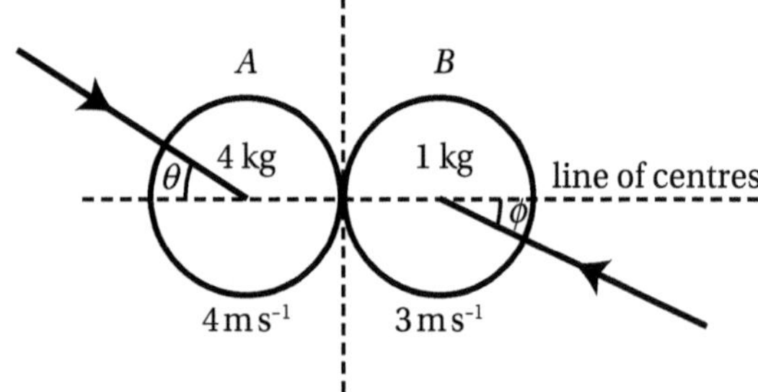

a $4\sin\theta = 3.2$

$4\cos\theta = 2.4$

$3\sin\phi = 1.8$

$3\cos\phi = 2.4$

Calculate the components of the initial velocities for A and B.

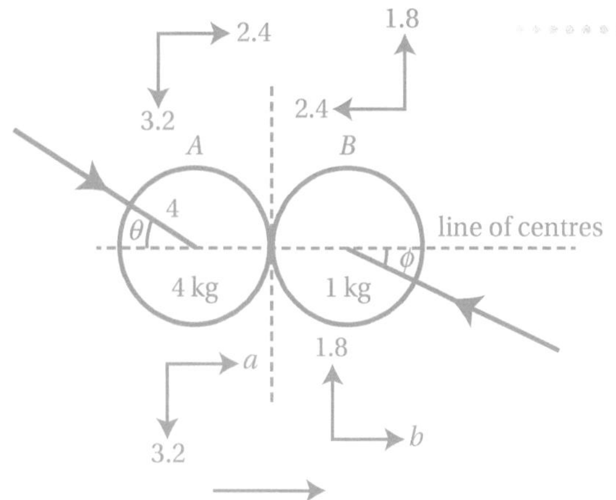

Put the components of the initial velocities above the relevant sphere and the final components below, so you don't get confused.

The components of the velocities perpendicular to the line of centres remain unchanged and can be put on the diagram as final velocity components immediately.

Continues on next page ...

$m_1u_1 + m_2u_2 = m_1v_1 + m_2v_2$

$(4 \times 2.4) - (1 \times 2.4) = 4a + b$

so $4a + b = 7.2$

Apply the principle of conservation and momentum along the line of centres.

$e = \frac{v_2 - v_1}{u_1 - u_2}$

$0.4(2.4 - (-2.4)) = b - a$

so $b - a = 1.92$

Apply Newton's experimental law along the line of centres.

$a = 1.056$, $b = 2.976$

Solve the simultaneous equations.

The components of the velocity of A are 1.056 and 3.2

so $v_A = \sqrt{1.056^2 + 3.2^2} = 3.37$ (to 3 s.f.)

$\tan^{-1}\left(\frac{3.2}{1.056}\right) = 71.7°$

$v_A = 3.37\ \text{m s}^{-1}$ at an angle of 71.7° to the line of centres

Find the velocity of A using Pythagoras' theorem and the direction using trigonometry.

The components of the velocity of B are 2.976 and 1.8

so $v_B = \sqrt{2.976^2 + 1.8^2} = 3.48$ (to 3 s.f.)

$\tan^{-1}\left(\frac{1.8}{2.976}\right) = 31.2°$

$v_B = 3.48\ \text{m s}^{-1}$ at an angle of 31.2° to the line of centres

Find the velocity of B using Pythagoras' theorem and the direction using trigonometry.

b $I = mv - mu$

Use impulse = change in momentum.

The impulse on the spheres is along the line of centres and the impulse on B is equal and opposite to the impulse on A. If one is easier to work out than the other you choose that one. In this case, there is nothing to choose between them.

For B:

$I = (1 \times 2.976) - (1 \times (-2.4)) = 5.376\ \text{N s}$

$I = 5.38\ \text{N s}$ (to 3 s.f.) along the line of centres

Substitute in the numbers and state the magnitude of the impulse. Be careful with the signs.

Impulsive tensions in strings

In the diagram, the particles A and B, of masses 2.5 kg and 1.5 kg respectively, are joined by a light, inextensible string that is straight but not under tension. Particle B is initially at rest and particle A is projected at an angle of 45° to the string with speed $4\sqrt{2}$ m s^{-1}.

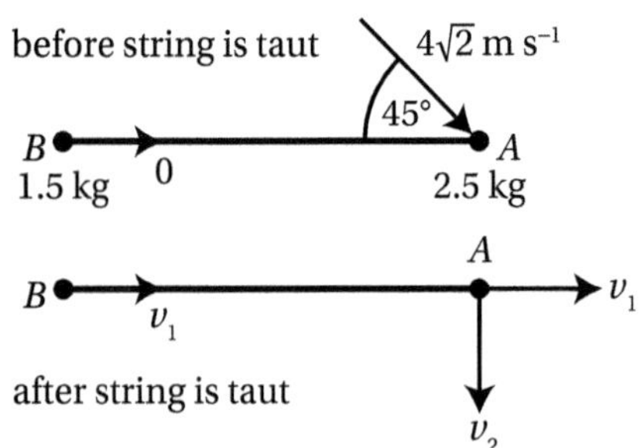

The diagram shows the velocities of A and B at the instants before and after the string becomes taut.

Rewind

In Chapter 3 you saw that when two particles are attached to the ends of a light elastic string and one is set in motion, an impulsive force was generated in the string when it becomes taut.

When the string becomes taut, there will be an impulse on both A and B generated by the tension in the string and the velocities of A and B will change. The new velocity of B along the string will be the same as the component of the new velocity of A along the string and in the same direction. The component of the velocity of A perpendicular to the string will be unchanged as the impulsive tension in the string acts along the string.

You can find v_1 and v_2 by using the principle of conservation of momentum.

Parallel to BA:

$$2.5 \times 4\sqrt{2} \times \cos 45 = 1.5v_1 + 2.5v_1 \Rightarrow v_1 = 2.5$$

Perpendicular to BA:

$$2.5 \times 4\sqrt{2} \times \sin 45 = 2.5v_2 \Rightarrow v_2 = 4$$

B starts to move along the length of the string with speed 2.5 m s^{-1} and A then starts to move with speed $\sqrt{2.5^2 + 4^2} = \sqrt{22.25} = 4.717$ m s^{-1} at an angle $\tan^{-1}\dfrac{4}{2.5}$ to the line of the string.

Impulsive tension $= mv_1 - mu = (1.5 \times 2.5) - 0 = 3.75$ N s. This will be the same for both A and B.

Key point 8.5

For particles connected by a light inextensible string, you need to split the velocities into components parallel and perpendicular to the string.

You then apply the principle of conservation of momentum parallel and perpendicular to the string.

WORKED EXAMPLE 8.13

A light, inextensible string has particles A and B, each of mass 400 g, attached to either end. The string and particles rest on a smooth table. The particle at A is hit with an impulse of 8 N s at an angle of 30° to the string, which is straight but not taut and at rest. What is the velocity of B after the impulse at the instant the string becomes taut?

$400\text{ g} = 0.4\text{ kg}$ — Convert g to kg.

$\text{Impulse} = mu$ — Calculate the initial speed of A using impulse = change in momentum.

$8 = 0.4u$

$u = 20\text{ m s}^{-1}$ at 30° to the string

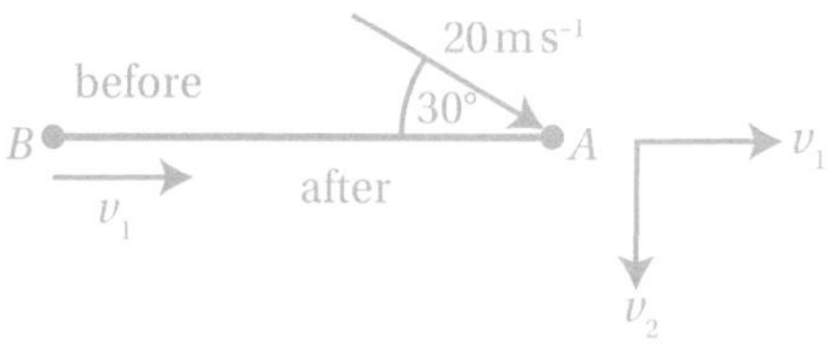

Draw a clear diagram showing the velocity of A immediately before the string starts to move and the components of the velocities of A and B, parallel and perpendicular to the string, immediately afterwards.

Parallel to the line of the string:

$0.4 \times 20\cos 30 = 0.4v_1 + 0.4v_1 \Rightarrow v_1 = 5\sqrt{3}$

The velocity of B after the impulse is $5\sqrt{3}\text{ m s}^{-1}$ along BA.

EXERCISE 8C

1. A smooth sphere, A, of mass 2 kg, is moving on a smooth horizontal surface with velocity $(3\mathbf{i} + 2\mathbf{j})\text{ m s}^{-1}$ when it collides with a second smooth sphere, B, of mass 3 kg, moving on the same surface with velocity $(2\mathbf{i} + 3\mathbf{j})\text{ m s}^{-1}$. The line of centres of the two spheres at the moment of collision is parallel to the $\mathbf{i}$ direction and the coefficient of restitution between the two spheres is 0.3. Find the velocities of A and B immediately after the collision.

2. A smooth sphere, P, of mass 5 kg, is moving on a smooth horizontal surface with velocity $(3\mathbf{i} + \mathbf{j})\text{ m s}^{-1}$ when it collides with a second smooth sphere, Q, of mass 2 kg, moving on the same surface with velocity $(\mathbf{i} + 3\mathbf{j})\text{ m s}^{-1}$. The line of centres of the two spheres at the moment of collision is parallel to the $\mathbf{i}$ direction and the coefficient of restitution between the two spheres is 0.4. Find the velocities of P and Q immediately after the collision.

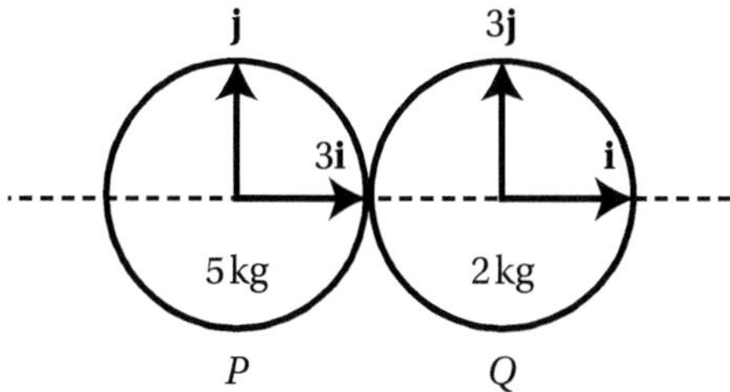

3 A smooth sphere, A, of mass 3 kg, is moving on a smooth horizontal surface with velocity $(2\mathbf{i}+3\mathbf{j})\ \text{m s}^{-1}$ when it collides with a second smooth sphere, B, of mass 2 kg, which is at rest. The line of centres of the two spheres, at the moment of collision, is parallel to the $\mathbf{i}$ direction and the coefficient of restitution between the two spheres is 0.4. Find the magnitude and direction of the velocities of A and B immediately after the collision.

4 Two smooth spheres, A and B, of masses 3 kg and 1 kg, respectively, collide as shown in the diagram. Immediately before the collision, A is moving at $5\ \text{m s}^{-1}$ at an angle θ above the line of centres, where $\sin\theta = \frac{4}{5}$. B is initially at rest. The coefficient of restitution between the two spheres is 0.4. Find the magnitude and direction of the velocities of A and B immediately after the collision.

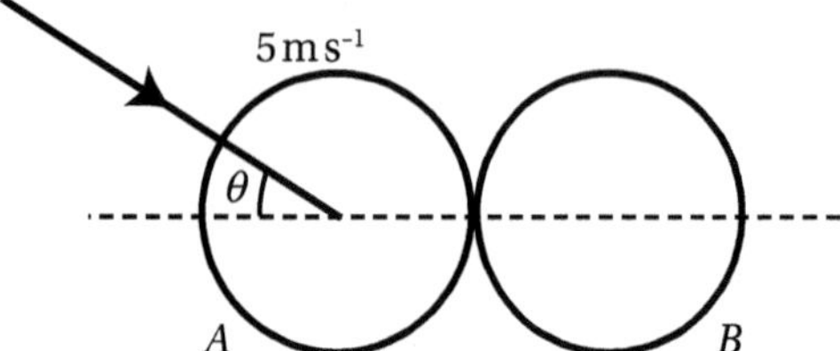

5 A smooth sphere, A, of mass 2 kg, is moving at $6\ \text{m s}^{-1}$ on a smooth horizontal surface when it collides with a second smooth sphere, B, of mass 1 kg, moving on the same surface with velocity $3\ \text{m s}^{-1}$. At the moment of collision, A is moving at 30° to the line of centres and B is moving at 40° to the line of centres towards A, as shown in the diagram. If the coefficient of restitution between the two spheres is 0.3, find the magnitude and direction of the velocities of A and B immediately after the collision.

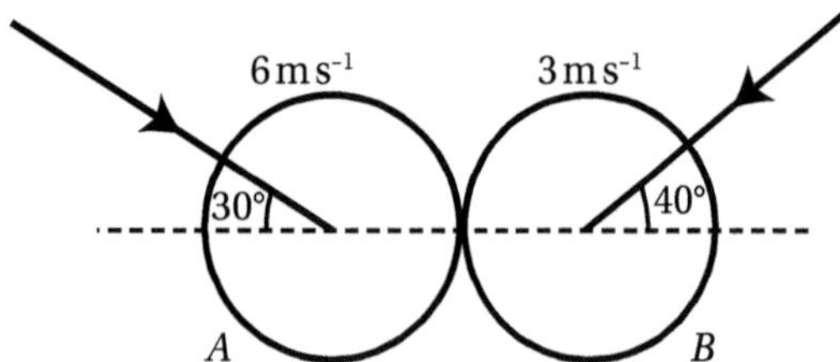

6 A smooth plastic ball, P, of mass 500 g, is moving at $6\ \text{m s}^{-1}$ on a smooth horizontal surface when it collides with a smooth metal ball, Q, of mass 2 kg, moving on the same surface with velocity $10\ \text{m s}^{-1}$. At the moment of collision, A is moving at 30° to the line of centres and B is moving at 30° to the line of centres towards A, as shown in the diagram. If the coefficient of restitution between the two spheres is 0.45, find the magnitude and direction of the velocities of P and Q immediately after the collision.

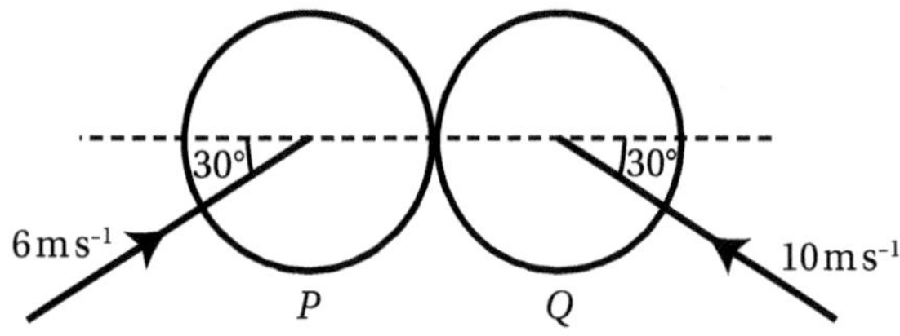

7 A particle A, of mass 3 kg, is attached by a straight, light inextensible string to a particle B of mass 2 kg. B is initially at rest and A is projected with speed 5 m s^{-1} so that, when the string is about to move, A is moving at 45° to the string, as in the diagram. Find:

a the speed of B immediately after the string becomes taut

b the magnitude of the impulsive tension in the string.

8 A particle A, of mass 2 kg, is attached by a light inextensible string to a stationary particle B of mass 1 kg. The string is initially straight but not under tension. A is hit with a blow of impulse 12 N s at 45° to the string and away from B, as in the diagram Find:

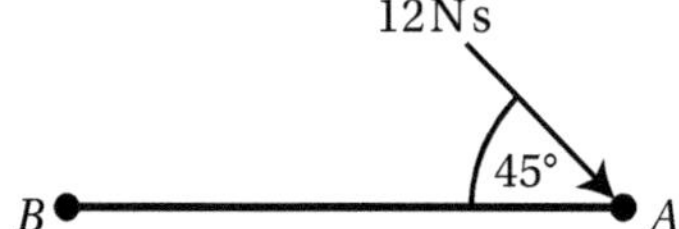

a the initial speed of A as a result of the impulse

b the speed of A immediately after the string becomes taut.

9 A particle A, of mass $2m$ kg, is attached by a light inextensible string to a stationary particle B of mass m kg. A is projected with speed 6 m s^{-1} so that, when the string is about to move into tension, A is moving at 60° to the string, as in the diagram. Find:

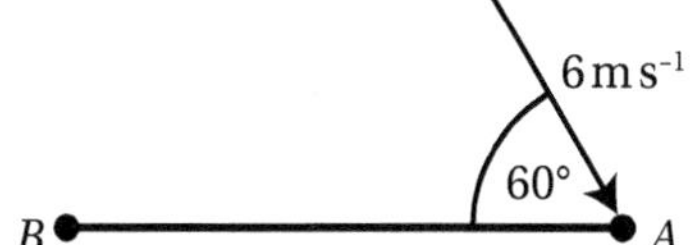

a the magnitude and direction of the speed A immediately after the string becomes taut

b the magnitude of the impulsive tension in the string

c the loss in kinetic energy in the system as a result.

Checklist of learning and understanding

- The impulse, I, of a constant force F acting for a time t is $I = Ft$.
- The impulse, I, of a variable force F acting for a time $t_1 \leqslant t \leqslant t_2$ is $I = \int_{t_1}^{t_2} F\,\mathrm{d}t$.
- The impulse of a force acting on a body is equal to the change in momentum.
- When an object moving at speed u collides at an angle θ with a smooth, flat surface and rebounds:
  - the impulse acts at right angles to the surface and is equal to the change in momentum in that direction
  - the component of the velocity parallel to the surface remains unchanged
  - the component of the velocity perpendicular to the surface is multiplied by $-e$, where e is the coefficient of restitution between the object and the surface.
- For particles connected by a light inextensible string, you need to split the velocities into components parallel and perpendicular to the string.
- You then apply the principle of conservation of momentum in directions parallel and perpendicular to the string, for the situations before and after the string becomes taut.

Mixed practice 8

1 A particle P of mass 1.2 kg is moving in a straight line with speed 6 m s^{-1} when it is deflected through an angle θ by an impulse of magnitude I N s. The impulse acts at right angles to the initial direction of motion of P (see diagram). The speed of P immediately after the impulse acts is 8 m s^{-1}. Find the value of θ and the value of I.

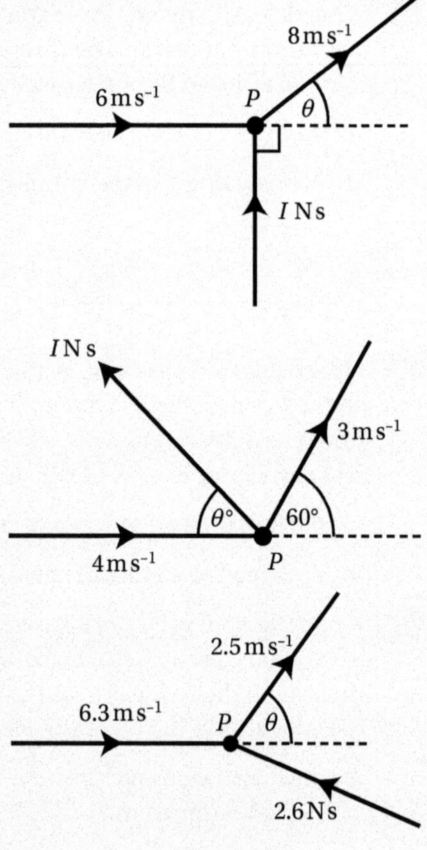

2 A particle P of mass 0.4 kg is moving horizontally with speed 4 m s^{-1} when it receives an impulse of magnitude I N s, in a direction which makes an angle $(180 - \theta)°$ with the direction of motion of P. Immediately after the impulse acts P moves horizontally with speed 3 m s^{-1}. The direction of motion of P is turned through an angle of 60° by the impulse (see diagram). Find I and θ.

© OCR, GCE Mathematics, Paper 4730, January 2010

3 A particle P of mass 0.5 kg is moving in a straight line with speed 6.3 m s^{-1}. An impulse of magnitude 2.6 N s applied to P deflects its direction of motion through an angle of θ, and reduces its speed to 2.5 m s^{-1} (see diagram). By considering an impulse-momentum triangle, or otherwise,

i show that $\cos\theta = 0.6$,

ii find the angle that the impulse makes with the original direction of motion of P.

© OCR, GCE Mathematics, Paper 4730, January 2009

4 A small ball of mass 0.6 kg is moving with speed 8 m s^{-1} when it receives an impulse of magnitude 5 N s. The speed of the ball immediately afterwards is 6 m s^{-1}. The angle between the directions of motion before and after the impulse acts is α. Using an impulse-momentum triangle or otherwise, find α.

5 A ball of mass 0.5 kg is moving with speed 22 m s^{-1} in a straight line when it is struck by a bat. The impulse exerted by the bat has magnitude 15 N s and the ball is deflected through an angle of 90° (see diagram). Find

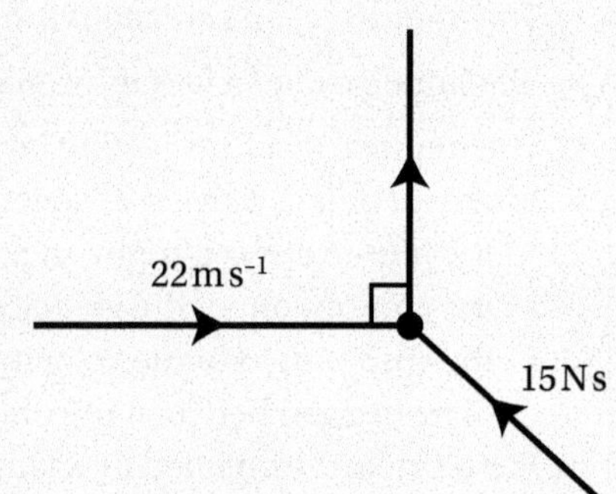

i the direction of the impulse,

ii the speed of the ball immediately after it is struck.

© OCR, GCE Mathematics, Paper 4730, January 2011

6 A particle P of mass 0.05 kg is moving on a smooth horizontal surface with speed $2\ \mathrm{m\,s^{-1}}$, when it is struck by a horizontal blow in a direction perpendicular to its direction of motion. The magnitude of the impulse of the blow is I N s. The speed of P after the blow is $2.5\ \mathrm{m\,s^{-1}}$.

i Find the value of I.

Immediately before the blow P is moving parallel to a smooth vertical wall. After the blow P hits the wall and rebounds from the wall with speed $\sqrt{5}\ \mathrm{m\,s^{-1}}$.

ii Find the coefficient of restitution between P and the wall.

7 Two uniform smooth spheres A and B, of equal radius, have masses 6 kg and 3 kg respectively. They are moving on a horizontal surface when they collide. Immediately before the collision the velocity of A has components $4\ \mathrm{m\,s^{-1}}$ along the line of centres towards B, and $v\ \mathrm{m\,s^{-1}}$ perpendicular to the line of centres. B is moving with speed $8\ \mathrm{m\,s^{-1}}$ along the line of centres towards A (see diagram). The coefficient of restitution between the spheres is e.

i Find, in terms of e, the component of the velocity of A along the line of centres immediately after the collision.

ii Given that the speeds of A and B are the same immediately after the collision, and that $3e^2 = 1$, find v.

8 Two uniform smooth spheres A and B, of equal radius, have masses 5 kg and 3 kg, respectively, They are moving on a horizontal surface, and they collide. Immediately before the collision, A is moving with speed $10\ \mathrm{m\,s^{-1}}$ at an angle α to the line of centres, where $\sin\alpha = 0.6$, and B is moving along the line of centres with speed $15\ \mathrm{m\,s^{-1}}$ (see diagram). The coefficient of restitution between the spheres is 0.6. Find the speed and direction of motion of each sphere after the collision.

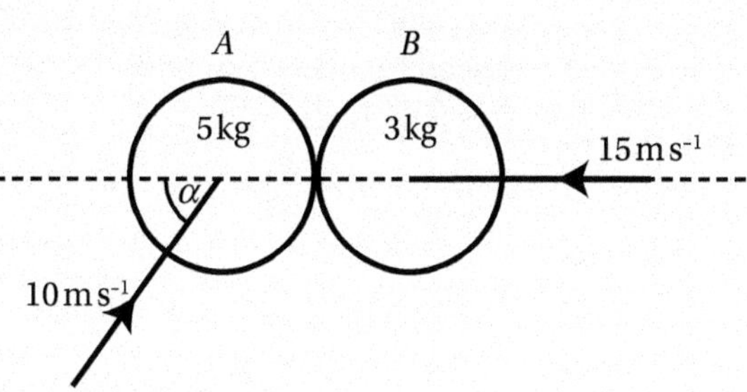

 **9** Two uniform smooth spheres A and B of equal radius are moving on a horizontal surface when they collide. A has mass 0.1 kg and B has mass 0.4 kg. Immediately before the collision A is moving with speed 2.8 m s^{-1} along the line of centres, and B is moving with speed 1 m s^{-1} at an angle θ to the line of centres, where $\cos\theta = 0.8$ (see diagram). Immediately after the collision A is stationary. Find

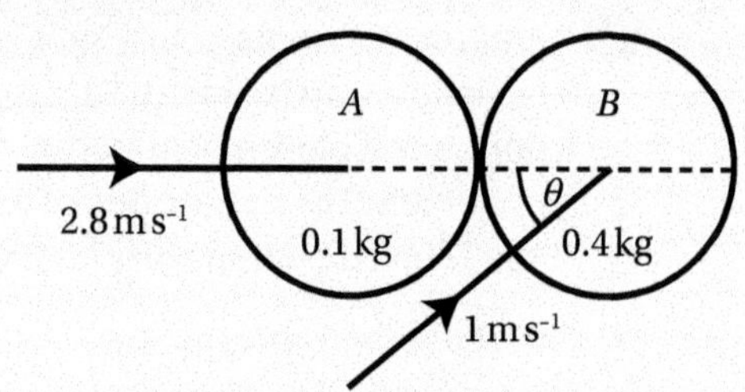

i the coefficient of restitution between A and B,

ii the angle turned through by the direction of motion of B as a result of the collision.

© OCR, GCE Mathematics, Paper 4730/01, June 2014

 **10** Two uniform smooth spheres A and B of equal radius are moving on a horizontal surface when they collide. A has mass 0.1 kg and B has mass 0.2 kg. Immediately before the collision A is moving with speed 3 m s^{-1} along the line of centres, and B is moving away from A with speed 1 m s^{-1} at an acute angle θ to the line of centres, where $\cos\theta = 0.6$ (see diagram).

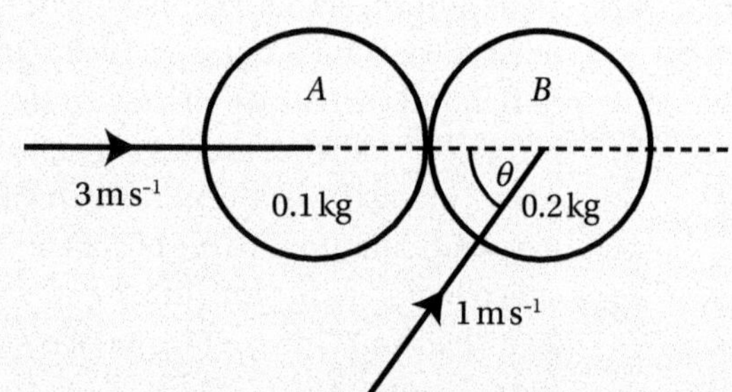

The coefficient of restitution between the spheres is 0.8. Find

i the velocity of A immediately after the collision,

ii the angle turned through by the direction of motion of B as a result of the collision.

© OCR, GCE Mathematics, Paper 4730/01, June 2013

 **11** Two uniform smooth spheres A and B, of equal radius and equal mass, are moving towards each other on a horizontal surface. Immediately before they collide, A has speed 0.3 m s^{-1} along the line of centres and B has speed 0.6 m s^{-1} at an angle of 30° to the line of centres (see diagram).

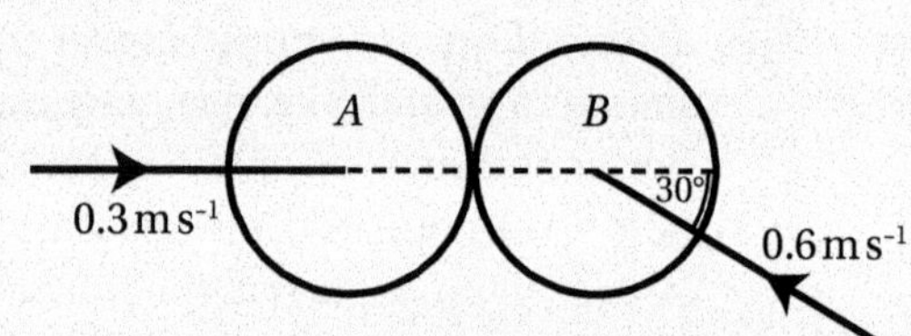

After the collision, the direction of motion of B is at right angles to its original direction of motion. Find

i the speed of B after the collision,

ii the speed and direction of motion of A after the collision,

iii the coefficient of restitution between A and B.

© OCR, GCE Mathematics, Paper 4730/01, January 2013

12 Two uniform smooth spheres A and B, of equal radius, have masses 2 kg and m kg respectively. They are moving on a horizontal surface when they collide. Immediately before the collision, A has speed 5 m s^{-1} and is moving towards B at an angle of α to the line of centres, where $\cos \alpha = 0.6$. B has speed 2 m s^{-1} and is moving towards A along the line of centres (see diagram). As a result of the collision, A's loss of kinetic energy is 7.56 J, B's direction of motion is reversed and B's speed after the collision is 0.8 m s^{-1}. Find

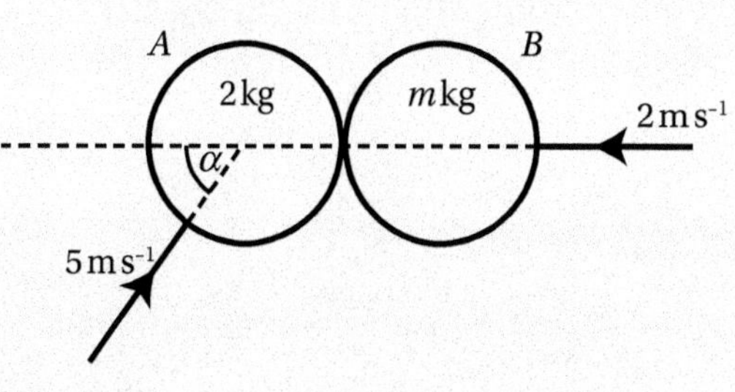

i the speed of A after the collision,

ii the component of A's velocity after the collision, parallel to the line of centres, stating with a reason whether its direction is changed to the left or to the right,

iii the value of m,

iv the coefficient of restitution between A and B.

© OCR, GCE Mathematics, Paper 4730, June 2012

13 Two uniform smooth spheres A and B, of equal radius, have masses $2m$ kg and m kg respectively. They are moving in opposite directions on a horizontal surface and they collide. Immediately before the collision, each sphere has speed u m s^{-1} in a direction making an angle α with the line of centres (see diagram). The coefficient of restitution between A and B is 0.5.

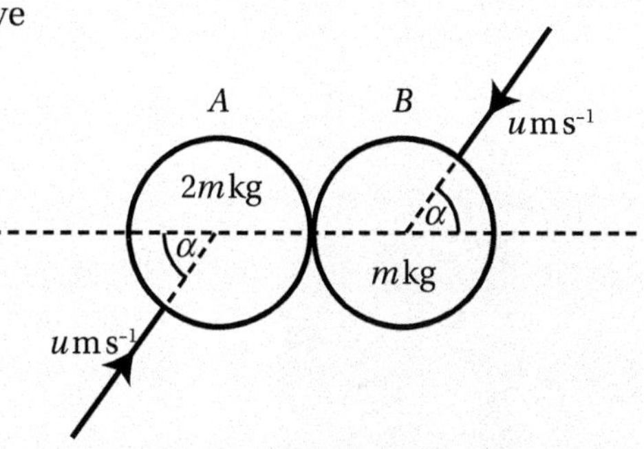

i Show that the speed of B is unchanged as a result of the collision.

ii Find the direction of motion of each of the spheres after the collision.

© OCR, GCE Mathematics, Paper 4730, January 2012

14 A particle P, of mass 3.6 kg, is attached by a light inextensible string to a particle Q, of mass 1.5 kg. Q is initially stationary and P is projected with speed 4.5 m s^{-1} so that when the string is about to move into tension, P is moving at 30° to the string. Find, correct to three significant figures:

i the speed of Q immediately after the string becomes taut

ii the magnitude of the impulsive tension in the string.

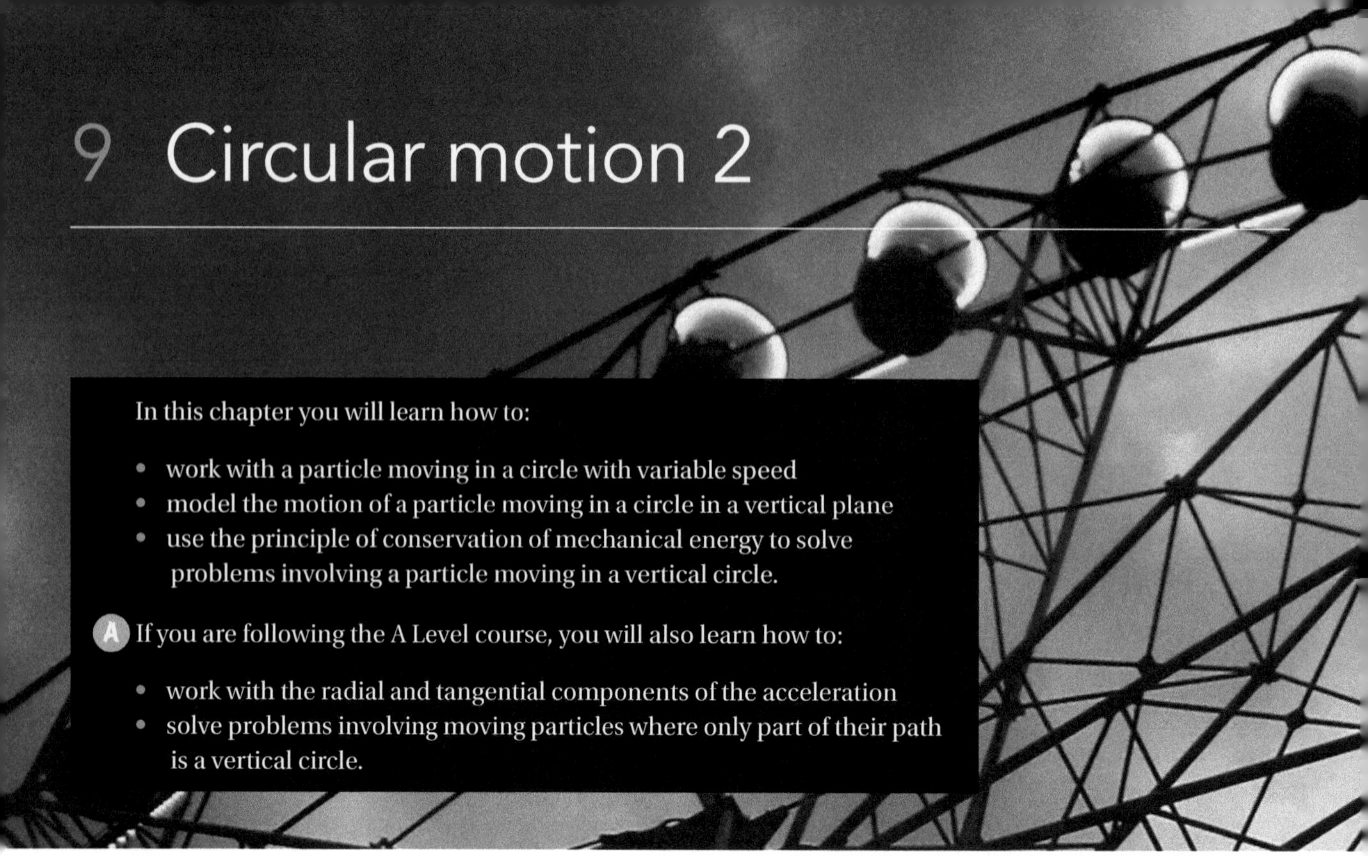

9 Circular motion 2

In this chapter you will learn how to:

- work with a particle moving in a circle with variable speed
- model the motion of a particle moving in a circle in a vertical plane
- use the principle of conservation of mechanical energy to solve problems involving a particle moving in a vertical circle.

A If you are following the A Level course, you will also learn how to:

- work with the radial and tangential components of the acceleration
- solve problems involving moving particles where only part of their path is a vertical circle.

Before you start…

Chapter 1	You should know the principle of conservation of mechanical energy (using kinetic energy and gravitational potential energy).	1 A cyclist is travelling at 4 m s^{-1} along a road when he reaches an incline making an angle of 5° with the horizontal. If the cyclist does not pedal to maintain his speed, how far along the road will he reach, assuming there is no resistance?
Chapter 4	You should be able to model motion in a horizontal circle.	2 A particle moves in a circular orbit of radius 3 m at a constant angular speed of 0.4 rad s^{-1}. What is the linear speed of the particle?
A **A Level Mathematics Student Book 1**	You should be able to model motion of a particle under constant acceleration using the equations of motion.	3 A ball is hit at an angle of 30° to the horizontal at a speed of 5 m s^{-1} from a height of 1 m above the ground. Calculate the maximum height above the ground reached by the ball.
A **A Level Mathematics Student Book 2**	You should be able to label the forces acting on an object resting on an inclined plane at an angle θ to the horizontal.	4 A 2 kg box is on the point of sliding down a plane inclined at 30° to the horizontal. Find the normal reaction between the box and the inclined plane. 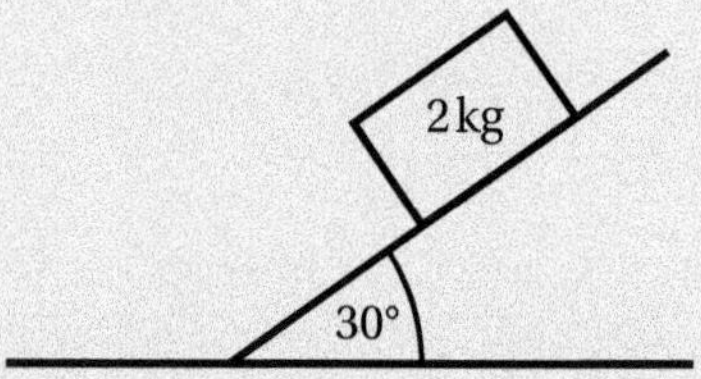

What is circular motion with variable speed?

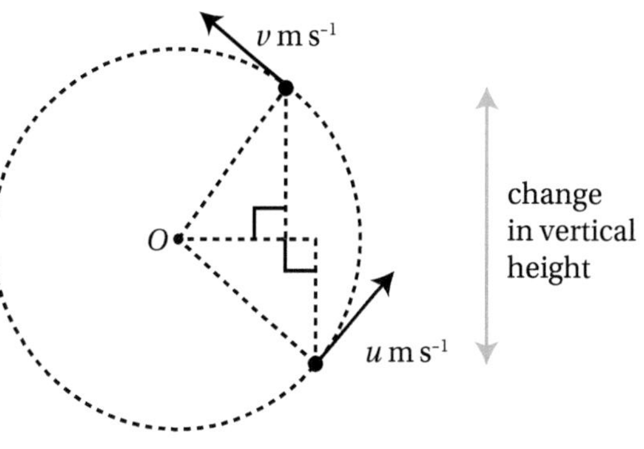

In Chapter 4 you considered the speed of a particle moving in a horizontal circle as constant, however the velocity was not since the direction of the tangential vector (the velocity vector) changes as the particle moves in a horizontal circle.

An important example of circular motion with variable speed is when a particle is moving in a vertical circle. You can consider what is happening to a particle when it moves around a vertical circle, from an initial speed u to a final speed v.

Section 1: Conservation of mechanical energy

Key point 9.1

You can use the principle of conservation of mechanical energy to determine the speed of a particle at any point in a vertical circular orbit.

Rewind

You learned about the conservation of mechanical energy in Chapter 1.

WORKED EXAMPLE 9.1

A smooth bead of mass 50 g is threaded onto a smooth circular wire of radius 2 m and centre O fixed in a vertical plane. The bead is projected from its lowest point A with speed 12 m s^{-1}.

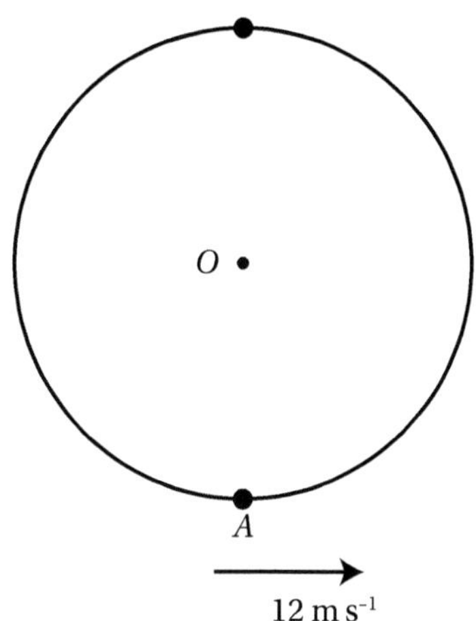

Find the speed of the bead when it reaches its highest point B in its motion.

$u_A = 12$ m s^{-1} and the vertical distance bead travels, AB, is 4 m.

Write down any information that may be helpful from the diagram. Include the zero level for gravitational potential energy.

Set the gravitational potential energy to equal zero at the horizontal line passing through the lowest point of the vertical circle, A.

Continues on next page ...

At the point A:

$GPE + KE = mgh_A + 0.5mu_A^2$

$= 0.05 \times g \times 0 + 0.5 \times 0.05 \times 12^2$

$= 3.6$

Calculate the gravitational potential energy and kinetic energy of the bead at A.

At the point B:

$GPE + KE = mgh_B + 0.5mu_B^2$

$= 0.05 \times g \times 4 + 0.5 \times 0.05 \times u_B^2$

$= 1.96 + 0.025u_B^2$

Calculate the gravitational potential energy and kinetic energy of the bead at B.

Since energy is conserved:

$3.6 = 1.96 + 0.025u_B^2$

By the principle of conservation of mechanical energy, the total energy at A is equal to the total energy at B.

$0.025u_B^2 = 3.6 - 1.96$

$u_B^2 = 65.6$

$u_B = 8.10\ \text{m s}^{-1}$ (3 s.f.)

You can rearrange to make u_B^2 the subject.

If you want to find the forces acting on a particle as it moves in a vertical circle, you can use the principle of conservation of mechanical energy to find the speed at any point and then apply Newton's second law ($F = ma$).

Acceleration towards the centre of circular motion is $\frac{v^2}{r}$, so you can calculate the force towards the centre.

Acceleration towards the centre of motion is known as a **radial acceleration**.

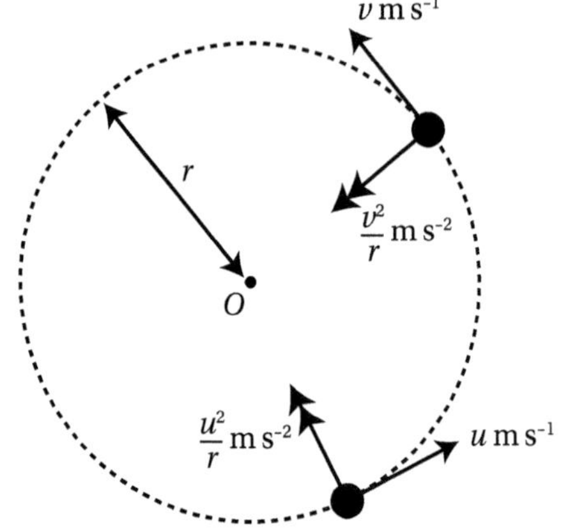

Focus on ...

In Focus on ... Problem solving 1 you solve a problem involving the impulse–momentum principle as well as conservation of mechanical energy to find the speed of a particle moving in a vertical circular orbit.

Rewind

You learned about acceleration in horizontal circular motion in Chapter 4.

Key point 9.2

Once you know the speed of a particle at a particular point in a circular path, you can:

- find the acceleration towards the centre by using $a = \frac{v^2}{r}$
- use Newton's second law to find the force towards the centre of the circle.

Fast forward

(A) The linear speed of the particle moving in a vertical circle is changing, so there is a component of acceleration (and hence also a force) acting on the particle in the direction tangential to the circle. You will find out about this in Section 2.

WORKED EXAMPLE 9.2

A smooth bead of mass 50 g is threaded onto a smooth circular wire of radius 2 m and centre O fixed in a vertical plane. The bead is projected from its lowest point A with speed 12 m s^{-1}.

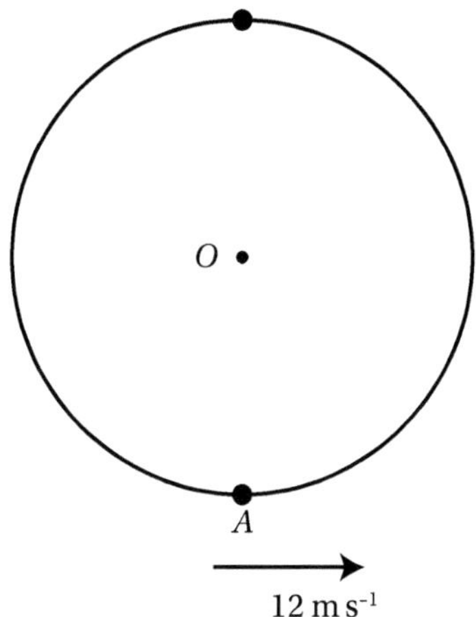

What is the magnitude of the normal reaction force of the wire on the bead when the bead is in the same horizontal line as the centre of the circle?

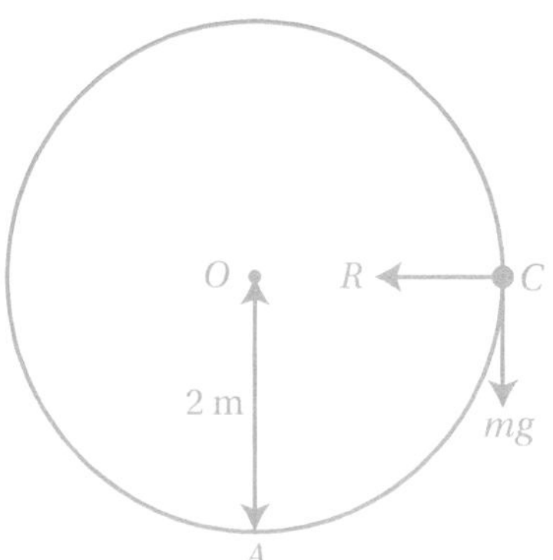

Write down any information that may be helpful on the diagram.

$u_A = 12$ m s^{-1} and the vertical distance the bead travels, AO, is 2 m. Set the gravitational potential energy to equal zero at the horizontal line passing through the lowest point of the vertical circle, A. Let C denote the position of the bead on the circular wire and R the normal reaction force of the wire on the bead.

Decide on the zero level for gravitational potential energy. You first need to find the speed of the bead at the point C when the bead is in the same horizontal line as the centre of the circle.

Continues on next page ...

At the point A:

$GPE + KE = mgh_A + 0.5mu_A^2$

$= 0.05 \times g \times 0 + 0.5 \times 0.05 \times 12^2$

$= 3.6$

Calculate the gravitational potential energy and kinetic energy of the bead at A.

At the point C:

$GPE + KE = mgh_C + 0.5mu_C^2$

$= 0.05 \times g \times 2 + 0.5 \times 0.05 \times u_C^2$

$= 0.98 + 0.025u_C^2$

Calculate the gravitational potential energy and kinetic energy of the bead at the new point C.

Since energy is conserved:

$3.6 = 0.98 + 0.025u_C^2$

By the principle of conservation of mechanical energy, the total energy at A is equal to the total energy at C.

$0.025u_C^2 = 3.6 - 0.98$

$u_C^2 = 104.8$

$u_C = 10.2\ \text{m s}^{-1}$ (3 s.f.)

Using $F = ma$ towards the centre O:

$R = 0.05 \times a$

$= 0.05 \times \frac{v^2}{r}$

$= 0.05 \times \frac{104.8}{2}$

$R = 2.62\ \text{N}$

$\frac{mv^2}{r}$ is equal to the resultant force towards the centre of the circular motion. It is the normal reaction of the wire on the bead that provides this force.

When a point in the circular motion is being considered whose radius is at an angle to the horizontal, you need to include in $F = ma$ the component of the weight towards the centre. This is shown in Worked example 9.3.

WORKED EXAMPLE 9.3

A particle of mass 0.2 kg is attached to one end of a light inextensible string of length 0.6 m. The other end of the string is attached to a fixed point O and is free to rotate in a vertical circle. The particle is hanging in equilibrium at its lowest point when it is projected with a horizontal speed of u m s^{-1}.

a Find an expression for the tension in the string when it makes an angle of θ with the downward vertical through O.

b Find the range of values of u for which the particle will perform a complete circle.

a Set the gravitational potential energy to equal zero at the horizontal line passing through the lowest point of the vertical circle. Call this point A.

Write down any information that may be helpful and draw a diagram. Include the zero level for gravitational potential energy.

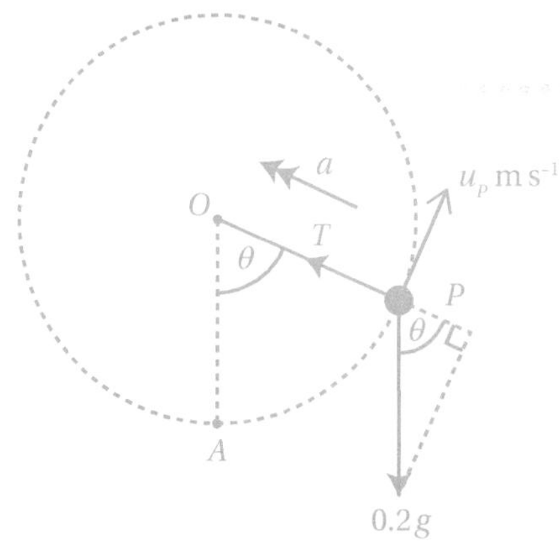

Note that only the radial acceleration is marked on the diagram since this is all you need to solve the problem, but there will also be a tangential component.

Let the particle be at position P in its circular orbit when it makes an angle of θ with the downward vertical.

Include any extra labels that might be helpful when trying to refer to position in the circular orbit.

At the lowest point, A:

Calculate the gravitational potential energy and kinetic energy of the particle at A.

$$\text{GPE} + \text{KE} = mgh_A + 0.5mu_A^2$$

$$= 0.2 \times g \times 0 + 0.5 \times 0.2 \times u^2$$

$$= 0.1u^2$$

Continues on next page ...

At the point P:

$GPE + KE = mgh_p + 0.5mu_p^2$

$= 0.2 \times g \times 0.6(1 - \cos\theta) + 0.5 \times 0.2 \times u_p^2$

$= 0.12\,g(1 - \cos\theta) + 0.1u_p^2$

Calculate the gravitational potential energy and kinetic energy of the particle at P, where h_P is the vertical height above point A.

Since energy is conserved:

$0.1u^2 = 0.12g(1 - \cos\theta) + 0.1u_p^2$

By the principle of conservation of mechanical energy, the total energy at A is equal to the total energy at P.

$u_p^2 = u^2 - 1.2g(1 - \cos\theta)$

You now have an expression for the tangential speed at P.

$$a = \frac{v^2}{r} = \frac{u^2 - 1.2g(1 - \cos\theta)}{0.6}$$

Use this speed in the formula for acceleration in circular motion.

Resolving the forces in the radial direction of the circular motion,

You can now resolve the forces in the same direction as the tension.

$F = ma$

$T - 0.2g\cos\theta$

$$= 0.2 \times \frac{u^2 - 1.2g(1 - \cos\theta)}{0.6}$$

$$T = \frac{1}{3}u^2 - 0.4g + 0.6g\cos\theta$$

Rearrange to find an expression for tension in terms of u, g and θ.

b For the particle to make a full circle the speed must be large enough so that the string is taut at the highest point in the circular motion.

For the particle to move in a full circle the string must have some tension in order to keep the string taut.

You want $T \geqslant 0$ when $\theta = 180°$:

$$\frac{1}{3}u^2 - 0.4g + 0.6g\cos 180 \geqslant 0$$

At the highest point in the movement the angle made with the downward vertical is 180°.

$$\frac{1}{3}u^2 - 0.4g - 0.6g \geqslant 0$$

$$\frac{1}{3}u^2 \geqslant 1g$$

You can rearrange to find u. This will give a lower bound for the value that the initial speed can take in order for the particle to complete a full circle.

$u^2 \geqslant 3 \times 1g$

$u \geqslant \sqrt{29.4}$

$u \geqslant 5.42\ \text{m s}^{-1}$ (3 s.f.)

Key point 9.3

If a particle connected to a light inextensible string moving in vertical circles is to complete full circles, the tension in the string must be greater than or just equal to zero at the highest point of the vertical circular orbit.

WORKED EXAMPLE 9.4

A particle of mass 0.1 kg is attached to one end of a light rod of length 0.4 m. The other end of the rod is attached to a fixed point O and is free to rotate in a vertical circle. The particle is hanging in equilibrium at its lowest point when it is projected with a horizontal speed of u m s^{-1}. Find:

a an expression for the speed of the particle when the rod is at an angle of θ with the upward vertical through O

b the set of values of u for which the particle will perform a complete circle.

a $m = 0.1$ kg, length of rod is 0.4 m and initial speed is u m s^{-1}.

Write down any information that may be helpful from the diagram. Include the zero level for gravitational potential energy.

Set the gravitational potential energy to equal zero at the horizontal line passing through the lowest point of the vertical circle. Call this point A.

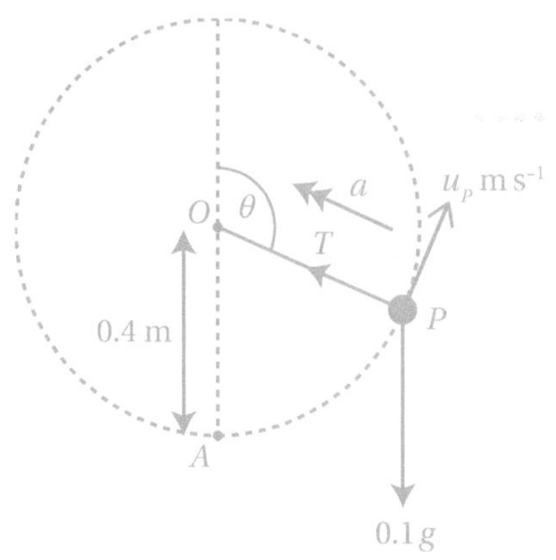

Note that only the radial acceleration is marked on the diagram since this is all you need to solve the problem, but there will also be a tangential component.

Let the particle be at position P in its circular orbit when it makes an angle of θ with the upward vertical through O.

Write down helpful information from the question. Include any extra symbols that might be helpful when trying to refer to position in the circular orbit.

At the lowest point, A:

Calculate the gravitational potential energy and kinetic energy of the particle at A, where h_A is the vertical height at A (the bottom of the circle is taken to be height = 0).

$$\text{GPE} + \text{KE} = mgh_A + 0.5mu_A^2$$

$$= 0.1 \times g \times 0 + 0.5 \times 0.1 \times u^2$$

$$= 0.05u^2$$

Continues on next page ...

At the point P:

Calculate the gravitational potential energy and kinetic energy of the particle at P, where h_p is the vertical height above point A.

$$GPE + KE = mgh_p + 0.5mu_p^2$$
$$= 0.1 \times g \times 0.4(1 + \cos\theta) + 0.5 \times 0.1 \times u_p^2$$
$$= 0.04g(1 + \cos\theta) + 0.05u_p^2$$

Since energy is conserved:

By the principle of conservation of mechanical energy, the total energy at A is equal to the total energy at P.

$$0.05u^2 = 0.04g(1 + \cos\theta) + 0.05u_p^2$$
$$u_p^2 = u^2 - 0.8g(1 + \cos\theta)$$

b For the particle to make a full circle the speed must be greater than zero when the particle is at the highest point in the circular orbit.

Unlike a string, a rod cannot go slack. Therefore, the speed of the particle at the highest point must be greater than zero for the particle to move in complete vertical circles.

You want $u_p \geqslant 0$ when $\theta = 0°$,

At the highest point in the movement the angle made with the downward vertical is 0°.

$$u^2 - 0.8g(1 + \cos 0) \geqslant 0$$
$$u^2 - 0.8g(1 + 1) \geqslant 0$$
$$u^2 - 1.6g \geqslant 0$$

You can rearrange to find u. This will give a lower bound for the value that the initial speed can take in order for the particle to complete a full circle.

$$u^2 \geqslant 1.6g$$
$$u \geqslant \sqrt{1.6g}$$
$$u > 3.96 \text{ m s}^{-1} \text{ (3 s.f.)}$$

Key point 9.4

If a particle connected to a light rod moving in vertical circles is to complete full circles, the speed of the particle must be greater than zero at the highest point of its circular orbit. The same condition is true if the particle is representing a bead threaded onto a smooth circular wire.

WORK IT OUT 9.1

A particle P of mass m kg is attached to one end of a light inextensible string of length r m. The other end of the string is attached to a fixed point O. The particle hangs in equilibrium with the string taut at position O. The particle is then set in motion with a horizontal speed of u m s^{-1} so that the particle moves in a vertical circle. What conditions are necessary for the particle to complete the vertical circle? Which solution is correct? Can you identify the errors in the incorrect solutions?

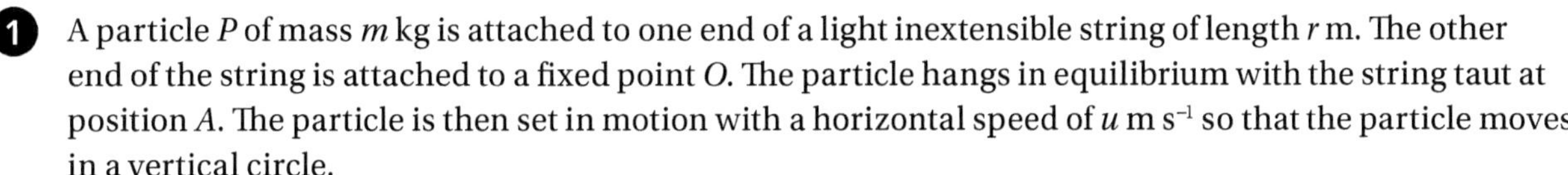

Solution 1	Solution 2	Solution 3
The particle will complete vertical circles if the speed at the top of the circle is greater than zero.	The particle will complete vertical circles if the initial speed $u=\sqrt{2gr}$ m s^{-1}.	The particle will complete vertical circles if the speed of the particle is enough to keep the string taut at the top of the circle.

EXERCISE 9A

Unless otherwise instructed, when a numerical value for the acceleration due to gravity is needed, use $g = 9.8$ m s^{-2}.

1 A particle P of mass m kg is attached to one end of a light inextensible string of length r m. The other end of the string is attached to a fixed point O. The particle hangs in equilibrium with the string taut at position A. The particle is then set in motion with a horizontal speed of u m s^{-1} so that the particle moves in a vertical circle.

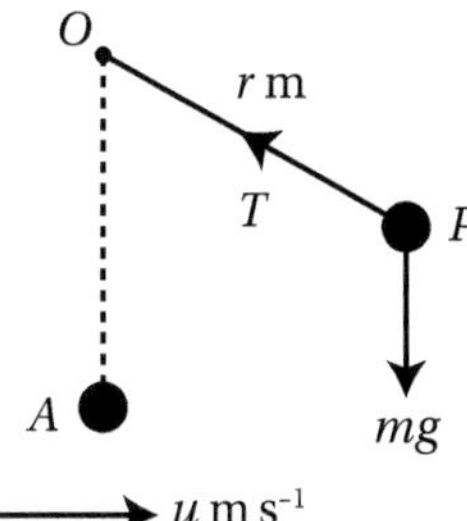

a **i** If $r = 1$ and $u = 3$, find the speed of the particle when angle AOP is 20°.

ii If $r = 3$ and $u = 9$, find the speed of the particle when angle AOP is 110°.

b **i** If $r = 2.3$ and $u = 3.2$, find the acceleration towards centre O when angle AOP is 35°.

ii If $r = 0.75$ and $u = 5.3$, find the acceleration towards centre O when angle AOP is 70°.

c **i** If $r = 2$, $u = 4$ and $m = 2$, find the tension in the string when angle AOP is 30°.

ii If $r = 0.9$, $u = 6$ and $m = 1.2$, find the tension in the string when angle AOP is 130°.

d **i** If $r = 1.5$ and $u = 4$, find the angle made between OP and the downward vertical when the speed of the particle is 2 m s^{-1}.

ii If $r = 0.75$ and $u = 3.2$, find the angle made between OP and the upward vertical when the speed of the particle is 0.8 m s^{-1}.

2 A smooth bead is threaded onto a smooth circular wire fixed in a vertical plane, with centre O and radius r. The bead is projected from the lowest point B with initial speed u m s^{-1}.

a If $u^2 = 7gr$, find the speed of the bead when it passes through the general point A where OA makes an angle of θ with the downward vertical.

b If $u^2 = 2gr$, find the greatest height reached by the bead above the lowest point B of the circular wire.

c If $u^2 = 5gr$, find the speed of the bead when it passes through the point C that is level with the centre O.

d If $u^2 = 9gr$, find the speed of the bead when it passes through the highest point D of the circular wire.

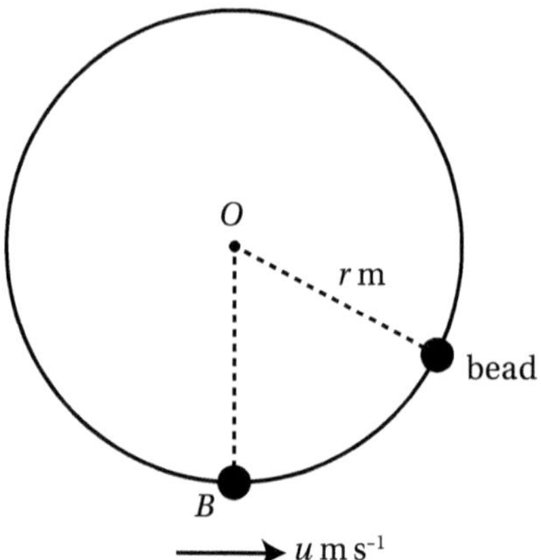

3 A smooth bead is threaded onto a smooth circular wire fixed in a vertical plane, with centre O and radius a. The bead is projected from the lowest point with initial speed u m s^{-1}. Determine if the bead will make a full circle and, if not, find the maximum vertical height reached by the bead, when the initial speed u is given by:

a $u^2 = ga$ b $u^2 = \frac{2}{3}ga$ c $u^2 = 4ga$

4 A particle of mass 0.5 kg is attached to one end of a light rod OA of length 0.4 m. The rod is free to rotate in a vertical plane about O. The particle is held at rest with OA horizontal and then released.

a Calculate the speed of the particle as it passes through the lowest point.

b Find the tension in the rod at this lowest point.

5 A particle of mass 0.5 kg is attached to one end of a light inextensible string OA of length 0.4 m. The particle is hanging in equilibrium at the lowest point B when it is set in motion with a speed of u m s^{-1}. If the string remains taut during the particle's motion, write an expression for the speed of the particle when OA makes an angle of θ with the downward vertical OB.

6 A particle P of mass 1.2 kg is attached to one end of a light rod of length 1.5 m. The other end of the rod is attached to a fixed point O and it is free to rotate about O. The rod is hanging vertically with P below O when the particle is set in motion with a horizontal speed of u m s^{-1}. Find the minimum value of u for which the particle will perform a complete circle.

7 A light inextensible string of length r m has a particle P of mass m kg attached at one end. The other end is attached to a fixed point O and the particle P describes complete vertical circles, centre O. Given that the speed of the particle at the lowest point is 2 times the speed of the particle at its highest point, find the tension in the string when the particle is at the highest point.

8 A light inelastic string of length 2 m has one end attached to a fixed point O. A particle P of mass 0.5 kg is attached to the other end. The particle P is held with OP horizontal and the string taut.

a If the particle P is released from rest, what is the maximum speed and where will this occur in the circular orbit?

b If the particle P is projected vertically downwards with speed $\sqrt{2g}$, find the tension in the string when OP makes an angle of θ with the horizontal.

c Given that the string will break when the tension in the string is g N, find the angle between the string and the horizontal when the string breaks.

9 A smooth hemispherical bowl, centre O and of radius 15 cm, is fixed on a horizontal surface such that the top of the bowl is parallel with the horizontal surface. A smooth marble P of mass 25 g is held in place on the inner surface such that, for the plane containing the centre and the marble, the line OP makes an angle 60° with the downward vertical. The particle is released from rest.

a Calculate the speed of the particle as it passes through the lowest point.

b Calculate the normal reaction force acting on the marble when the marble passes through the lowest point.

c If the model is refined to include friction, calculate the constant frictional force such that the marble comes to rest directly below the centre O and nowhere else before.

Explore

As you have seen, you can model motion in a vertical circle using energy. However, sometimes you just need to think about the limiting factors for an object to be able to move in a vertical circular path. This idea will help you tackle this problem from NRICH: www.cambridge.org/links/moscmec6004.

Section 2: Components of acceleration (a general model)

In the previous section, you used the conservation of mechanical energy to find the speed of a particle moving in a vertical circular orbit and used this to calculate the force directed towards the centre of motion (the radial direction).

You also need to be able to model the motion of the circular orbit and determine the tangential and radial components of the acceleration, not just the acceleration directed towards the centre.

The formula for acceleration of a particle moving in a circular orbit in Chapter 4 was based on the fact that the angular speed of the particle was constant. If you now consider that the angular speed is given by a function of time, you can create a general model for particles moving in a circular orbit.

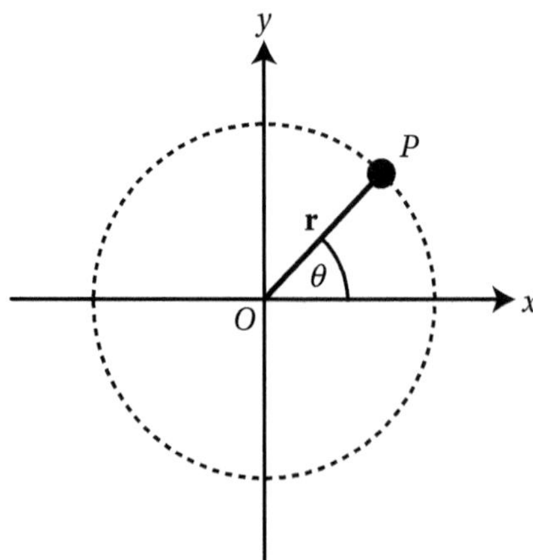

If you no longer have a constant linear or angular speed, you need to consider the angle as a function of time, $\theta(t)$. So you can say that the position vector is given by:

$$\mathbf{r} = \begin{pmatrix} r\cos\theta \\ r\sin\theta \end{pmatrix}$$

Differentiating with respect to time gives the **velocity vector** for angular speed:

$$\mathbf{v} = \frac{\mathrm{d}\mathbf{r}}{\mathrm{d}t} = \begin{pmatrix} -r\frac{\mathrm{d}\theta}{\mathrm{d}t}\sin\theta \\ r\frac{\mathrm{d}\theta}{\mathrm{d}t}\cos\theta \end{pmatrix} = \begin{pmatrix} -r\omega\sin\theta \\ r\omega\cos\theta \end{pmatrix}$$

$$= r\omega\begin{pmatrix} -\sin\theta \\ \cos\theta \end{pmatrix}$$

You can see that the magnitude of the velocity is $|\mathbf{v}| = r\frac{\mathrm{d}\theta}{\mathrm{d}t} = r\omega$.

If you differentiate again with respect to time you get the **acceleration vector** for angular speed:

$$\mathbf{a} = \frac{\mathrm{d}\mathbf{v}}{\mathrm{d}t} = \begin{pmatrix} -r\frac{\mathrm{d}^2\theta}{\mathrm{d}t^2}\sin\theta - r\left(\frac{\mathrm{d}\theta}{\mathrm{d}t}\right)^2\cos\theta \\ r\frac{\mathrm{d}^2\theta}{\mathrm{d}t^2}\cos\theta - r\left(\frac{\mathrm{d}\theta}{\mathrm{d}t}\right)^2\sin\theta \end{pmatrix} = \begin{pmatrix} -r\frac{\mathrm{d}^2\theta}{\mathrm{d}t^2}\sin\theta - r\omega^2\cos\theta \\ r\frac{\mathrm{d}^2\theta}{\mathrm{d}t^2}\cos\theta - r\omega^2\sin\theta \end{pmatrix}$$

$$= r\frac{\mathrm{d}^2\theta}{\mathrm{d}t^2}\begin{pmatrix} -\sin\theta \\ \cos\theta \end{pmatrix} - r\omega^2\begin{pmatrix} \cos\theta \\ \sin\theta \end{pmatrix}$$

Tip

Remember, here angular speed is not constant.

Rewind

You used vectors in A Level Mathematics Student Book 2.

The two most important directions as a particle moves in a circular path are the **radial direction** and the **tangential direction**. Now that you have found the velocity and acceleration vectors, you can look for the radial and tangential components of each.

For the velocity vector, you have a vector of magnitude $r\frac{d\theta}{dt}$ moving only in the direction $\begin{pmatrix}-\sin\theta\\ \cos\theta\end{pmatrix}$, which is the tangential direction.

For the acceleration vector, there are two parts.

The first part is a component of the vector in the direction $\begin{pmatrix}-\sin\theta\\ \cos\theta\end{pmatrix}$, with magnitude $r\frac{d^2\theta}{dt^2}=\frac{dv}{dt}$ and this is the **tangential component of the acceleration**.

The second part gives the **radial component of the acceleration** as $-\frac{v^2}{r}$ (since $\begin{pmatrix}\cos\theta\\ \sin\theta\end{pmatrix}$ is the radial vector).

If you want to find the magnitude of the acceleration vector, since the radial and tangential components are perpendicular, you can use Pythagoras' theorem.

Key point 9.5

$r\frac{d^2\theta}{dt^2}=\frac{dv}{dt}$ is the tangential (or transverse) component of the acceleration and $-\frac{v^2}{r}$ or $-r\left(\frac{d\theta}{dt}\right)^2$ is the radial component of the acceleration.

Did you know?

You can prove that the velocity vector is tangential to the circular path by using the displacement vector and the scalar product.

Rewind

This model is a more sophisticated model for circular motion, when angular speed is not constant. However, if you did have constant angular speed, $\frac{d\theta}{dt}=\omega$ is equal to a constant, then $\frac{d^2\theta}{d^2t}=0$ and the vector equation for the acceleration would simplify to the case you studied in Chapter 4.

Formula book

Radial acceleration is $\frac{v^2}{r}$ or $r\dot{\theta}^2$ towards the centre.

Tangential acceleration is $\dot{v}=r\ddot{\theta}$.

Using the notation developed in A Level Mathematics Student Book 1 you can refer to $r\frac{d^2\theta}{dt^2}=\frac{dv}{dt}$ as $r\ddot{\theta}$ and $\frac{v^2}{r}=r\left(\frac{d\theta}{dt}\right)^2$ as $r\dot{\theta}^2$ where the dot denotes differentiation with respect to time.

WORKED EXAMPLE 9.5

An athlete is running around the circular part of a running track of radius 5 m. He increases his speed uniformly from 4 m s^{-1} to 6 m s^{-1} in a 4 second period.

a Find an expression for the tangential and radial parts of the athlete's acceleration over this time period.

b What is the magnitude of the acceleration 2 seconds after the athlete starts to increase his speed?

Continues on next page ...

a The acceleration of the athlete will be given by $\frac{dv}{dt}$ in the tangential direction and $-\frac{v^2}{r}$ in the radial direction.

If a particle is moving in a circular path where speed is not constant then you need to look at the components of the acceleration in the radial and tangential directions.

The athlete's speed changes uniformly from 4 to 6 m s^{-1} over 4 seconds.

You can calculate the athlete's tangential component of the acceleration by using the uniform increase in speed from 4 m s^{-1} to 6 m s^{-1} in 4 seconds.

$\frac{dv}{dt}=\frac{6-4}{4}=0.5\text{ m s}^{-2}$

$\frac{dv}{dt}$ is the change in speed per change in time and this will give the tangential component of the acceleration.

$v=\int 0.5\,dt=0.5t+c$

You can integrate $\frac{dv}{dt}$ to get an expression for v in terms of t.

At $t=0$, $v=4$ so $v=0.5t+4$

You can use the initial conditions to find the constant of integration.

$a_r=-\frac{(0.5t+4)^2}{5}\text{ m s}^{-2}$

You can now substitute v into $-\frac{v^2}{r}$ to find the radial component of the acceleration.

b At $t=2$:

You can substitute the value for time into each component of the acceleration.

Radial acceleration is

$-\frac{(0.5\times2+4)^2}{5}=-5\text{ m s}^{-1}$.

Tangential acceleration is 0.5 m s^{-2}.

Thus:

To find the magnitude of the acceleration, you calculate the magnitude of the vector.

$|a|=\sqrt{0.5^2+(-5)^2}=\sqrt{25.25}$

$|a|=5.02\text{ m s}^{-2}$ (3 s.f.)

WORKED EXAMPLE 9.6

A smooth bead of mass m kg is threaded onto a smooth circular wire fixed in a vertical plane, centre O and radius r. The bead is projected from its lowest point A on the circular wire with speed u m s^{-1}.

a Find the speed of the bead when it passes through the point marked P on the diagram.
b Find the radial and transverse components of the acceleration of the bead at P.

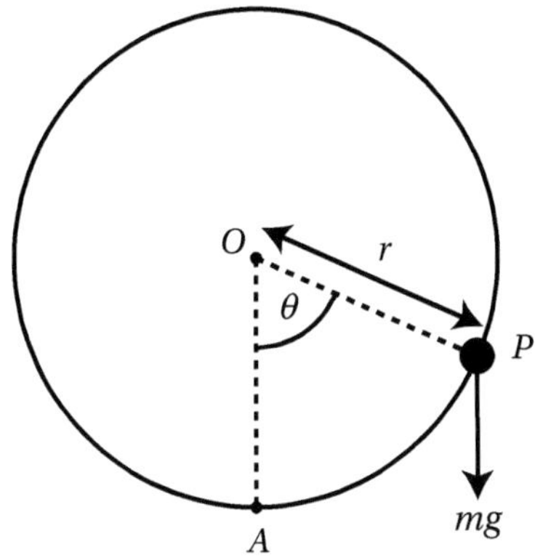

a The bead is at position P in its circular orbit when it makes an angle of θ with the downward vertical at O. Set the gravitational potential energy to equal zero at the horizontal line passing through the lowest point of the vertical circle at A.

Write down any information that maybe helpful from the diagram. Include where you will be measuring your gravitational potential energy from.

To find the speed of the bead, you can use the principle of conservation of mechanical energy.

At the point A:

$$\text{GPE} + \text{KE} = mgh_A + 0.5mu_A^2$$
$$= mg \times 0 + 0.5mu^2$$
$$= 0.5mu^2$$

Calculate the gravitational potential energy and kinetic energy of the bead at A.

At the point P:

$$\text{GPE} + \text{KE} = mgh_p + 0.5mu_p^2$$
$$= mgr(1 - \cos\theta) + 0.5mu_p^2$$

Calculate the gravitational potential energy and kinetic energy of the bead at P.

Since energy is conserved:

$$0.5mu^2 = mgr(1 - \cos\theta) + 0.5mu_p^2$$

By the principle of conservation of mechanical energy, the total energy at A is equal to the total energy at P.

$$u_p^2 = u^2 - 2gr(1 - \cos\theta)$$
$$u_p = \sqrt{u^2 - 2gr(1 - \cos\theta)}$$

You can rearrange to find u_P.

Continues on next page ...

b At the point P:

You need to find the components of the acceleration of the bead in the radial and tangential directions.

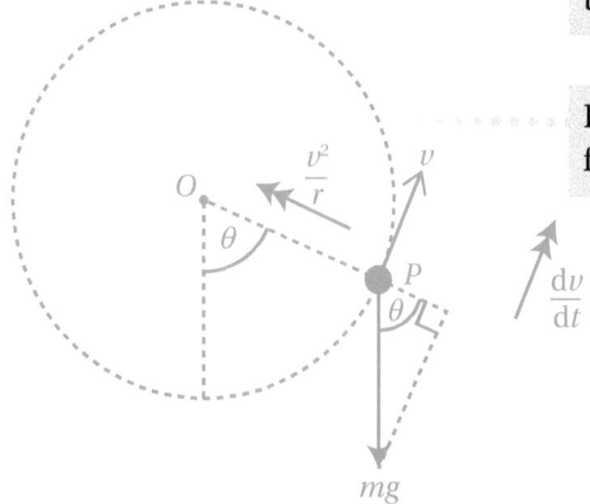

It is more convenient, for this part, to use v rather than u_P for the velocity at P.

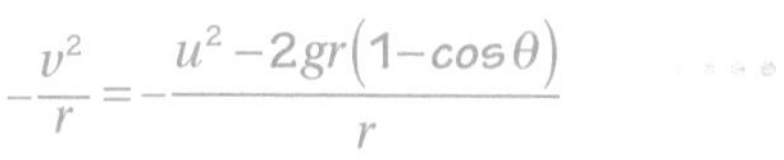

$$-\frac{v^2}{r} = -\frac{u^2 - 2gr(1-\cos\theta)}{r}$$

For the radial direction you can use your calculation from part **a** to find $\frac{-v^2}{r}$.

Using $F = ma$,

$$-mg\sin\theta = m\left(\frac{dv}{dt}\right)$$

so $\frac{dv}{dt} = -g\sin\theta$

For the tangential component, use the force acting on the bead in tangential direction, $-mg\sin\theta$, with Newton's second law.

EXERCISE 9B

Unless otherwise instructed, when a numerical value for the acceleration due to gravity is needed, use $g = 9.8$ m s^{-2}.

1 A particle is moving in a circular path of radius r.

a The particle's speed uniformly increases from u m s^{-1} to v m s^{-1} in t seconds.

i If $r = 3$, $u = 4$, $v = 9$ and $t = 7$, find an expression for the tangential and radial parts of the acceleration.

ii If $r = 0.8$, $u = 2.3$, $v = 7.3$ and $t = 3$, find an expression for the tangential and radial parts of the acceleration.

b The particle's speed uniformly decreases from u m s^{-1} to v m s^{-1} in t seconds.

i If $r = 1$, $u = 6$, $v = 2$ and $t = 4$, find an expression for the tangential and radial parts of the acceleration.

ii If $r = 1.2$, $u = 5.6$, $v = 2.3$ and $t = 1.5$, find an expression for the tangential and radial parts of the acceleration.

c The particle's tangential component of the acceleration is given by a_T.

i If $a_T = 2t + 1$, find an expression for the linear speed of the particle if at $t = 3$, $v = 3$.

ii If $a_T = e^{-t}$, find an expression for the linear speed of the particle if at $t = 0$, $v = 2$.

2 A car is driven around a roundabout of radius 40 m. Its speed increases uniformly from 5 m s^{-1} to 10 m s^{-1} in 8 seconds.

a Find expressions for the radial and tangential acceleration of the car.

b Find the magnitude of the acceleration after 3 seconds.

3 A rally car travelling at 25 m s^{-1} is accelerating around a circular bend of radius 55 m. If the speed of the car is increasing at a rate of 3 m s^{-2}, find the magnitude of the acceleration of the car after 3 seconds.

4 A particle of mass 0.45 kg describes complete vertical circles while attached to one end of a light inextensible string of length 1.5 m. The other end of the string is fixed at the point O. If the speed of the particle is 4 m s^{-1} at the highest point in the circular orbit, find the magnitude of the tangential acceleration when the string is horizontal.

5 A smooth bead of mass 50 g is threaded onto a smooth circular wire fixed in a vertical plane with centre O and radius 0.5 m. The bead is projected from its lowest point on the circular wire with a speed of 5 m s^{-1}. Find an expression for the magnitude of the acceleration when the bead and the centre of the circular wire are in the same horizontal line.

6 One end of a light inextensible string of length 1.5 m is attached to a fixed point O and the other end is attached to a particle P of mass 0.35 kg. With the string taut and horizontal, the particle P is projected with a velocity of 4 m s^{-1}, vertically downwards. The particle begins to move in a vertical circle with centre O. While the string remains taut, the angular displacement of OP from its initial position is θ radians and the speed of P is v m s^{-1}. Find, in terms of θ, the radial and tangential components of the acceleration of P.

A Section 3: Problem solving situations

Leaving a circular path

Sometimes a particle will only follow a circular path for a short period of time. Once it is no longer moving in a circle, it will need to be modelled as a particle moving freely under gravity.

WORKED EXAMPLE 9.7

A smooth solid hemisphere with radius 4 m and centre O is resting on a horizontal table with its flat face in contact with the table. A particle P of mass 5 kg starts to slip from rest at the highest point A on the hemisphere.

a If the hemisphere stays in a fixed position, find an expression for the normal reaction force of the particle to the surface of the hemisphere if the angle between OP and OA is θ.

b Find the angle between OP and OA when the particle leaves the surface of the hemisphere.

c Once the particle leaves the hemisphere, how could you model its subsequent movement?

d Find the distance away from the centre of the hemisphere when the particle first hits the table.

Continues on next page ...

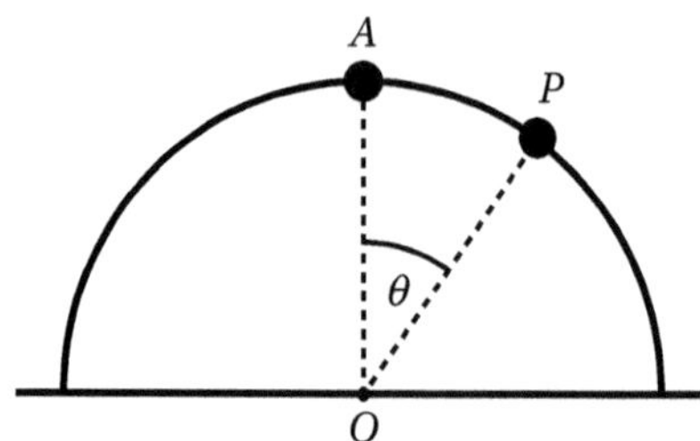

a $m = 5$ kg, radius $= 4$ m and initial speed $= 0$ m s^{-1}.

Set the gravitational potential energy to equal zero at the horizontal line passing through the point O.

> Write down any information that may be helpful from the diagram. Include where you will be measuring your gravitational potential energy from.

At the point A:

$$GPE + KE = mgh_A + 0.5mu_A^2$$
$$= 5 \times g \times 4 + 0.5 \times 5 \times 0^2$$
$$= 20g$$

> Calculate the gravitational potential energy and kinetic energy of the particle at A.

At the point P:

$$GPE + KE = mgh_P + 0.5mu_P^2$$
$$= 5 \times g \times 4\cos\theta + 0.5 \times 5 \times u_P^2$$
$$= 20g\cos\theta + 2.5u_P^2$$

> Calculate the gravitational potential energy and kinetic energy of the particle at P.

Since energy is conserved:

$$20g = 20g\cos\theta + 2.5u_P^2$$
$$u_P^2 = 8g(1 - \cos\theta)$$

> By the principle of conservation of mechanical energy, the total energy at A is equal to the total energy at P.

$$R - mg\cos\theta = -m\left(\frac{u_P}{r}\right)$$
$$R = mg\cos\theta - \frac{8mg(1-\cos\theta)}{4}$$
$$R = 3mg\cos\theta - 2mg$$

> Once you have calculated the speed you can use Newton's second law and $a = -\frac{v^2}{r}$ to find the normal reaction force R by resolving perpendicularly to the surface of the hemisphere.

Continues on next page ...

b When the particle leaves the surface, $R = 0$.

$3mg\cos\theta - 2mg = 0$

So $\cos\theta = \frac{2}{3}$

$\theta = 48.2°$

So the angle between OP and OA is $48.2°$ (3 s.f.)

The angle when the particle leaves the surface will be the instant when the normal reaction force between the particle and the surface is zero.

c You can model the particle as a projectile falling freely under gravity.

When the particle is no longer moving in a circular path it is now free to move as if it were a projectile, falling freely under gravity.

d The particle leaves the surface when $\theta = 48.2°$.

You first need to calculate the horizontal distance the particle travels before it leaves the surface of the hemisphere.

The horizontal distance between O and this point is given by $4\sin 48.2° = 2.98$ m (3 s.f.)

Once the particle leaves the surface of the hemisphere it falls under gravity. Let the positive vertical direction be in the direction A to O and the positive horizontal direction be away from O:

When the particle leaves the surface of the hemisphere it can be modelled as a projectile.

You need to set up a direction for the horizontal and vertical components of the velocity and displacement for a projectile.

$\theta = 48.2°$

Initial vertical speed $= u_p \sin\theta$

$= \sqrt{8g(1-\cos\theta)}\sin\theta$

$= 3.81\text{ m s}^{-1}$ (3 s.f.)

Horizontal speed $= u_p\cos\theta$

$= \sqrt{8g(1-\cos\theta)}\cos\theta$

$= 3.41\text{ m s}^{-1}$ (3 s.f.)

Continues on next page …

Acceleration due to gravity $= 9.8\ \text{m s}^{-2}$

Vertical height $= 4\cos\theta$

$$= 4 \times \frac{2}{3} = 2.67\ \text{m}$$

Using $s = ut + 0.5at^2$,

You can use the equations of motion for a particle moving with a constant acceleration to calculate horizontal and vertical components of velocity and displacement and the time of flight.

$2.67 = u_p t \sin\theta + 0.5 \times 9.8 \times t^2$

$2.67 = 3.81t + 4.9t^2$

$4.9t^2 + 3.81t - 2.67 = 0$

You have a quadratic equation in t and so can use the quadratic formula to find the positive value for t.

Using the quadratic formula:

$$t = \frac{-3.81 \pm \sqrt{3.81^2 - 4 \times 4.9 \times (-2.67)}}{9.8}$$

which gives $t = 0.446$ seconds

The horizontal distance travelled from the point where the particle leaves the surface of the hemisphere is given by $s = ut$:

$s = u_p \cos\theta \times t$

$s = 3.41 \times 0.446 = 1.52\ \text{m}$ (3 s.f.)

Total horizontal distance from O is given by:

$2.98 + 1.52 = 4.50\ \text{m}$ (3 s.f.)

Finally, you can combine the horizontal distances travelled by the particle before leaving the surface and after leaving the surface of the hemisphere.

Key point 9.6

When the normal reaction force between the particle and a surface is equal to zero, a particle loses contact with the surface.

WORKED EXAMPLE 9.8

A particle of mass m kg is attached to one end of a light inextensible string of length l metres. The other end of the string is attached to a fixed point O such that the particle hangs in equilibrium directly below O at A. The particle is set in motion with a horizontal speed of $2\sqrt{gl}$. At the point P, the string first goes slack.

a Find the vertical height of P above the starting position A where the string first goes slack.

At the point when the string first goes slack, the particle is released from the string.

b Find the maximum height the particle reaches above its starting position.

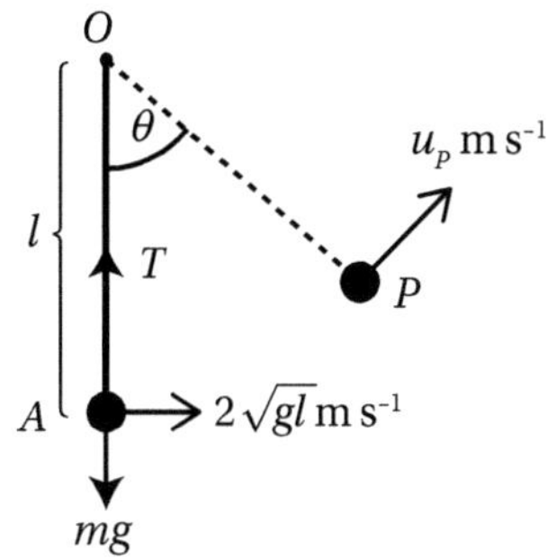

a Set the gravitational potential energy to equal zero at the horizontal line passing through the point A. Let θ be the angle formed between OP and the downward vertical OA. Let T be the tension in the string.

Write down any information that may be helpful from the diagram. Include where you will be measuring your gravitational potential energy from. Include any extra labels that might be helpful when trying to refer to position in the circular orbit.

At the point A:

$$\text{GPE} + \text{KE} = mgh_A + 0.5mu_A^2$$
$$= m \times g \times 0 + 0.5 \times m \times (2\sqrt{gl})^2$$
$$= 2mgl$$

Calculate the gravitational potential energy and kinetic energy of the particle at A.

At the point P:

$$\text{GPE} + \text{KE} = mgh_P + 0.5mu_P^2$$
$$= m \times g \times l(1 - \cos\theta) + 0.5 \times m \times u_P^2$$
$$= mgl(1 - \cos\theta) + 0.5mu_P^2$$

Calculate the gravitational potential energy and kinetic energy of the particle at P.

Continues on next page ...

Since energy is conserved:

$2mgl = mgl(1-\cos\theta) + 0.5mu_p^2$

$u_p^2 = 2gl(1+\cos\theta)$

By the principle of conservation of mechanical energy, the total energy at A is equal to the total energy at P.

$F = ma$

$T - mg\cos\theta = m\frac{v^2}{r}$

$T = mg\cos\theta + \frac{2mgl(1+\cos\theta)}{l}$

Once you have calculated the speed you can use Newton's second law and $a = \frac{v^2}{r}$ to find the tension T by resolving in the radial and tangential directions.

$T = mg\cos\theta + 2mg(1+\cos\theta) = 0$

When the string goes slack there is no tension in the string.

$\cos\theta + 2 + 2\cos\theta = 0$

$\cos\theta = \frac{-2}{3}$

$\theta = 132°$

You can rearrange to make $\cos\theta$ the subject and calculate a value for θ.

The vertical height above A where the string first becomes slack is:

$l(1-\cos\theta) = l\left(1 - \frac{-2}{3}\right) = \frac{5l}{3}$ m

You can find the vertical height using $\cos\theta$.

b When the particle is released from the string the particle can be modelled as a projectile.

For the motion of the particle, take the upward vertical as the positive direction.

It is important to define a direction to the projectile motion.

Vertical speed $= u_p \sin\theta$

$= \sqrt{2gl(1+\cos\theta)}\sin\theta$

$= \sqrt{\frac{2gl}{3}} \times \frac{\sqrt{5}}{3}$

$= \sqrt{\frac{10gl}{27}}$

The maximum height reached by the projectile is when the final vertical velocity equals zero.

Continues on next page ...

Using $v^2 = u^2 + 2as$:

$$0 = \frac{10gl}{27} - 2gs$$

$$s = \frac{5l}{27}$$

$$\text{Total distance} = \frac{5l}{3} + \frac{5l}{27} = \frac{50l}{27}\text{ m}$$

You can find the total vertical distance travelled by the particle by combining the projectile motion with the motion in its circular path.

WORK IT OUT 9.2

A smooth solid hemisphere with radius r m and centre O is placed in a fixed position on a horizontal plane with its flat face in contact with the horizontal plane. A particle P of mass m kg starts to move from rest from the highest point. When OP has turned through an angle of θ, if the particle is still on the surface of the hemisphere, find an expression for R, the normal reaction force of the hemisphere on the particle. Which solution is correct? Can you identify the errors in the incorrect solutions?

Solution 1

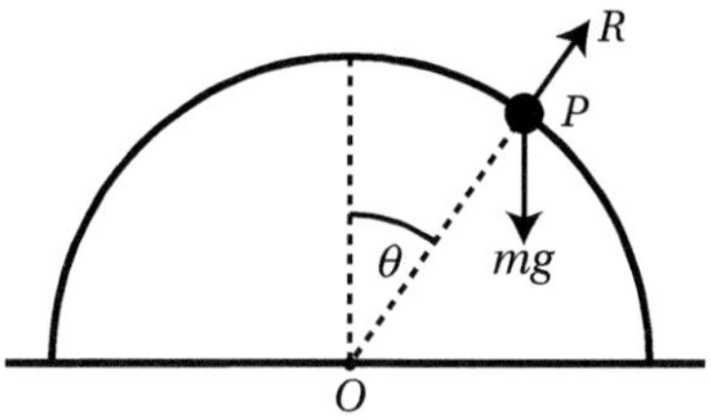

R
P
θ
mg
O

At P:

$mgr = \frac{1}{2}mv^2 + mgr\cos\theta$

$v^2 = 2gr(1 - \cos\theta)$

$F = ma$

$R - mg\cos\theta = \frac{mv^2}{r}$

$R = mg\cos\theta + \frac{m}{r}2gr(1 - \cos\theta)$

$R = mg\cos\theta + 2mg - 2mg\cos\theta$

$R = 2mg - mg\cos\theta$

$R = mg(2 - \cos\theta)$

Solution 2

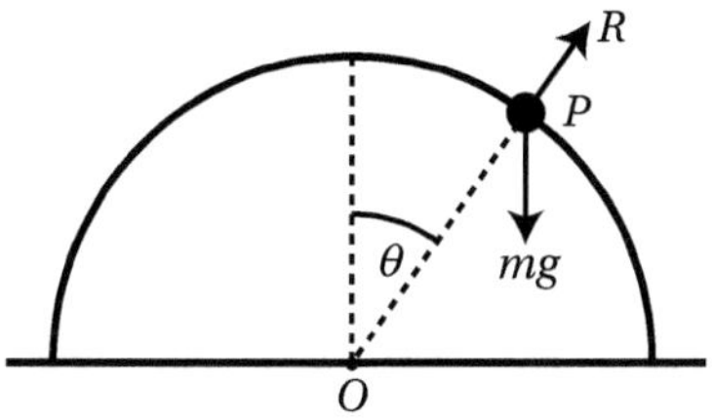

R
P
θ
mg
O

At P:

$mgr = \frac{1}{2}mv^2 + mgr\cos\theta$

$v^2 = 2gr(1 - \cos\theta)$

$F = ma$

$mg\cos\theta - R = \frac{mv^2}{r}$

$R = mg\cos\theta - \frac{m^2gr(1 - \cos\theta)}{r}$

$R = mg\cos\theta - 2gm + 2gm\cos\theta$

$R = mg(3\cos\theta - 2)$

Solution 3

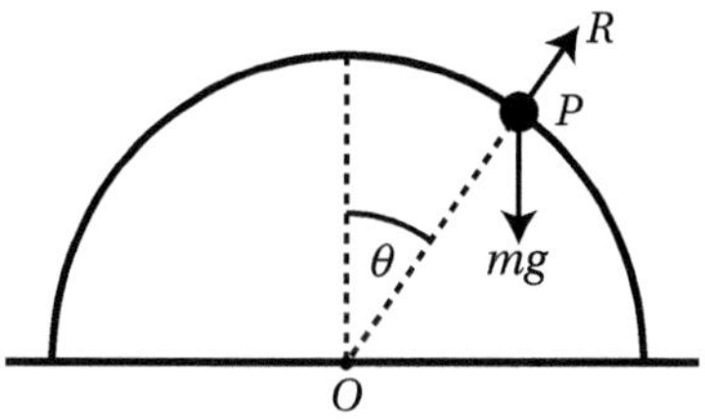

R
P
θ
mg
O

At P:

$mgr = \frac{1}{2}mv^2 + mgr\cos\theta$

$v^2 = 2gr(1 + \cos\theta)$

$F = ma$

$mg\cos\theta - R = \frac{mv^2}{r}$

$R = mg\cos\theta - \frac{m^2gr(1 + \cos\theta)}{r}$

$R = mg\cos\theta - 2gm - 2gm\cos\theta$

$R = -mg(\cos\theta + 2)$

EXERCISE 9C

Unless otherwise instructed, when a numerical value for the acceleration due to gravity is needed, use $g = 9.8\text{ m s}^{-2}$.

1 A smooth solid hemisphere with radius r metres and centre O is resting on a horizontal table with its flat face in contact with the table. A particle P of mass m kg is projected from a point A, the highest point of the hemisphere, parallel with the horizontal surface at an initial speed of $u\text{ m s}^{-1}$.

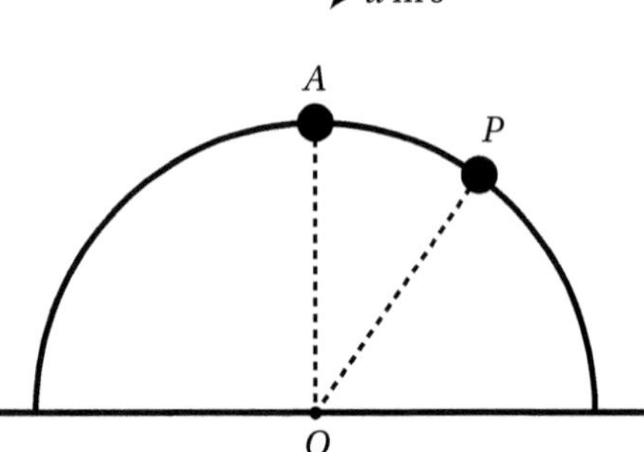

a **i** If $u = 2$ and $r = 1$, find the speed of the particle if the angle between OP and OA is 10°.

ii If $u = 5$ and $r = 1.3$, find the speed of the particle if the angle between OP and OA is 22°.

b **i** If $u = 2$, $r = 2.3$ and $m = 3$, find the normal reaction force acting on the particle at the surface of the hemisphere if the angle between OP and OA is 17°.

ii If $u = 5$, $r = 4.7$ and $m = 2.4$, find the normal reaction force acting on the particle at the surface of the hemisphere if the angle between OP and OA is 30°.

c **i** If $u = 2$ and $r = 1.75$, find the angle between OP and OA when the particle leaves the surface of the hemisphere.

ii If $u = 5$ and $r = 3$, find the angle between OP and the horizontal when the particle leaves the surface of the hemisphere.

d **i** If $u = 2$ and $r = 1.75$, find the speed of the particle when it leaves the surface of the hemisphere.

ii If $u = 5$ and $r = 3$, find the speed of the particle when it leaves the surface of the hemisphere.

2 A particle of mass 500 g is released from rest at the top of a smooth track which forms a quarter of circle, centre O of radius 50 cm, followed by a drop of 2 m to the ground.

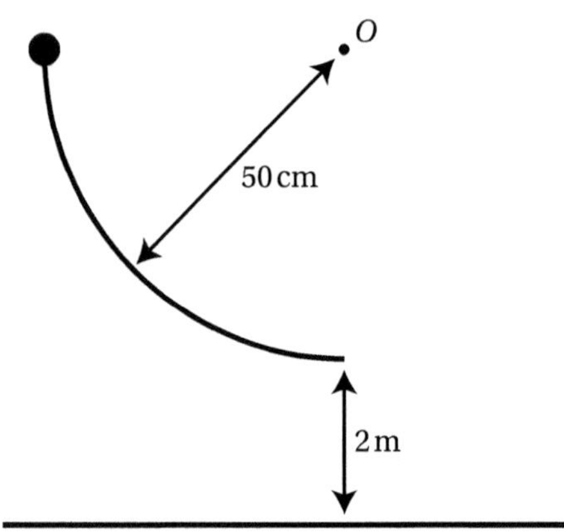

a Calculate the speed of the particle as it leaves the quarter circle part of the track.

b What is the total horizontal distance that the particle travels before it hits the ground?

3 A smooth piece of track XY is constructed so that it is in the shape of a circular arc. The arc XY has a radius of 2 m and subtends an angle of 30° at its centre O_{XY}. The points X and O_{XY} are on a line that is parallel to a horizontal surface, which is vertically 5 m below the point Y. O_{XY}, X and Y all lie in the same vertical plane. A particle P is released from rest at X.

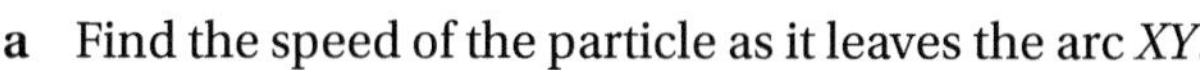

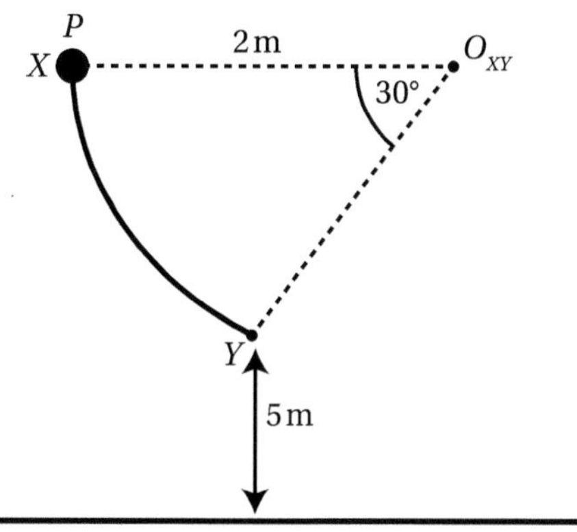

a Find the speed of the particle as it leaves the arc XY.

b Find the time taken for the particle to hit the ground after it has left Y.

c Find the horizontal distance that the particle P travels after it leaves the track before it hits the horizontal surface.

4 A smooth piece of track XY is constructed so that it is in the shape of a circular arc. The arc XY has a radius of 3 m and subtends an angle of 60° at its centre O_{XY}. The points X and O_{XY} are on a line that is parallel to a horizontal surface, which is vertically 2 m below point Y parallel to a horizontal surface. O_{XY}, X and Y all lie in the same vertical plane. A particle P is released from rest at X.

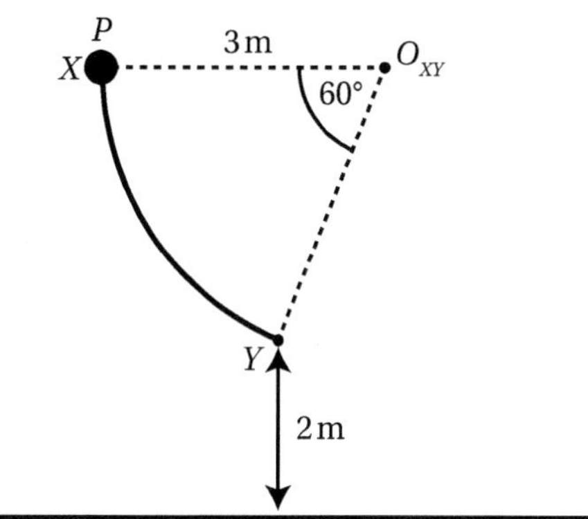

a Find the speed of the particle as it leaves the arc XY.

b Find the time taken for the particle to hit the ground after it has left Y.

c Find the horizontal distance that the particle P travels after it leaves the track before it hits the horizontal surface.

5 A smooth piece of track XY is constructed so that it is in the shape of a circular arc. The arc XY has a radius of 0.5 m and subtends an angle of 120° at its centre O_{XY}. The points X and O_{XY} are on a line that is that is parallel to a horizontal surface, which is vertically 4 m below from the point Y parallel to a horizontal surface. O_{XY}, X and Y all lie in the same vertical plane. A particle P is released from rest at X.

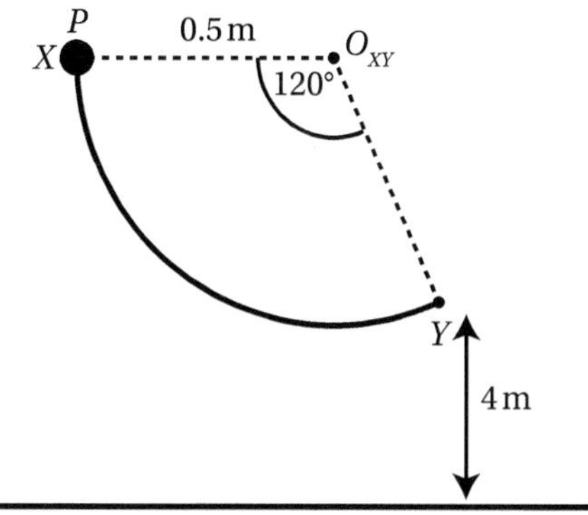

a Find the speed of the particle as it leaves the arc XY.

b Find the time taken for the particle to hit the ground after it has left Y.

c Find the horizontal distance the particle P travels after it leaves the track before it hits the horizontal surface.

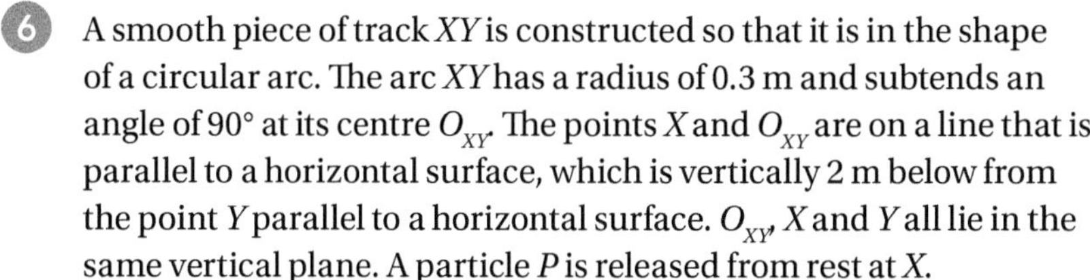

6 A smooth piece of track XY is constructed so that it is in the shape of a circular arc. The arc XY has a radius of 0.3 m and subtends an angle of 90° at its centre O_{XY}. The points X and O_{XY} are on a line that is parallel to a horizontal surface, which is vertically 2 m below from the point Y parallel to a horizontal surface. O_{XY}, X and Y all lie in the same vertical plane. A particle P is released from rest at X.

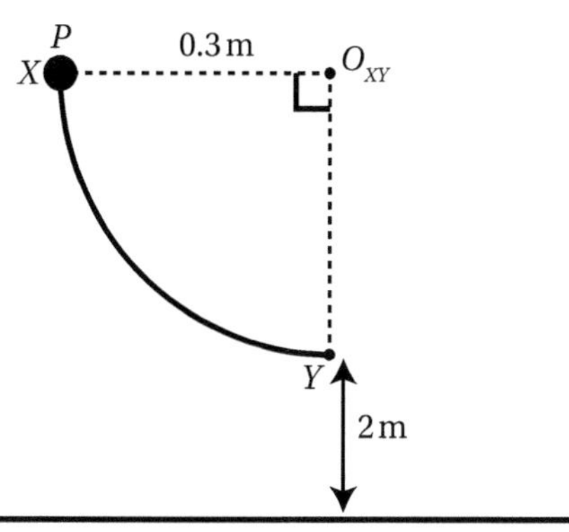

a Find the speed of the particle as it leaves the arc XY.

b Find the time taken for the particle to hit the ground after it has left Y.

c Find the horizontal distance the particle P travels after it leaves the track before it hits the horizontal surface.

7 A smooth solid hemisphere with centre O and radius 2 m is fixed with its flat surface in contact with a horizontal plane. A particle P is released from rest on the surface of the hemisphere, such that OP makes an angle of 5° with the upward vertical. The particle leaves the hemisphere at X. Find the angle between OX and the upward vertical.

8 A smooth sphere of centre O and radius 90 cm is fixed to a horizontal table. A particle P of mass 2 kg is released from rest at a point A on the surface of the sphere such that the acute angle formed between OA and the line perpendicular to the horizontal surface going through O is 25°. Find the speed of the particle when it leaves the surface of the sphere.

9 A light inextensible rope AB of length 4 m is attached at one end A to a horizontal beam 6 m above the horizontal ground and at the other end B to a seat. A horizontal platform 4 m above the horizontal ground has an acrobat of mass 65 kg holding the rope taut while sitting on the seat attached to the rope. The acrobat is released from rest and follows a circular arc. After the acrobat has travelled through an angle of 90°, measured from the starting position, the acrobat releases herself from the seat.

a What angle does AB make with the downward vertical when held taut by the acrobat on the platform?

b Calculate the tension in the rope when the acrobat is directly below A.

c Calculate the speed and direction of the acrobat as she leaves the rope.

10 A marble P of mass 30 g is attached to one end of a light inextensible string of length 60 cm. The other end of the string is attached to a fixed point O such that P hangs in equilibrium. The marble is set in motion with a horizontal speed of 3 m s^{-1}. Let θ be the angle OP makes with the downward vertical at O. If the string does not become slack:

a find an expression for the speed of P

b find an expression for the tension in the string in terms of θ

c show that the marble does not make full circles.

11 A smooth rubbish chute is built in two sections, AB and BC, each in the shape of an arc of a circle. The arc AB has a radius of 3 m and subtends an angle of 60° at its centre O_{AB}. The arc BC has a radius 7 m and subtends an angle of 45° at its centre O_{BC}. The points O_{AB}, O_{BC} and A, B and C all lie in the same vertical plane with O_{AB}, B and O_{BC} on the same vertical line.

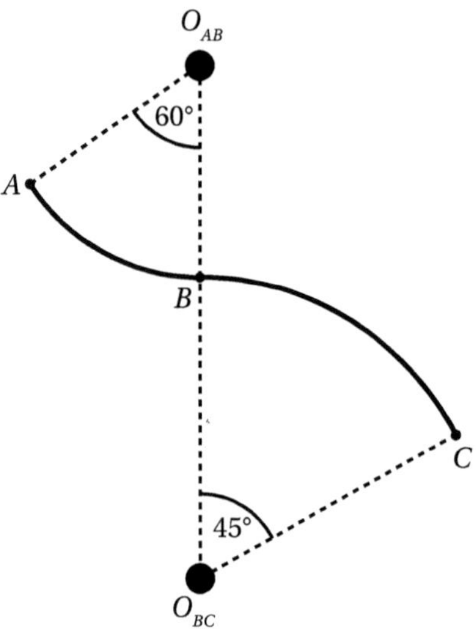

a If a bag containing rubbish of mass 3 kg is released from rest at A, calculate the speed at which the bag enters the arc BC.

A large container to collect the rubbish bags from the chute is positioned 2 m below C.

b Calculate the speed at which the rubbish bag reaches the large container below C.

c Determine whether or not the rubbish bag of mass 3 kg will lose contact with the chute before it reaches C.

Checklist of learning and understanding

- For a particle moving in a circular path of radius r with varying angular speed, you can find the velocity of the particle at any point in the path using the principle of conservation of mechanical energy. This is assuming that the particle is only subject to weight and a central force.
- The acceleration is directed towards the centre of the circular motion and you can use this to find the force in the same direction.
- If a particle connected to a light inextensible string moving in vertical circles is to complete full circles, then the tension in the string must be greater than or equal to zero throughout its circular orbit.
- If a particle connected to a light rod moving in vertical circles is to complete full circles, then the speed of the particle must be greater than zero throughout its circular orbit.

- $r\frac{d^2\theta}{dt^2}$ is the tangential (or transverse) component of the acceleration and $-\frac{v^2}{r}$ is the radial component of the acceleration.
- When a particle loses contact with a surface, the normal reaction force between the particle and the surface becomes zero.

Mixed practice 9

Unless otherwise instructed, when a numerical value for the acceleration due to gravity is needed, use $g = 9.8\ \mathrm{m\,s^{-2}}$.

1 A particle P of mass 750 kg is attached to one end of a light inextensible rope of length 0.8 metres. The other end of the rope is attached to a fixed point O. The particle hangs in equilibrium with the rope taut at position A. The particle is then set in motion with a horizontal speed of $4\ \mathrm{m\,s^{-1}}$ so that the particle moves in a vertical circle. Find the maximum height the particle reaches above A.

2 A particle P of mass 200 g is attached to one end of a light inextensible string of length 130 cm. The other end of the string is attached to a fixed point O. The particle hangs in equilibrium with the string taut at position A. The particle is then set in motion with a horizontal speed of $6\ \mathrm{m\,s^{-1}}$ so that the particle moves in a vertical circle. Find the tension in the string when the particle P is in the same horizontal line as the fixed point O.

3 A smooth solid hemisphere with radius 115 cm and centre O is resting on a horizontal table with its flat face in contact with the table. A particle P of mass 720 g is projected from the highest point parallel with the horizontal surface at an initial speed of $3\ \mathrm{m\,s^{-1}}$. When OP makes an angle of 83° with the horizontal, find the speed of the particle.

4 A particle of mass 0.4 kg is attached to one end of a light rod of length 2 m. The other end of the rod is attached to a fixed point O. The particle is hanging in equilibrium at its lowest point A when it is projected with a horizontal speed of $7\ \mathrm{m\,s^{-1}}$. Using the principle of conservation of mechanical energy, find the speed of the particle when the angle OP is 60° made with downward vertical OA.

5 One end of a light inextensible rope of length 1 m is attached to ball B of mass 700 g and the other end is attached to a fixed point A. The particle is hanging in equilibrium at C when it is set in motion with a horizontal speed of $5\ \mathrm{m\,s^{-1}}$. Calculate the tension in the rope when AB makes an angle of 30° with the downward vertical AC.

A 6 A hollow circular cylinder is fixed with its axis horizontal. The inner surface of the cylinder is smooth and has a radius of 1.05 m. A particle P of mass 0.6 kg is projected horizontally with speed $5\ \mathrm{m\,s^{-1}}$ from the lowest point A so that P moves in a vertical circle centre O, which is perpendicular to the axis of the cylinder. The angle AOP is θ.

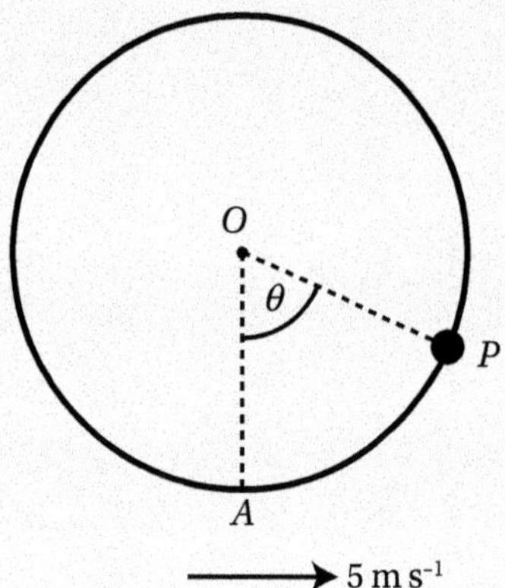

i While P is in contact with the inner surface of the cylinder, the speed is $v\ \mathrm{m\,s^{-1}}$. Find an equation for v^2 by using the principle of conservation of mechanical energy.

ii For what value of θ will the particle P leave the inner surface of the cylinder?

7 A light inextensible string of length of length 3 m has one end attached to a fixed point O and the other end attached to a particle P of mass 400 g. P moves in a vertical circle with centre O and radius 3 m. When P is at the highest point on the circle it has a speed of 7 m s^{-1}. Determine the tension in the string when P is at its lowest point in the circular orbit.

8 A light rod of length a m is freely hinged to a fixed point O, while at the other end is attached to a particle P of mass m kg. The particle starts at rest from a point vertically below O and is projected horizontally with speed u m s^{-1}. The particle moves in complete circles. Find the set of values of u for which this happens.

9 A particle of mass 0.4 kg is attached to a fixed point O by a light inextensible string of length 0.5 m. The particle is projected horizontally with speed 6 m s^{-1} from the point 0.5 m vertically below O. The particle moves in a complete circle. Find the tension in the string when

i the string is horizontal,

ii the particle is vertically above O.

10 A smooth sphere of radius r m and centre O has a particle P of mass m kg sitting at rest at the highest point of the sphere. The particle is projected horizontally with speed u m s^{-1} and the subsequent motion of P is down the sphere. P loses contact with the sphere when OP makes an angle of θ with the upward vertical.

i Find an expression for $\cos\theta$ in terms of u, r and g (the acceleration due to gravity).

ii Determine the minimum value of u in terms of r and g for which P leaves the surface of the sphere the instant it is projected.

11 A light rod OP of length r m has a particle of mass m kg attached at the point P. The rod is free to rotate in a vertical plane about a fixed point O. The greatest force acting along the rod is $10mg$ N.

i At which point in the particle's circular orbit does the force along the rod reach this greatest value?

ii Find the speed of the particle at the point where the force acting along the rod is greatest.

iii Find the magnitude of the force acting along the rod when the speed is $\sqrt{6rg}$.

12

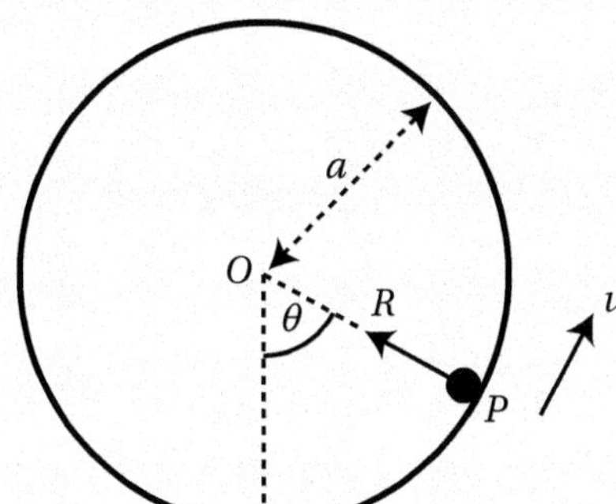

A hollow cylinder has internal radius a. The cylinder is fixed with its axis horizontal. A particle P of mass m is at rest in contact with the smooth inner surface of the cylinder. P is given a horizontal velocity u, in a vertical plane perpendicular to the axis of the cylinder, and begins to move in a vertical circle. While P remains in contact with the surface, OP makes an angle of θ with the downward vertical, where O is the centre of the circle. The speed of P is v and the magnitude of the force exerted on P by the surface is R (see diagram).

i Find v^2 in terms of u, a, g and θ and show that $R = \frac{mu^2}{a} + mg(3\cos\theta - 2)$

ii Given that P just reaches the highest point of the circle, find u^2 in terms of a and g, and show that in this case the least value of v^2 is ag.

iii Given instead that P oscillates between $\theta = \pm\frac{1}{6}\pi$ radians, find u^2 in terms of a and g.

© OCR, GCE Mathematics, Paper 4730, June 2009

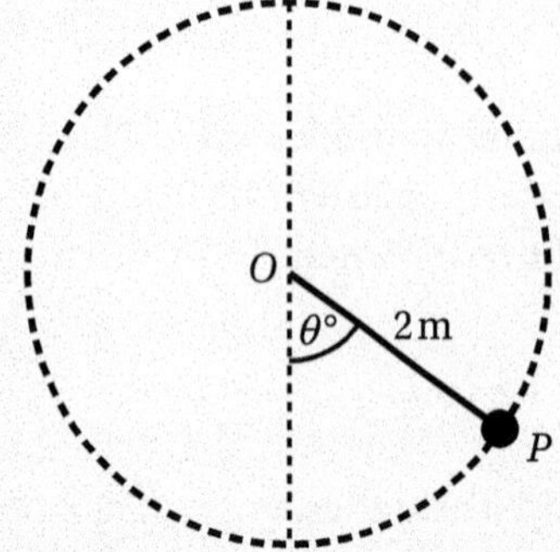

A particle P of mass 0.4 kg is attached to one end of a light inextensible string of length 2 m. The other end of the string is attached to a fixed point O. With the string taut the particle is travelling in a circular path in a vertical plane. The angle between the string and the downward vertical is $\theta°$ (see diagram). When $\theta = 0$ the speed of P is 7 m s^{-1}.

i At the instant when the string is horizontal, find the speed of P and the tension in the string.

ii At the instant when the string becomes slack, find the value of θ.

© OCR, GCE Mathematics, Paper 4730/01, January 2008

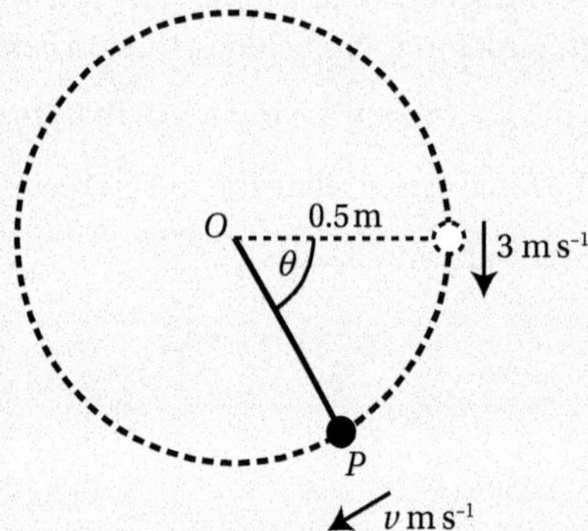

One end of a light inextensible string of length 0.5 m is attached to a fixed point O. A particle P of mass 0.2 kg is attached to the other end of the string. With the string taut and horizontal, P is projected with a velocity of 3 m s^{-1} vertically downwards. P begins to move in a vertical circle with centre O. While the string remains taut the angular displacement of OP is θ radians from its initial position, and the speed of P is v m s^{-1} (see diagram).

i Show that $v^2 = 9 + 9.8\sin\theta$.

ii Find, in terms of θ, the radial and tangential components of acceleration of P.

iii Show that the tension in the string is $(3.6 + 5.88\sin\theta)$ N and hence find the value of θ at the instant when the string becomes slack, giving your answer correct to 1 decimal place.

© OCR, GCE Mathematics, Paper 4730, January 2009

  **15** One end of a light inextensible string of length 0.8 m is attached to a fixed point O. A particle P of mass 0.3 kg is attached to the other end of the string. P is projected horizontally from the point 0.8 m vertically below O with speed 5.6 m s^{-1}. P starts to move in a vertical circle with centre O. The speed of P is v m s^{-1} when the string makes an angle θ with the downward vertical.

i While the string remains taut, show that $v^2 = 15.68(1 + \cos\theta)$, and find the tension in the string in terms of θ.

ii For the instant when the string becomes slack, find the value of θ and the value of v.

iii Find, in either order, the speed of P when it is at its greatest height after the string becomes slack, and the greatest height reached by P above its point of projection.

  **16** A particle P is attached to a fixed point O by a light inextensible string of length 0.7 m. A particle Q is in equilibrium suspended from O by an identical string. With the string OP taut and horizontal, P is projected vertically downwards with speed 6 m s^{-1} so that it strikes Q directly (see diagram). P is brought to rest by the collision and Q starts to move with speed 4.9 m s^{-1}.

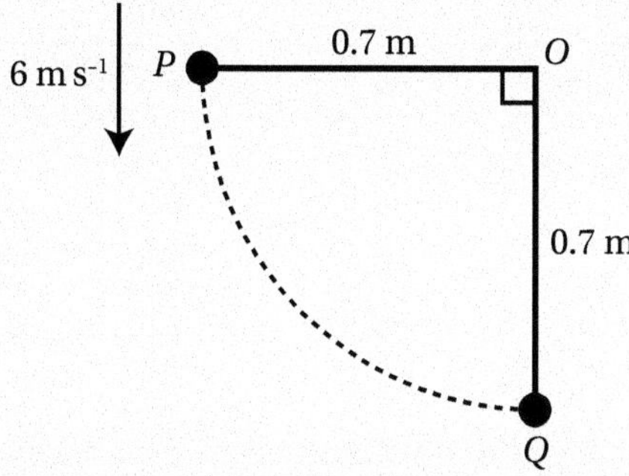

i Find the speed of P immediately before the collision. Hence find the coefficient of restitution between P and Q.

ii Given that the speed of Q is v m s^{-1} when OQ makes an angle θ with the downward vertical, find an expression for v^2 in terms of θ, and show that the tension in the string OQ is $14.7m(1 + 2\cos\theta)$ N, where m kg is the mass of Q.

iii Find the radial and transverse components of the acceleration of Q at the instant that the string OQ becomes slack.

iv Show that $V^2 = 0.8575$, where V m s^{-1} is the speed of Q when it reaches its greatest height (after the string OQ becomes slack). Hence find the greatest height reached by Q above its initial position.

Rewind

Recall how to find the coefficient of restitution from Chapter 3.

10 Centres of mass 2

A This chapter is for A Level students only.
In this chapter you will learn how to:

- use integration to find centres of mass of rods of variable density, uniform laminas and uniform solids of revolution
- apply your knowledge of centres of mass to problems of equilibrium, including suspension of a lamina and toppling or sliding of a lamina acted on by several forces.

Before you start...

A Level Mathematics Student Book 2	You should be able to integrate functions of the type: $\int_{x_1}^{x_2} x\mathrm{f}(x)\mathrm{d}x$.	1 Evaluate: $\int_1^3 x\ln x\,\mathrm{d}x$
A Level Mathematics Student Book 2	You should understand the moment of a force and be able to calculate moments.	2 Find the moment of a force of $\begin{pmatrix}0\\3\end{pmatrix}$ N acting at the point with position vector $\begin{pmatrix}5\\0\end{pmatrix}$ m about the point with position vector $\begin{pmatrix}2\\0\end{pmatrix}$ m.
A Level Mathematics Student Book 2	You should be able to use the coefficient of friction and the inequality $F \leqslant \mu R$.	3 A particle rests on a horizontal rough surface. A horizontal force is applied such that the particle is on the point of sliding. Find the value of the frictional force, in terms of μ, given that the mass of the particle is 2 kg.

Centres of mass, safety and stability

An object placed on a horizontal plane may topple over. An object placed on a rough inclined plane may topple over or slide. If an external force is applied to an object on a rough plane (horizontal or inclined) the object may topple over or slide. By analysing the forces on an object, including its weight, and the moments of those forces, you can determine whether the object will remain stationary, topple over or slide. You can assess the stablility of objects, such as a tractor on a hillside, and consider the safety implications.

Did you know?

Ships contain ballast below the waterline that lowers the centre of mass of the vessel. The ballast has to be adjusted carefully depending on the weight and distribution of the cargo, to ensure the ship is stable in a range of conditions at sea. The *Hoegh Osaka* left Southampton on 3 January 2015 but while still in the Solent it developed a severe list (tilt). The rudder and propeller were out of the water and the Captain could not control the ship. The crew were evacuated to safety and the 51 000 tonne vessel was grounded on a sandbank to prevent capsize. The calculations that should have led to a safe distribution of ballast and cargo were inaccurate and the centre of mass of the loaded vessel was too high. This is a very practical example of the need for an accurate method for assessing the location of the centre of mass of a three-dimensional body.

Section 1: Centres of mass by integration

The centre of mass of an object can be found by integration.

- When a rod has variable density that can be expressed as a function $f(x)$ you can use integration to find the centre of mass.
- When a lamina has a shape that can be expressed as a function $f(x)$ you can use integration to find the centre of mass.
- You can also use integration to find the centre of mass of a symmetrical solid of revolution defined by function $f(x)$. The centre of mass will lie on the axis of revolution.
- It is usually better to use standard results, if possible. If the shapes are non-standard, or the mass density is not uniform, integration is needed. You will also be expected to use integration to derive some of the standard results.

Centre of mass of a rod of variable density

Rods may be designed to be non-uniform. For example, it may be desirable to reinforce a rod where it is expected to be subject to the greatest force.

Key point 10.1

The centre of mass of a rod of length a metres with variable density function $f(x)$ is given by:

$$\bar{x} = \frac{\int_0^a x f(x)\,dx}{\int_0^a f(x)\,dx}$$

Tip

You learned about density in GCSE. It is usually the mass per unit volume of a solid object, and is measured in kg m^{-3}.

When working with a one-dimensional object such as a rod, density is mass per unit length, measured in kg m^{-1}.

Rewind

You learned in Chapter 5, Section 1, how to find the centre of mass of a composite body in one dimension.

Tip

Rods are assumed to be one-dimensional.

Tip

$\int_0^a f(x)\,dx$ is the mass of the rod.

WORKED EXAMPLE 10.1

A metal bar 8 metres long is modelled as a rod with mass density function $f(x) = 50 - x$ kg m^{-1}. Find the distance of the centre of mass from the denser end.

Use $\bar{x} = \dfrac{\int_0^a x\mathrm{f}(x)\,\mathrm{d}x}{\int_0^a \mathrm{f}(x)\,\mathrm{d}x}$ — Use the formula for centre of mass. Let $\bar{x}$ be the position of the centre of mass from one end of the bar.

$$\bar{x} = \frac{\int_0^8 x(50 - x)\,\mathrm{d}x}{\int_0^8 50 - x\,\mathrm{d}x}$$

$$\bar{x} = \frac{\int_0^8 50x - x^2\,\mathrm{d}x}{\int_0^8 50 - x\,\mathrm{d}x}$$

Substitute in the density function and the limits.

$$\bar{x} = \frac{\left[25x^2 - \frac{x^3}{3}\right]_0^8}{\left[50x - \frac{x^2}{2}\right]_0^8}$$

Integrate.

$$\bar{x} = \frac{1600 - \frac{512}{3}}{400 - 32}$$

$\bar{x} = 3.88$ m (3 s.f.)

$\therefore$ The centre of mass is 3.88 m from the denser end. — The rod is denser where $x = 0$, because $f(x)$ is 50 kg m^{-1} at this end but 42 kg m^{-1} at the other end.

Centre of mass of a uniform lamina defined by a function f(x)

If a lamina is not a standard shape, you may be able to model the shape using a mathematical function.

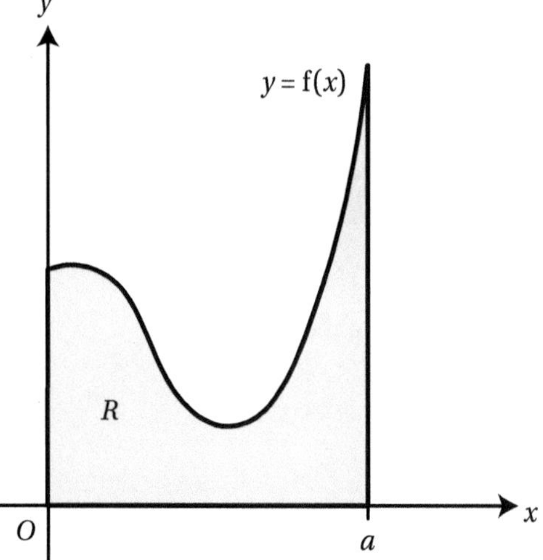

In this example, the region R represents a uniform lamina. R is defined by the function $f(x)$ and the lines $x = a$, $y = 0$ and $x = 0$.

> **Tip**
>
> Because the lamina is uniform, mass is proportional to area. You can work with area rather than mass.

> **Tip**
>
> These formulae can be derived by imagining the region R to be divided into many small rectangles and summing along the x-axis.

Key point 10.2

The coordinates of the centre of mass of a uniform lamina defined by $f(x)$ and the lines $x = a$, $y = 0$ and $x = 0$, are given by integration:

$$\bar{x} = \frac{\int_0^a x\,f(x)\,dx}{\int_0^a f(x)\,dx} \qquad \bar{y} = \frac{\frac{1}{2}\int_0^a (f(x))^2\,dx}{\int_0^a f(x)\,dx}$$

It is often convenient to use these rearrangements of the formulae:

$A\bar{x} = \int_0^a x\,f(x)\,dx$	$A\bar{y} = \frac{1}{2}\int_0^a (f(x))^2\,dx$

where A is the area of the lamina.

> **Tip**
>
> The formula for $\bar{x}$ is the same for a rod of variable density $f(x)$ and for a lamina defined by $f(x)$.

WORKED EXAMPLE 10.2

A lamina has three straight edges along the lines $x = 0$, $x = 2$ and $y = 0$.

The fourth edge is a curve modelled by $f(x) = x^2 + 4$, as shown.

Find the x-coordinate of the centre of mass of the lamina.

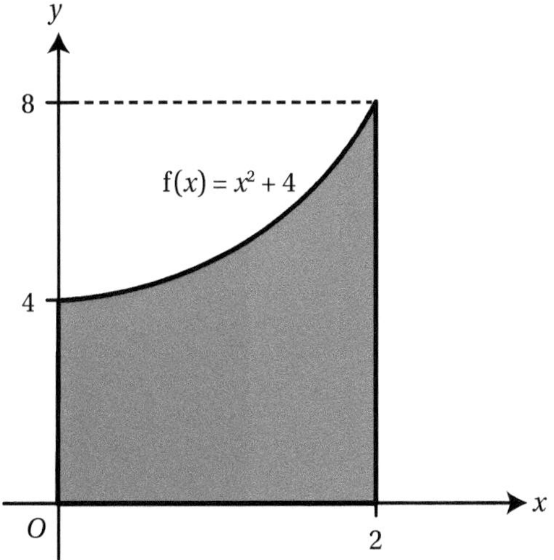

Continues on next page ...

$$\bar{x} = \frac{\int_0^a x\,\mathrm{f}(x)\,dx}{\int_0^a \mathrm{f}(x)\,dx}$$

$$\bar{x} = \frac{\int_0^2 x^3 + 4x\,dx}{\int_0^2 x^2 + 4\,dx}$$

Substitute for the function $\mathrm{f}(x)$, multiplying out the expression for $x\mathrm{f}(x)$.

$$\bar{x} = \frac{\left[\frac{x^4}{4} + 2x^2\right]_0^2}{\left[\frac{x^3}{3} + 4x\right]_0^2} = \frac{12}{10\frac{2}{3}} = 1\frac{1}{8}$$

Integrate.

Check that the value of $\bar{x}$ looks sensible.

You can use integration to find the centre of mass of a right-angled isosceles triangle, as in Worked example 10.3.

WORKED EXAMPLE 10.3

Use integration to find the centre of mass of the uniform triangular lamina shown.

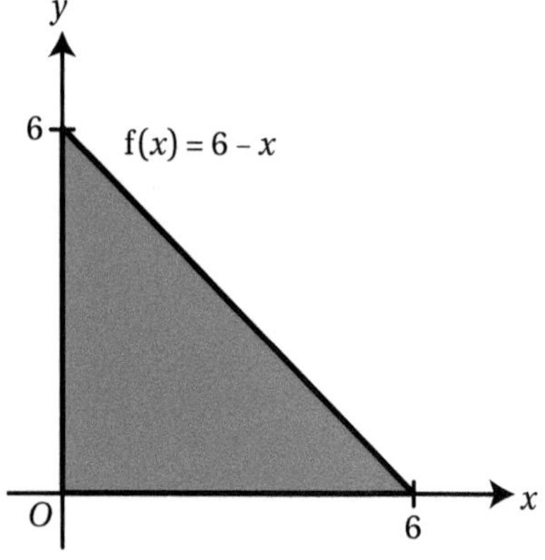

$\bar{x} = \bar{y}$

The lamina is in the shape of an isosceles triangle so the centre of mass lies on its axis of symmetry.

$$\bar{x} = \frac{\int_0^a x\,\mathrm{f}(x)\,dx}{\int_0^a \mathrm{f}(x)\,dx}$$

Use the formula for the centre of mass of a lamina by integration.

$$\bar{x} = \frac{\int_0^6 6x - x^2\,dx}{\int_0^6 6 - x\,dx} \quad \therefore \bar{x} = \frac{\left[3x^2 - \frac{x^3}{3}\right]_0^6}{\left[6x - \frac{x^2}{2}\right]_0^6}$$

$$\bar{x} = \frac{36}{18} = 2$$

$$\begin{pmatrix}\bar{x}\\ \bar{y}\end{pmatrix} = \begin{pmatrix}2\\ 2\end{pmatrix}$$

WORKED EXAMPLE 10.4

In the right-angled uniform triangular lamina ABC, $\hat{C} = 90°$, $CB = a$ and $CA = b$.

Use integration to find the centre of mass of the lamina. State the distances of the centre of mass from CB and CA.

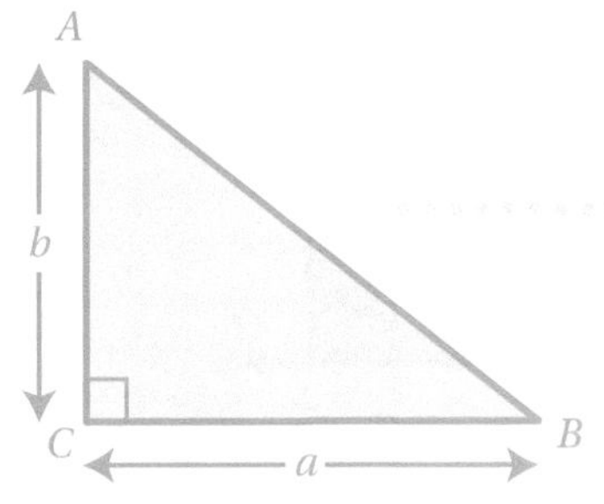

Draw the triangle. Let CB be the x-axis and CA be the y-axis.

Gradient of $AB = -\frac{b}{a}$

Find the equation of edge AB.

$\Rightarrow y = -\frac{b}{a}x + b$

$A\bar{x} = \int_0^a x\left(-\frac{b}{a}x + b\right)dx$

Use $A\bar{x} = \int_0^a x\text{f}(x)\text{d}x$, with your equation for f(x).

$A\bar{x} = \int_0^a -\frac{b}{a}x^2 + bx\,dx$

$A\bar{x} = \left[-\frac{bx^3}{3a} + \frac{bx^2}{2}\right]_0^a$

Integrate from $x = 0$ to $x = a$.

$A\bar{x} = -\frac{ba^3}{3a} + \frac{ba^2}{2} = \frac{ba^2}{6}$

Substitute limits to find $A\bar{x}$.

$A\bar{y} = \frac{b^2a}{6}$

You could use integration to find $A\bar{y}$, but in this case consider that you could have chosen CA to be the x-axis and CB the y-axis, then a and b would be swapped over.

$A = \frac{1}{2}b \times a$

Find A using the formula for the area of a triangle. There is no need for integration here.

$\Rightarrow \begin{pmatrix}\bar{x}\\ \bar{y}\end{pmatrix} = \begin{pmatrix}\frac{a}{3}\\ \frac{b}{3}\end{pmatrix}$

You can check this result using the coordinates of the vertices.

The centre of mass lies $\frac{b}{3}$ from CB and $\frac{a}{3}$ from CA.

Rewind

Recall from Chapter 5 that the centre of mass of a triangular lamina lies at the intersection of its medians.

WORKED EXAMPLE 10.5

Use integration, together with the inverse function $f^{-1}(x)$, to find the y-coordinate of the centre of mass of the uniform lamina defined by the straight lines $x = 2$, $y = 0$, and $f(x) = x^3$.

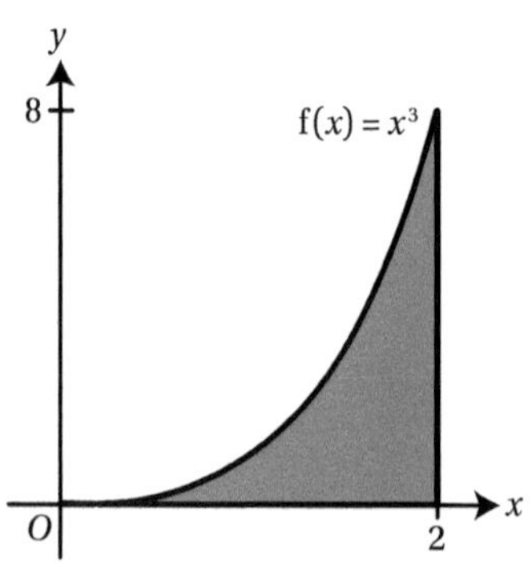

$$\bar{x} = \frac{\int_0^8 x \times x^{\frac{1}{3}} dx}{\int_0^8 x^{\frac{1}{3}} dx}$$

The technique here is to find the x-coordinate of the centre of mass of the uniform lamina defined by the inverse function bounded by $x = 8$, $y = 0$ and $f^{-1}(x) = \sqrt[3]{x}$.

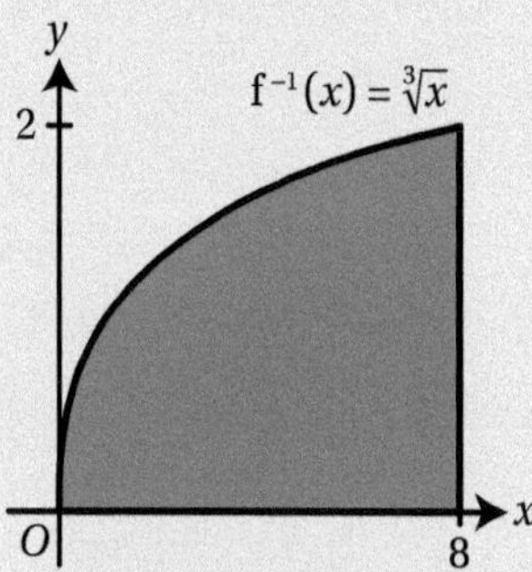

This will be the y-coordinate of the centre of mass of empty figure defined by $x = 0$, $y = 8$ and $y = f(x)$.

$$\bar{x} = \frac{\left[\frac{3x^{\frac{7}{3}}}{7}\right]_0^8}{\left[\frac{3x^{\frac{4}{3}}}{4}\right]_0^8}$$

$$\therefore \bar{x} = 4\frac{4}{7}$$

The denominator represents the area of the 'inverse' lamina which is 12.

$$m_1 y_1 + m_2 y_2 = M\bar{y}$$

$$12 \times 4\frac{4}{7} + 4\bar{y} = 16 \times 4$$

$$\bar{y} = 2\frac{2}{7}$$

The y-coordinate of the centre of mass of the required lamina can then be calculated by subtraction.

The area of the bounding box is 16, the area between $f(x)$ and the x-axis is 4 and the area between $f^{-1}(x)$ and the x-axis is 12.

You can check this answer using the formula given in Key point 10.2.

Rewind

Finding inverse functions is covered in A Level Mathematics Student Book 2, Chapter 2.

Centre of mass of a uniform solid of revolution

A **solid of revolution** is the solid three-dimensional shape formed by rotating a function about an axis. In the diagram, the x-axis is the axis of revolution. The centre of mass lies on the axis of revolution.

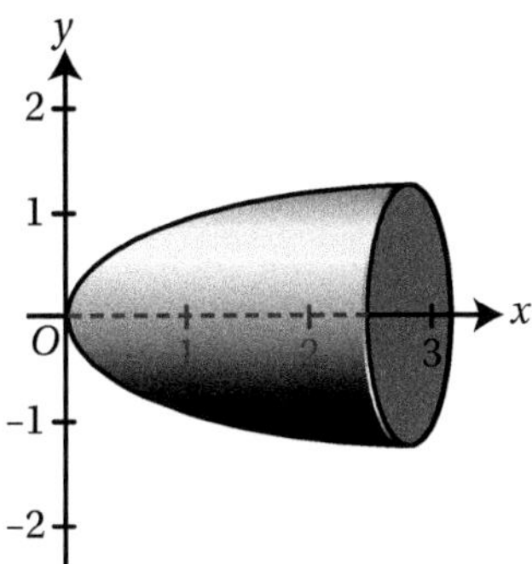

The formula can be derived by imagining the solid to be divided into many small discs and summing along the x-axis.

Key point 10.3

The position of the centre of mass of a uniform solid of revolution with radius defined by $f(x)$ is:

$$\bar{x} = \frac{\int_0^a \pi x y^2 \, dx}{\int_0^a \pi y^2 \, dx}$$

where $\int_0^a \pi y^2 \, dx$ is the volume of the solid of revolution.

Rewind

Finding the volume of a solid of revolution is covered in Pure Core Student Book 2.

It can be more convenient to use the formula in the form:

$$V\bar{x} = \int_0^a \pi x y^2 dx$$

where V is the volume of the solid.

Tip

Since the solid is uniform, you can work with volume rather than mass.

WORKED EXAMPLE 10.6

The region R is bounded by the curve $y = \sqrt{4 - x^2}$ for $0 \leqslant x \leqslant 2$, the x-axis and y-axis.

R is rotated through 2π radians about the x-axis to produce a solid of revolution. Show by integration that the centre of mass of the solid has x-coordinate $\frac{3}{4}$.

Continues on next page ...

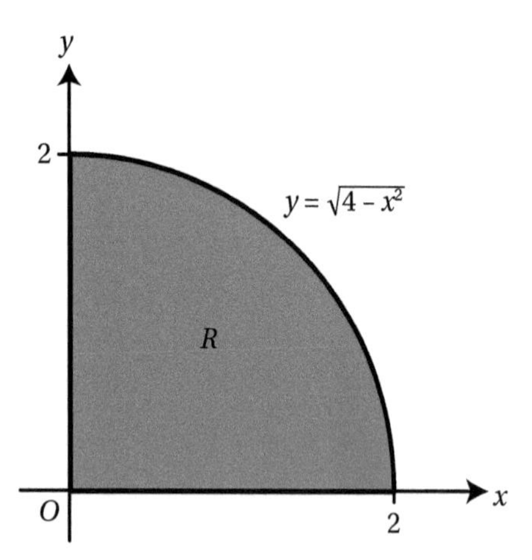

The region is a quarter disc of radius 2, centre (0, 0), $0 \leqslant x \leqslant 2$.

The solid of revolution is a hemisphere.

The formula book gives a formula for the centre of mass of a hemisphere, but you are required to 'show by integration' so you cannot just quote this result.

$$\bar{x} = \frac{\int_0^2 \pi x(4 - x^2)\,dx}{\int_0^2 \pi(4 - x^2)\,dx}$$

Use the formula for the centre of mass of a volume of revolution by integration.

$$\bar{x} = \frac{\int_0^2 4x - x^3\,dx}{\int_0^2 4 - x^2\,dx}$$

Cancel π and expand the brackets in the numerator.

$$\bar{x} = \frac{\left[2x^2 - \frac{x^4}{4}\right]_0^2}{\left[4x - \frac{x^3}{3}\right]_0^2}$$

Write down the integrals and substitute the limits.

$$\Rightarrow \bar{x} = \frac{2 \times 2^2 - \frac{2^4}{4}}{4 \times 2 - \frac{2^3}{3}} = \frac{4}{\frac{16}{3}}$$

$$\Rightarrow \bar{x} = \frac{3}{4}, \text{ as required.}$$

WORKED EXAMPLE 10.7

Use integration to show that the centre of mass of a uniform solid right circular cone of height h lies $\frac{h}{4}$ from its base.

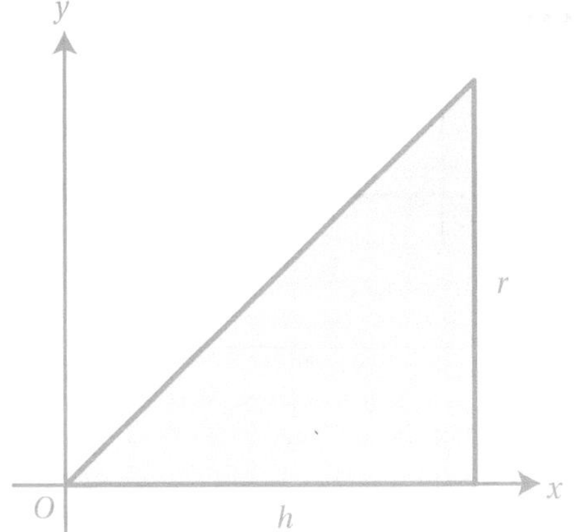

Let r be the radius of the cone.

You can generate the solid cone by rotating a right-angled triangular region about the x-axis.

$\text{Gradient} = \frac{r}{h} \Rightarrow y = \frac{r}{h}x$

Find the equation of the hypotenuse.

$$\bar{x} = \frac{\int_0^h \pi x \times \left(\frac{rx}{h}\right)^2 dx}{\int_0^h \pi \left(\frac{rx}{h}\right)^2 dx}$$

Use the formula for the centre of mass of a solid of revolution.

$$\bar{x} = \frac{\int_0^h x^3\, dx}{\int_0^h x^2\, dx}$$

Cancel $\pi \times \left(\frac{r}{h}\right)^2$.

$$\bar{x} = \frac{\left[\frac{x^4}{4}\right]_0^h}{\left[\frac{x^3}{3}\right]_0^h} = \frac{h^4}{4} \times \frac{3}{h^3}$$

Integrate and substitute limits.

$$\bar{x} = \frac{3h}{4}$$

Simplify.

The centre of mass is $\frac{3h}{4}$ from the vertex.

$\Rightarrow$ The centre of mass is $\frac{h}{4}$ from the base of the cone.

In Worked example 10.7, you could have used $f(x) = r - \frac{r}{h}x$ to generate the cone as a solid of revolution.

This would have led directly to $\frac{h}{4}$ but the integration would have required more steps.

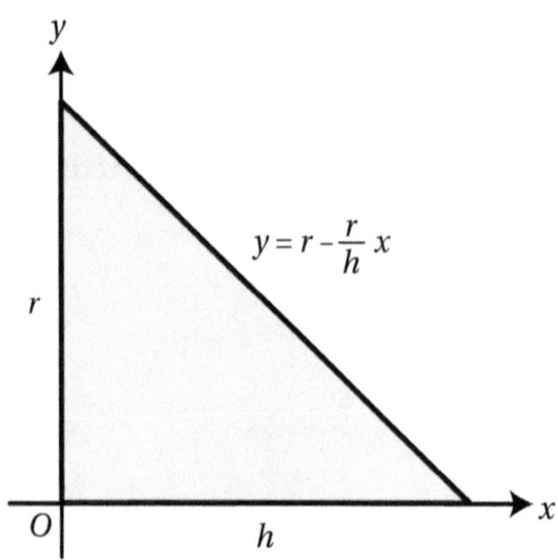

WORKED EXAMPLE 10.8

The region R is bounded by the line $y = \frac{1}{2}x + 3$ for $0 \leqslant x \leqslant 4$, the x-axis and y-axis.

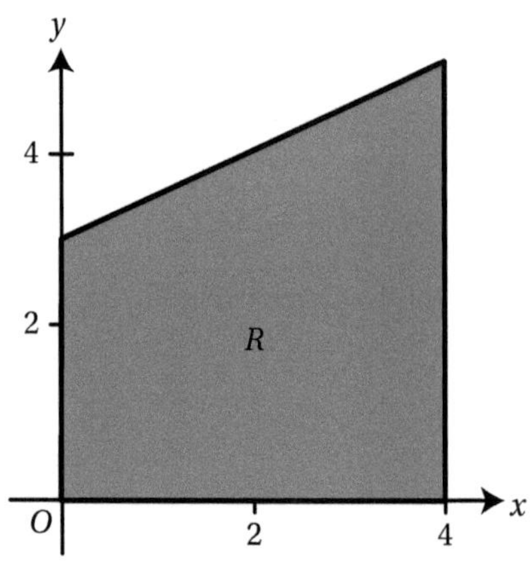

R is rotated through 2π radians about the x-axis to produce a solid of revolution. Calculate the x-coordinate of the centre of mass of the solid.

$$\bar{x} = \frac{\int_0^4 \pi x \times \left(\frac{1}{2}x+3\right)^2 dx}{\int_0^4 \pi \left(\frac{1}{2}x+3\right)^2 dx}$$

Use the formula for the centre of mass of a volume of revolution by integration.

The solid formed is a frustum of a cone.

$$= \frac{\int_0^3 \frac{x^3}{4} + 3x^2 + 9x \, dx}{\int_0^3 \frac{x^2}{4} + 3x + 9 \, dx}$$

Cancel π and expand the brackets in the numerator.

$$= \frac{\left[\frac{x^4}{16} + x^3 + \frac{9x^2}{2}\right]_0^4}{\left[\frac{x^3}{12} + \frac{3x^2}{2} + 9x\right]_0^4} = \frac{152}{\frac{196}{3}}$$

Write down the integrals and substitute the limits.

$\bar{x} \approx 2.33$

When integrating to find the centre of mass, you may need to use any of the integration techniques you have already learned.

WORKED EXAMPLE 10.9

The region R is bounded by the curve $y = \sin x$, $y = 0$ and $0 \leqslant x \leqslant \frac{\pi}{2}$.

R is rotated through 2π radians about the x-axis. Find the x-coordinate of the centre of mass of the solid formed.

Use the formula for the centre of mass of a volume of revolution.

$$\bar{x} = \frac{\int_0^{\frac{\pi}{2}} x\sin^2 x \, dx}{\int_0^{\frac{\pi}{2}} \sin^2 x \, dx}$$

You need to express $\sin^2 x$ using a double angle identity:

$\cos 2x = 1 - 2\sin^2 x$

$\therefore \sin^2 x = \frac{1}{2} - \frac{1}{2} \times \cos 2x$

$$\bar{x} = \frac{\int_0^{\frac{\pi}{2}} \frac{1}{2}x - \frac{x}{2}\cos 2x \, dx}{\int_0^{\frac{\pi}{2}} \frac{1}{2} - \frac{1}{2}\cos 2x \, dx}$$

Substitute for $\sin^2 x$.

You need to integrate $\frac{x}{2}\cos 2x$ by parts.

$$\bar{x} = \frac{\left[\frac{x^2}{4}\right]_0^{\frac{\pi}{2}} - \left[\frac{x\sin 2x}{4}\right]_0^{\frac{\pi}{2}} + \int_0^{\frac{\pi}{2}} \frac{\sin 2x}{4} dx}{\left[\frac{x}{2} - \frac{\sin 2x}{4}\right]_0^{\frac{\pi}{2}}}$$

Integrate using integration by parts and being careful with + and – signs.

$$\bar{x} = \frac{\left[\frac{x^2}{4}\right]_0^{\frac{\pi}{2}} - \left[\frac{x\sin 2x}{4}\right]_0^{\frac{\pi}{2}} - \left[\frac{\cos 2x}{8}\right]_0^{\frac{\pi}{2}} dx}{\left[\frac{x}{2} - \frac{\sin 2x}{4}\right]_0^{\frac{\pi}{2}}}$$

$$\bar{x} = \frac{\frac{\pi^2}{16} - \left(-\frac{1}{8} - \frac{1}{8}\right)}{\frac{\pi}{4}}$$

Substitute limits.

$\bar{x} = 1.10$ rad (3 s.f.)

Check your solution using your calculator, if possible.

EXERCISE 10A

1. Use integration to find the centre of mass of a rod of length 2 metres with mass density function: $f(x) = 10 + x(2 - x)$ kg m^{-1}, $0 \leqslant x \leqslant 2$.

2. A javelin is modelled as a rod of length 2.65 metres of mass density $f(x) = 0.23(2.65 - x)x^{1.5}$, $0 \leqslant x \leqslant 2.65$, where x is measured from the tail end. Calculate the distance of the centre of mass of the javelin from its tail end.

3. A uniform triangular lamina is in the shape of a right-angled triangle ABC, $\hat{A} = 90°$, $AB = 8$ cm and $AC = 5$ cm.

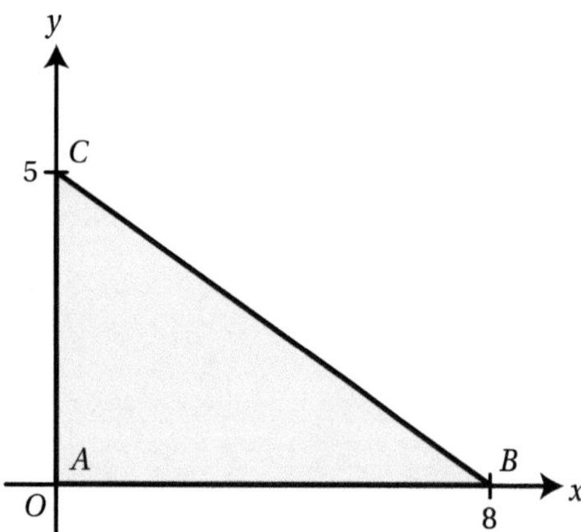

   a Find the equation of the line passing through CB.

   b Use integration to find the coordinates of the centre of mass of the lamina.

4. Use integration to find the centre of mass of a uniform lamina bounded by $y = 2\sqrt{x}$, $y = 0$ and $x = 1$.

5. Use integration to show that the distance of the centre of mass of a uniform solid cone of height $3r$ metres and base radius r metres is $\frac{9r}{4}$ from its vertex.

6. A uniform triangular lamina is bounded by the line $y = 8 - x$, and the positive x- and y-axes. Use integration to find the centre of mass of the triangular lamina.

7. The shape of a solid toy can be modelled by rotating the graph of $y = x\sqrt{5 - x}$, $0 \leqslant x \leqslant 5$, where x is measured in cm, through 360° about the x-axis.

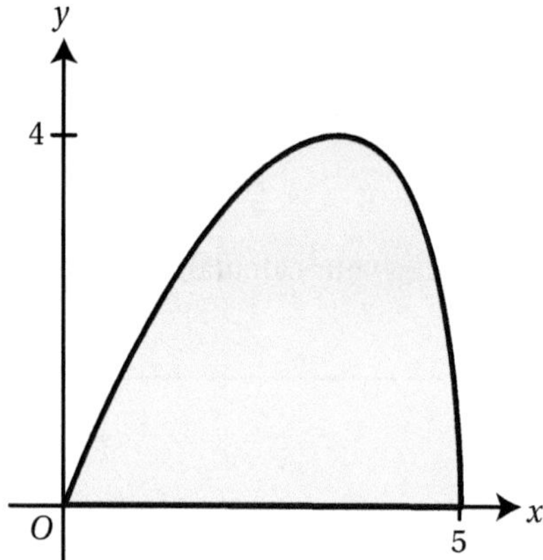

   Assuming the solid formed is uniform, find the centre of mass of the toy.

8 The region bounded by the line $y = x + 6$, $y = 0$ and $0 \leqslant x \leqslant 4$ is rotated though 360° about the x-axis to form a truncated cone (frustum). Use integration to find the centre of mass of the frustum.

9 A uniform lamina is bounded by the curve $y = kx^2$, the line $x = 3$ and the x-axis. Find:

a the area of the lamina in terms of k

b the x-coordinate of the centre of mass of the lamina

c the y-coordinate of the centre of mass of the lamina in terms of k.

10 A uniform lamina is bounded by the curve $y = 9 - x^2$ and the x-axis, $-3 \leqslant x \leqslant 3$. Find the y-coordinate of the centre of mass of the lamina.

11 A uniform lamina is defined by the positive x-axis, the positive y-axis and the curve with equation:

$y = \sqrt{R^2 - x^2}$.

Use integration to find the position of the centre of mass of the lamina, in terms of R.

12 The region bounded by the line $y = \cos x$, $y = 0$ and $0 \leqslant x \leqslant \frac{\pi}{2}$ is rotated though 2π radians about the x-axis to form a solid figure. Use integration to find the x-coordinate of the centre of mass of the solid.

Section 2: Equilibrium of a rigid body

A **rigid body** is a single or composite object consisting of particles, rods, wires, laminas and solids that is fixed in shape. It is in equilibrium if the resultant force acting on the body is zero and the resultant moment acting on the body is also zero.

Suspension of a lamina from a point

The moment of the weight and reaction about the point of suspension are both zero, as the line of action of both forces passes through the point of suspension.

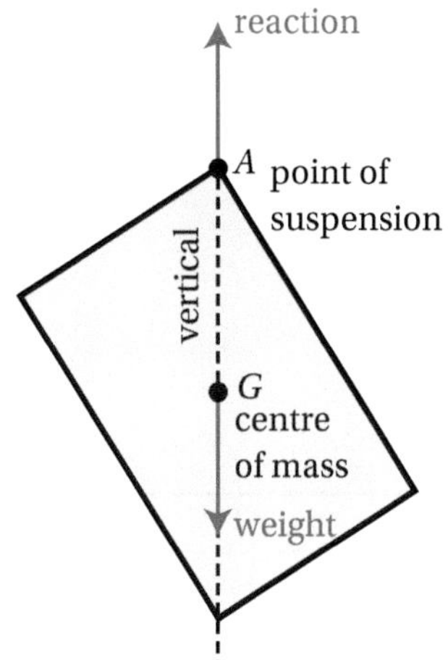

Key point 10.4

If a rigid body is freely suspended, it will hang with its centre of mass vertically below the point of suspension.

You can apply this principle to solve problems.

WORKED EXAMPLE 10.10

A uniform lamina has its centre of mass G at the point (5, 8) as shown. A is a point on the edge of the lamina at (2, 12). Find the angle between the line $y = 8$ and the vertical when the lamina is freely suspended from A.

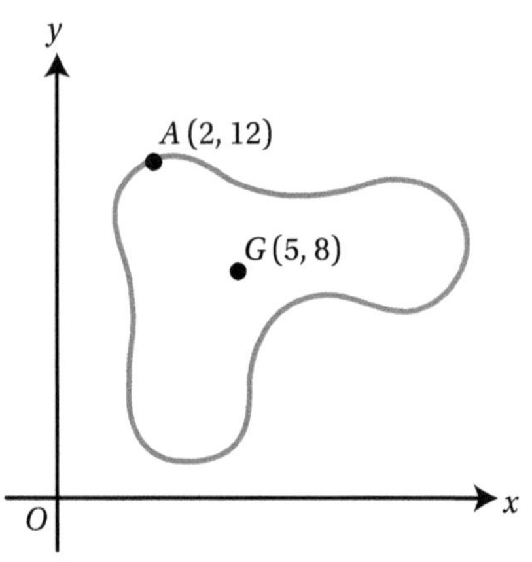

The lamina will hang with the centre of mass G vertically below A.

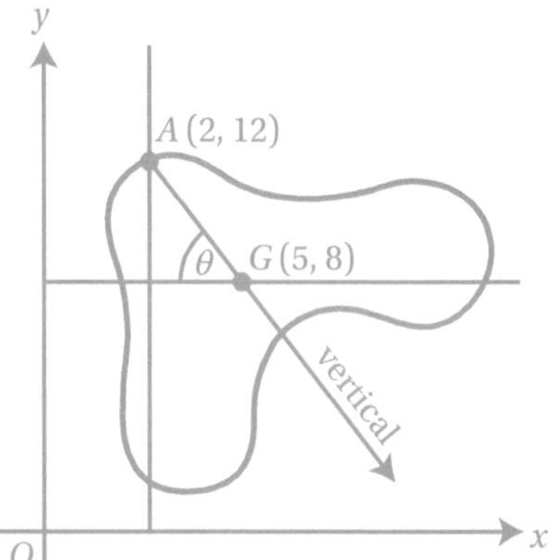

Draw a vertical line through A and the line $y = 8$. There is no need to rotate the diagram.

$$\tan\theta = \frac{12-8}{5-2} = \frac{4}{3}$$

Let the angle between AG and $y = 8$ be θ.

$$\therefore \theta = 53.1°$$

WORKED EXAMPLE 10.11

A composite lamina of mass M kg is made from a uniform rectangular lamina and a uniform isosceles triangular lamina abutting as shown.

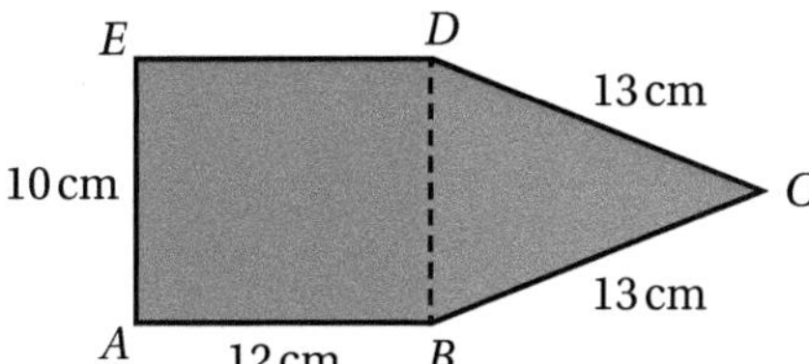

a Find the distance of the centre of mass from AB and from AE.

The lamina is freely suspended from D.

b Find the angle between DB and the vertical.

The lamina remains suspended from D but now has a point mass kM kg attached at C. The lamina now hangs with AB horizontal.

c Find the exact value of k.

If a perpendicular is drawn from C to DB it makes two 5 : 12 : 13 triangles.

a Area of rectangular lamina = 120 cm^2

Area of triangular lamina = 60 cm^2

The mass of each component is directly proportional to area so you can work with area.

$$(120+60)\begin{pmatrix}\bar{x}\\ \bar{y}\end{pmatrix}=120\begin{pmatrix}6\\ 5\end{pmatrix}+60\begin{pmatrix}16\\ 5\end{pmatrix}$$

$$\begin{pmatrix}\bar{x}\\ \bar{y}\end{pmatrix}=\begin{pmatrix}9\frac{1}{3}\\ 5\end{pmatrix}$$

Let the x-axis pass through AB and the y-axis pass through AE.

Let vertex A be (0, 0).

Remember that the centre of mass of an isosceles triangular lamina is one-third the distance from the centre of the base to the opposite vertex.

b

D
θ
vertical
5 cm
G
$2\frac{2}{3}$ cm
B

Draw in the vertical through D, which passes through the centre of mass G.

Continues on next page ...

$\tan\theta = \dfrac{2\frac{2}{3}}{5}$

$\Rightarrow \theta \approx 28.1°$

Calculate θ.

c

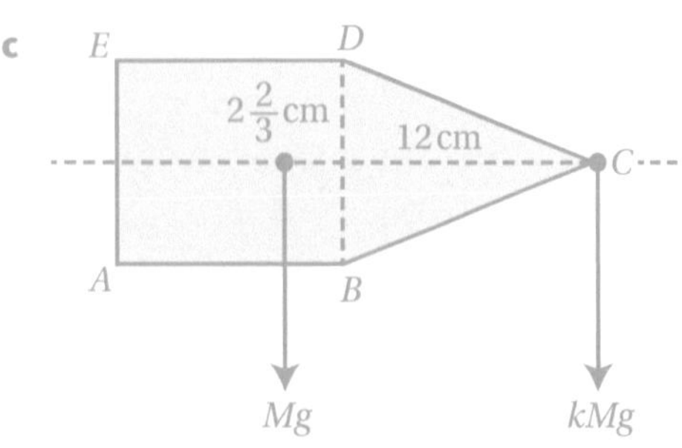

$2\frac{2}{3} \times Mg - 12 \times kMg = 0$

$k = \dfrac{2}{9}$

Take moments about the midpoint of DB, to work out the value of k.

As the lamina is hanging in equilibrium the resultant moment is zero.

An object may be attached to a point or surface by a hinge. The hinge allows the object to rotate, like hinges connecting a door to its door frame. There is always a reaction force at the hinge, but this can often be eliminated from calculations by choosing a suitable point about which to take moments so that the moment of the reaction force is zero. If you need to calculate the reaction force at the hinge it can be useful to resolve the reaction force into perpendicular components.

Rewind

Taking moments is covered in A Level Mathematics Student Book 2, Chapter 22.

WORKED EXAMPLE 10.12

A uniform rectangular lamina $ABCD$, $AB = 18$ cm, $BC = 12$ cm, is smoothly pivoted at A to a horizontal surface. It rests in equilibrium against a fixed smooth block of height 10 cm. The mass of the lamina is 4 kg. AB makes an angle of 45° with the horizontal. Calculate:

a the magnitude of the force exerted by the block on the lamina

b the magnitude and direction of the reaction on the lamina at the hinge.

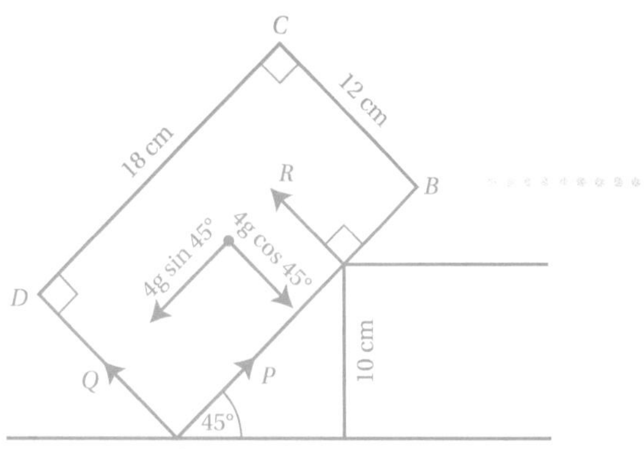

Draw a diagram showing the forces acting on the lamina.

The reaction of the hinge on the lamina has been resolved into components P and Q, parallel to the edges of the lamina.

The reaction, R, of the smooth block on the lamina is normal to edge AB.

The weight of the block has been resolved into components parallel to the edges of the lamina.

Continues on next page ...

a $R \times \sqrt{0.1^2 + 0.1^2} + 4g\frac{\sqrt{2}}{2} \times 0.06 = 4g\frac{\sqrt{2}}{2} \times 0.09$

$0.1414R = 4g\frac{\sqrt{2}}{2} \times 0.03$

$\Rightarrow R = 5.88$ N

The lamina is in equilibrium.

Take moments about A, thus eliminating the reaction force from the calculation.

Since the rod is in equilibrium the anticlockwise moment is equal to the clockwise moment.

The centre of mass of the lamina is 6 cm from AB and 9 cm from AD.

b $P - 4g\frac{\sqrt{2}}{2} = 0$

$\Rightarrow P = 27.7$ N

There is zero resultant force parallel to AD.

$Q + R - 4g\frac{\sqrt{2}}{2} = 0$

$\Rightarrow Q = 27.72 - 5.881$

$\Rightarrow Q = 21.8$ N

There is zero resultant force parallel to AB.

$\sqrt{27.72^2 + 21.84^2} = 35.3$ N

Use Pythagoras' theorem to calculate the magnitude of the reaction at the hinge.

$\tan^{-1}\left(\frac{21.84}{27.72}\right) = 38.2°$

Use trigonometry to find the direction of the reaction at the hinge.

The reaction force is at 38.2° to AB.

WORKED EXAMPLE 10.13

A piece of uniform wire AB of length 20 cm is bent to form three sides of a rectangle, 1 cm, 18 cm and 1 cm, and then freely suspended from a hinge at A. Calculate the angle between AB and the vertical.

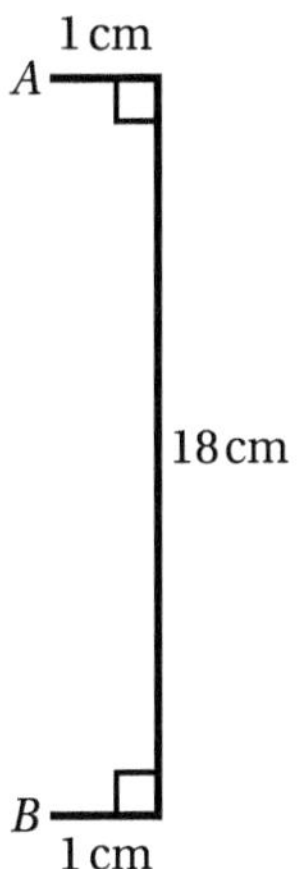

Let the midpoint of AB be $O\,(0, 0)$, and the centre of mass be at G.

The wire is symmetrical so $\overline{y} = 0$.

Continues on next page ...

$20 \times OG = 1 \times 0.5 + 18 \times 1 + 1 \times 0.5$

Since the wire is uniform, mass is proportional to length, so you can work with length to find the centre of mass.

Calculate $\bar{x}$, OG, using $M\bar{x} = m_1\bar{x}_1 + m_2\bar{x}_2$

$\Rightarrow OG = \frac{19}{20} = 0.95 \text{ cm}$

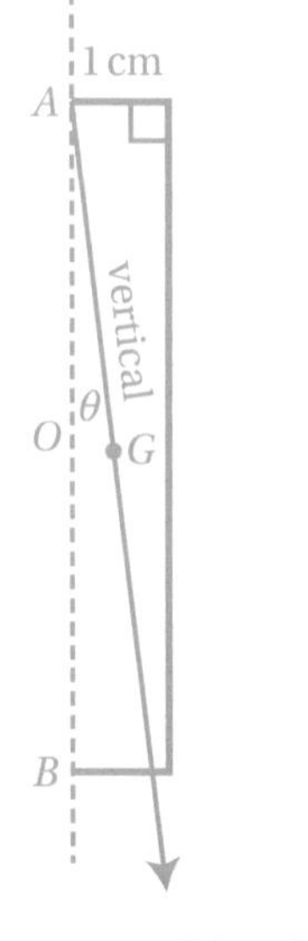

Add a vertical line to the diagram from A passing through G.

Let θ be angle between AB and vertical.

$\tan\theta = \frac{OG}{OA} = \frac{0.95}{9}$

$\theta \approx 6.03°$

WORKED EXAMPLE 10.14

A composite lamina of mass M kg is made from two rectangular laminas joined as shown. There is an axis of symmetry passing between the midpoints of AF, BE and CD.

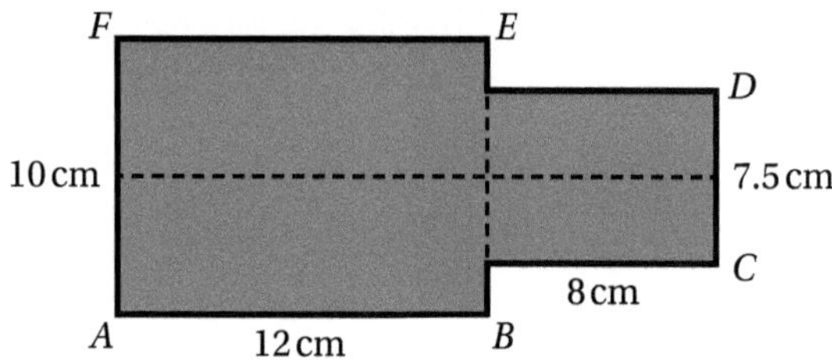

a Find the distance of the centre of mass from AB and from AF.

The lamina is freely suspended from a hinge at E.

b Find the angle between EB and the vertical.

The lamina remains suspended from E but now has a point mass kM kg attached at C. The lamina now hangs with AB horizontal.

c Find the exact value of k.

Continues on next page ...

a Area of larger rectangular lamina = 120 cm²

Area of smaller rectangular lamina = 60 cm²

$$(120+60)\begin{pmatrix}\bar{x}\\ \bar{y}\end{pmatrix}=120\begin{pmatrix}6\\ 5\end{pmatrix}+60\begin{pmatrix}16\\ 5\end{pmatrix}$$

$$\begin{pmatrix}\bar{x}\\ \bar{y}\end{pmatrix}=\begin{pmatrix}9\frac{1}{3}\\ 5\end{pmatrix}$$

The mass of each component is directly proportional to area so you can work with area. Work out the distances of the centres of mass of each rectangle from AB and AF, using $M\begin{pmatrix}\bar{x}\\ \bar{y}\end{pmatrix}=m_1\begin{pmatrix}\bar{x}_1\\ \bar{y}_1\end{pmatrix}+m_2\begin{pmatrix}\bar{x}_2\\ \bar{y}_2\end{pmatrix}$, taking vertex A as (0, 0).

b

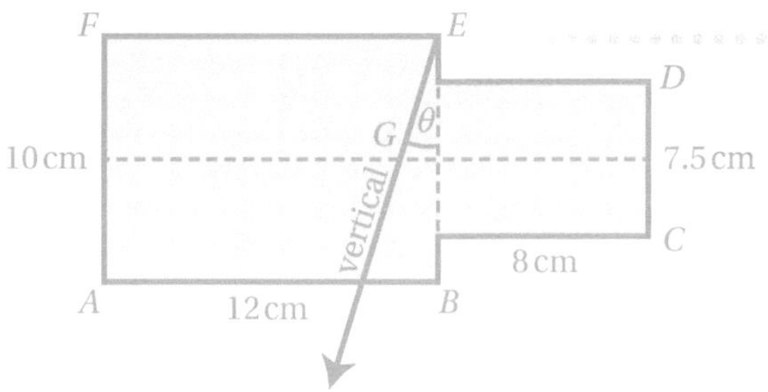

The centre of mass G will be vertically below E when the lamina is suspended. Draw in the vertical through E, which passes through G.

$$\tan\theta=\frac{12-9\frac{1}{3}}{5}=\frac{2\frac{2}{3}}{5}$$

$\therefore \theta = 28.1°$ (3 s.f.)

Use trigonometry to calculate the required angle.

c $2\frac{2}{3}\times Mg = 8\times kMg$

$$k=\frac{1}{3}$$

The weight of the lamina acts at G. Take moments about the midpoint of EB, to work out the value of k.

Tip

In part **a** of Worked example 10.13 the location of the centre of mass in the y-direction could have been found directly since it will lie on the line of symmetry.

Explore

If a point on the rim of a lamina is attached to a fixed point, and the lamina is free to rotate, it will hang with its centre of mass vertically below the point of attachment. But what is there to stop it resting with its centre of mass vertically above the point of attachment? In this 'upside-down' situation forces and moments sum to zero, as required for equilibrium. Why, in practice, does the lamina hang with the centre of mass below the point of attachment?

Toppling of a lamina when there is sufficient friction to prevent sliding

If a lamina is placed on a rough inclined plane, it may slide down the plane or it may topple over.

A lamina will be in stable equilibrium if a vertical line through the centre of mass of the lamina lies within its line of contact (the line from the top-most point of contact to the bottom-most) with the plane. It will not topple.

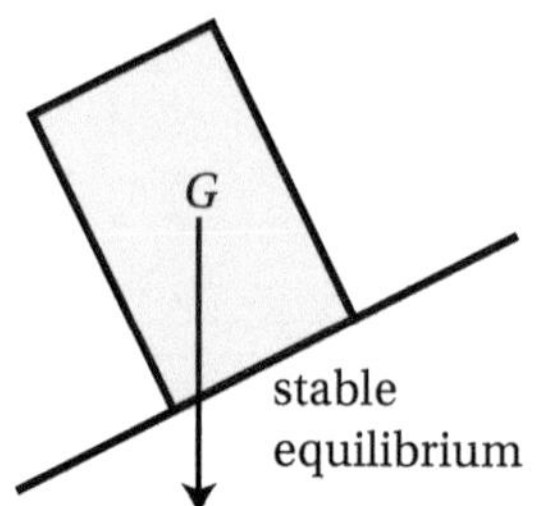

A lamina will be in unstable (limiting) equilibrium if its centre of mass lies vertically above the end of its line of contact with the plane. It is about to topple.

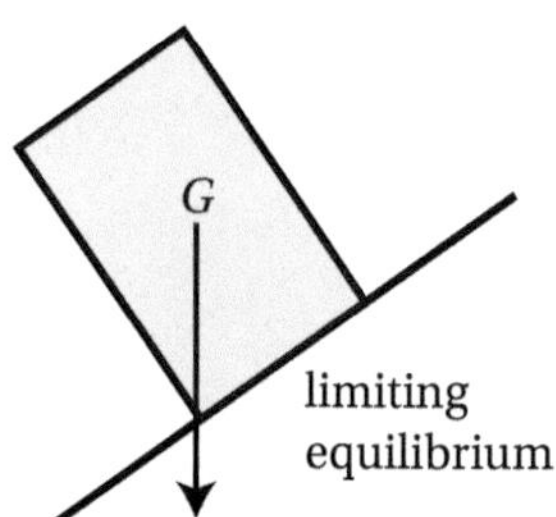

A lamina will topple if its centre of mass lies vertically above a point on the inclined plane outside its line of contact with the plane.

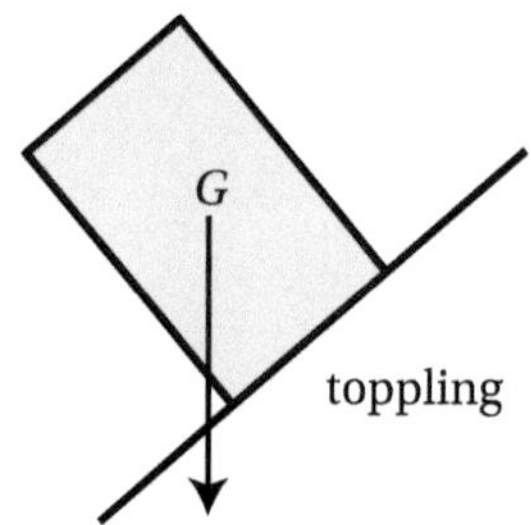

Key point 10.5

If there is sufficient friction at the surface to prevent sliding, the lamina topples if its centre of mass lies vertically above a point on the inclined plane outside its line of contact with the plane.

Tip

Use a diagram to find the position of the centre of mass of the lamina above its line of contact with the inclined plane.

WORKED EXAMPLE 10.15

A rectangular lamina measures 10 cm by 8 cm. It rests with one of its shorter sides on an inclined plane. Friction between the lamina and the inclined plane is sufficiently large to prevent sliding. Find the maximum inclination of the plane to the horizontal that will allow the lamina to rest in equilibrium.

Continues on next page ...

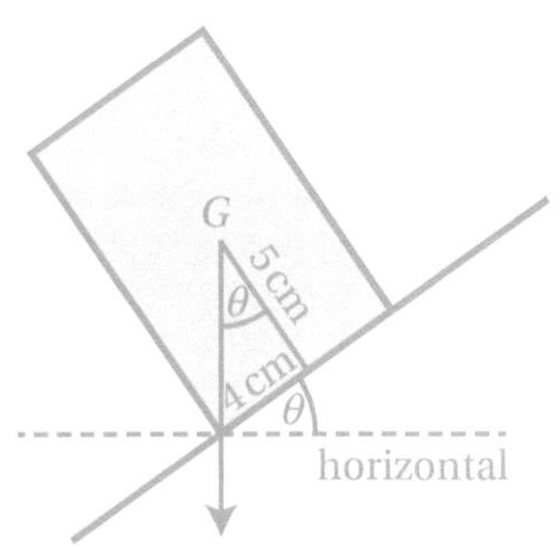

Draw a sketch, showing the angle between the plane and the horizontal.

When the lamina is in unstable equilibrium with its centre of mass vertically above its line of contact with the plane, the inclination of the plane is maximised.

$\theta \leqslant \tan^{-1}\left(\frac{4}{5}\right)$

$\therefore \theta \leqslant 38.7°$

Use trigonometry to find an upper bound for θ.

The inclination of the plane must be no more than 38.7°.

WORKED EXAMPLE 10.16

A rectangular lamina, measuring 15 cm by 7.5 cm, has a square removed from one corner as shown.

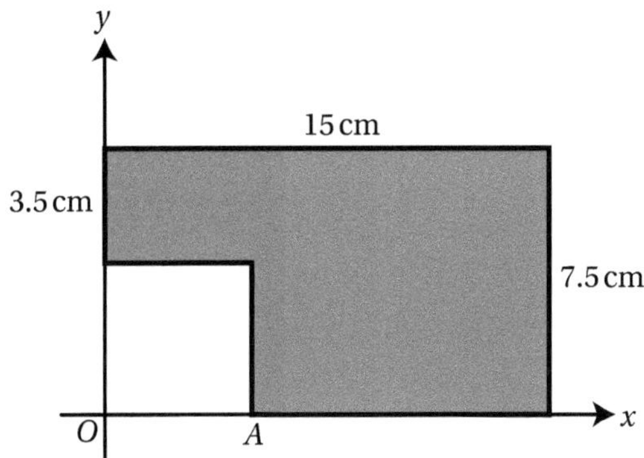

a Find the centre of mass of the lamina.

The lamina is placed on a rough inclined plane and rests in limiting equilibrium on the point of toppling about point A.

b Find the angle of inclination of the plane to the horizontal.

a The centre of mass of the missing square lies at: $\begin{pmatrix} 2 \\ 2 \end{pmatrix}$ cm

Area of lamina $= 15 \times 7.5 - 16\text{ cm}^2 = 96.5\text{ cm}^2$

$96.5\begin{pmatrix} \bar{x} \\ \bar{y} \end{pmatrix} = 112.5\begin{pmatrix} 7.5 \\ 3.75 \end{pmatrix} - 16\begin{pmatrix} 2 \\ 2 \end{pmatrix}$

$\begin{pmatrix} \bar{x} \\ \bar{y} \end{pmatrix} = \begin{pmatrix} 8.41 \\ 4.04 \end{pmatrix}$ cm (to 3 s.f.)

Find the area of the lamina by subtraction.

Use $M\begin{pmatrix} \bar{x} \\ \bar{y} \end{pmatrix} = m_1\begin{pmatrix} \bar{x}_1 \\ \bar{y}_1 \end{pmatrix} - m_2\begin{pmatrix} \bar{x}_2 \\ \bar{y}_2 \end{pmatrix}$, to find the centre of mass of the composite lamina.

Continues on next page ...

b

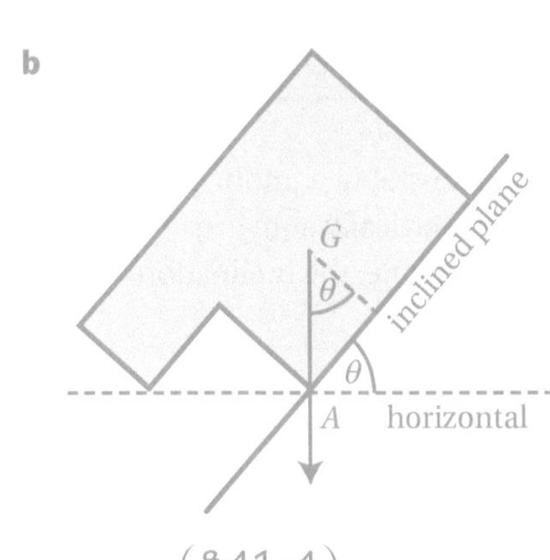

Draw a sketch.

The centre of mass is resting above A. The lamina is in unstable equilibrium.

$$\theta \approx \tan^{-1}\left(\frac{8.41-4}{4.04}\right)$$

$$\therefore \theta = 47.5° \text{ (to 3 s.f.)}$$

Calculate the angle made by the plane with the horizontal using trigonometry.

Toppling or sliding of an object on an inclined plane

If a force is applied to an object resting on a rough surface, the turning moment may cause the object to topple before it slides. In other cases, the resultant force may be sufficient to cause the object to slide before it topples.

Consider the forces acting on an object resting in stable equilibrium on a rough inclined plane.

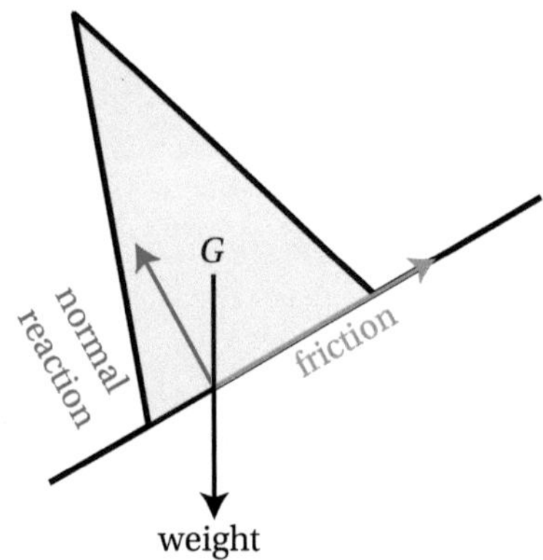

The weight acts vertically downwards through G, the centre of mass. The normal reaction and friction are both considered to act at the point on the inclined plane that the weight passes through.

Tip

If the object is about to topple, its centre of mass lies vertically above the end of its line of contact with the plane – so the normal reaction and frictional force both act at the point that the object would topple about.

Rewind

You met the coefficient of friction in A Level Mathematics Student Book 2, Chapter 21.

Remember: $F \leqslant \mu R$

In the limiting case where the object is about to slide:

$F = \mu R$.

WORKED EXAMPLE 10.17

A uniform solid cylinder is resting in equilibrium with its end on a rough plane inclined at a variable angle α to the horizontal. The cylinder has diameter 0.6 metres and height 1.8 metres.

a Assuming the plane is sufficiently rough to prevent sliding, find the maximum value of α that would allow the cylinder to continue to rest in equilibrium.

The coefficient of friction between the cylinder and the plane is $\frac{2}{9}$.

b As α is increased, show that the cylinder will slide before it topples.

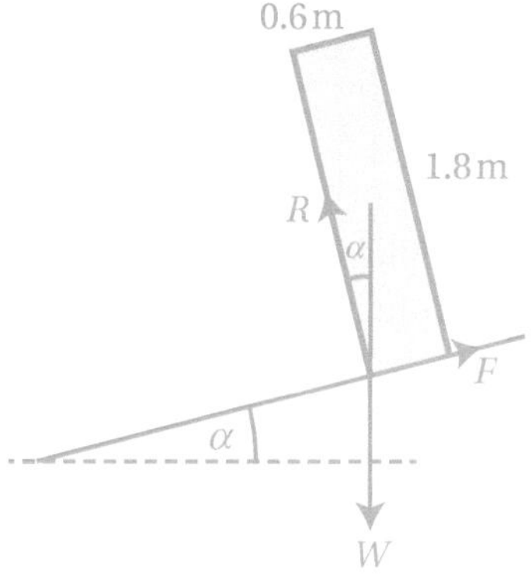

Draw a diagram showing the forces.

When the cylinder is in unstable equilibrium, its centre of mass lies directly above the outer edge of its base.

The centre of mass of the cylinder lies on its axis of symmetry at a height of 0.9 m above the base.

a $\tan\alpha = \frac{0.3}{0.9}$

$\therefore \alpha = 18.4°$

b The cylinder slides down the plane if:

$W\sin\alpha > \mu R$ and $R = W\cos\alpha$

$\therefore W\sin\alpha > \frac{2}{9}W\cos\alpha$

$\tan\alpha > \frac{2}{9}$

and $\alpha > 12.5°$

$\therefore$ The cylinder starts to slide when α exceeds 12.5° but does not topple until α exceeds 18.4°.

Consider the component of the weight acting parallel to the plane. The cylinder slides down the plane if the component of the weight acting down the plane exceeds the limiting value of friction, μR.

Resolve perpendicular to the plane to find the magnitude of R in terms of W, and use

$\frac{\sin\alpha}{\cos\alpha} = \tan\alpha$

An object resting on a horizontal plane may topple over if an applied force causes a resultant turning moment.

WORKED EXAMPLE 10.18

A cardboard box in the form of a cuboid and its contents, with a combined mass of 0.35 kg, rests in equilibrium on a rough horizontal plane. The contents of the box are evenly distributed and the centre of mass of the box lies at its geometric centre. The diagram shows a vertical cross-section through the centre of the box, *WXYZ*.

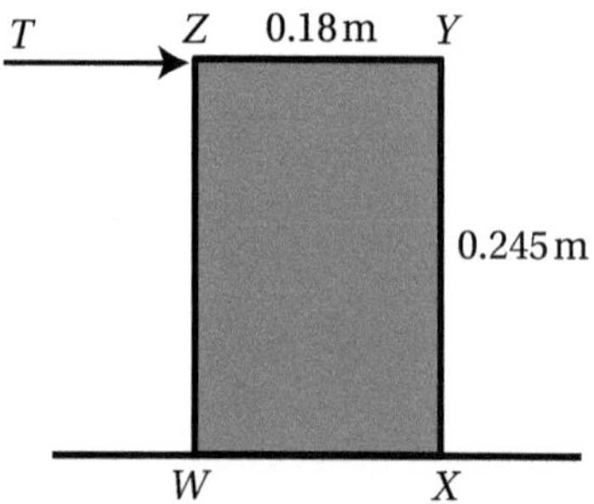

A horizontal force of magnitude T N acts on a horizontal line through Z. The coefficient of friction between the box and the plane is μ. As T gradually increases from zero, the box slides before it topples if $\mu < k$. Show that $k = \frac{18}{49}$.

Take moments about X:

$T \times 0.245 - 0.35g \times 0.09 > 0$

$T > 1.26$ N

The box will topple about X if the moment of T exceeds the moment of the weight of the box. At the point of toppling the normal reaction from the surface acts through X.

Resultant force // to WX:

$T - \mu R > 0$, and $R = 0.35g$ N

$\therefore T > 0.35g\mu$ N

$T > 3.43\mu$ N

The box will slide if there is a resultant force parallel to the plane surface.

$\therefore 3.43\mu < 1.26$

$\mu < \frac{18}{49}$

$\therefore k = \frac{18}{49}$

The box will slide before it topples if: $3.43\mu < T \leqslant 1.26$

WORKED EXAMPLE 10.19

A uniform solid cube, of side 10 metres and mass m kg, rests on a rough horizontal plane. The diagram shows a vertical cross-section $ABCD$ through the centre of mass of the cube. A force, H N, is applied at the midpoint of CD, acting at an angle of $\theta°$ above the horizontal as shown such that $\theta < 45°$.

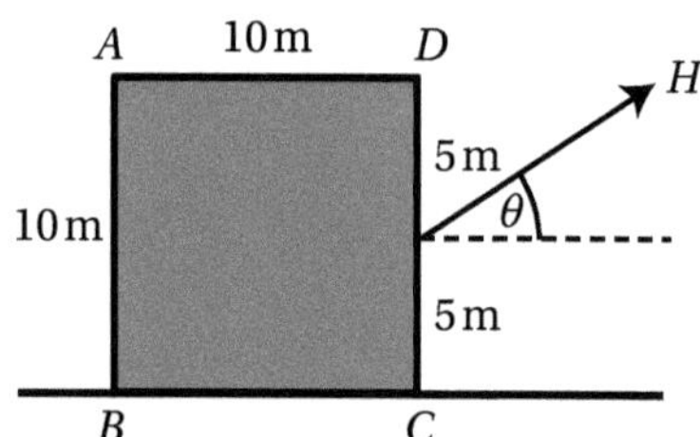

Continues on next page ...

a Assuming that the cube would not slide but is on the point of toppling about C, find an expression for H in terms of m, g and θ.

b Assuming that the cube would not topple but is on the point of sliding along the plane, show that:

$H = \frac{\mu mg}{\cos\theta + \mu\sin\theta}$ where μ is the coefficient of friction between the cube and the plane.

c Find an inequality for μ if the cube is to slide before it topples.

a Take moments about C:

$mg \times 5 = H\cos\theta \times 5$

$\therefore H = \frac{mg}{\cos\theta}$

The cube will topple about C if the moment of H exceeds the moment of the weight of the box. At the point of toppling the normal reaction from the surface acts through C.

b Resolve perpendicular to the surface, and let the normal reaction at the surface be R:

$H\sin\theta + R = mg \quad \therefore R = mg - H\sin\theta$

The cube is on the point of sliding if the resultant force parallel to the plane surface is zero.

Resolve // to surface:

$H\cos\theta = \mu R$

$\therefore H\cos\theta = \mu(mg - H\sin\theta)$

$H\cos\theta + \mu H\sin\theta = \mu mg$

$\therefore H = \frac{\mu mg}{\cos\theta + \mu\sin\theta}$

Rearrange to make H the subject: friction takes its limiting value, μR newtons.

c $\frac{\mu mg}{\cos\theta + \mu\sin\theta} < \frac{mg}{\cos\theta}$

$\mu\cos\theta < \cos\theta + \mu\sin\theta$

$\mu(\cos\theta - \sin\theta) < \cos\theta$

$\mu < \frac{\cos\theta}{\cos\theta - \sin\theta}$

The cube will slide before it topples if

$\frac{\mu mg}{\cos\theta + \mu\sin\theta} < H < \frac{mg}{\cos\theta}$

EXERCISE 10B

In questions 1–4 the x-axis lies in a horizontal plane and the y-axis in a vertical plane.

1. A lamina with centre of mass at the point $G(5, 8)$ is freely suspended from the point $X(10, 10)$. Find the angle between GX and the line $y = 10$.
2. A lamina with centre of mass at the point $G(4, 4)$ is freely suspended from the point $X(12, 16)$. Find the angle between GX and the line $y = 16$.
3. A lamina with centre of mass at the point $G(7, 1)$ is freely suspended from the point $X(3, 5)$. Find the angle between GX and the line $y = 5$.
4. A lamina with centre of mass at the point $G(25, 10)$ is freely suspended from the point $X(20, 15)$. Find the angle between GX and the line $y = 15$.
5. A uniform rectangular lamina with side lengths 15 cm and 10 cm is freely suspended from one vertex. Find the angle between the longer side and the vertical.
6. A uniform rectangular lamina with side lengths 18 cm and 25 cm is freely suspended from one vertex. Find the angle between the shorter side and the vertical.

7 A uniform lamina in the shape of an equilateral triangle ABC of side 25 cm has an equilateral triangle of side 10 cm removed from vertex C as shown.

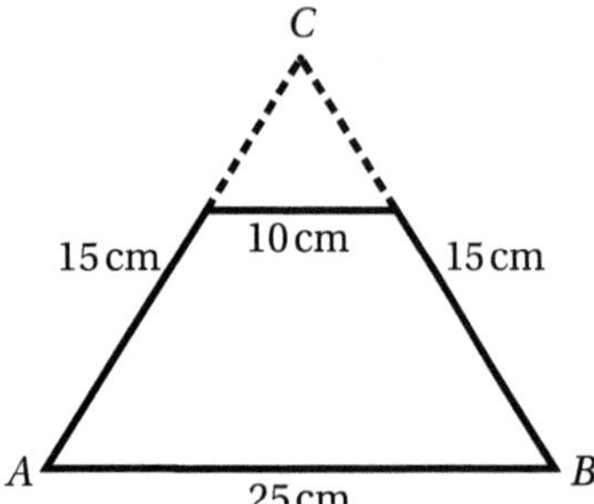

a Find the distance of the centre of mass from AB.

The lamina is freely suspended from A.

b Find the angle between AB and the vertical.

8 A rectangular lamina, measuring 15 cm by 7.5 cm, has a quarter disc removed from one corner as shown.

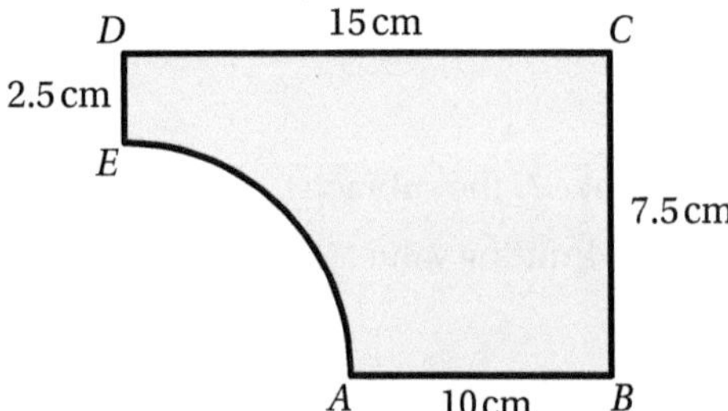

a Find the distance of the centre of mass of the lamina from AB and DE.

The lamina is placed on an inclined plane so that its centre of mass is vertically above the point A and rests in equilibrium.

b Find the inclination of the plane to the horizontal.

9 A uniform rectangular lamina $ABCD$ has mass 10 kg. The side AB measures 60 cm and the side BD measures 40 cm. A uniform circular lamina, of mass 5 kg, and radius 10 cm, is fixed to the rectangular lamina to form a sign. The centre of the circular lamina is 20 cm from AB and BC, as shown.

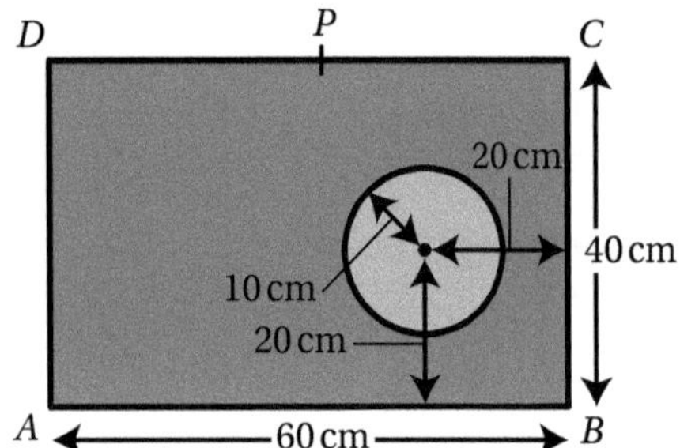

a Find the distances of the centre of mass from AB and AD.

The sign is freely suspended from P, the midpoint of DC.

b Calculate the angle between AD and the vertical when the sign hangs in equilibrium.

10 A uniform solid cylinder of height 0.5 metres and radius 0.1 metre rests with one of its plane faces on a rough plane inclined at θ to the horizontal. There is sufficient friction between the cylinder and the plane to prevent slipping. Calculate the value of θ if the cylinder is on the point of toppling.

11 A solid cone of base radius r cm and height $5r$ cm rests with its circular base on a rough plane inclined at θ to the horizontal. There is sufficient friction between the cone and the plane to prevent slipping. Calculate the value of θ if the cone is on the point of toppling.

12 A solid cone of base radius 50 cm and height h metres rests with its circular base on a rough plane inclined at 30° to the horizontal. There is sufficient friction between the cone and the plane to prevent slipping. Calculate the exact value of h, given the cone is on the point of toppling.

13 A piece of wire AB of length 20 cm is bent to form an arc of a quarter-circle, and then suspended freely from A.

a Calculate the angle between AB and the vertical.

The arc of wire remains in suspension at A when a force, F, is applied to the arc at its midpoint along a tangent, upwards. The mass of the arc of wire is 200 grams.

b Find the magnitude of F required to maintain the arc of wire in equilibrium with OX, the axis of symmetry, horizontal.

14 A uniform rectangular lamina $ABCD$ of mass of mass m kg rests with AB on horizontal ground, which is rough enough to prevent slipping. AB measures 30 cm and BC measures 20 cm. A force, F, is applied to the lamina at C at an angle of 30° below the horizontal. Find the magnitude of F, in terms of m, if the lamina is on the point of toppling about B.

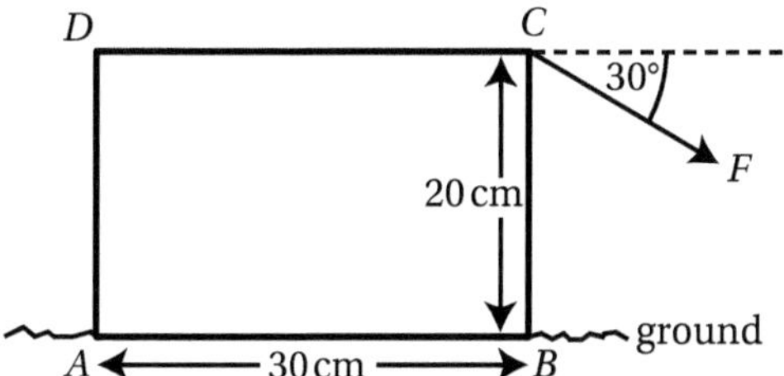

15 A uniform rectangular lamina $ABCD$ of mass 10 kg rests with AB on a horizontal rough plane. AB measures 25 cm and BC measures 50 cm. The coefficient of friction between the plane and the block is 0.2. A horizontal force, F, is applied to the lamina at C.

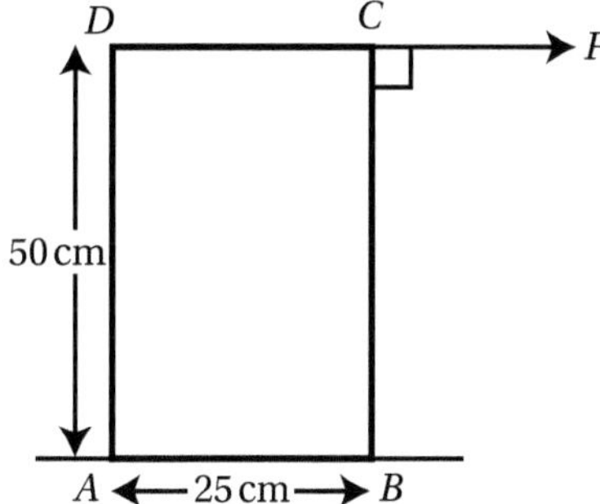

a Find the value of F if the lamina is on the point of slipping along the plane.

b Find the value of F if the lamina is on the point of toppling about B.

16 **a** The region bounded by the x-axis, the line $x = \ln 4$ and the curve $y = \frac{1}{2}e^{\frac{x}{2}}$, for $0 \leqslant x \leqslant \ln 4$, is occupied by a uniform lamina. Find, in exact form, the coordinates of the centre of mass of this lamina.

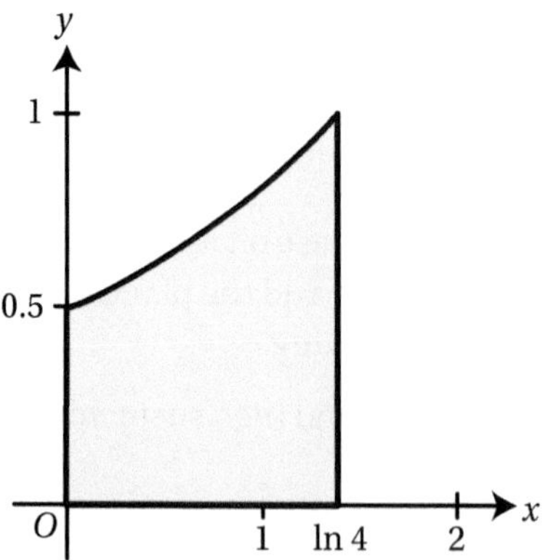

b The region bounded by the x-axis, the line $x = 1$ and the curve $y = 2\ln(2x)$, for $\frac{1}{2} \leqslant x \leqslant 1$, is occupied by a second uniform lamina. By using your answer to part **a**, calculate, to 3 significant figures, the x-coordinate of the centre of mass of the second lamina.

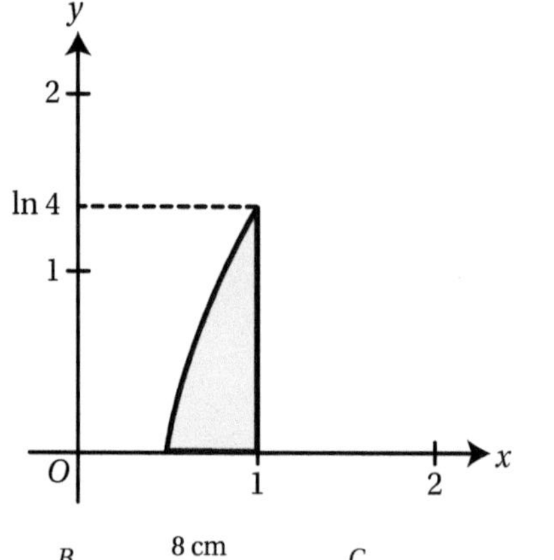

17 **i**

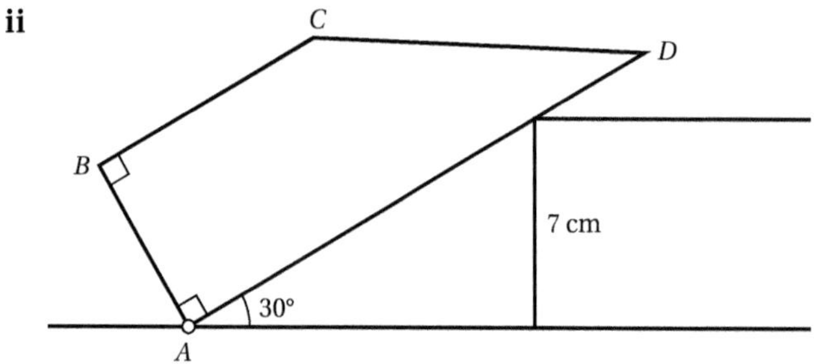

Fig. 1

A uniform lamina $ABCD$ is in the form of a right-angled trapezium. $AB = 6$ cm, $BC = 8$ cm and $AD = 17$ cm (see Fig. 1). Taking x- and y-axes along AD and AB respectively, find the coordinates of the centre of mass of the lamina.

ii

C
D
B
7 cm
30°
A

Fig. 2

The lamina is smoothly pivoted at A and it rests in a vertical plane in equilibrium against a fixed smooth block of height 7 cm. The mass of the lamina is 3 kg. AD makes an angle of 30° with the horizontal (see Fig. 2). Calculate the magnitude of the force which the block exerts on the lamina.

© OCR, GCE Mathematics, Paper 4729/01, June 2008

Checklist of learning and understanding

- The centre of mass of any symmetrical uniform lamina or solid lies on its axis or axes of symmetry.
- The centre of mass of a rod of variable density, f(x), can be found by integration: $\bar{x} = \dfrac{\int_0^a x\,\mathrm{f}(x)\,\mathrm{d}x}{\int_0^a \mathrm{f}(x)\,\mathrm{d}x}$
- The centre of mass of a uniform lamina with shape defined by f(x) is found by integration:

$$\bar{x} = \frac{\int_0^a x\,\mathrm{f}(x)\,\mathrm{d}x}{\int_0^a \mathrm{f}(x)\,\mathrm{d}x} \qquad \bar{y} = \frac{\frac{1}{2}\int_0^a (\mathrm{f}(x))^2\,\mathrm{d}x}{\int_0^a \mathrm{f}(x)\,\mathrm{d}x}$$

- The centre of mass of a uniform solid of revolution is found by integration: $\bar{x} = \dfrac{\int_0^a \pi x y^2\,\mathrm{d}x}{\int_0^a \pi y^2\,\mathrm{d}x}$
- If a rigid body is freely suspended, it will hang with its centre of mass vertically below the point of suspension.
- If there is sufficient friction at the surface to prevent sliding, the position of the centre of mass of a lamina above its line of contact with the inclined plane allows you to work out whether it will topple.
- You can use your knowledge of friction and moments to determine whether a body placed on a rough surface will slide or topple.

Mixed practice 10

1 A uniform rod AB of mass 5 kg and length 8 metres is suspended from two cables fixed to the rod at C and D. The rod hangs horizontally, with $AC = 2$ metres and $AD = 5$ metres. A 3 kg packet, modelled as a point mass, is placed on the rod at B. Calculate:

a the distance AG given G is the centre of mass of the combined rod and packet

b the tensions in the cables at C and D.

2 The diagram shows a uniform lamina in the shape of two rectangles attached together, $AWEF$ and $WBCD$, as shown. AF measures 4 cm, AW measures 5 cm, WB measured 4 cm and BC measures 7 cm.

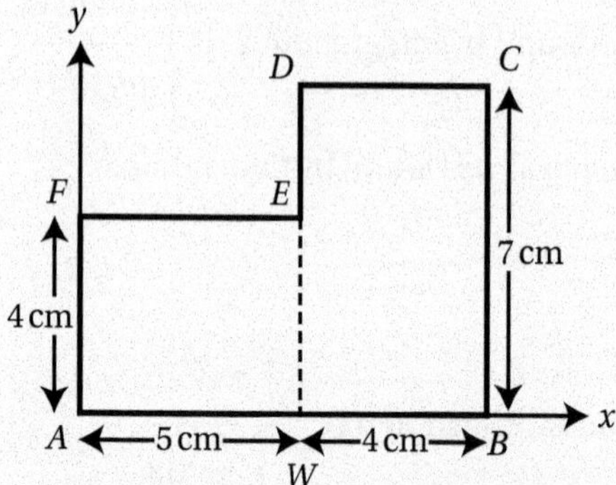

a Find the position of the centre of mass from AB and from AF.

The lamina is freely suspended from C.

b Find the angle between BC and the vertical when the lamina is in equilibrium.

3 A uniform rectangular lamina $ABCD$ has mass 2.2 kg. AB is 10 cm long and BC is 8 cm long. A uniform square lamina of mass 1.6 kg and side length 4 cm is attached onto the rectangular lamina with one edge along the middle of the shorter side of the rectangular lamina. The diagram shows the system.

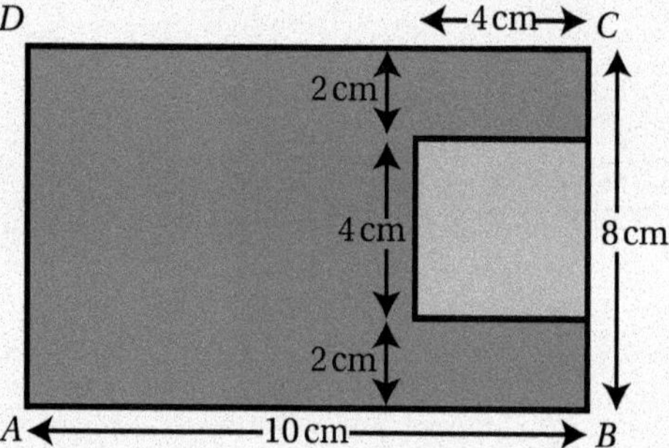

a Explain why the centre of mass is 4 cm from AB.

b Find the distance of the centre of mass from AD.

The composite body is freely suspended from D.

c Find the angle between DC and the vertical when the body hangs in equilibrium.

4 A straight rod AB has length a. The rod has variable density, and at a distance x from A its mass per unit length is given by $k\left(4-\sqrt{\frac{x}{a}}\right)$, where k is a constant. Find the distance from A of the centre of mass of the rod.

5

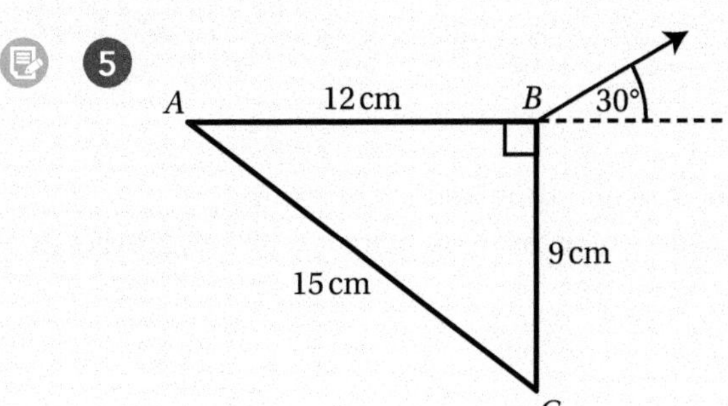

A uniform right-angled triangular lamina ABC with sides $AB = 12$ cm, $BC = 9$ cm and $AC = 15$ cm is freely suspended from a hinge at vertex A. The lamina has mass 2 kg and is held in equilibrium with AB horizontal by means of a string attached to B. The string is at an angle of 30° to the horizontal (see diagram). Calculate the tension in the string.

6

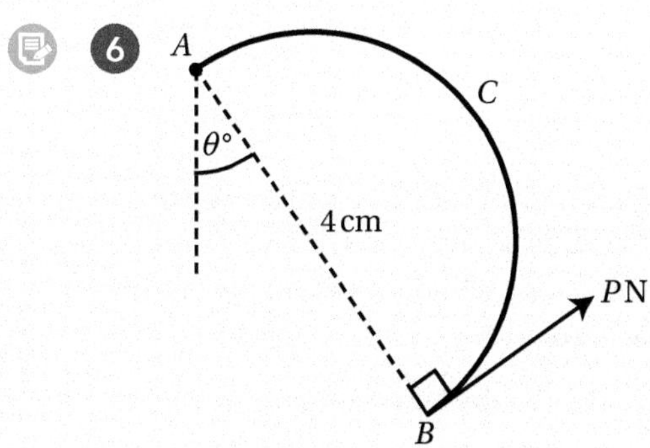

A uniform semicircular arc ACB is freely pivoted at A. The arc has mass 0.3 kg and is held in equilibrium by a force of magnitude P N applied at B. The line of action of this force lies in the same plane as the arc, and is perpendicular to AB. The diameter of AB has length 4 cm and makes an angle of $\theta°$ with the downward vertical (see diagram).

i Given that $\theta = 0$, find the magnitude of the force acting on the arc at A.

ii Given instead that $\theta = 30$, find the value of P.

7 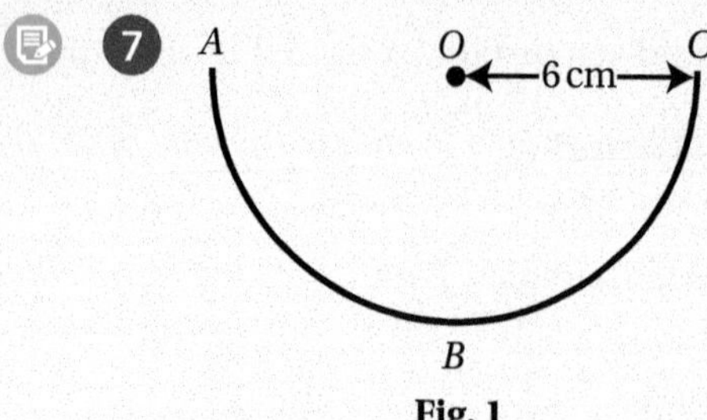

Fig. 1

i A uniform piece of wire, ABC, forms a semicircular arc of radius 6 cm. O is the midpoint of AC (see Fig. 1). Show that the distance from O to the centre of mass of the wire is 3.82 cm, correct to 3 significant figures.

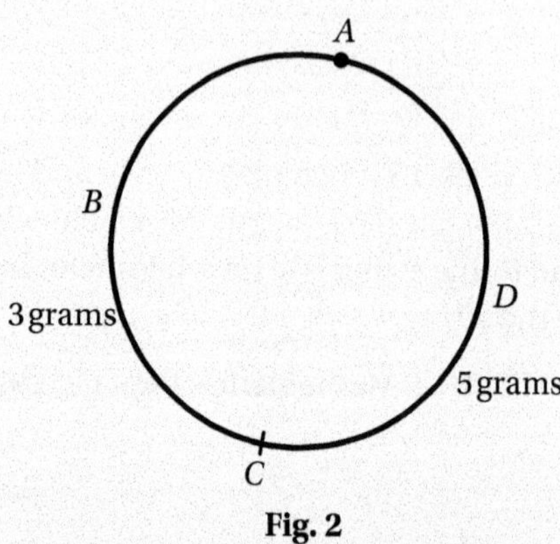

Fig. 2

ii Two semicircular pieces of wire, ABC and ADC, are joined together at their ends to form a circular hoop of radius 6 cm. The mass of ABC is 3 grams and the mass of ADC is 5 grams. The hoop is freely suspended from A (see Fig. 2). Calculate the angle which the diameter AC makes with the vertical, giving your answer correct to the nearest degree.

8 A uniform solid is made of a hemisphere with centre O and radius 0.6 m, and a cylinder of radius 0.6 m and height 0.6 m. The plane face of the hemisphere and a plane face of the cylinder coincide. (The formula for the volume of a sphere is $\frac{4}{3}\pi r^3$.)

i Show that the distance of the centre of mass of the solid from O is 0.09 m.

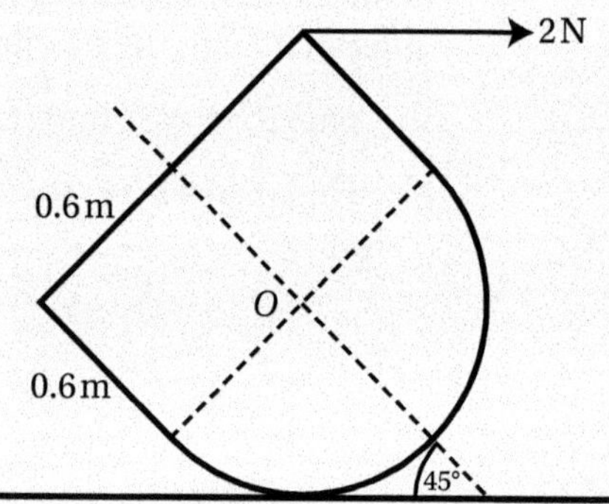

ii The solid is placed with the curved surface of the hemisphere on a rough horizontal surface and the axis inclined at 45° to the horizontal. The equilibrium of the solid is maintained by a horizontal force of 2 N applied to the highest point on the circumference of its plane face (see diagram). Calculate

a the mass of the solid,

b the set of possible values of the coefficient of friction between the surface and the solid.

9 A straight rod AB has length a. The rod has variable density, and at a distance x from A its mass per unit length is $k\,\mathrm{e}^{-\frac{x}{a}}$, where k is a constant. Find, in an exact form, the distance of the centre of mass of the rod from A.

© OCR, GCE Mathematics, Paper 4731, June 2011

10 The region bounded by the x-axis, the y-axis, the line $x = \ln 3$, and the curve $y = \mathrm{e}^{-x}$, for $0 \leqslant x \leqslant \ln 3$, is occupied by a uniform lamina. Find, in an exact form, the coordinates of the centre of mass of this lamina.

© OCR, GCE Mathematics, Paper 4731, June 2010

11 **a** The region bounded by the x-axis, the line $x = 2$ and the curve $y = \frac{x^2}{4}$ for $0 \leqslant x \leqslant 2$, is occupied by a uniform lamina. Find, in exact form, the coordinates of the centre of mass of this lamina.

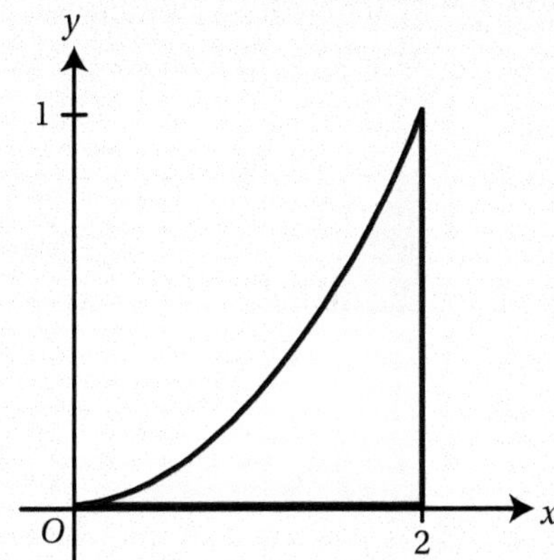

b The region bounded by the x-axis, the line $x = 1$ and the curve $y = 2\sqrt{x}$, for $0 \leqslant x \leqslant 1$, is occupied by a second uniform lamina. By using your answer to part **a**, calculate, to 3 significant figures, the x-coordinate of the centre of mass of the second lamina.

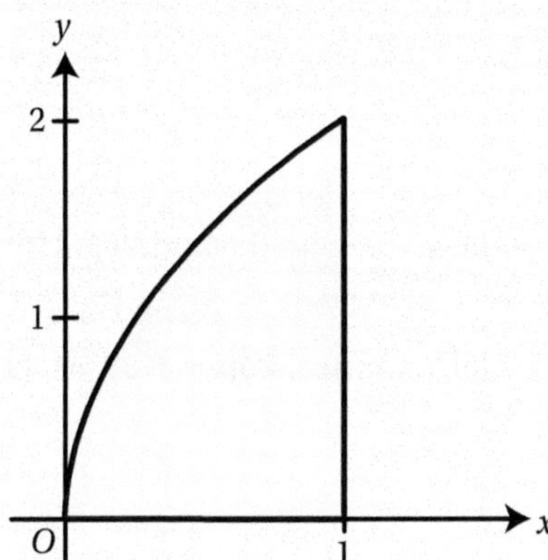

  **i** A uniform semicircular lamina has radius 4 cm. Show that the distance from its centre to its centre of mass is 1.70 cm, correct to 3 significant figures.

ii

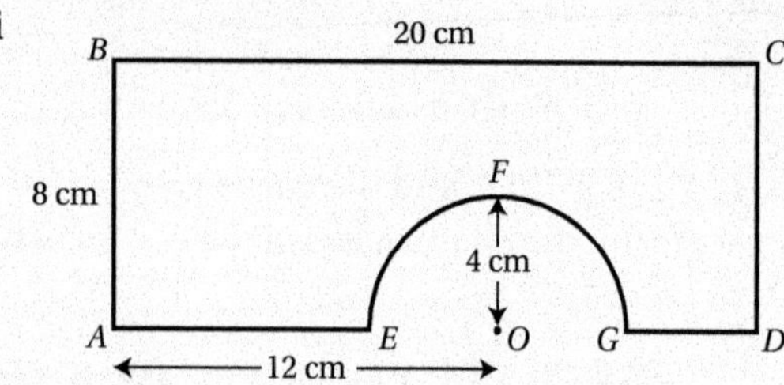

Fig. 1

A model bridge is made from a uniform rectangular board, $ABCD$, with a semicircular section, EFG, removed. O is the mid-point of EG. $AB = 8$ cm, $BC = 20$ cm, $AO = 12$ cm and the radius of the semicircle is 4 cm (see Fig. 1).

a Show that the distance from AB to the centre of mass of the model is 9.63 cm, correct to 3 significant figures.

b Calculate the distance from AD to the centre of mass of the model.

iii

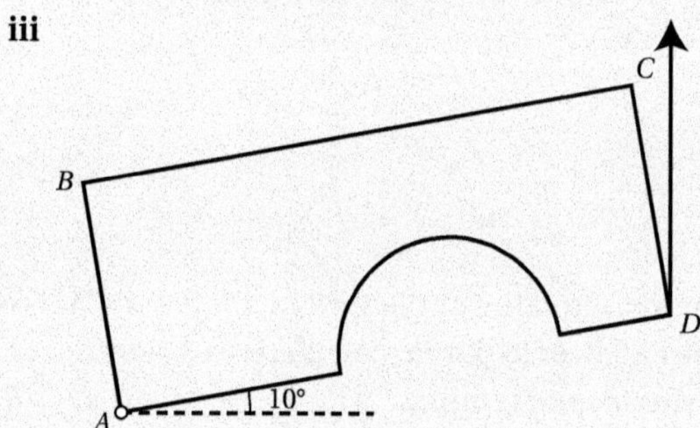

Fig. 2

The model bridge is smoothly pivoted at A and is supported in equilibrium by a vertical wire attached to D. The weight of the model is 15 N and AD makes an angle of 10° with the horizontal (see Fig. 2). Calculate the tension in the wire.

FOCUS ON ... PROOF 2

This section is for A Level students only.

In Chapter 5, the formulae for the centres of mass of uniform triangular laminas were stated and used without proof. This Focus on ... section explores why the centre of mass lies at the intersection of the medians. It then shows how you can set up proofs of the formulae, based on this fact and making use of vector arguments.

Consider the statement: the centre of mass of a uniform triangular lamina lies at the intersection of the medians.

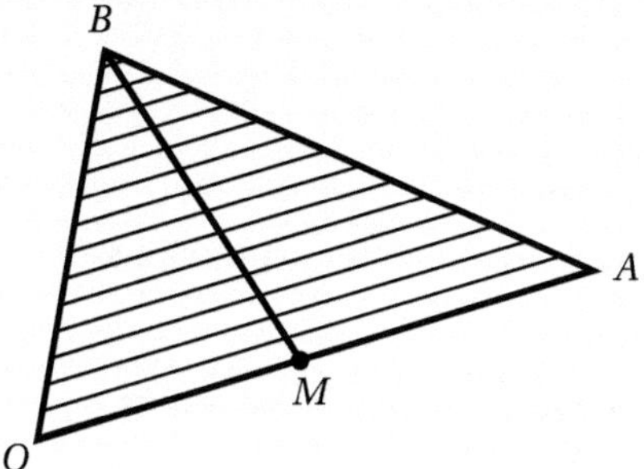

You learned that the centre of mass of a uniform lamina lies on any axis of symmetry. A uniform triangular lamina does not have an axis of symmetry unless it is isosceles. In the diagram the lamina has been divided into many trapezia parallel to *OA*. You can approximate these trapezia as uniform rods having centres of mass lying on *BM*, the median from *B* to *OA*. Since the centres of mass of all of the rods lie on *BM* it follows that the centre of mass of the whole lamina lies on *BM*. The same argument would apply if you started from the other two vertices, so the centre of mass must lie at the intersection of the medians, known as the centroid.

Questions

1 Prove that the intersection of the medians of a triangle lies at a point that is two-thirds of the distance along the medians measured from the vertices.

Vectors can be very useful in geometry and you can use them in proofs.

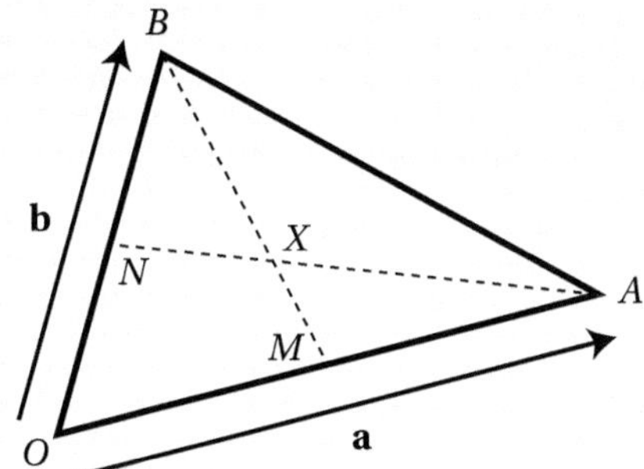

Let the midpoint of *OA* be *M* and the midpoint of *OB* be *N*. Consider the medians *AN* and *BM*. Let the intersection of these be *X*.

You can use vectors to find alternative expressions for the position of X.

$\overrightarrow{OX} = \overrightarrow{OA} + \overrightarrow{AX}$

$\overrightarrow{AX} = \lambda \overrightarrow{AN}$

$\overrightarrow{OX} = \overrightarrow{OB} + \overrightarrow{BX}$

$\overrightarrow{BX} = \mu \overrightarrow{BM}$

X lies part-way along AN and BM; you use λ and μ to indicate this; you are trying to prove that $\lambda = \mu = \frac{2}{3}$.

$\overrightarrow{OX} = \overrightarrow{OA} + \lambda \overrightarrow{AN}$

$\overrightarrow{OX} = \overrightarrow{OB} + \mu \overrightarrow{BM}$

Use the vectors **a** and **b**, together with the constants λ and μ, to find two alternative vector expressions for $\overrightarrow{OX}$.

You may now equate coefficients of **a** and **b** in the two expressions to get two simultaneous equations. Solve these to find values for λ and μ.

You should be able to prove that point X is two-thirds along the medians from the vertices.

2 Prove that for a uniform triangular lamina: $\begin{pmatrix} \bar{x} \\ \bar{y} \end{pmatrix} = \left(\frac{x_1 + x_2 + x_3}{3}, \frac{y_1 + y_2 + y_3}{3} \right)$

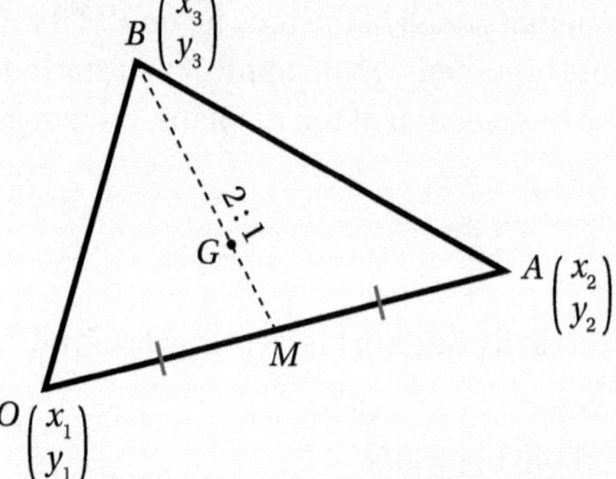

Consider a triangle having vertices with position vectors $\mathbf{o}\begin{pmatrix} x_1 \\ y_1 \end{pmatrix}$, $\mathbf{a}\begin{pmatrix} x_2 \\ y_2 \end{pmatrix}$ and $\mathbf{b}\begin{pmatrix} x_3 \\ y_3 \end{pmatrix}$.

Let the midpoint of OA be M and the centre of mass be G. Remember that the centre of mass, G, of the triangle lies on MB, such that $MG : GB$ is $1 : 2$.

The position vector of the centre of mass, **G**, is then given by:

$$\begin{pmatrix} \bar{x} \\ \bar{y} \end{pmatrix} = \begin{pmatrix} x_1 \\ y_1 \end{pmatrix} + \overrightarrow{OM} + \overrightarrow{MG} = \begin{pmatrix} x_1 \\ y_1 \end{pmatrix} + \overrightarrow{OM} + \frac{1}{3}\overrightarrow{MB}$$

Find vector expressions for $\overrightarrow{OM}$ and $\overrightarrow{MB}$ in terms of $x_1, y_1, \ldots, x_3, y_3$ and substitute them to prove the formula.

A FOCUS ON ... PROBLEM SOLVING 2

This section is for A Level students only.

Alternative approaches

Focus on ... Problem solving 1 set out a step-by-step method for solving a Mechanics problem.

You know that there are different methods for solving a quadratic equation such as factorisation, completing the square or the quadratic formula. You choose the method that takes you most quickly to the result(s) you need.

Here, the focus is on two Mechanics problems that can be approached in different ways.

Problem 1

An elastic string of unstretched length l has one end fixed at point O. A bob is attached to the other end and dropped from O. Find the maximum speed of the bob in the subsequent motion.

Method 1

You can use conservation of energy to derive an expression for v^2 in terms of the extension of the elastic string, x.

$$mg(l+x)=\frac{\lambda x^2}{2l}+\frac{1}{2}mv^2$$

You need to be very careful with your definitions of distances. If you do this successfully you will derive the equation:

$$v^2=-50x^2+200x+150$$

You can find the value of x for which v^2 is maximised by completing the square:

$$v^2=-50[(x^2-4x)-3]$$

$$\therefore\ v^2=-50[(x-2)^2-7]$$

When $x=2$, v takes its maximum value of $\sqrt{350}$.

In a simple question this approach may be 'a sledgehammer to crack a nut'.

A side benefit of this approach is that you can use the expression for v^2 to find the maximum extension of the string, by solving $-50x^2+200x+150=0$.

Method 2

When speed is maximised, acceleration is zero, likewise the resultant force.

Resultant force:

$$mg-\frac{\lambda x}{l}=0$$

This takes you straight to $x=\frac{mgl}{\lambda}$.

You can substitute your value of x into the energy equation to find v^2:

$$mg(l+x)=\frac{\lambda x^2}{2l}+\frac{1}{2}mv^2$$

This approach involves less algebra and quickly gets you to v.

To carry on and find the maximum extension of the string you would need to set $v=0$ in the general energy equation:

$$mg(l+x)=\frac{\lambda x^2}{2l}+\frac{1}{2}mv^2$$

You will need to solve a quadratic equation.

The common theme is application of the principle of conservation of energy: $mg(l+x)=\frac{\lambda x^2}{2l}+\frac{1}{2}mv^2$.

Problem 2

A small smooth sphere sliding across a smooth surface is acted on by an impulse directed towards the centre of the sphere. The speed of the sphere is increased from u to v and its direction of motion is diverted through angle α. Values for u, v and α are given. Find the magnitude, I, and direction, β, of the impulse.

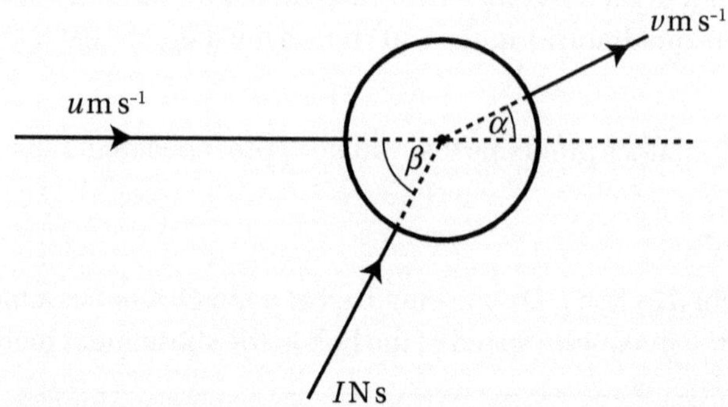

Method 1

You can use an impulse-momentum triangle:

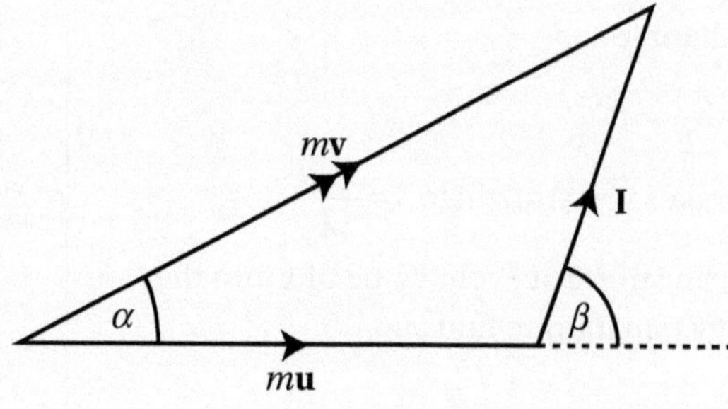

You can use the cosine rule to find the value of I from values given for u, v and α.

$I^2 = (mu)^2 + (mv)^2 - 2 \times mu \times mv \times \cos\alpha$

You will have an expression for I in terms of m, unless the value of m is also given.
You can use the sine rule in the vector triangle and hence find β:

$$\frac{\sin\beta}{mv} = \frac{\sin\alpha}{I}$$

You must take care with your vector triangle. Make sure that the directions of the arrows on the sides make sense.
Don't forget to put momentums in the triangle rather than velocities to make the triangle dimensionally consistent.
Little algebraic rearrangement is necessary in this solution.

Method 2

You can resolve the final velocity into components and use conservation of momentum.

$\parallel$ to $\mathbf{u}$: $mu + I\cos\beta = mv\cos\alpha$
$\perp$ to $\mathbf{u}$: $mv\sin\alpha = I\sin\beta$

These are simultaneous equations and you need to eliminate either I or β.

You obtain:

$$mu + \frac{mv\sin\alpha}{\sin\beta} = mv\cos\alpha$$

Substitute the values for u, v and α to obtain β and hence I.

You must take care to resolve velocities and to apply conservation of momentum correctly.
Simultaneous equations are a standard technique, but you need to take care with your rearrangements.

Questions

1 An elastic string is fixed at one end at the point O. A bob of mass 200 g is attached to the other end of the string. The string has natural length 50 cm and its modulus of elasticity is 3.92 N. The bob is held next to O and dropped. Find:

a the maximum speed of the bob as it descends

b the maximum extension of the string.

Solve this problem by both of the methods described for Problem 1 and compare your answers.

2 A smooth sphere of mass 2.5 kg is sliding across a smooth horizontal floor with a speed 2 m s^{-1} when it receives an impulse acting towards its centre. The sphere slows to a speed of 1.2 m s^{-1} and its direction of motion is diverted through 60°. Find the magnitude and direction of the impulse.

Solve this problem by both of the methods described for Problem 2 and compare your answers.

FOCUS ON ... MODELLING 2

The simple pendulum

A simple pendulum consists of an inextensible string of length l fixed at one end with a mass m attached to the other end; you can call the mass the bob. The bob will hang in equilibrium immediately below the fixing unless it is displaced. If the bob is displaced out of the vertical and then released, it will swing back and forth along the arc of a circle.

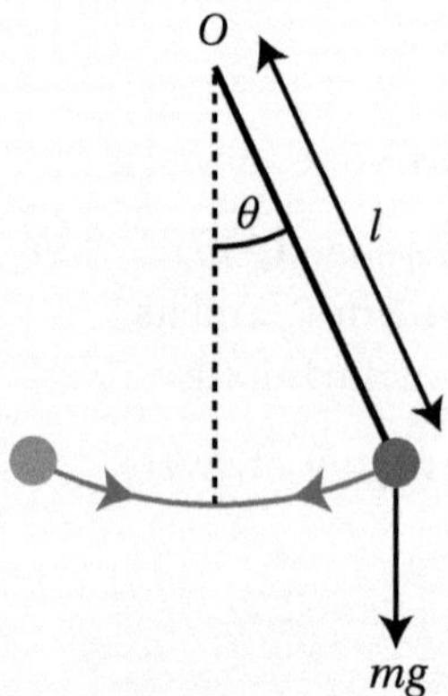

Assuming that any resistances to motion are negligible, you can derive an equation of motion of the pendulum bob. You need to consider the transverse acceleration of the pendulum bob, and apply Newton's second law:

$$ml\ddot{\theta} = -mg\sin\theta$$

This equation of motion simplifies to:

$$\ddot{\theta} + \frac{g}{l}\sin\theta = 0$$

Like free fall under gravity, the equation of motion of a pendulum bob is independent of mass. Thus the solution of the equation would be the same for a 10 g bob and a 2.5 kg bob.

It would be possible to solve $\ddot{\theta} + \frac{g}{l}\sin\theta = 0$ by numerical methods, but the theory of the simple pendulum relies on some of your work on complex numbers in Pure Core Student Book 2. You also learned that $\sin\theta = \theta - \frac{\theta^3}{3!} + \frac{\theta^5}{5!} - \cdots$ so that, when close to 0, all terms are vanishingly small except the first. Thus, if θ is close to 0 then $\sin\theta \approx \theta$.

Now the equation of motion for the pendulum bob can be approximated to:

$$\ddot{\theta} + \frac{g}{l}\theta = 0$$

This is now similar in form, but not the same as, the equation for simple harmonic motion:

$$\ddot{\theta} + \omega^2\theta = 0 \text{ where } \omega^2 = \frac{g}{l}$$

So the pendulum equation can be solved using your knowledge of simple harmonic motion.

Questions

1 Use the theory of simple harmonic motion to write down an expression for how θ varies with time, in terms of g and l, given that the pendulum bob is displaced so that the string makes an angle θ_{max} with the vertical and then released.

2 Work out the period of oscillation for a simple pendulum of length 2.45 m, as a multiple of π.

3 Sketch a graph of angular displacement against time, i.e. θ against t, given that a bob, attached to an inextensible string of length 2.45 m, is displaced to $\frac{\pi}{24}$ radians from the vertical and then released.

4 Assume that $\theta = \frac{\pi}{24}\cos 2t$. Differentiate to find an expression for $\dot{\theta}$. Also, derive an expression for the transverse velocity v from the angular velocity $\dot{\theta}$.

5 Find the maximum value for the transverse velocity to 4 significant figures.

How accurate is the model?

To get an idea of the accuracy of the model you can compare the velocity calculated using the simple harmonic motion approximation to the velocity calculated using conservation of mechanical energy.

$$mgl \times (1 - \cos\theta_{max}) = \text{KE at bottom of swing}$$
$$= \frac{1}{2}m \times v^2_{max}$$
$$\therefore v_{max} = \sqrt{2gl(1 - \cos\theta_{max})}$$

Question

6 **a** With $\theta_{max} = \frac{\pi}{24}$ and $l = 2.45$ metres, as previously, calculate v_{max} from the energy equation, to 4 significant figures.

b Find the percentage error predicted in v_{max} by the SHM model.

c Repeat Questions 3–6b for pendulums with these different starting displacements:

i $\frac{\pi}{12}$ **ii** $\frac{\pi}{6}$

CROSS-TOPIC REVIEW EXERCISE 2

1 A particle A, of mass 2 kg, is moving in a straight line with velocity v m s^{-1} at time t s. It is acted on by a force F N, in the direction of the line of motion of A, which is defined as:

$F = 0$ for $t < 0$

$F = 3t - 1$ for $t \geq 0$.

a Find an expression for v in terms of t for $t \geq 0$.

b If the velocity of A is 5 m s^{-1} when $t = 0$, find the velocity of A when $t = 5$ s.

c A particle, P, of mass 2 kg, is acted on by a force $[(2t - 1)\mathbf{i} + 4\mathbf{j}]$ N for $t \geq 0$. When $t = 0$, the particle has velocity $(\mathbf{i} - \mathbf{j})$ m s^{-1}. Find the velocity of P when $t = 5$ s.

2 A particle P of mass 0.8 kg is moving in a straight line with speed 6.5 m s^{-1}. An impulse of magnitude 4 N s deflects P through an angle θ, and reduces its speed to 3 m s^{-1} (see diagram).

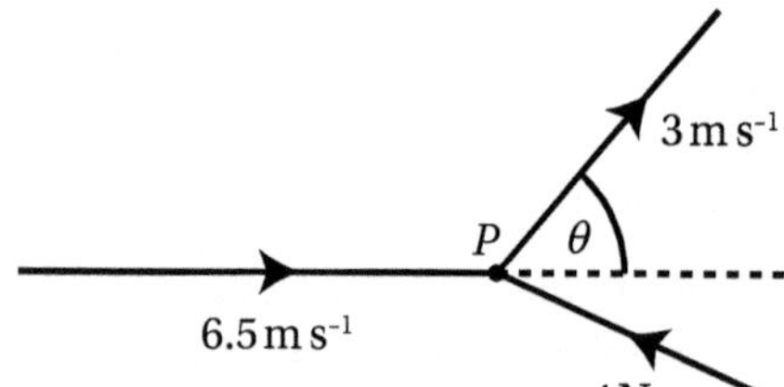

By considering an impulse-momentum triangle:

a Show that $\cos\theta = \frac{35}{52}$.

b Find the angle that the impulse makes with the original direction of motion of P.

3 A small ball is moving across a horizontal plane floor when it strikes a smooth vertical wall. The coefficient of restitution between the ball and the wall is e. Just before impact the direction of motion of the ball makes an angle of 60° with the wall. Immediately after impact its direction of motion makes an angle of 45° with the wall.

a Find the fraction of the kinetic energy of the ball that is lost in the impact.

b Find the value of e.

4 A light rod of length 0.75 metres has one end freely hinged at a fixed point O and a particle P of mass m kg attached to the other end. The rod is set in motion and P makes complete circles about O. The speed of P at the top of the circle is half of its speed at the bottom of the circle. Find the maximum speed of P in terms of g.

5 A region A is defined by the curve $y^2 = 10x$, the line $x = 2.5$ and the x-axis. A uniform solid is formed by rotating A through 2π radians about the x-axis.

a Show that the volume of the solid is $\frac{125\pi}{4}$.

b Show further that the x-coordinate of the centre of mass of the solid is $1\frac{2}{3}$.

6 A particle of mass 0.8 kg is moving in a straight line on a smooth horizontal surface. A horizontal force then acts on the particle for 4 seconds. This force acts in the direction of motion of the particle and at time t seconds has magnitude $(5t - 2)$ newtons. When $t = 4$, the velocity of the particle is 50 m s^{-1}.

a Find the magnitude of the impulse of the force on the particle between $t = 0$ and $t = 4$.

b Hence find the velocity of the particle when $t = 0$.

c Find the value of t when the velocity of the particle is 70 m s^{-1}.

7 Two smooth uniform spheres A and B of equal radius have masses 1.5 kg and 0.75 kg. They are moving on a smooth horizontal plane when they collide. Immediately before the collision the speed of A is 3 m s^{-1} and the speed of B is 2 m s^{-1}. When they collide, the line joining their centres makes an angle α with the direction of motion of A and an angle β with the direction of motion of B, as shown in the diagram. It is given that $\tan\alpha = \frac{3}{4}$ and $\tan\beta = \frac{5}{12}$.

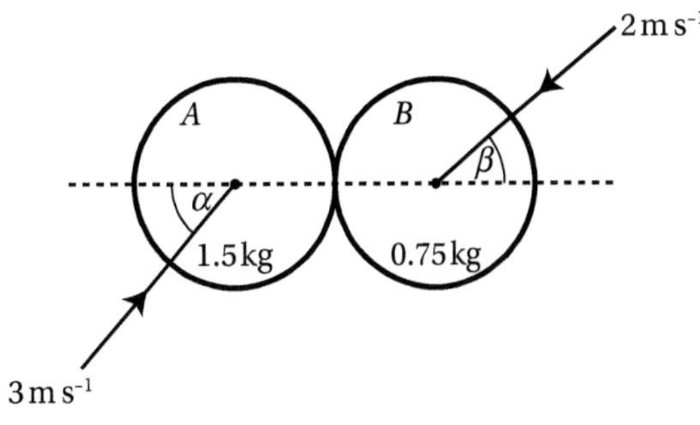

a Find the components of the velocities of A and B perpendicular and parallel to the lines of centres immediately before the collision.

The coefficient of restitution between A and B is $\frac{1}{2}$.

b Find the speed of each sphere after the collision.

8 A particle P of mass m kg is attached to one end of a light inextensible string of length 0.5 metres. The other end of the string is attached to a fixed point O. The particle is hanging in equilibrium at point A, directly below O, when it is given a horizontal speed of 4.5 m s^{-1}. When OP has turned through an angle θ and the string is still taut, the tension in the string is T.

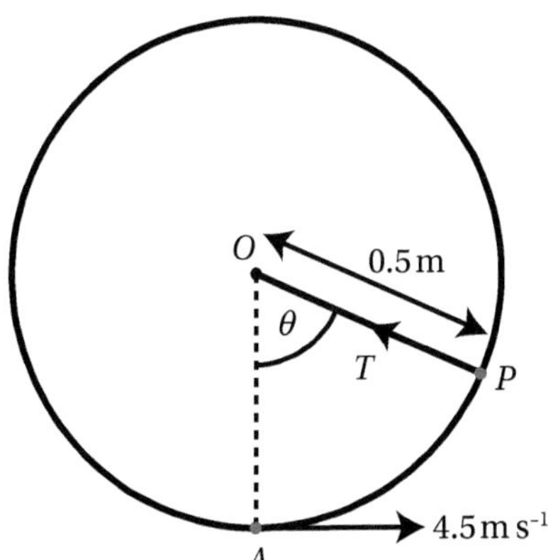

a Find an expression for T.

b Find the height above A at the instant when the string goes slack.

c Find the maximum height above A reached by P before it starts to fall down again.

9 A smooth sphere S lies at rest on a smooth horizontal plane. A second identical sphere R, moving on the plane, collides with the sphere S. Immediately before the collision the direction of motion of R makes an angle α with the line joining the centres of the spheres. Immediately after the collision the direction of motion of R makes an angle β with the line joining the centres of the spheres. The coefficient of restitution between the spheres is e.

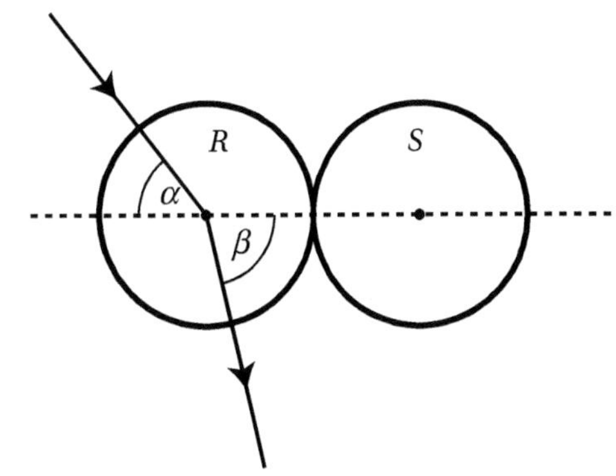

Show that $(1 - e)\tan\beta = 2\tan\alpha$.

10 A uniform solid consists of a hemisphere of radius r and a cylinder of base radius r and height h, fixed together so that the bases coincide. The solid can rest in equilibrium with any point on the curved surface of the hemisphere in contact with a horizontal plane. Find h in terms of r.

11 A particle is placed at the highest point P on the outer surface of a fixed smooth hemisphere of radius a and centre O. The hemisphere is placed with its plane face on a horizontal surface. The particle is projected horizontally from P with speed u ($u < ag$) and initially moves along the surface of the sphere. The particle leaves the sphere at point Q, where OQ makes an angle θ with the upward vertical through O, as shown.

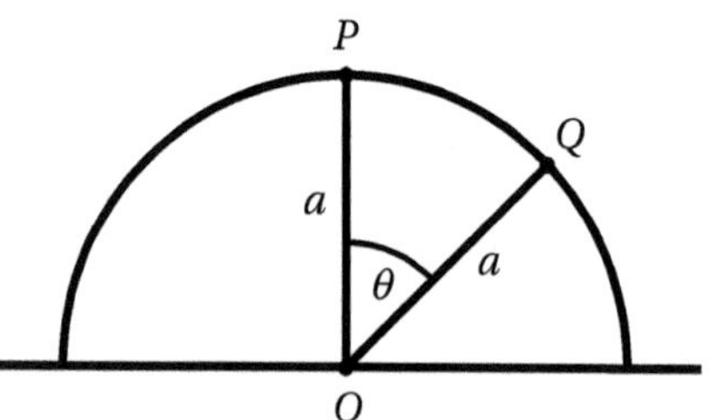

a Find an expression for $\cos\theta$ in terms of u, g and a.

After the particle leaves the surface of the hemisphere, it strikes the horizontal surface with speed $\sqrt{\frac{3ag}{2}}$.

b Find the value of θ.

12 A child's toy is formed by joining two solid cones so that their circular bases coincide. The cones have the same uniform mass density and the same base radius. The heights of the cones are $1.5h$ and h.

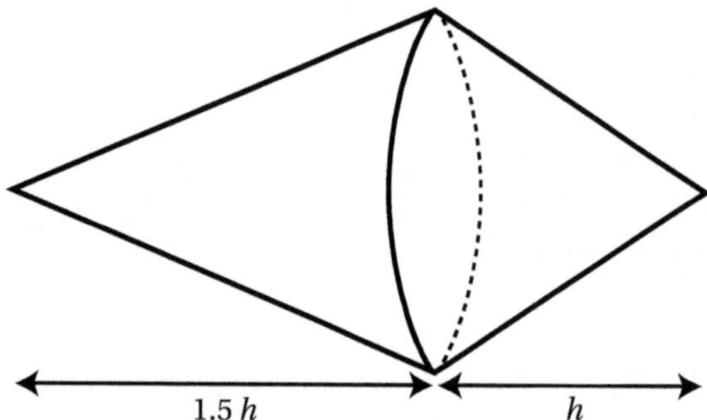

a Find the distance of the centre of mass of the toy from the vertex of the larger cone.

The toy is now placed on horizontal ground with the sloping surface of the smaller cone in contact with the ground. The object rests in equilibrium but is on the point of toppling.

b Find the radius of the base of the cones as an exact multiple of h.

13 Two uniform smooth spheres A and B, of equal radius, have masses $2m$ kg and m kg respectively. The spheres are moving on a horizontal surface when they collide. Before the collision, A is moving with speed a m s^{-1} in a direction making an angle α with the line of centres and B is moving towards A with speed b m s^{-1} in a direction making an angle β with the line of centres (see diagram). After the collision, A moves with velocity 2 m s^{-1} in a direction perpendicular to the line of centres and B moves with velocity 2 m s^{-1} in a direction making an angle of 45° with the line of centres. The coefficient of restitution between A and B is $\frac{2}{3}$.

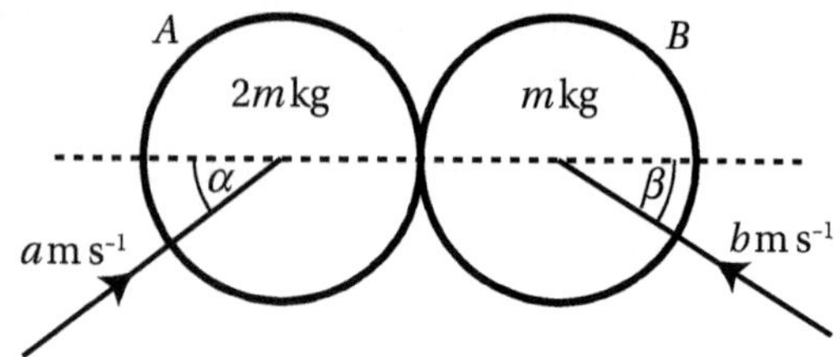

i Show that $a\cos\alpha = \frac{5}{6}\sqrt{2}$ and find $b\cos\beta$.

ii Find the values of a and α.

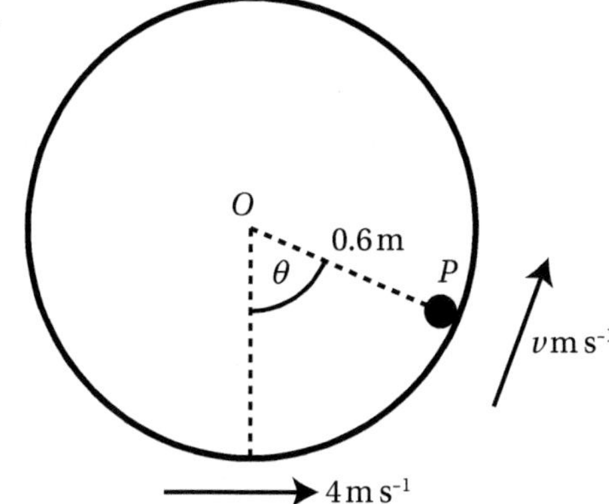

A hollow cylinder is fixed with its axis horizontal. The inner surface of the cylinder is smooth and has radius 0.6 m. A particle P of mass 0.45 kg is projected horizontally with speed 4 m s^{-1} from the lowest point of a vertical cross-section of the cylinder and moves in the plane of the cross-section, which is perpendicular to the axis of the cylinder. While P remains in contact with the surface, its speed is v m s^{-1} when OP makes an angle θ with the downward vertical at O, where O is the centre of the cross-section (see diagram). The force exerted on P by the surface is R N.

i Show that $v^2 = 4.24 + 11.76 \cos\theta$ and find an expression for R in terms of θ.

ii Find the speed of P at the instant when it leaves the surface.

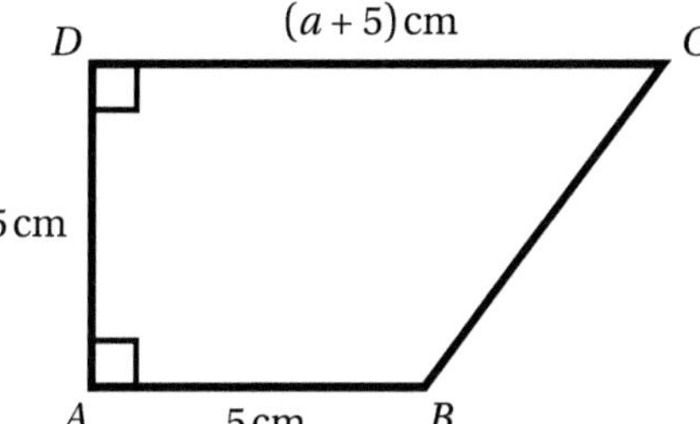

The diagram shows the cross-section through the centre of mass of a uniform solid prism. The cross-section is a trapezium $ABCD$ with AB and CD perpendicular to AD. The lengths of AB and AD are each 5 cm and the length of CD is $(a + 5)$ cm.

i Show the distance of the centre of mass of the prism from AD is

$$\frac{a^2+15a+75}{3(a+10)}\text{cm.}$$

The prism is placed with the face containing AB in contact with a horizontal surface.

ii Find the greatest value of a for which the prism does not topple.

The prism is now placed on an inclined plane which makes an angle θ with the horizontal. AB lies along a line of greatest slope with B higher than A.

iii Using the value for a found in part **ii**, and assuming the prism does not slip down the plane, find the greatest value of θ for which the prism does not topple.

AS LEVEL PRACTICE PAPER

Time allowed: 1 hour and 15 minutes

The total mark for this paper is 60.

The acceleration due to gravity is denoted by g m s^{-2}. Unless otherwise instructed, when a numerical value is needed, use $g = 9.8$.

1 A smooth bead is threaded onto a smooth circular wire with centre O and radius 1 metre. The circular wire is fixed in a vertical plane. The bead is projected from its lowest point on the wire with speed $\sqrt{g}$. Calculate the maximum vertical height, in metres, above the point of projection that the bead reaches. **[3 marks]**

2 The string on a guitar is plucked, creating a wave. The velocity, v, of the wave depends upon the mass of the string, m, its length, l, and the tension T in the string so that $v = km^a l^b T^c$.

a Write down the dimensions of tension. **[1 mark]**

b Find a, b and c, given that k is a dimensionless constant. **[3 marks]**

c Comment on whether it was necessary to state that k is a dimensionless constant in part **b**. **[1 mark]**

3 A car of mass 1000 kg moves along a horizontal road against a constant resistive force of 300 N.

a Find the maximum speed, in m s^{-1}, at which the car can move if the engine cannot exert more than 12 kW. **[2 marks]**

A tow rope is now attached to the car, which pulls a trailer of mass 250 kg. The resistance to motion for the trailer is 200 N and the resistance to car's motion has not changed. Let T be the tension in the rope and, at the instant the speed is 8 m s^{-1}, the engine is working at 12 kW.

b Find the driving force for the car. **[2 marks]**

c What modelling assumptions have been made about the tow rope? **[2 marks]**

d Use Newton's second law to write an expression for the acceleration of the car in terms of T. **[3 marks]**

e Find the tension in the tow rope. **[3 marks]**

4 A particle P is attached to one end of a string of length l. The other end of the string is attached to a fixed point O. A second particle Q of the same mass is attached to one end of another identical string, while the other end of the string is attached to the first particle P. The whole system moves with a constant angular speed of ω rad s^{-1} about the downward vertical through O. The upper string OP makes an angle of α with the downward vertical through O and the lower string PQ makes an angle of β with the downward vertical through P.

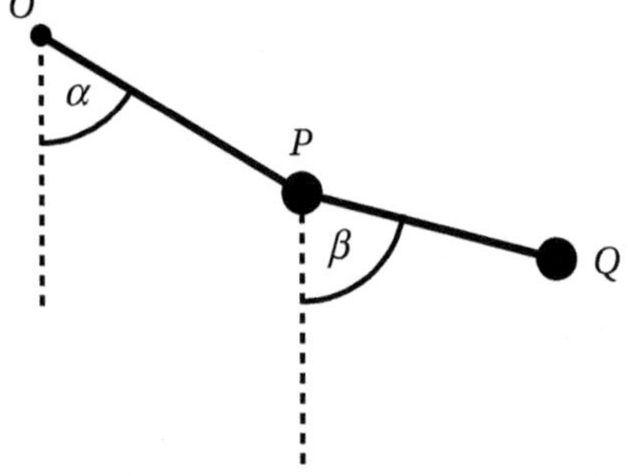

a State two assumptions that you should make about the string in order to model the circular motion of P and Q. **[1 mark]**

b By considering the forces and the circular motion at Q, show that
$\tan\beta = \frac{l\omega^2}{g}(\sin\alpha + \sin\beta)$ **[4 marks]**

c By considering the forces and the circular motion at P and part **b** show that
$\tan\alpha = \frac{l\omega^2}{2g}(2\sin\alpha + \sin\beta)$ **[4 marks]**

5 Two small spheres, A and B, of masses $2m$ and $3m$, respectively, are attached to opposite ends of a light inextensible string of length l. They are placed next to each other on a horizontal table and sphere A is projected vertically upward with a speed of $\sqrt{gl}$ m s^{-1}.

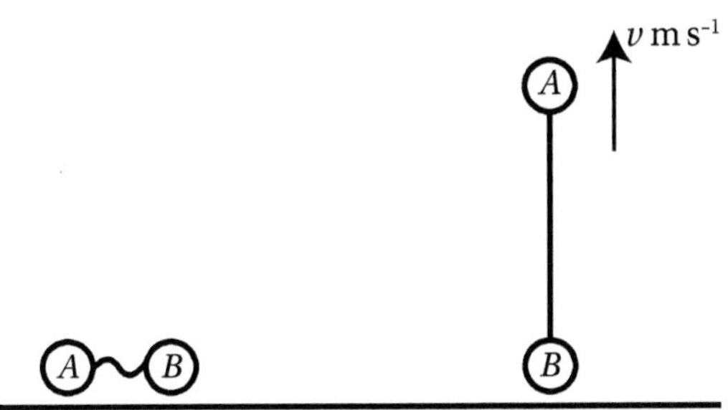

a Find the speed of sphere A at the instant the string becomes taut. **[2 marks]**

b Comment on how the modelling assumption 'the two spheres are placed next to each other' will affect your answer to part **a**. **[2 marks]**

c Show, using that the law of conservation of momentum, that, at the instant immediately after the string becomes taut, the velocity of B is $0.8\sqrt{gl}$ m s^{-1}. **[2 marks]**

d State the magnitude of the impulse in the string. **[1 mark]**

e Calculate the maximum height that sphere A reaches above the horizontal table when it first comes to instantaneous rest. **[3 marks]**

f Calculate the loss in kinetic energy due to the tightening of the string. **[3 marks]**

6 Two smooth spheres, X and Y, with masses 0.6 kg and 0.4 kg, respectively, are moving on a smooth horizontal surface. The spheres are moving towards each other and before they collide each sphere is moving at a speed of 5 m s^{-1}. After the collision X moves with a speed of 2.4 m s^{-1} in the opposite direction to its initial motion.

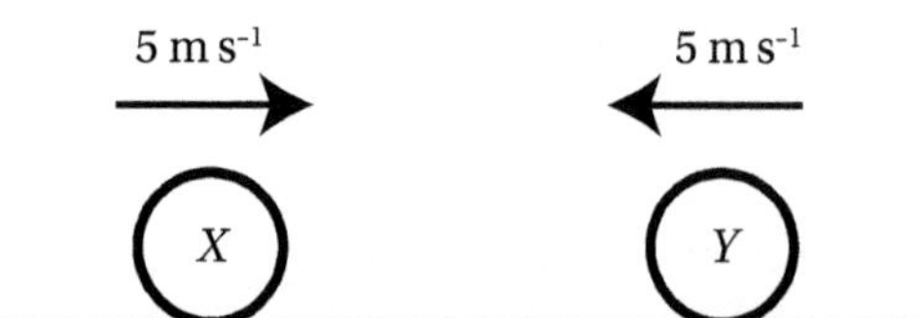

a State the direction in which the sphere Y moves after the collision. **[1 mark]**

b Calculate the coefficient of restitution between the two spheres. **[5 marks]**

7 A particle of mass 25 kg slides down a slope at 30° to the horizontal. The particle increases its speed from 3 m s^{-1} to 5 m s^{-1} while sliding down 8 m of the slope.

a Calculate the gain in kinetic energy of the particle. **[2 marks]**

b Calculate the work done against the resistance to motion. **[4 marks]**

There is a constant frictional force between the particle and the slope, and this force is the only resistance to motion.

c Calculate the coefficient of friction between the particle and the slope to 3 significant figures. **[3 marks]**

d For what value of the coefficient of friction (to 3 significant figures) would the particle slide down the slope at a constant speed? **[3 marks]**

A LEVEL PRACTICE PAPER

Time allowed: 1 hour and 30 minutes

The total mark for this paper is 75.

The acceleration due to gravity is denoted by g m s^{-2}. Unless otherwise instructed, when a numerical value is needed, use $g = 9.8$.

1 A ball is released from rest and falls from a height of k metres above a horizontal table. Given that the ball rebounds to a height h metres, find an expression for the coefficient of restitution in terms of k and h. **[3 marks]**

2 The force that two objects, of masses m_1 and m_2, exert on each other is given by $F = \frac{Gm_1m_2}{d^2}$, where d is the distance in metres between the two objects and G is a constant. Find the dimensions of G. **[3 marks]**

3 A light elastic spring with natural length 30 cm rests on a smooth horizontal table. One end is attached to a fixed point O, while the other end is attached to a particle of mass 300 g. The particle is held 20 cm away from O. The modulus of elasticity of the spring is 300 N. Find the elastic potential energy in the spring. **[3 marks]**

4 A particle of mass m is attached to one end of a light elastic string of modulus of elasticity mg and natural length l. The other end of the string is attached to a fixed point O on a smooth table so that the particle is moving in a horizontal circle with centre O.

a Find an expression for the force towards the centre of motion, if r is the radius of the circular motion. **[2 marks]**

b Given that the particle is moving at $\frac{k}{\pi}$ revolutions per second, find an expression for the radius of the circular motion. **[4 marks]**

c For $l = 1$ metre, sketch a graph of r against k. **[2 marks]**

If the tension in the 1 metre elastic string reaches mg N the string will break.

d Comment on your sketch from part **c** with reference to the values of k that can be chosen for this model. **[2 marks]**

5 A particle P is moving along the x-axis, initially starting at the origin O. At time t seconds, the velocity of P is v m s^{-1} in the direction of x increasing, where:

$v = t^2$ for $0 \leqslant t \leqslant 2$ and $v = 4e^{2-t}$ for $t > 2$. When $t = 0$, P is at O.

a Sketch a graph of v against t for $0 \leqslant t \leqslant 4$. **[2 marks]**

b Calculate the acceleration of P at $t = 2.5$ seconds. **[2 marks]**

c Calculate the total distance travelled by P in the first 4 seconds. **[3 marks]**

6 A light elastic string of modulus of elasticity $\frac{4}{\sqrt{3}}g$ N and natural length 4 m is attached to two points, A and B, which are 4 m apart in a horizontal line. Two particles, X and Y, each of mass 1 kg, are attached to fixed points of the string such that the unstretched lengths of AX and YB are each 1 m. The system is in equilibrium with the angle XAB equal to YBA, both denoted by α.

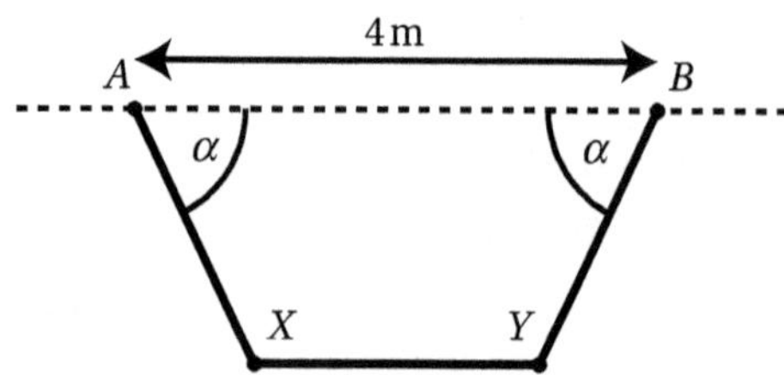

a Show that the tension in AX is given by $g\,\text{cosec}\,\alpha$ and in XY is given by $g\cot\alpha$. **[3 marks]**

b Show that $\tan\alpha - \sin\alpha = \frac{\sqrt{3}}{2}$. **[6 marks]**

c Verify that $\alpha = 60°$ is a solution to the equation found in part **b**. **[1 mark]**

7 A smooth sphere with centre A and mass 2 m is moving with speed $2v$ m s^{-1} when it collides with a second smooth sphere with centre B and mass m moving at a speed of v m s^{-1}. The velocities of the spheres immediately before impact are inclined at angles of 60° and 90°, respectively, to the direction AB at the moment of impact.

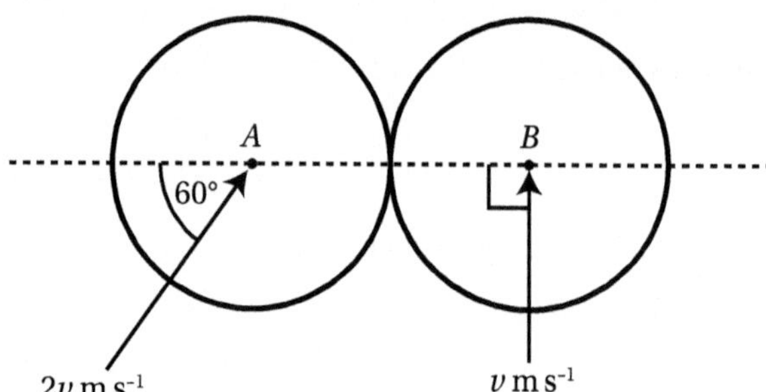

The coefficient of restitution between the spheres is 0.5.

a Calculate the speed and direction of the spheres after impact. **[5 marks]**

b Calculate the loss of kinetic energy as a result of the impact. **[2 marks]**

8 An aeroplane of mass 1250 kg travels vertically downwards while moving in a quarter circle and then travels horizontally.

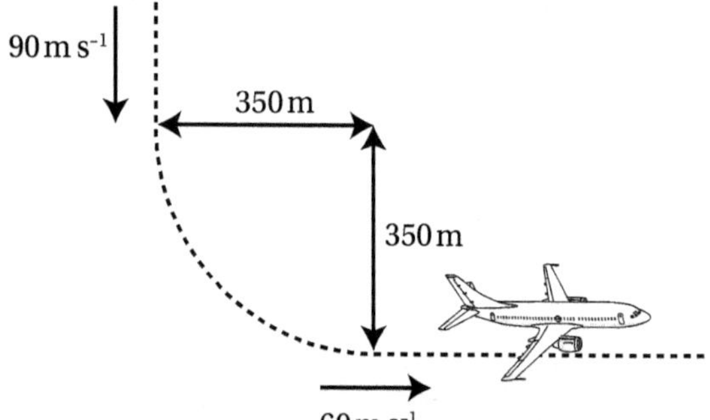

The circle has radius 350 m and the linear speed of the plane reduces uniformly from 90 m s^{-1} to 60 m s^{-1} during the 15 seconds it takes the plane to turn through the quarter circle. Let t be the time after the plane enters the quarter turn.

a Find expressions for the radial and tangential components of the acceleration of the plane during the turn. **[4 marks]**

b While the plane is in the turn, there is a constant resistive force. Calculate the energy lost due to resistances to motion in the turn, in kJ. **[2 marks]**

When the plane is halfway through the quarter circle, it releases a parcel. The plane is 200 m vertically above the horizontal ground. The particle is modelled as a projectile once it has been released.

c Calculate the speed with which the parcel is released. **[4 marks]**

d Calculate the time taken for the parcel to reach the ground. **[3 marks]**

9 A solid object is formed by rotating the area under the curve $y=\frac{1}{x}$ around the x-axis between the lines $x=a$ and $x=b$ with $0<a<b$.

a Show that the distance of the centre of mass from $x=a$ is $\dfrac{a\left(a-b-b\ln\left(\frac{a}{b}\right)\right)}{b-a}$. **[5 marks]**

A solid object is created in this way, with $a=1$ and $b=5$. The solid shape is placed on a rough inclined plane, at an angle of θ to the horizontal, with the largest flat face of the shape in contact with the inclined plane, and does not slide.

b Find the angle θ at the point of toppling, to 3 significant figures. **[2 marks]**

c At what angle θ would the solid object slide down the inclined plane, if the coefficient of friction between the object and the inclined plane is 0.6? **[2 marks]**

d Given that the coefficient of friction between the inclined plane is 0.6, will the shape topple or slide as the angle θ is increased? **[1 mark]**

10 A car P of mass 1250 kg starts at A and moves along a horizontal road with a driving force 2000 N and a variable resistance to motion force that is proportional to the square of the distance from A. At the instant when P is a distance of 20 m from A, the resultant force is 1920 N.

a If x metres is the distance AP, find an equation for the resultant force F in terms of the distance x. **[2 marks]**

b Find the work done, in kJ, by the car when the car has travelled a distance of 30 metres. **[3 marks]**

c Given that the car starts from rest at A, find the speed of the car when it is at a distance of 30 metres from the point A. **[4 marks]**

FORMULAE

The following formulae will be given on the AS and A Level assessment papers:

Kinematics

Motion in a straight line	**Motion in two dimensions**
$v = u + at$	$\mathbf{v} = \mathbf{u} + \mathbf{a}t$
$s = ut + \frac{1}{2}at^2$	$\mathbf{s} = \mathbf{u}t + \frac{1}{2}\mathbf{a}t^2$
$s = \frac{1}{2}(u+v)t$	$\mathbf{s} = \frac{1}{2}(\mathbf{u}+\mathbf{v})t$
$v^2 = u^2 + 2as$	$\mathbf{v}.\mathbf{v} = \mathbf{u}.\mathbf{u} + 2\mathbf{a}.\mathbf{s}$
$s = vt - \frac{1}{2}at^2$	$\mathbf{s} = \mathbf{v}t - \frac{1}{2}\mathbf{a}t^2$

Newton's experimental law

Between two smooth spheres $v_1 - v_2 = -e(u_1 - u_2)$
Between a smooth sphere with a fixed plane surface $v = -eu$

Motion in a circle

Tangential velocity is $v = r\dot{\theta}$

Radial acceleration is $\frac{v^2}{r}$ or $r\dot{\theta}^2$ towards the centre

Tangential acceleration is $\dot{v} = r\ddot{\theta}$

Centres of mass

Triangular lamina: $\frac{2}{3}$ along median from vertex

Solid hemisphere, radius r: $\frac{3}{8}r$ from centre

Hemispherical shell, radius r: $\frac{1}{2}r$ from centre

Circular arc, radius r, angle at centre 2α: $\frac{r \sin \alpha}{\alpha}$ from centre

Sector of circle, radius r, angle at centre 2α: $\frac{2r \sin \alpha}{3\alpha}$ from centre

Solid cone or pyramid of height h: $\frac{1}{4}h$ above the base on the line from centre of base to vertex

Conical shell of height h: $\frac{1}{3}h$ above the base on the line from centre of base to vertex

Answers

All answers are given to 3 significant figures, where appropriate.

Chapter 1

Before you start...

1 15 km
2 11 300 N
3 20 m s^{-2}
4 8cos 20° N, 8sin 20° N

Exercise 1A

1 60 J
2 20.4 kJ
3 2.68 m
4 5.88 J
5 125 J
6 a 30 000 J b 18 000 J
7 3550 J
8 23 100 J

Exercise 1B

1 5.04 kJ
2 96.9 kg
3 37.8 km h^{-1}
4 a 14.0 J b 14.0 J c 1.40 m
5 17.1 kJ
6 a 147 kJ b 97.2 kJ
7 6.61 m s^{-1}
8 4950 N
9 38.6 kN
10 1.63 N
11 Proof
12 6.98 m s^{-1}

Exercise 1C

1 1230 J
2 196 kJ
3 5.40 m
4 306 g
5 a 27.6 J b 11.0 J
c 38.6 J d 41.4 m s^{-1}
6 a 1690 J b 6390 J c 14.6 m s^{-1}
d Model Anita as particle leaving the surface of the springboard and entering the water, no resistance to motion.
7 a 2.62 J b 1.71 J
c 4.32 J d 12.2 m s^{-1}
8 2070 J
9 a 58.8 J b 12.3 m s^{-1}
10 90.0 N
11 a 600 J b 4040 J
c 64.3 m

Exercise 1D

1 117 J
2 1.96 kJ
3 73.3 m
4 23.0
5 55.2°
6 20.7 J
7 169 J
8 30.8 m
9 a 454 J b 454 J
10 a 840 J b 574 J c 5.16 m s^{-1}

Exercise 1E

1 310 kW
2 4.08 kW
3 30.1 kW
4 16.7 kW
5 41.7 N
6 149 W
7 14.1 MJ
8 340 W
9 a 5880 J s^{-1} b 756 J s^{-1} c 6640 W
10 10.7 N
11 0.237 m s^{-2}
12 $u = 15.6$ m s^{-1}
13 $k = 3.03$
14 a 5.75 s b 8.33 m s^{-2}

Mixed practice 1

1 6800 J
2 30.5 m

3 196 W

4 i 104 J ii 20.9 W

5 i 58.8 J ii 12.7 m s^{-1}

6 i 625 N ii 8380 W

7 i 0.125 m s^{-2} ii 10.6 m s^{-1}

8 a 3810 J b 2090 J

c 6.38 m s^{-1}

9 i $k = 16.5$ ii 35.7 m s^{-1}

10 i $k = 103$ ii 17 000 W

11 i Proof ii 958 W

12 i 900 N ii 0.275 m s^{-2}

13 i Proof ii 26.5 m s^{-1}

iii 0.801 m s^{-2}

14 i Proof ii 1.04 m s^{-2}

iii 41 900 W

15 a $t = 3.45$ b 10.8 m s^{-2}

16 i 31.4 m s^{-1} ii 22.7 m s^{-1}

iii 1.22 m s^{-2}

17 i $P = 19\,200$ ii 31.7 m s^{-1}

18 i 560 J ii 4120 J

iii 55.4 m

19 i Proof ii 3.60 s

20 i 0.313 m s^{-2} ii 234 m

21 i 750 N ii 9000 W

iii 14 000 W iv 6.42°

22 96 W

23 a 9750 W b 3375 W c 6075 W

Chapter 2

Before you start...

1 a r^4 b r^{12}

c $\frac{1}{16}$ d $\sqrt{2}$

2 $x = \pm\sqrt{\frac{(t+1)y}{zt^3}}$

3 $x = 4, y = -2$

4 $P = \frac{2}{9}$

5 a $\frac{4}{3}\pi \times 3^3 = 36\pi$ b $4\pi \times 3^2 = 36\pi$

6 m s^{-1}

7 q $= \frac{5}{4} = 1.25$ rad

8 5 m s^{-1}

9 $a = 0.7$ m s^{-2}

10 $a = 4$ m s^{-2}

11 $v = 6.26$ m s^{-1} if $g = 9.8$ m s^{-2}

Exercise 2A

1 a LT^{-2} b LT^{-2}

c MLT^{-2} d MLT^{-2}

e MLT^{-1} f Dimensionless

g L^3 h ML^{-3}

i ML^{2}T^{-2} j ML^{-1}T^{-2}

2 Dimensionless

3 Dimensionless

4 a ML^{2}T^{-2} b Yes

5 a ML^{2}T^{-2} b The same

6 Dimensionless

7 MLT^{-3}

8 a ML^{2}T^{-2} b MLT^{-2}

9 M^{-1}L^{3}T^{-2}

10 ML^{2}T^{-1}

Exercise 2B

1 a L b L^2 c L^3

2 a MLT^{-1} b ML^{2}T^{-2}

c ML^2 d L

3 L

4 a Consistent b Not consistent

c Consistent d Consistent

e Not consistent

5 a T^{-2} b Consistent

6 a $m\frac{d^2x}{dt^2} = -kx$ b MT^{-2}

7 a ML^{2}T^{-1}

b MLT^{-1}, not the same

c [angular momentum] = L[linear momentum]

8 a ML^{2}T^{-2} b The same

9 a $E = \frac{Fl}{xA}$ b ML^{-1}T^{-2}

10 a $\frac{gx}{2v^2}\sec^2\theta$

b Change the x to x^2

Work it out 2.1

Solution 2 is correct.

Exercise 2C

1 ML^2T^{-3}

2 L^2T^{-2}

3 T^{-3}

4 MLT^{-3}

5 Proof

6 a Proof

b Yes. As the angle must be dimensionless, ω must have the inverse dimension of t, so the dimension of ω can be determined as T^{-1}.

7 $\alpha = 1$

8 a Dimensionless b 50 dB

9 a LT^{-2}

b $[A] = T^{-1}$

c $[B] = T^{-2}$

10 $\tan\theta = \frac{v^2}{rg}$

Exercise 2D

1

Quantity	Dimension	SI unit
Time	T	second (s)
Mass	M	kilogram (kg)
Weight (mg)	MLT^{-2}	newton (N)
length (displacement)	L	metre (m)
Area	L^2	m^2
Volume	L^3	m^3
Velocity	LT^{-1}	m/s or m s^{-1}
Acceleration	LT^{-2}	m/s^2 or m s^{-2}
Acceleration due to gravity	LT^{-2}	m/s^2 or m s^{-2}
Force (ma)	MLT^{-2}	newton (N)
Kinetic energy ($\frac{1}{2}mv^2$)	ML^2T^{-2}	joule (J)
Gravitational potential energy (mgh)	ML^2T^{-2}	joule (J)
Work done (force × distance moved)	ML^2T^{-2}	joule (J)
Moment of a force (force × distance)	ML^2T^{-2}	newton metre (N m)
Power (rate of doing work $\frac{dw}{dt}$)	ML^2T^{-3}	watt (W)
Momentum (mv)	MLT^{-1}	kg m s^{-1}
Impulse (force × time)	MLT^{-1}	newton second (N s)
Moment of inertia ($\sum mr^2$)	ML^2	kg m^2
Angular velocity $\left(\omega = \frac{d\theta}{dt}\right)$	T^{-1}	rad/s or rad s^{-1}
Density $\left(\frac{\text{mass}}{\text{volume}}\right)$	ML^{-3}	kg/m^3 or kg m^{-3}
Pressure $\left(\frac{\text{force}}{\text{area}}\right)$	$ML^{-1}T^{-2}$	pascal (Pa)
Periodic time (time for one complete cycle)	T	second (s)
Frequency $\left(\frac{1}{\text{periodic time}}\right)$	T^{-1}	hertz (Hz)
Surface tension $\left(\frac{\text{energy}}{\text{area}}\right)$	MT^{-2}	kg/second^2 or kg s^{-2}

Mixed practice 2

1 a T b LT^{-3}

2 Proof

3 a $[\text{Tension}] = MLT^{-2}$

b i Inconsistent, $\frac{mv}{r}$ is the incorrect term.

ii Consistent

iii Inconsistent, $g\cos\theta$ is the incorrect term.

4 a ML^2T^{-2} b 52 J

5 a L b MT^{-2}

6 $\alpha = 1, \beta = 2$ and $\gamma = -1$. $F = \frac{mv^2}{r}$

7 a MLT^{-2}

b $\beta = \gamma$ as the two masses must make a similar contribution to the attractive force.

c $F = \frac{Gm_1m_2}{r^2}$

8 a T^{-2} b $[A] = T^{-1}$ c $B = \frac{g}{l}$

9 a MT^{-2} b $d = A\sqrt{\frac{S}{\rho g}}$

c 1.98 if $g = 9.8$

10 a [Tension] = MLT^{-2}

b $\alpha=-1, \beta=\frac{1}{2}, \gamma=-\frac{1}{2}. f=\frac{1}{2l}\sqrt{\frac{F}{\mu}}$

11 a $ML^{-1}T^{-2}$ **b** $ML^{-1}T^{-1}$

c $\alpha=2, \beta=1$

12 $\alpha=1, \beta=2, \gamma=1. F=k\rho v^2 A.$

13 a MT^{-2} **b** ML^{-3}

c $h=\frac{AS}{\rho rg}$ **d** 98 mm

Chapter 3

Before you start...

1 $x=-\frac{1}{2}, y=2$

2 $(-7.47, -17.9), (1.47, -0.0557)$

3 10.8 m s^{-1} if $g=9.8$ m s^{-2}

4 a m s^{-1} **b** m s^{-2} **c** N

5 7.5 m s^{-2}

6 0.8 J

Exercise 3A

1 a 2250 kg m s^{-1} **b** 22.5 kg m s^{-1}

c 0.2 kg m s^{-1} **d** 20 000 kg m s^{-1}

e 28 000 kg m s^{-1}

2 900 m s^{-1}

3 0.8 tonnes

4 120 N s

5 720 N s

6

Positive direction		
Initial velocity (m s^{-1})	Final velocity (m s^{-1})	Impulse (N s)
4 ⟶	6 ⟶	$(+6m)-(+4m)=+2m$
4 ⟶	2 ⟶	$2m-4m=-2m$
4 ⟶	6 ⟵	$-6m-4m=-10m$
8 ⟵	3 ⟵	$-3m--8m=5m$
3 ⟵	8 ⟶	$8m--3m=11m$

7 5 m s^{-1}

8 240 s

9 20 m s^{-1}

10 10 m s^{-1}

11 17.5 N s away from the wall

12 50 N s away from the wall

13 125 N

14 150 N

Work it out 3.1

Solution 3 is the only possible answer.

Exercise 3B

1

m_1	m_2	u_1	u_2	v_1	v_2
3	4	+10	+2	$\frac{14}{3}$	+6
2	4	+6	−2	−2	2
2	5	8	+2	+0.5	+5
2	5	+8	−2	−1	+1.6

2 2.25 m s^{-1}

3 1.2 m s^{-1}

4 14 m s^{-1}

5 a 6.67 m s^{-1} **b** 4 m s^{-1}

6 0.125 m s^{-1} in *A*'s original direction of travel

7 0.96 kg

8 5.56 m s^{-1}

9 10 m s^{-1}

10 9.6 m s^{-1}. The balls being spherical, the balls being the same size, the impact being along the line of centres, the contact being smooth.

11 a $v_1=\frac{5m-9}{m+3}, v_2=\frac{9-5m}{m+3}$ **b** 5 kg and $\frac{3}{7}$ kg

Exercise 3C

1

	i	ii	iii	iv	v
a	−1.2 m s^{-1}	−10 m s^{-1}	0	−32 m s^{-1}	−6 m s^{-1}
b	5.2*m*	20*m*	60*m*	72*m*	16*m*
c	7.28*m*	0	1800*m*	288*m*	32*m*

2 Both change direction. Velocity of *P* is 1.4 m s^{-1} and of *Q* is 3.1 m s^{-1}

3 a 0.2 m s^{-1} towards *A*

b $\frac{1}{20}$

4 a $\frac{3}{4}$ b 42 N s c 84 J

5 a $\frac{mV}{J}$ b $mV+J$

c $\frac{1}{2}m\left(\left(\frac{J}{m}\right)^2-V^2\right)$

6 a 20 m s^{-1} b 0.625

c 46.9 J

7 $\frac{1}{2}$

8 a Velocity of A is 7.12 m s^{-1} and of B is 4.08 m s^{-1}, moving in opposite directions to each other.

b 6.048 N s

9 0.72 m

10 a Velocity of A is $0.25u$ m s^{-1} and of B is $4u$ m s^{-1}, both in the original direction of motion.

b 4.375 mu^2

11 Velocity of A is 3.3 m s^{-1} and of B is 5.7 m s^{-1}, both in the original direction of motion.

12 $1:e^2$

13 a Velocity of A is 3.6 m s^{-1} and B is 5.4 m s^{-1}, both in the original direction of motion.

b 0.6

14 a 4.2 m s^{-1}

b 0.8

c −0.288 N s

15 $\frac{\sqrt{g}}{2}(2+\sqrt{5})=6.63$ N s

16 $\frac{\sqrt{35}}{7}$

17 $e>\frac{1}{9}$

18 $e>\frac{10}{17}$

19 a 10 m s^{-1} b 30 N s

Mixed practice 3

1 a −2.6 Ns b 0.75 m s^{-1}

2 a 1.6 kg b 2.4 kg

3 2.4 m s^{-1} in the direction of the second roller skater

4 3.375 m s^{-1} in the direction of initial motion

5 i a 0.096 kg b 1.2 kg m s^{-1}

ii 3.25 m s^{-1}

6 i 1.46 m s^{-1} ii 1.08 m

7 i $\frac{13}{30}$ m s^{-1} ii 2 m

8 i Proof

ii $4m-1.5=v(m+0.5)$

iii $v=1.5$ m s^{-1}

9 i 0.2 m s^{-1}and B has changed direction

ii a 1 m s^{-1} b 14 400 N s

10 i 1.5 m s^{-1}

ii As 2.8 > 2.75 there are no more collisions

11 i 2.27 N s ii 0.775

12 i 0.12 kg

ii a 0.14 kg b 0.02 kg, 0.42 kg

13 1 m s^{-1} and 2 m s^{-1} away from each other

14 i $\frac{2u}{5}$ ii Proof iii Proof

iv Speed of A is $\frac{u}{5}$ away from the wall and speed of B is $\frac{3u}{5}$ towards the wall.

Chapter 4

Before you start...

1 10.5 cm

2 $\begin{pmatrix}-5\\7\end{pmatrix}$

3 53.1°

4 $v=3t+2$, $s=\frac{3}{2}t^2+2t+3$

5 $\frac{5\pi}{6}$ rad

Work it out 4.1

Solution 3 is correct.

Exercise 4A

1 a i 10.2 m s^{-1} ii 0.422 m s^{-1}

b i 1.75 m ii 16 m

c i 0.167 rad s^{-1} ii 22.4 rad s^{-1}

d i 0.251 m s^{-1} ii 3.14 m s^{-1}

2 a i 0.419 rad s^{-1} ii 71.6 m

b i 4.19 rad s^{-1} ii 2.39 m

c i 0.105 rad s^{-1} ii 47.7 m

3 10 rad s^{-1}

4 a 0.107 rad s^{-1} b 58.9 s

5 a 0.140 rad s^{-1} b 1.40 cm s^{-1}
c 7.16 m

6 0.25 rad s^{-1}

7 a 57.3 s b 0.219 rad s^{-1}

8 a Its orbit is circular and its angular speed is constant.
b i $0.000\,249 \text{ rad s}^{-1}$
ii 31.9 km s^{-1}

Exercise 4B

1 a i 0.313 m ii 1.29 m
b i 3.57 m ii 1.41 m
c i 2.26 m s^{-1} ii 1.46 m s^{-1}
d i 3 rad s^{-1} ii 12.2 rad s^{-1}

2 a i 4 m s^{-2}
ii 8 N
b i 3.78 m s^{-2} ii 11 000 N
c i $a = 0.0148 \text{ m s}^{-2}$ ii $F = 0.002\,96$ N

3 0.447 N

4 $a = 1.38 \text{ m s}^{-2}$, $F = 2070$ N

5 a 60 N b 21.6 N

6 Emily will feel an increase in force by a factor of $\frac{4}{3}$.

7 a 26.4 km h^{-1}
b No, it is not a sensible estimate; it is too small. This is a very low speed to drive around a bend of 55 m radius.

8 $\mu = 0.0209$

9 $v = 13.0 \text{ m s}^{-1}$

10 a Assume the only friction force acting on car is from road surface. Assume car is on point of slipping away from centre.
b i 47.8 km h^{-1} ii 52.0 km h^{-1}
c For asphalt, reduce max safe speed from 47.8 km h^{-1} to 28.2 km h^{-1} when wet.
For concrete, reduce max safe speed from 52.0 km h^{-1} to 37.8 km h^{-1} when wet.
d Depends on where the road is to be built. For example, in a city with a low speed limit asphalt would be cheaper and suitable.

11 a Proof b Proof
c Proof d Proof
e Proof

Exercise 4C

1 a i 20.9 N ii 41.9 N
b i 36 N ii 47.3 N
c i 2.27 rad s^{-1} ii 2.29 rad s^{-1}
d i 39.4° ii 83.5°

2 a $\theta = 88.6°$ b $\omega = 3.36 \text{ rad s}^{-1}$
c $T = 106$ N d $m = 5.18$ kg

3 64.9°

4 Proof

5 a 13.4 N b 6.76 rad s^{-1}

6 Proof

7 a $\frac{4}{5}mg + \frac{324}{625}m\omega^2$
b $\frac{432}{625}m\omega^2 - \frac{3}{5}mg$
c $\omega > 2.92 \text{ rad s}^{-1}$

8 a 1.94 rad s^{-1} b 56.6 N
c 5.66 N, compression

9 a $\frac{5}{3}mg$ N b $4\sqrt{\frac{rg}{15}} \text{ m s}^{-1}$

10 a 41.6 N b 3.27 rad s^{-1}
c 18.4 N, away from the centre B so the rod is in compression.

11 $T = 36.9$ N, $r = 1.21$ m

12 Max speed 21.8 m s^{-1}, min speed 5.05 m s^{-1}

13 Proof

Mixed practice 4

1 a 1.6 rad s^{-1} b 3.93 s
c 2.56 N

2 a

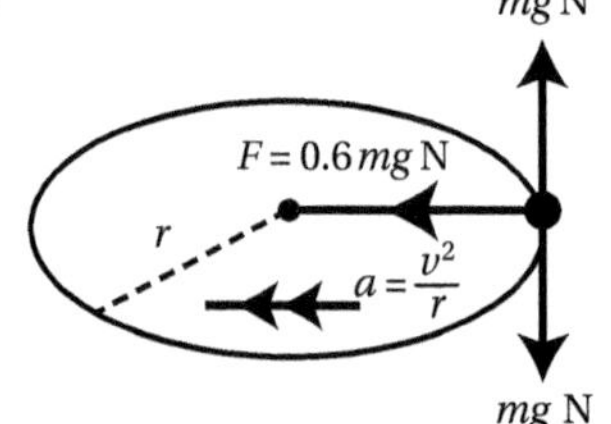

b 1.33 m s^{-1}

3 a $13.4\ \text{m s}^{-2}$ b $6.72\ \text{N}$

4 1300 N

5 Proof

6 $12.5\ \text{rad s}^{-1}$

7 a $\frac{25mg}{7}$ b $2\sqrt{42gL}$

c There was no frictional force acting.

8 a $22.7\ \text{km h}^{-1}$

b i $13.3\ \text{km h}^{-1}$ ii $30.4\ \text{km h}^{-1}$

9 i 3.27 N ii $\omega = 1.81\ \text{rad s}^{-1}$

iii $\omega = 2.26\ \text{rad s}^{-1}$

10 i 11.4 N in *AP* and 1.60 N in *BP*

ii $6.51\ \text{rad s}^{-1}$

11 i Proof ii $4.16\ \text{rad s}^{-1}$

12 i 44.3 N in *AP* and 19.8 N in *BP*

ii $2.97\ \text{m s}^{-1}$

13 a Proof b $\frac{mv^2}{l} - mg\sin\theta$

c Proof

14 i $\mu = 0.5$ ii $5.72\ \text{rad s}^{-1}$

Chapter 5

Before you start...

1 $\begin{pmatrix} -4.5 \\ 4.5 \\ 6 \end{pmatrix}$

Exercise 5A

1 151 cm

2 3 kg

3 72 cm

4 7.5 cm

5 $\bar{x} = 4.30, \bar{y} = 3.70$

6 $\bar{x} = 4.14, \bar{y} = 4.57$

7 $\bar{x} = 4.89, \bar{y} = 5.22$

8 $\begin{pmatrix} -1.25 \\ 2.25 \end{pmatrix}$ cm

9 $x = 5$ cm, $y = 3$ cm

Exercise 5B

1 (5.5, 4)

2 (3.5, 3.5)

3 (1.5 cm, 0.866 cm)

4 a (3, 2) b (2, 4)

c $\left(\frac{2}{3}, 1\frac{2}{3}\right)$ d $\left(-\frac{1}{3}, \frac{1}{3}\right)$

e $(-3, -\frac{1}{3})$

5 2.12 cm

6 a $(2, 1\frac{1}{3})$ b $(3, 1\frac{1}{3})$

c (2.83, 0.645) d (4.94, 1.96)

7 9.74 cm

8 9.44 cm

9 1.57 rad

Work it out 5.1

Solution 1 is correct.

Exercise 5C

1 a $(2\frac{5}{18}, 2)$ b $\left(2\frac{1}{14}, 1\frac{4}{7}\right)$

c $\left(2\frac{9}{14}, 2\frac{3}{7}\right)$ d $\left(2\frac{4}{9}, 1\frac{17}{18}\right)$

e $\left(2\frac{11}{27}, 1\frac{26}{27}\right)$ f $\left(2\frac{2}{15}, 1\frac{13}{15}\right)$

g (3.49, 4.16) h (4.18, 4.57)

2 0.616 m

3 16.3 cm from *AD*, 10.8 cm from *AB*

4 $\frac{5a}{24}$ from x

5 5.5 kg

6 6.43 cm

7 1.5 cm from *AB* and 5 cm from *AC*

8 (3.89, 3.42)

9 19.0 cm

10 0.114 m from *AB* and 0.611 m from *BC*

11 14.3 cm

12 8.37 cm

13 7.83 cm

14 Proof

Mixed practice 5

1 1.9 m

2 $\bar{x} = 10.6, \bar{y} = 7.71$

3 $\bar{x} = 6.67, \bar{y} = 3.87$

4 3.11 cm

5 2.51 cm

6 (4.31, 12.6)

7 0.0612 m

8 $\bar{x} = 0499$ m

9 $\bar{y} = 2$ cm, $\bar{x} = -1$ cm

10 $x = 0.482$ cm

11 0.94 m

Focus on ... Proof 1

1 Proof

2 $\omega^2 - \omega_0{}^2 = 2\alpha\theta$, $\theta = \omega t - \frac{1}{2}\alpha t^2$,
$\theta = \frac{1}{2}(\omega_0 + \omega)t$, if $\theta_0 = 0$.

3 50 rad s^{-1}

Focus on ... Problem solving 1

1 $\sqrt{2.26}$ m

2 0.9π s

3 5.3 m s^{-1}

Focus on ... Modelling 1

1 6.6 m s^{-1}

2 2.05 m

3 Yes, the ball hits the bell.

4 $h = 2.21$ m

Cross-topic review 1

1 $\alpha = 1, \beta = 2, \gamma = 1$

2 a $\boldsymbol{I} = 30$ kg m s^{-1}

b $\boldsymbol{v} = 16$ m s^{-1}

3 9.87 N

4 56.6°

5 36 kW

6 Proof

7 0.654 s

8 2 m s^{-1} away from the wall

9 (–0.675, 0)

10 a MLT^{-2} b $ML^{-1}T^{-2}$

11 0.775 m

12 1.29 m^3

13 $\left(\frac{7}{3}, \frac{7}{3}\right)$

Chapter 6

Before you start...

1 196 J

2 661 J

3 0.0120 N

4 2

Exercise 6A

1 12.5 J

2 5 J

3 5π J

4 625 J

5 $k = 90$ N m^{-2}

6 $a = 64$

7 74.0 J

8 9.70 m s^{-1}

9 75.9 m s^{-1}

10 4730

11 $d = 39.5$ m

12 $5x + \frac{2x^3}{3 - 4x^2}$, 78.7 m

Work done $\frac{2}{3}x^3 - 4x^2 + 5x$

Work it out 6.1

Solution 2 is correct.

Exercise 6B

1 26.6 N

2 42.9 N

3 220 N

4 0.124 m

5 0.104 m

6 33.7 N

7 33.3 N

8 0.446 m

9 3.38 J

10 32.6 J

11 523 N

12 0.542 m

13 0.226 m

14 a 0.895 m b 30.6 m s^{-2} upwards

15 Proof

16 1.50 m

17 $OQ = 0.987$ m

18 a 5.5 J b 5.91 m s^{-1}

Exercise 6C

1 a 102 J b 14.5 W

2 a 88.0 J b 2.65 m s^{-1}

3 6°

4 a 1.93 m s^{-1} b 1.23 m

5 16.0 s

6 1.00 m s^{-1}

7 24.1 N

8 a Proof b 3.21 m s^{-2}

9 a 0.105 m s^{-2} b 9.60 m s^{-1}

10 a Proof b 22.2 m s^{-1}

Exercise 6D

1 a i 812 J ii 62 J iii 50 J

b $a = 5.5$ c $x = 20$

2 a i 16.8 J ii 45.8 J

b i 4.87 m s^{-1} ii 3.96 m s^{-1}

c 1.5 m s^{-1}

3 a i 22 W ii 0.75 W

b $x = 2$m c $x = -8$m or 2m

4 $40\mathbf{i} + 80\mathbf{j}$ m

5 1500 J

6 45.0 m s^{-1}

7 8100 W

8 $15.25\mathbf{i} + 30.5\mathbf{j}$ m s^{-1}

9 a $\mathbf{i} + 5\mathbf{j}$ N

b 135 W c 173 J

10 a $240\mathbf{i} - 427\mathbf{j}$ m s^{-1}

b 255 kW c 296 kJ

Mixed practice 6

1 47 J

2 a $5\mathbf{i} + 5t\mathbf{j}$ N b 60 W c 40 J

3 a $\frac{0.8}{t}\mathbf{i} + 0.4\mathbf{j}$ m s^{-2} b $\mathbf{v} = 0.55\mathbf{i} + 0.6\mathbf{j}$

c 3.51 W

4 1.5 m

5 a $\mathbf{F} = 3.90\mathbf{i} + 7.50\mathbf{j}$

b 60.6 W

6 i 8.82 m s^{-2} ii 3.25 m s^{-1}

7 i 3.00 m

ii 1.43 m s^{-2} upwards

8 i 1.03 m ii 24.0 m s^{-2}

9 i 2.70 m s^{-1} ii 2.01 m

10 i Proof ii Proof

11 ii Proof ii 10.6 m s^{-1}

12 2.75 s

13 9.40 m s^{-1}

14 41.7 m

15 i 80 m s^{-1}, Proof ii Proof

16 i 800 N ii 19.9 m s^{-1}

iii 88.2 m s^{-2}

17 i Proof

ii a 2.72 m b 6.85 m s^{-1} c 24.2 m s^{-2}

18 a mg is the weight of a mass of m kg at sea level, where g is the acceleration due to gravity. The variable weight model gives $\frac{km}{R^2}$ as the weight of a mass of m kg at sea level.

b 3.98×10^{14} m^3 s^{-2}

c 2.4×10^9 J (2.4 GJ)

19 a $-mr\omega^2(\cos\omega t\,\mathbf{i} + \sin\omega t\,\mathbf{j})$

b $mr\omega^2$

c $\frac{1}{2}m\,r^2\omega^2$

d Proof

Mixed practice 8

1 $\theta = 41.4°$, $I = 6.35$ N s

2 $I = 1.442$ N s, $\theta = 46.1°$

3 i Proof ii 157.4°

4 71.4°

5 i 42.8° to the initial direction

ii 20.4 m s^{-1}

6 i 0.075 N s ii $\frac{2}{3}$

7 i $-4e$ ii 4 m s^{-1}

8 A: 10 m s^{-1} at an angle of 36.9° above the horizontal away from B, B: 8 m s^{-1} in the opposite direction to its initial motion.

9 i 0.75 b 15.1°

10 i 0.12 m s^{-1} to the right along the line of centres

ii 31.7°

11 i $\sqrt{0.12}$ m s^{-1}

ii 0.393 m s^{-1} to the left along the line of centres

iii 0.691

12 i 4.176 m s^{-1}

ii 1.2 m s^{-1} to the left

iii 3 kg iv 0.4

13 i Proof

ii B has α below the line of centres. A moves up perpendicular to line of centres.

14 a 2.75 m s^{-1}

b 4.13 N s

Chapter 9

Before you start...

1 9.37 m

2 1.2 m s^{-1}

3 1.32 m

4 17.0 N

Work it out 9.1

Solution 3 is correct.

Exercise 9A

1 a i 2.80 m s^{-1} ii 1.45 m s^{-1}

b i 0.908 m s^{-2} ii 24.6 m s^{-2}

c i 27.7 N ii 1.80 N

d i 53.7° ii 69.7°

2 a $v = \sqrt{gr(5 + 2\cos\theta)}$

b $h = r$

c $v = \sqrt{3gr}$ d $v = \sqrt{5gr}$

3 a No, maximum height $h = \frac{1}{2}a$

b No, maximum height $h = \frac{1}{3}a$

c No, maximum height $h = 2a$

4 a 2.8 m s^{-1} b 14.7 N

5 $v = \sqrt{u^2 - 0.8g + 0.8g\cos\theta}$

6 $u > \sqrt{6g}$ for a full circle to occur.

7 $\frac{1}{3}mg$

8 a $v = 2\sqrt{g}$ when P hangs vertically below O

b $1.5g\sin\theta + 0.5g$ N c 19.5°

9 a 1.21 m s^{-1} b 0.49 N

c $F = 1.56$ N

Exercise 9B

1 a i Tangential $\frac{5}{7}$ m s^{-2}, radial $-\frac{\left(\frac{5}{7}t+4\right)^2}{3}$ m s^{-2}

ii Tangential $\frac{5}{3}$ m s^{-2}, radial $-\frac{\left(\frac{5}{3}t+2.3\right)^2}{0.8}$ m s^{-2}

b i Tangential -1 m s^{-2}, radial $-(6-t)^2$ m s^{-2}

ii Tangential $\frac{-11}{5}$ m s^{-2},

radial $-\frac{\left(5.6-\frac{11}{5}t\right)^2}{1.2}$ m s^{-2}

c i $t^2 + t - 9$ ii $3 - e^{-t}$

2 a Radial component $-\frac{\left(\frac{5}{8}t+5\right)^2}{40}$,

tangential component $\frac{5}{8}$.

b 1.34 m s^{-2}

3 21.2 m s^{-2}

4 g

5 $|a| = 31.9\text{ m s}^{-2}$

6 Radial component $2g\sin\theta - \frac{32}{3}\text{ m s}^{-2}$, tangential component is $g\cos\theta\text{ m s}^{-2}$.

Work it out 9.2

Solution 2 is correct.

Exercise 9C

1 a i 2.07 m s^{-1} ii 5.18 m s^{-1}

b i 20.3 N ii 1.30 N

c i 41.9° ii 71.8°

d i 3.57 m s^{-1} ii 5.29 m s^{-1}

2 a $\sqrt{g} = 3.13\text{ m s}^{-1}$

b 2m

3 a 4.43 m s^{-1} b 0.692 s c 1.53 m

4 a 7.14 m s^{-1} b 0.371 s c 2.29 m

5 a 2.91 m s^{-1} b 1.06 s c 2.69 m

6 a 2.42 m s^{-1} b 0.639 s c 1.55 m

7 48.4°

8 2.31 m s^{-1}

9 a 60° b 1270 N

c 5.36 m s^{-1} in the direction 30° to the horizontal

10 a $v = \sqrt{9 - 2g(0.6 - 0.6\cos\theta)}$

b $T = 0.88\cos\theta - 0.14$

c Proof

11 a 5.42 m s^{-1} b 10.4 m s^{-1}

c It will lose contact with the chute.

Mixed practice 9

1 81.6 cm

2 1.62 N

3 3.03 m s^{-1}

4 5.42 m s^{-1}

5 21.6 N

6 i $v^2 = 25 - 2.1g + 2.1g\cos\theta$

ii $\theta = 98.2°$

7 26.1 N

8 $u > \sqrt{2g(a - a\cos\theta)}$

9 i 21.0 N ii 9.2 N

10 a $\cos\theta = \frac{u^2}{3gr} + \frac{2}{3}$ b $u = \sqrt{gr}$

11 a When P is vertically below O

b $3\sqrt{gr}$ c $5.5mg$

12 i $v^2 = u^2 - 2ga(1 - \cos\theta)$, proof

ii $u^2 = 5ag$, proof

iii $u^2 = ag(2 - \sqrt{3})$

13 i 3.13 m s^{-1} and 1.96 N

ii 99.6°

14 i Proof

ii Radial $18 + 19.6\sin\theta$, tangential $g\cos\theta$

iii −37.8°

15 i $T = 2.94(2 + 3\cos\theta)$

ii $\theta = 132°$, $v = 2.29\text{ m s}^{-1}$

iii height = 0.148 m, speed = 1.52 m s^{-1}

16 i $v = 7.05\text{ m s}^{-1}$, $e = 0.695$

ii $v^2 = 10.29 + 13.72\cos\theta$, proof

iii radial acceleration = -4.9 m s^{-2}, transverse acceleration = -8.49 m s^{-2}

iv Proof, height = 1.18 m

Chapter 10

Before you start...

1 2.94

2 9 N m clockwise

3 $2g\mu$

Exercise 10A

1 $\bar{x} = 1$ m

2 1.47 m

3 a $y = 5 - 0.625x$ b $\begin{pmatrix}\bar{x}\\ \bar{y}\end{pmatrix} = \begin{pmatrix}\frac{8}{3}\\ \frac{5}{3}\end{pmatrix}$ cm

4 (0.6, 0.75)

5 Proof

6 $\left(2\frac{2}{3}, 2\frac{2}{3}\right)$ cm

7 (0, 3)

8 (0, 2.33)

9 a $9k$ b 2.25 c $2.7k$

10 3.6

11 $\bar{x} = \frac{4R}{3\pi}$

12 0.467

Exercise 10B

1 21.8°

2 56.3°

3 45.0°

4 45.0°

5 33.7°

6 54.2°

7 a 5.57 cm b 24.0°

8 a 4.09 cm from AB, 8.64 cm from DE

b 41.7°

9 a 20 cm from AB, $33\frac{1}{3}$ cm from AD

b 9.46°

10 21.8°

11 38.7°

12 $200\sqrt{3}$

13 a 15.2° b 1.77 N

14 $F = \frac{\sqrt{3}mg}{2}$

15 a $F = 2g$ b $F = 2.5g$

16 a $\bar{x} = 2\ln 4 - 2, \bar{y} = \frac{3}{8}$

b $\bar{x} = 0.824$

17 i $\begin{pmatrix} \bar{x} \\ \bar{y} \end{pmatrix} = \begin{pmatrix} 6.52 \\ 2.64 \end{pmatrix}$ cm

ii 9.09 N

Mixed practice 10

1 a 4.5 m

b $T_D = 65.3$ N, $T_C = 13.1$ N

2 a 2.88 cm from AB, 5.13 cm from AF

b 43.2°

3 a Proof b 5.5 cm

c 36.0°

4 $\bar{x} = \frac{12a}{25}$

5 26.1 N

6 i 0.936 N ii 1.55 N

7 i Proof ii 9°

8 i Proof

ii a 4.65 kg b $\mu \geqslant 0.0439$

9 $\frac{a(e-2)}{e-1}$

10 $\bar{x} = 1 - \frac{1}{2}\ln 3, \bar{y} = \frac{1}{3}$

11 a (1.5, 0.3) b 0.6

12 i Proof

ii a Proof b 4.43 cm

iii 6.64 N

Focus on ... Proof 2

1 Proof

2 Proof

Focus on ... Problem solving 2

1 a 3.5 m s^{-1}

b 0.809 m

2 4.36 N s, at 36.6° to original direction of motion

Focus on ... Modelling 2

1 $\theta = \theta_{max} \cos\sqrt{\frac{g}{l}}t$

2 $T = \pi$

3

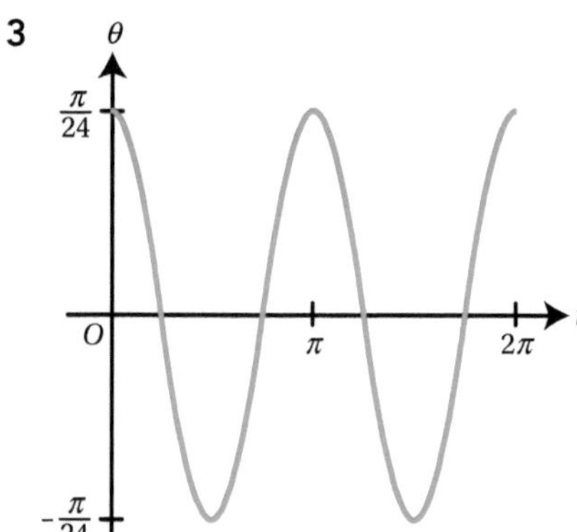

4 a $\dot{\theta} = -2 \times \frac{\pi}{24} \times \sin 2t$

$v = -2.45 \times 2 \times \frac{\pi}{24} \times \sin 2t$

5 $= 0.6414 \text{ m s}^{-1}$

6 a $v_{max} = 0.641 \text{ m s}^{-1}$

b 0.06%

c i $|v_{max}| \approx 1.2828 \text{ m s}^{-1}$ from SHM model. $v_{max} \approx 1.2792 \text{ m s}^{-1}$ from the energy equation (the bob is going 0.3% slower than the SHM model predicts).

ii $|v_{max}| \approx 2.5656 \text{ m s}^{-1}$ from SHM model. $v_{max} \approx 2.5364 \text{ m s}^{-1}$ from the energy equation (the bob is going 1.2% slower than the SHM model predicts).

Cross-topic review 2

1 a $v = \frac{3}{4}t^2 - \frac{t}{2} + c$ b 21.3 m s^{-1}

c $11\mathbf{i} + 9\mathbf{j}$

2 a Proof b $153.7°$

3 a $\frac{1}{2}$ b $e = \frac{\sqrt{3}}{3}$

4 $2\sqrt{g}$

5 a Proof b Proof

6 a 32 N s b 10 m s^{-1}

c 4.8 s

7 a Sphere A:

$\parallel$ to line of centres $3 \cos \alpha = \frac{12}{5} \text{ m s}^{-1}$

$\perp$ to line of centres $3 \sin \alpha = \frac{9}{5} \text{ m s}^{-1}$

Sphere B:

$\parallel$ to line of centres $2 \cos \beta = \frac{24}{13} \text{ m s}^{-1}$

$\perp$ to line of centres $3 \sin \beta = \frac{10}{13} \text{ m s}^{-1}$

b Speed of $A = 1.82 \text{ m s}^{-1}$, speed of $B = 2.52 \text{ m s}^{-1}$

8 a $T = 3mg \cos \theta + 20.9m$

b 0.855 m

c 0.943 m

9 Proof

10 $h = r$

11 a $\cos \theta = \frac{u^2 + 2ga}{3ga}$ b $\theta = 60°$

12 a $\frac{11h}{8}$ b $\frac{\sqrt{2}h}{4}$

13 i Also, $b \cos \beta = 2\sqrt{\frac{2}{3}}$

ii $a = 2.32$ m/a, $\alpha = 5$p.5°

$b = 1.70$ m/s, $\beta = 56.3°$

14 i Proof

$R = 3.18 + 13.23 \cos \theta$

ii $v = 1.19 \text{ m s}^{-1}$

15 i Proof ii $5\sqrt{3}$ cm

iii 60°

AS Level practice questions

1 0.5 m

2 a MLT^{-2}

b $a = -0.5, b = 0.5, c = 0.5$

c It was necessary since the dimensions of k would affect the solution found in part **b**.

3 a 40 m s^{-1} b 1500 N

c Light and inextensible.

d $a = \frac{1200 - T}{1000}$ e $T = 400$ N

4 a Light and inextensible

b Proof c Proof

5 a $2\sqrt{gl}$

b It will affect how high above the horizontal A can move before the string goes taut. The speed of A will be larger if A is not directly above B.

c Proof

d $2.4m\sqrt{gl}$

e $\frac{33}{25}l$

f $\frac{12}{5}mgl$

6 a Y is moving in the opposite direction to its initial motion.

b 0.85

7 a 200 J

b 780 J

c 0.460

d 0.577

A Level practice questions

1 $e=\sqrt{\frac{h}{k}}$

2 $M^{-1}L^{3}T^{-2}$

3 5 J

4 a $T=\frac{(r-l)mg}{l}$

b $r=\frac{lg}{g-4lk^2}$

c

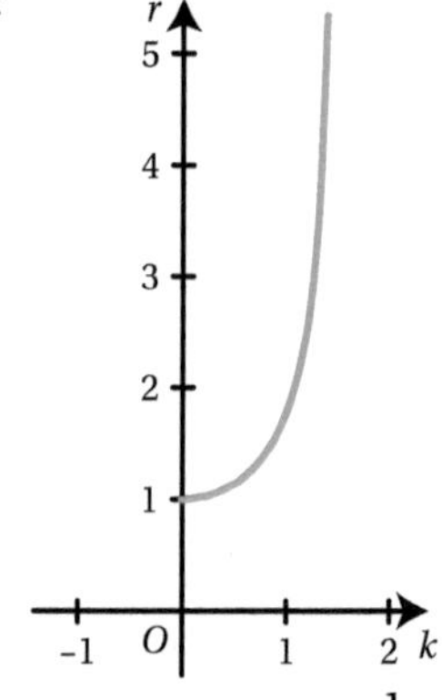

d Asymptote at $k=\frac{1}{2}\sqrt{g}$. $1<r<2$ so that the string does not break, so $0<k<\frac{1}{2}\sqrt{\frac{g}{2}}$.

5 a

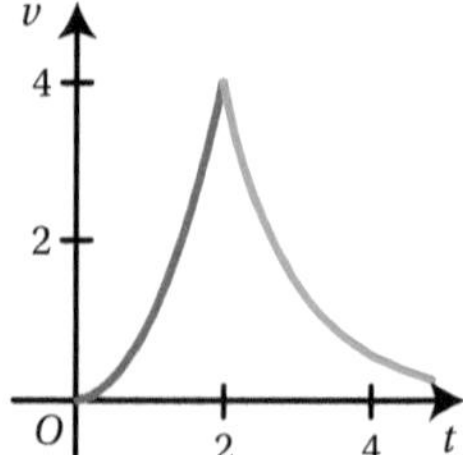

b -2.43 m s^{-2}

c 6.13 m

6 a Proof

b Proof

c Proof

7 a Sphere A: $v\frac{\sqrt{13}}{2}\text{ m s}^{-1}$, angle 74°

Sphere B: $v\sqrt{2}$, angle 45° to the direction AB before the impact.

b $\frac{1}{4}mv^2$

8 a Radial: $\frac{(90-2t^2)}{350}$, tangential: -2 m s^{-2}

b 7100 kJ

c 85.3 m s^{-1}

d 2.72 seconds

9 a Proof

b 44.7°

c 31.0°

d It will slide.

10 a $F=2000-\frac{x^2}{5}$

b 58.2 kJ

c 9.65 m s^{-1}

Glossary

Acceleration vector: The rate of change of the velocity vector of an object.

Angular speed: The rate at which an object is rotating, measured as the angle in radians turned through in unit time.

Centre of mass: A single point at which the mass of an object can be considered to be located.

Centripetal force: The force directed towards the centre of a circle that hold a moving object in a circular path.

Composite body: An object made from a combination of shapes.

Conical pendulum: A particle attached to the end of a string or rod suspended from a pivot point; the particle moves in a horizontal circle with constant angular speed, with the string or rod tracing out the curved surface of a cone.

Dimensions: These describe what type of quantity you are measuring. In mechanics the usual dimensions used to describe a quantity are combinations of mass (M), length (L) and time (T).

Displacement: Distance moved in a particular direction.

Elastic limit: When an elastic spring or string is stretched beyond its elastic limit it does not return to its original length when the force is removed.

Elastic potential energy: Energy stored in an elastic string when stretched or an elastic spring when stretched or compressed.

Elastic spring: A spring that can be stretched or compressed when a force is applied and will return to its original length when the force is removed.

Elastic string: A string that can be stretched when a force is applied and will return to its original length when the force is removed.

Energy: The capacity of a physical system to do work.

Gravitational potential energy: energy possessed by an object because of its height above an arbitrary fixed level.

Impulse: The product of the force on an object and the time for which the force acts, which results in a change in the object's momentum.

Kinetic energy: Energy that a body possesses by virtue of being in motion.

Lamina: A two-dimensional object.

Mechanical energy: The sum of the kinetic energy and gravitational potential energy of an object.

Modulus of elasticity: Theoretically the force required to double the length of an elastic string or spring, or to compress the length of an elastic spring to zero.

Momentum: The product of mass and velocity of a moving object.

Oblique impact: A collision at an angle to the line joining the centres of two colliding objects.

Perfectly elastic collision: A collision in which there is no loss of kinetic energy.

Power: The rate at which energy is transferred when a force does work.

Propulsive forces: forces that promote movement.

Radial acceleration: Acceleration towards the centre of circular motion.

Radial direction: The direction along a radius of a circle.

Resistive forces: forces that oppose movement.

Scalar quantity: A quantity that has only magnitude but not direction.

SI: The international system of units based on seven base units, including the kilogram, metre and second.

Stiffness: The force required for unit extension of an elastic string or spring or for unit compression of an elastic spring.

Tangential direction: The direction along a tangent at a point of a curve.

Tension: A force that is transmitted through a string or rod.

Thrust (in a spring): A force that opposes a compressive force.

Tractive force: The driving force of an engine.

Uniform lamina: A two-dimensional object that has constant mass per unit area.

Vector quantity: A quantity that has both magnitude and direction.

Velocity vector: The rate of change of the position of an object. The magnitude gives the speed and the vector direction gives the direction of the motion.

Work done: A force does work when it moves an object.

Work–energy principle: An essential idea in mechanics that enables us to calculate the work necessary to cause a change in energy.

Index

Acknowledgements

The authors and publishers acknowledge the following sources of copyright material and are grateful for the permissions granted. While every effort has been made, it has not always been possible to identify the sources of all the material used, or to trace all copyright holders. If any omissions are brought to our notice, we will be happy to include the appropriate acknowledgements on reprinting.

Thanks to the following for permission to reproduce images:

Cover image: huskyomega/Getty Images

Back cover: Fabian Oefner www.fabianoefner.com

Robin Bush/Getty Images; SSPL/Getty Images; VIPDesignUSA/Getty Images; Fine Art Images/Heritage Images/Getty Images; N.J. Simrick/Getty Images; Steve Lindridge/Getty Images; Chad Baker/Getty Images; Marin Tomas/Getty Images; acro_phuket/getty Images; Katjaaa/Getty Images; Andy Caulfield/Getty Images; salvador74/Getty Images; Iurii Kovalenko/Getty Images; Preyansh Chandak/EyeEm/Getty Images; Joan Esver/EyeEm/Getty Images; Martin Ruegner/Getty Images.